Econometric Society Monographs No. 16

Misspecification tests in econometrics

Econometric Society Monographs

Editors:

Jean-Michel Grandmont *Centre d'Études Prospectives
    d'Économie Mathématique Appliquées à la Planification,
    Paris*
Charles F. Manski *University of Wisconsin, Madison*

The Econometric Society is an international society for the
advancement of economic theory in relation to statistics and
mathematics. The Econometric Society Monograph Series
is designed to promote the publication of original research
contributions of high quality in mathematical economics
and theoretical and applied econometrics.

Other titles in the series:

Werner Hildenbrand, Editor *Advances in economic theory*
Werner Hildenbrand, Editor *Advances in econometrics*
G. S. Maddala *Limited-dependent and qualitative variables in
    econometrics*
Gerard Debreu *Mathematical economics*
Jean-Michel Grandmont *Money and value*
Franklin M. Fisher *Disequilibrium foundations of equilibrium
    economics*
Bezalel Peleg *Game theoretic analysis of voting in committees*
Roger Bowden and Darrell Turkington *Instrumental variables*
Andreu Mas-Colell *The theory of general economic equilibrium*
James J. Heckman and Burton Singer *Longitudinal analysis of
    labor market data*
Cheng Hsiao *Analysis of panel data*
Truman F. Bewley, Editor *Advances in economic theory–Fifth
    World Congress*
Truman F. Bewley, Editor *Advances in econometrics–Fifth
    World Congress* (Volume I)
Truman F. Bewley, Editor *Advances in econometrics–Fifth
    World Congress* (Volume II)
Hervé Moulin *Axioms of cooperative decision making*

Misspecification tests in econometrics

THE LAGRANGE MULTIPLIER PRINCIPLE AND OTHER APPROACHES

L. G. GODFREY

Department of Economics, University of York

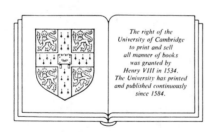

The right of the
University of Cambridge
to print and sell
all manner of books
was granted by
Henry VIII in 1534.
The University has printed
and published continuously
since 1584.

CAMBRIDGE UNIVERSITY PRESS

Cambridge

New York   New Rochelle   Melbourne   Sydney

Published by the Press Syndicate of the University of Cambridge
The Pitt Building, Trumpington Street, Cambridge CB2 1RP
32 East 57th Street, New York, NY 10022, USA
10 Stamford Road, Oakleigh, Melbourne 3166, Australia

First published 1988

Printed in the United States of America

Library of Congress Cataloging-in-Publication Data
Godfrey, L. G.
Misspecification tests in econometrics: the Lagrange multiplier
principle and other approaches/L. G. Godfrey.
p. cm.
Bibliography: p.
ISBN 0-521-26616-5

1. Econometrics. 2. Econometric models. 3. Multiplier
(Economics) I. Title. II. Title: Lagrange multiplier.
HB139.G63 1988
330'.028–dc 19   88-7296

British Library Cataloguing in Publication Data
Godfrey, L. G.

Misspecification tests in econometrics:
the Lagrange multiplier principle and
other approaches

1. Econometric models. Estimation and testing
I. Title
330'.0724

ISBN 0 521 26616 5

To Christine, James and Robert

Contents

Preface

In the past ten years, there have been rapid developments in the field of testing for misspecification in both applied and theoretical econometrics. The idea that a model must be tested before it can be taken to be an adequate basis for studying economic behaviour has become widely accepted. Modern empirical analyses usually include testing for a number of specification errors, and the range of tests available to applied workers has increased enormously. Theoretical research has produced new general approaches to testing and a better understanding of the properties of tests and the relationships between them. The purpose of this book is to bring together a large number of results on misspecification tests in such a way that a wide audience of applied and theoretical researchers, graduate students and professional economists will find its contents useful. General results are, therefore, often illustrated by examples, and the familiar linear model provides the framework for the main discussion, with the extensions required for testing non-linear models being outlined.

Attention is restricted to testing for misspecification, so that other topics in inference – for example, tests of theoretical constraints in demand systems – are not considered. Also, in order to keep the book to a manageable length, I have not covered tests for non-nested hypotheses, but have instead provided references to suitable surveys and collections of recent work.

The chapters are divided into numbered sections and sub-sections. Equations are numbered by section, not by chapter. If reference is made to an equation appearing in another chapter, then this is made clear in the text. The first chapter provides the theoretical underpinnings of the various general approaches to be considered in subsequent chapters. It was used as the basis of a course for master's students in the Department of Statistics, Australian National University, during a most enjoyable visit. The second chapter deals with a systematic numerical inequality among the classical Lagrange multiplier, likelihood ratio and Wald statistics that has received considerable attention in the literature and explores its generality and implications. Of the three classical tests, the Lagrange multiplier procedure is often regarded as the most suitable for constructing misspecification tests because, unlike the other two approaches, it does not require the estimation of the alternative model. The Lagrange multiplier principle, therefore, merits special consideration in this book and it is the subject of extended analysis in the third chapter. The third chapter also contains a discussion of non-standard cases to which the results of Chapter 1 cannot be applied without modification. One important concept derived from the analysis of Chapter 3 is that of a locally equivalent alternative (LEA). The use of LEAs reveals interesting theoretical relationships and also makes it clear that many misspecification tests can be implemented simply by adding extra regressors to the model being evaluated and then testing their significance.

The last three chapters cover a large number of tests for various specification errors in the context of multiple regression equations, simultaneous equation systems, and models with qualitative or limited dependent variables. A wide range of specific misspecifications is examined (including omitted variables, incorrect functional form, errors-in-variables, non-normality, autocorrelation and heteroscedasticity) as are several general tests that do not require the formulation of an alternative hypothesis. In many cases, it is shown that a check for misspecification, whatever its origins, can be implemented as a test for omitted variables. This result simplifies the analysis of important topics such as the construction of joint tests for a number of specification errors and the impact of selecting the wrong alternative hypothesis. It also provides applied workers with a very convenient method for calculating test statistics.

I have received a great deal of help during the preparation of this book. I owe a special debt to my wife Christine, who read through the whole manuscript and made many valuable comments and suggestions. I would also like to thank Professor Chuck Manski and two anonymous reviewers for their careful and constructive reports on the first draft. Trevor Breusch provided detailed comments on the first chapter, and other parts of the book draw upon results obtained in our joint work over the years. The results of joint research with Mike Wickens, who stimulated my interest in econometrics, also play a significant role. The revision of the manuscript was supported by the Economic and Social Research Council (UK) under project reference number B00232137. I am grateful to Francis Brooke (formerly of Cambridge University Press) for his help, and to Sal Cuthbert, Jo Hall, Barbara Olive, Gail Slavin and Vanessa Windass for typing a difficult manuscript with speed and efficiency. Finally, my greatest thanks go to Christine, Robert and James, who put up with me while I was writing this book.

CHAPTER 1

Approaches to testing the hypothesis of adequate specification

1.1 Introduction

Tests for misspecification play an important role in the evaluation of econometric models, and the need for such tests has been stressed by several authors. For example, Hendry (1980, p. 403) suggests that the three golden rules of econometrics are 'test, test and test,' and Malinvaud (1981, p. 1370) argues that the research aims of econometricians should include the special requirement that more emphasis be put on the testing of the specification. One purpose of this chapter is to consider some basic issues in testing for specification error. These issues, which are discussed in Sections 1.2 and 1.3, include the arguments for and against employing an alternative specification when testing the model under scrutiny, the interpretation of test statistics and their potential value in respecification following the rejection of a tentatively entertained model.

Some of the available statistical procedures and the relationships between them are also discussed at a rather general level in preparation for the detailed examination of tests of particular interest to economists and econometricians which appears in subsequent chapters. A large part of this discussion is presented in Section 1.4, which focuses on the likelihood ratio, Wald and Lagrange multiplier tests (sometimes referred to collectively as the trinity of classical tests). The emphasis on these three tests is justified in part by the fact that they are widely used in econometrics. Also a detailed discussion of these procedures makes it simpler to examine related tests that are potentially useful, but less familiar to applied workers; several such procedures are considered in Section 1.5.

A common feature of the classical tests developed in the framework of maximum likelihood estimation is that they involve the specification of the more general statistical model serving as the alternative hypothesis. It has been argued that there is sometimes little information about the nature of the specification errors present in the model being evaluated, so that more general tests are required. There is considerable theoretical interest in this approach to assessing model adequacy, and Section 1.6 contains a discussion of the general tests of Hausman (1978) and White (1982). This

1

discussion uses some of the results of Section 1.4 to examine the relationships between general specification tests and the classical tests in special cases. The unifying work by Newey (1985a) and Tauchen (1985) which extends the results of Hausman and White is also considered.

Finally, a summary of the main points and some qualifications are offered in Section 1.7.

1.2   Testing without an alternative hypothesis

Suppose that the unknown stochastic process which generated the n-dimensional observation vector $y = (y_1, \ldots, y_n)'$ is to be modelled and that the adequacy of the specified model is to be assessed.[1] If the selected model is specified by the null hypothesis H_0, then it is necessary to test the consistency of H_0 with the sample data. The hypothesis H_0 is said to be *simple* if it completely specifies the joint density function of y and is otherwise said to be *composite*. Most specifications in econometrics are characterized by hypotheses of the latter type and involve unknown parameters which are not determined by H_0. Such parameters are referred to as *nuisance parameters*, but this technical terminology in no way implies that such parameters are uninteresting.

Let $T = T(y)$ be a statistic constructed for the purpose of testing H_0.[2] Cox and Hinkley (1974, p. 66) argue that T should satisfy the following criteria:

(a)   the distribution of T when H_0 is true should be known, at least approximately, and should not depend upon the values of any nuisance parameters (sometimes it is not feasible to obtain the small sample distribution of T under H_0 and only the asymptotic or limit null distribution will be known); and

(b)   the larger the sample value of T the stronger the evidence of departure from H_0 of the type it is required to test.

Note that no alternative specification to H_0 is required to derive T, and accordingly this procedure is often called a *pure significance test*.

The absence of an alternative hypothesis is the source of both the weakness and strength of the pure significance test. Under a given

---

[1] We use 'adequacy' rather than 'truth' or 'validity' because econometric models are usually better regarded as more or less useful approximations to the actual process as opposed to complete and accurate representations of it.

[2] In order to economize on notation, we shall not distinguish between a random variable and its observed value except where there is the possibility of confusion.

alternative it is usually possible to find a specific test which will outperform a pure significance test. The relatively high power of a specific test may, however, be bought at the price of a lack of sensitivity to other alternatives, so that it may be inferior to the pure significance test when used in an inappropriate situation (see the interesting comments on this point by Ramsey, 1974).

A further problem associated with the pure significance test is that, without a specific alternative hypothesis, it may be difficult to choose from the potentially large number of plausible test statistics available. This choice will, however, be made bearing in mind the type of departures from H_0 which are meaningful. Of course, there may be several types of departure from H_0 which are of interest. For example, when testing for non-normality in the disturbances of a linear regression model, it would seem natural to consider both skewness and kurtosis.[3] More generally, if there are s types of departure with corresponding test statistics $T_1, \ldots, T_s$, then one can either carry out the s tests separately or combine them in an appropriate way to obtain a single test statistic: the latter course clearly requires that the joint distribution of $T_1, \ldots, T_s$ under H_0 be obtained. An obvious disadvantage of the first approach is that it is difficult to calculate the overall significance level. This probability will lie between the maximum of the individual significance levels and their sum. If, therefore, each test is carried out with a significance level of α, the significance level of the overall test will be between α and $s\alpha$. When there is a high degree of dependence between the individual significance tests, the actual overall significance level may be somewhat smaller than its upper bound of $s\alpha$, whereas if the tests are independent it is given by $1 - (1 - \alpha)^s$.

The alternative approach involving a single test of the joint significance of $T_1, \ldots, T_s$ does not suffer from the same drawback and either the small sample or the asymptotic significance level will be known. It has, however, been argued that, in the event of the rejection of H_0, the joint test provides no information about the causes of the inconsistency of H_0 with the data, while consideration of the s individual test statistics may provide such information. The very nature of pure significance tests suggests that we cannot expect too much guidance in respecifying a rejected model. Moreover, if H_0 is rejected as being inadequate, it seems unwise to use inference which is valid only under H_0 to guide its reformulation, the marginal distributions of the statistics T_i under an unspecified alternative being unknown.

[3] Measures of skewness and excess kurtosis would have to be calculated from estimated residuals, rather than the unobservable disturbances. A discussion of appropriate large-sample tests is given by White and MacDonald (1980).

Pure significance tests have not been widely used in econometrics, possibly because of the difficulty in deciding which procedures are useful in the absence of a formally specified alternative and also because it may be generally felt that the information available permits the selection of more powerful specific tests.

1.3   Testing with an alternative hypothesis

A natural approach to the testing of a particular specification of interest is to embed it in some more general model in such a way that the former can be derived from the latter by imposing a set of parametric restrictions. The adequacy of the tentatively entertained null model can then be assessed by checking whether these restrictions are consistent with the sample data. The null hypothesis H_0 is accordingly identified with these parametric constraints.[4]

As will be seen in the next section, the asymptotic theory for various tests derived within this framework has been examined in some detail, and many useful results are available. However, several relevant general comments can be made prior to mathematical analysis.

First, it is important to note that, of the null and alternative models, only the former is being tested and that its rejection should not entail the automatic acceptance of the latter. The case against the unquestioning adoption of the model of the alternative hypothesis is strengthened by the fact that tests may be quite powerful against alternatives for which they were not designed. (The Durbin–Watson test is a familiar example of a procedure known to be sensitive to several quite different types of misspecification.)

Some researchers have attempted to exploit the sensitivity of tests to unspecified errors by adopting alternatives that have instrumental, rather than intrinsic, interest. In such cases, alternative models are selected in the hope of obtaining reasonable power against a wide range of specification errors, and not because they reflect precise ideas about possible inadequacies of the null model. The distinction between the pure significance tests discussed in the previous section and parametric restriction tests is clearly blurred when this approach is adopted.

As with pure significance tests, it is sometimes useful to check for several different types of misspecification, and the previous comments on the choice between a single overall test and a collection of individual tests

---

[4] In an important article, Hausman (1978) has proposed an approach which does not require that the null hypothesis be given in parametric form. Hausman's procedure and its relationship to other techniques will be discussed below.

remain pertinent. Indeed, Ramsey and Kmenta (1980) suggest that the major difficulty with using specification tests is in isolating and identifying the separate effects in the presence of more than one misspecification. (This problem is examined in Chapter 3.)

Tests based upon nesting the model of interest in a more general specification are extremely important and receive much of our attention in what follows. It is shown that, with an appropriate choice of alternative hypothesis, this approach will often yield tests originally proposed as pure significance tests. Indeed, the most widely known general checks of the adequacy of an econometric model can all be reinterpreted in this way. It will, therefore, be convenient to discuss tests derived without an alternative hypothesis (see Section 1.6) after tests of parametric hypotheses have been examined (see Section 1.5).

There is a third approach to checking model adequacy. It is possible to derive tests when the alternative is fully specified but does not contain the null model as a special case. Such procedures are known as tests of non-nested hypotheses and are often obtained using results contained in the influential papers by Cox (1961, 1962). In order to keep this work to a manageable length, this type of test is not covered. The interested reader should consult the collection of articles edited by White (1983b), the surveys by McAleer (1983) and MacKinnon (1983), and the references cited in these works.

1.4   The likelihood ratio, Wald and Lagrange multiplier tests

The likelihood ratio (LR), Wald (W) and Lagrange multiplier (LM) tests of parametric restrictions are examined in this section. Although the main concern here is how these procedures can be used to derive checks for the misspecification of economic models, the discussion is fairly general. Clearly, the assumptions underlying this general treatment should constitute an adequate basis for subsequent econometric applications. In particular, given that many economic variables are specified as having systematic components which vary from one observation to another and that dynamic relationships are frequently used, the mathematical assumptions should allow for non-identical distributions of the observations and for general dependence. These requirements suggest that Crowder's (1976) results will be of value, and it is not surprising that his work is often cited in the econometric literature (e.g., see Breusch and Pagan, 1980; Engle, 1984). Following Crowder (1976), suppose that the (possibly vector-valued) observations $y_0, y_1, \ldots, y_n$ have conditional probability density functions $f_t(y_t | \mathscr{F}_{t-1}; \theta)$ where the functional form of $f_t(\cdot)$ is known, θ is an m-dimensional parameter vector and $\mathscr{F}_{t-1} = (y_{t-1}, y_{t-2}, \ldots, y_0)$ denotes the 'previous history.' (The dependence of the functions $f_t(\cdot)$ on non-stochastic variables will not be shown explicitly.) If $L_n(\theta)$ denotes the likelihood function conditional upon y_0, then its (natural) logarithm is

$$l_n(\theta) = \ln L_n(\theta) = \Sigma_1^n \ln f_t(y_t | \mathscr{F}_{t-1}; \theta). \tag{4.1}$$

It will be assumed that the null hypothesis to be tested is composite and takes the form of s ($s < m$) linear constraints on the elements of θ. The parametric restrictions under test will be written as

$$H_0: R\theta - r^0 = 0, \tag{4.2}$$

where the elements of the s by m matrix R are known constants, as are those of the s-dimensional vector r^0. Further, the rank of R is s, so that there are no redundant restrictions. This set-up is general enough to cover the tests for model misspecification that are to be discussed.

The assumptions

The following assumptions which are compiled from Cox and Hinkley (1974), Crowder (1976) and Silvey (1959) are sufficient for many econometric applications. Some special cases of econometric interest which are not covered by these assumptions are considered in Chapter 3.

(i)   The true parameter value θ^t is interior to the parameter space Θ which is finite dimensional, closed and bounded.

(ii)   The probability distributions defined by any two different values of θ are distinct.

(iii)   The first- and second-order partial derivatives of $l_n(\theta)$ with respect to the elements of θ are continuous throughout some neighbourhood of the true parameter value. Moreover, the third-order partial derivatives are such that the quantities $n^{-1}|\partial^3 l_n(\theta)/\partial\theta_i\partial\theta_j\partial\theta_k|$ ($i, j, k = 1, \ldots, m$) exist and are bounded by integrable functions in such a neighbourhood.

(iv)   If the *score vector* $\partial l_n(\theta)/\partial\theta$ is denoted by $d_n(\theta)$ and the *Hessian* $\partial^2 l_n(\theta)/\partial\theta\partial\theta'$ by $D_n(\theta)$, then when the argument θ is the true parameter value θ^t,

$$E[d_n(\theta^t)] = 0 \tag{4.3}$$

and

$$V[d_n(\theta^t)] = -E[D_n(\theta^t)] = \mathscr{I}_n(\theta^t), \tag{4.4}$$

where $E[\cdot]$ and $V[\cdot]$ denote expectation and variance–covariance matrices, respectively, and $\mathscr{I}_n(\theta^t)$ is the *information matrix*. Equations (4.3) and (4.4) require that the relevant integrals converge and that the effective range of integration be independent of θ.

(v) The matrix $\mathscr{I}_n(\theta)$ is positive definite at $\theta = \theta^t$ and in an open neighbourhood of the true value which implies that θ^t is locally identifiable (see Rothenberg, 1971). This assumption involves restricting n so that it is greater than or equal to m and may have other implications; for example, there must be no perfect multicollinearity in the regressor matrix of a normal linear regression model.

(vi) The eigenvalues of $\mathscr{I}_n(\theta^t)$ all tend to infinity as $n \to \infty$ so that information accrues steadily as the sample size increases without limit. This assumption is used in establishing consistency of maximum likelihood estimators. Schmidt (1976, pp. 85–6) discusses a regression model in which it is not satisfied and the usual least-squares estimator is not consistent.

(vii) Under the θ^t-distribution, the probability limit of $-[\mathscr{I}_n(\theta^t)]^{-1}D_n(\theta^t)$ is I_m, the m by m identity matrix. Also, the probability limit of $[D_n(\theta)]^{-1}D_n(\theta^t)$ is I_m for θ in a neighbourhood of θ^t. (As will be seen below, these assumptions are useful when obtaining a relationship between maximum likelihood estimators and the score $d_n(\theta^t)$ by means of a Taylor series expansion.)

(viii) Consider the vector of first-order partial derivatives of $l_n(\theta)$ evaluated at the true parameter value, that is,

$$d_n(\theta^t) = \Sigma_1^n \partial l_t(\theta^t)/\partial\theta. \tag{4.5}$$

Let w be an arbitrary m-dimensional non-stochastic vector with $w'w < \infty$, and let X_t be defined as $w'\partial l_t(\theta^t)/\partial\theta$. The following conditions are satisfied: the ratio of $\Sigma_1^n E(X_t^2|\mathscr{F}_{t-1})$ to $\Sigma_1^n E(X_t^2)$ tends to 1 as $n \to \infty$; and $E(X_\tau^2)$ is negligible relative to $\Sigma_1^n E(X_t^2)$ for all τ. These conditions permit the use of a central limit theorem for martingales when considering the asymptotic distribution of $d_n(\theta^t)$ (see Crowder, 1976). (The use of such theorems can be based upon other sets of assumptions; e.g., see Brillingsley, 1961; McLeish, 1974.) Crowder shows that $[\mathscr{I}_n(\theta^t)]^{-\frac{1}{2}}d_n(\theta^t)$ is asymptotically distributed as $N(0, I_m)$.

This somewhat lengthy list of assumptions provides the justification for the application of central limit theorems and the use of Taylor series approximations which are fundamental to parametric hypothesis testing in the context of maximum likelihood estimation. As indicated above, assumptions (i) to (vii) are used to prove consistency and to derive an approximate relationship between estimators and the score $\partial l_n(\theta^t)/\partial\theta$. This relationship will be considered below and is combined with assumption (viii) to prove that estimators are asymptotically normal. In studies not specifically directed towards time-series applications, assumption (viii) is sometimes replaced by the more direct condition

(viii')   The vector $[\mathscr{I}_n(\theta^t)]^{-\frac{1}{2}}d_n(\theta^t)$ is asymptotically normally distributed with zero mean vector and covariance matrix I_m,

or some similar condition (see, e.g., Holly, 1982).

In many econometric specifications, it is further assumed that

(ix)   The elements of $\mathscr{I}_n(\theta^t)$ are $O(n)$, and $\lim_{n \to \infty} n^{-1}\mathscr{I}_n(\theta^t)$ exists and is a finite non-singular matrix.[5]

This assumption will be adopted in order to simplify comparisons with other work and also for convenience of exposition.

As Cox and Hinkley (1974) point out, there are close links between the construction of significance tests of parametric hypotheses and the estimation of the null and alternative models. It will, therefore, be convenient to consider certain properties of maximum likelihood estimators (MLE). Before we examine MLEs and their asymptotic behaviour, however, some simplifications of notation are made. In what follows, subscripts are often introduced to denote partitioning of matrices and vectors, and, in order to avoid too cumbersome a notation, the subscript n is omitted from terms depending on the sample; for example, $l(\cdot)$ is used rather than $l_n(\cdot)$. Also the distinction between the true value θ^t and a variable vector θ is no longer made. This distinction is important when stating assumptions (i) to (ix), but is not needed in the analysis that follows because there should be no risk of confusion. This treatment of the distinction is quite conventional (see, e.g., Cramer, 1986; and Rothenberg, 1973).

Finally, the dependence of the information matrix on the parameter value will not usually be shown unless it is essential to a particular argument. Thus this matrix will usually be written as $\mathscr{I}$, rather than $\mathscr{I}_n(\theta^t)$. It should be remembered, however, that $\mathscr{I}$ is not a constant matrix, and indeed if it were a constant matrix, assumption (vi) would not be satisfied.

Maximum likelihood estimation

The likelihood function $L(\theta)$, or equivalently the log-likelihood function $l(\theta)$, can be maximized subject to the restrictions of H_0 or with these

---

[5] The use of the order statements $o(\cdot)$, $O(\cdot)$, $o_p(\cdot)$ and $O_p(\cdot)$ follows the definitions of Cramér (1946, p. 122) and Mann and Wald (1943). The restriction on $\mathscr{I}_n(\theta^t)$ is also imposed in much of the literature on deriving estimators with desirable asymptotic properties; see, e.g., Hendry (1976).

constraints on θ ignored. The restricted and unrestricted MLE so derived will be denoted by $\hat{\theta}$ and $\tilde{\theta}$, respectively.[6] (Clearly, $l(\tilde{\theta})$ cannot be smaller than $l(\hat{\theta})$.) Under the assumptions listed above, $\tilde{\theta}$ is consistent and asymptotically normally distributed whether or not H_0 is true. One standard approach to deriving the asymptotic distribution of $\tilde{\theta}$ is to employ a two-term Taylor expansion of $d(\theta)$ about $\tilde{\theta}$; that is,

$$d(\theta) = d(\tilde{\theta}) + D(\theta, \tilde{\theta})(\theta - \tilde{\theta}), \tag{4.6}$$

where $D(\theta, \tilde{\theta})$ denotes the matrix of second derivatives of $l(\cdot)$ with rows evaluated at possibly different points on the line segment between θ and $\tilde{\theta}$ (see Crowder, 1976, p. 45).

It will be useful to convert (4.6) into a relationship in which the left-hand-side variable is $O_p(1)$. Crowder's results imply that $\mathscr{I}^{-\frac{1}{2}}d(\theta)$ is $O_p(1)$ since this vector is asymptotically distributed as $N(0, I_m)$, and so we consider

$$\mathscr{I}^{-\frac{1}{2}}d(\theta) = \mathscr{I}^{-\frac{1}{2}}d(\tilde{\theta}) + \mathscr{I}^{-\frac{1}{2}}D(\theta, \tilde{\theta})(\theta - \tilde{\theta})$$
$$= \mathscr{I}^{-\frac{1}{2}}d(\tilde{\theta}) + \mathscr{I}^{\frac{1}{2}}[\mathscr{I}^{-1}D(\theta, \tilde{\theta})](\theta - \tilde{\theta}). \tag{4.7}$$

The next step in the standard approach is to argue that the first-order conditions for a maximum of $l(\cdot)$ imply that $d(\tilde{\theta}) = 0$. Strictly speaking, there is the possibility that $\tilde{\theta}$ will not be an interior point of Θ and $d(\tilde{\theta}) \neq 0$; the probability of this event will tend to zero as $n \to \infty$ under the assumptions above. Using $d(\tilde{\theta}) = 0$, equation (4.7) can be rewritten as

$$\mathscr{I}^{-\frac{1}{2}}d(\theta) = \mathscr{I}^{\frac{1}{2}}[\mathscr{I}^{-1}D(\theta, \tilde{\theta})](\theta - \tilde{\theta})$$
$$= \mathscr{I}^{\frac{1}{2}}(\tilde{\theta} - \theta) + \mathscr{I}^{\frac{1}{2}}[\mathscr{I}^{-1}D(\theta, \tilde{\theta}) + I_m](\theta - \tilde{\theta}).$$

Crowder's conditions imply that $\operatorname{plim}\mathscr{I}^{-1}D(\theta, \tilde{\theta}) = -I_m$ (see Crowder, 1976, Sections 3 and 4). It follows that the probability limit of $[\mathscr{I}^{-1}D(\theta, \tilde{\theta}) + I_m]$ is a matrix of zeros, so that the former matrix is $o_p(1)$. Now $\mathscr{I}^{-\frac{1}{2}}d(\theta)$ is $O_p(1)$ and $\mathscr{I}^{\frac{1}{2}}$ is $O(n^{\frac{1}{2}})$, so that $(\tilde{\theta} - \theta)$ is $O_p(n^{-\frac{1}{2}})$ and $\mathscr{I}^{\frac{1}{2}}[\mathscr{I}^{-1}D(\theta, \tilde{\theta}) + I_m](\theta - \tilde{\theta})$ is $o_p(1)$. (The results on the asymptotic (stochastic) orders of magnitudes of products are based upon the findings of Mann and Wald, 1943.) We can, therefore, write

$$\mathscr{I}^{-\frac{1}{2}}d(\theta) = \mathscr{I}^{\frac{1}{2}}(\tilde{\theta} - \theta) + o_p(1). \tag{4.8}$$

Further, since the $o_p(1)$ term of (4.8) is asymptotically negligible relative to the other two terms which are both $O_p(1)$, we can express the relationship

---

[6] It would be more accurate to denote these estimators by $\hat{\theta}_n$ and $\tilde{\theta}_n$, but the subscript n is again omitted to simplify notation.

as

$$\mathscr{I}^{-\frac{1}{2}}d(\theta) \overset{a}{=} \mathscr{I}^{\frac{1}{2}}(\tilde{\theta} - \theta),$$

where $\overset{a}{=}$ denotes an equality which holds apart from asymptotically irrelevant terms.

The $\overset{a}{=}$ notation will often be employed. Its use does not require that the left-hand-side variable be scaled to be $O_p(1)$. It is the relative asymptotic orders of magnitude that are important, and any terms that are omitted must be of a lower order than those retained. Also it is sometimes convenient to subtract the left-hand-side variable from both sides of the relationship to give it the form $0 \overset{a}{=} \ldots$.

Returning to (4.8) and the derivation of the asymptotic distribution of $\tilde{\theta}$, since $\mathscr{I}^{-\frac{1}{2}}d(\theta)$ converges in distribution to $N(0, I_m)$ and this vector differs from $\mathscr{I}^{\frac{1}{2}}(\tilde{\theta} - \theta)$ by terms that converge in probability to zero, it follows that

$$\mathscr{I}^{\frac{1}{2}}(\tilde{\theta} - \theta) \overset{a}{\sim} N(0, I_m),$$

where $\overset{a}{\sim}$ should be read as 'is asymptotically distributed as.' For cases in which assumption (ix) on the behaviour of $\mathscr{I}$ is satisfied, we can write the results on asymptotic distributions as

$$n^{-\frac{1}{2}}d(\theta) \overset{a}{\sim} N(0, \lim_{n \to \infty} n^{-1}\mathscr{I})$$

and

$$n^{\frac{1}{2}}(\tilde{\theta} - \theta) \overset{a}{\sim} N(0, \lim_{n \to \infty} n\mathscr{I}^{-1}).$$

The asymptotic distribution of the constrained MLE $\hat{\theta}$ under H_0 can also be obtained by examining sets of first-order conditions. The restricted MLE $\hat{\theta}$ is obtained by solving the constrained optimization problem

$$\underset{\theta}{\text{maximize }} l(\theta)$$

$$\text{subject to } (R\theta - r^0) = 0.$$

It will be useful to introduce the Lagrangean

$$\Lambda(\theta, \lambda) = l(\theta) + \lambda'(R\theta - r^0), \tag{4.9}$$

where $\lambda = (\lambda_1, \ldots, \lambda_s)'$ is a vector of multipliers.

The elements of $\hat{\theta}$ then satisfy

$$d(\hat{\theta}) + R'\hat{\lambda} = 0 \tag{4.10}$$

and

$$(R\hat{\theta} - r^0) = 0, \tag{4.11}$$

where $\hat{\lambda}$ is the vector of estimated multipliers.

Assuming that H_0 is true and linearizing (4.10) about the true parameter θ, we have

$$d(\theta) + D(\theta)(\hat{\theta} - \theta) + R'\lambda \stackrel{a}{=} 0 \qquad (4.12)$$

and

$$R(\hat{\theta} - \theta) = 0. \qquad (4.13)$$

We first introduce a norming matrix $\mathscr{I}^{-\frac{1}{2}}$ in (4.12), since it is known that $\mathscr{I}^{-\frac{1}{2}} d(\theta)$ is asymptotically distributed as $N(0, I_m)$ and the large sample distributions of $(\hat{\theta} - \theta)$ and $\hat{\lambda}$ are required. Equation (4.12) then becomes

$$\mathscr{I}^{-\frac{1}{2}}d(\theta) + \mathscr{I}^{-\frac{1}{2}}D(\theta)(\hat{\theta} - \theta) + \mathscr{I}^{-\frac{1}{2}}R'\lambda \stackrel{a}{=} 0. \qquad (4.14)$$

Consider the second term on the left-hand side of (4.14) which is

$$\mathscr{I}^{-\frac{1}{2}}D(\theta)(\hat{\theta} - \theta) = \mathscr{I}^{-\frac{1}{2}}D(\theta).\mathscr{I}^{-\frac{1}{2}}\mathscr{I}^{\frac{1}{2}}(\hat{\theta} - \theta).$$

Now $\mathscr{I}^{-\frac{1}{2}}D(\theta).\mathscr{I}^{-\frac{1}{2}} = \mathscr{I}^{\frac{1}{2}}[\mathscr{I}^{-1}D(\theta)].\mathscr{I}^{-\frac{1}{2}}$ has a probability limit equal to $-I_m$ under the above assumptions (see (vii)). Combining this result with (4.14), we obtain

$$\mathscr{I}^{-\frac{1}{2}}d(\theta) - \mathscr{I}^{\frac{1}{2}}(\hat{\theta} - \theta) + \mathscr{I}^{-\frac{1}{2}}R'\lambda \stackrel{a}{=} 0. \qquad (4.15)$$

The next step is to eliminate $(\hat{\theta} - \theta)$ from (4.15) by using (4.13). It will be useful to define the s by m matrix A by

$$A = [R\mathscr{I}^{-1}R']^{-\frac{1}{2}}R\mathscr{I}^{-\frac{1}{2}}. \qquad (4.16)$$

This matrix has two important properties:

(a) $AA' = I_s$; and
(b) $A\mathscr{I}^{\frac{1}{2}}(\hat{\theta} - \theta) = [R\mathscr{I}^{-1}R']^{-\frac{1}{2}}R(\hat{\theta} - \theta) = 0$ (from (4.13)).

Pre-multiplying (4.15) by A, therefore, yields

$$A\mathscr{I}^{-\frac{1}{2}}d(\theta) + A\mathscr{I}^{-\frac{1}{2}}R'\lambda \stackrel{a}{=} 0$$

and, as

$$A\mathscr{I}^{-\frac{1}{2}}R' = [R\mathscr{I}^{-1}R']^{-\frac{1}{2}}R\mathscr{I}^{-1}R' = [R\mathscr{I}^{-1}R']^{\frac{1}{2}},$$

this relationship can be rewritten as

$$[R\mathscr{I}^{-1}R']^{\frac{1}{2}}\hat{\lambda} \stackrel{a}{=} -A\mathscr{I}^{-\frac{1}{2}}d(\theta).$$

Property (a) of matrix A together with Crowder's (1976) result on the asymptotic distribution of $\mathscr{I}^{-\frac{1}{2}}d(\theta)$ implies that $-A\mathscr{I}^{-\frac{1}{2}}d(\theta)$ converges in distribution to $N(0, I_s)$, so that we have the important result that if H_0 is true, then

$$[R\mathscr{I}^{-1}R']^{\frac{1}{2}}\hat{\lambda} \stackrel{a}{\sim} N(0, I_s). \qquad (4.17)$$

Under assumption (ix)–that is, the elements of $\mathscr{I}$ are $O(n)$ and $\lim n^{-1}\mathscr{I}$ is non-singular–(4.17) can be replaced by the equivalent expression

$$n^{-\frac{1}{2}}\hat{\lambda} \overset{a}{\sim} N(0, \lim n^{-1}[R\mathscr{I}^{-1}R']^{-1}).$$

This result on the large sample behaviour of $\hat{\lambda}$ can be employed to obtain the asymptotic null distribution of $\hat{\theta}$, for example, from equation (4.12). It can be shown that, under H_0, $n^{\frac{1}{2}}(\hat{\theta} - \theta)$ is asymptotically normally distributed with zero mean vector and finite covariance matrix; that is, $(\hat{\theta} - \theta)$, like $(\tilde{\theta} - \theta)$, is $O_p(n^{-\frac{1}{2}})$.[7] It follows that $(\hat{\theta} - \tilde{\theta}) = [(\hat{\theta} - \theta) - (\tilde{\theta} - \theta)]$ is at most $O_p(n^{-\frac{1}{2}})$ and for the purpose of studying significance tests it is useful to obtain relationships linking $(\hat{\theta} - \tilde{\theta})$ to $d(\hat{\theta})$ and $\hat{\lambda}$. If we linearize $d(\hat{\theta})$ about $\tilde{\theta}$, then since the difference between $\hat{\theta}$ and $\tilde{\theta}$ will be small under H_0 (being $O_p(n^{-\frac{1}{2}})$), we have

$$d(\hat{\theta}) \overset{a}{=} d(\tilde{\theta}) + D(\tilde{\theta})(\hat{\theta} - \tilde{\theta}), \text{ or}$$

$$d(\hat{\theta}) \overset{a}{=} D(\tilde{\theta})(\hat{\theta} - \tilde{\theta}), \tag{4.18}$$

since $d(\tilde{\theta}) = 0$.

Expression (4.18) is an example of a relationship in which the $\overset{a}{=}$ notation is used without norming the variables so that the largest order of magnitude is $O_p(1)$. Consider a typical element of $d(\hat{\theta})$ which, by Taylor's formula, can be written as

$$d_i(\hat{\theta}) = d_i(\tilde{\theta}) + \sum_j D_{ij}(\tilde{\theta})(\hat{\theta}_j - \tilde{\theta}_j)$$

$$+ \frac{1}{2}\sum_k\sum_j (\hat{\theta}_j - \tilde{\theta}_j)[\partial^3 l(\bar{\theta}, \tilde{\theta})/\partial\theta_i\partial\theta_j\partial\theta_k](\hat{\theta}_k - \tilde{\theta}_k),$$

where $\partial^3 l(\bar{\theta}, \tilde{\theta})/\partial\theta_i\partial\theta_j\partial\theta_k$ denotes a third-order derivative evaluated at a point on the line segment between $\hat{\theta}$ and $\tilde{\theta}$. The left-hand-side variable, $d_i(\hat{\theta})$, is $O_p(n^{\frac{1}{2}})$. The first term on the right-hand side is zero and the second term is $O_p(n^{\frac{1}{2}})$ since it is a sum of a finite number of products of the $D_{ij}(\tilde{\theta})$ which are $O_p(n)$ and the $(\hat{\theta}_j - \tilde{\theta}_j)$ which are $O_p(n^{-\frac{1}{2}})$. The third term on the right-hand side is, however, only $O_p(1)$ since the third-order derivatives are $O_p(n)$ and $(\hat{\theta}_j - \tilde{\theta}_j)(\hat{\theta}_k - \tilde{\theta}_k)$ is $O_p(n^{-1})$. Thus the third term is asymptotically negligible and can be omitted to obtain (4.18).

Equations (4.10) and (4.18) then yield the asymptotically valid approximation

$$D(\tilde{\theta})(\hat{\theta} - \tilde{\theta}) + R'\hat{\lambda} \overset{a}{=} 0 \tag{4.19}$$

---

[7] See Rothenberg (1973, chap. 2) for a detailed derivation of the distribution of $\hat{\theta}$.

The relationship between the various test criteria can now be examined using (4.17) to (4.19).

Asymptotic null distributions of LR, W and LM tests

Consider first the LR procedure which is based upon a comparison of the supremum of $l(\theta)$ when H_0 is imposed with that achieved when the parametric restrictions $R\theta - r^0 = 0$ are ignored. The LR statistic is

$$LR = 2[l(\tilde{\theta}) - l(\hat{\theta})]. \tag{4.20}$$

Given the assumptions on the partial derivatives of $l(\cdot)$ and the fact that $\hat{\theta}$ and $\tilde{\theta}$ only differ by $O_p(n^{-\frac{1}{2}})$ when H_0 is true, we can use the quadratic approximation

$$l(\hat{\theta}) \stackrel{a}{=} l(\tilde{\theta}) + \tfrac{1}{2}(\hat{\theta} - \tilde{\theta})'D(\tilde{\theta})(\hat{\theta} - \tilde{\theta}), \tag{4.21}$$

the term in $(\hat{\theta} - \tilde{\theta})$ vanishing because $d(\tilde{\theta}) = 0$ and the term consisting of the sum of the quantities

$$\frac{1}{6}[\partial l^3(\bar{\theta}, \tilde{\theta})/\partial\theta_i\partial\theta_j\partial\theta_k](\hat{\theta}_i - \tilde{\theta}_i)(\hat{\theta}_j - \tilde{\theta}_j)(\hat{\theta}_k - \tilde{\theta}_k) \quad (i, j, k = 1, m)$$

being omitted because it is $O_p(n^{-\frac{1}{2}})$ and so is asymptotically negligible relative to retained terms which are $O_p(1)$. Thus, under H_0,

$$LR \stackrel{a}{=} -(\hat{\theta} - \tilde{\theta})'D(\tilde{\theta})(\hat{\theta} - \tilde{\theta})$$

or, from (4.19),

$$LR \stackrel{a}{=} -\hat{\lambda}'RD(\tilde{\theta})^{-1}R'\hat{\lambda}.$$

But $-D(\tilde{\theta})^{-1} = -D(\tilde{\theta})^{-1}\mathscr{I}\mathscr{I}^{-1}$

and $\operatorname{plim} - D(\tilde{\theta})^{-1}\mathscr{I} = \operatorname{plim} - D(\theta)^{-1}\mathscr{I} = I_m$,

so that LR has the same asymptotic null distribution as $\hat{\lambda}'R\mathscr{I}^{-1}R'\hat{\lambda}$ which in view of (4.17) is central χ^2 with s degrees of freedom; that is, LR $\stackrel{a}{\sim} \chi^2(s)$ on H_0.

The W criteria are motivated by the observation that $\tilde{\theta}$ is consistent for θ and, under H_0, $R\theta - r^0 = 0$ so that $(R\tilde{\theta} - r^0)$ will tend to a null vector. The W test is then a test of the joint significance of the elements of $R\tilde{\theta} - r^0$. Note that if H_0 is true then $R\theta = r^0$ and so

$$(R\tilde{\theta} - r^0) = R(\tilde{\theta} - \theta) = R\mathscr{I}^{-\frac{1}{2}}\mathscr{I}^{\frac{1}{2}}(\tilde{\theta} - \theta). \tag{4.22}$$

Next pre-multiply (4.22) by $(R\mathscr{I}^{-1}R')^{-\frac{1}{2}}$ and recall that the matrix A is defined as in (4.16) to obtain

$$(R\mathscr{I}^{-1}R')^{-\frac{1}{2}}(R\tilde{\theta} - r^0) \stackrel{a}{=} A\mathscr{I}^{\frac{1}{2}}(\tilde{\theta} - \theta). \tag{4.23}$$

The right-hand side of (4.23) converges in distribution to $N(0, I_s)$ because $AA' = I_s$ and $\mathscr{I}^{\frac{1}{2}}(\tilde{\theta} - \theta) \overset{a}{\sim} N(0, I_m)$. The W test is then based upon the result that

$$(R\tilde{\theta} - r^0)'[R\mathscr{I}^{-1}R']^{-1}(R\tilde{\theta} - r^0) \overset{a}{\sim} \chi^2(s)$$

if H_0 is true. A feasible test statistic can be derived by replacing θ in $\mathscr{I}^{-1}$ by the consistent estimator $\tilde{\theta}$ without affecting the asymptotic null distribution. Using an obvious notation, the W statistic can be written as

$$W = (R\tilde{\theta} - r^0)'[R\tilde{\mathscr{I}}^{-1}R']^{-1}(R\tilde{\theta} - r^0). \qquad (4.24)$$

Significantly large values of W lead to the rejection of H_0.

Finally, the LM test as described by Aitchison and Silvey (1958) involves a test of the significance of the estimated multipliers. The form of an appropriate test statistic is apparent from (4.17) which implies that $\hat{\lambda}'R\mathscr{I}^{-1}R'\hat{\lambda}$ will converge in distribution to $\chi^2(s)$ when H_0 is true. Replacing θ in $\mathscr{I}$ by $\hat{\theta}$ where $(\hat{\theta} - \theta)$ is $o_p(1)$ on H_0 yields the feasible test statistic

$$LM = \hat{\lambda}'R\hat{\mathscr{I}}^{-1}R'\hat{\lambda} \qquad (4.25)$$

which, in common with LR and W, has a limit null distribution of $\chi^2(s)$.

It is interesting to note that if $\hat{\mathscr{I}}^{-1}$ in (4.25) is replaced by $-D(\tilde{\theta})$ (and this change is asymptotically valid under H_0 because plim $-D(\tilde{\theta}).\hat{\mathscr{I}}^{-1} = I_m$), then the resulting variant of the LM statistic is equal to the approximation to LR derived from (4.21). This result indicates a close relationship between LR and LM. The links between W and LM may be clarified by considering an alternative derivation of the former statistic.

The W test is derived by examining

$$(R\tilde{\theta} - r^0) = R(\tilde{\theta} - \hat{\theta}) \overset{a}{=} (R\tilde{D}^{-1}R')\hat{\lambda},$$

using $R\hat{\theta} - r^0 = 0$ and (4.19). Now if $z \sim N(0, \Sigma_{zz})$, Σ_{zz} being a non-singular s by s matrix, then $Kz \sim N(0, K\Sigma_{zz}K')$ for any fixed non-singular matrix K and

$$z'\Sigma_{zz}^{-1}z = (Kz)'[K\Sigma_{zz}K']^{-1}(Kz) \sim \chi^2(s).$$

Accordingly, since $(R\tilde{D}^{-1}R')$ is non-singular, the χ^2 type test of the significance of $(R\tilde{D}^{-1}R')\hat{\lambda}$ is the same as that for $\hat{\lambda}$ alone, that is, as the LM test.

The Aitchison–Silvey LM test may have considerable appeal to economists since it involves checking whether or not the shadow prices of the imposed restrictions are too high, and such ideas are familiar from economic analysis. An exactly equivalent procedure was, however, proposed by Rao (1948) from a completely different viewpoint some time before the publication of the Aitchison and Silvey (1958) article. If (4.10) is combined with (4.25), then it will be seen that

$$\text{LM} = d(\hat{\theta})'.\hat{\mathscr{I}}^{-1}d(\hat{\theta}). \tag{4.26}$$

In this form, the LM statistic is for obvious reasons referred to as the *efficient score statistic*. The motivation for proposing (4.26) is that, if H_0 is true, then $\hat{\theta}$ and $\tilde{\theta}$ should be close to each other and so $d(\hat{\theta})$ should be close to $d(\tilde{\theta})$ which is a null vector, implying that it is reasonable to test the joint significance of the elements of $d(\hat{\theta})$. An appropriate procedure must, of course, take account of any singularities in the asymptotic distribution of $d(\hat{\theta})$ under H_0. In many of the cases to be discussed, singularities occur because some elements of $d(\hat{\theta})$ equal zero for all samples.

It should be noted that the asymptotic null distributions of W and LM would not be affected if the required estimates of $\mathscr{I}$ were evaluated using any estimator $\dot{\theta}$ which was consistent under H_0, or indeed if $\mathscr{I}$ were replaced by any matrix G such that $\operatorname{plim}\mathscr{I}^{-1}G = I_m$ on H_0. Obvious choices for G are the negative Hessian $-D(\theta)$ and the matrix $\Sigma_1^n(\partial l_t(\theta)/\partial\theta)(\partial l_t(\theta)/\partial\theta)'$ as suggested by Berndt, Hall, Hall and Hausman (1974). However, small-sample behaviour may be sensitive to changes in the weighting matrices of the quadratic forms of the LM and W procedures. The available evidence for econometric tests is discussed in later chapters.

The use of the Berndt et al. (1974) approximation to $\mathscr{I}$ leads to a very simple form of the LM statistic. If $W(\theta)$ is the n by m matrix with typical element $\partial l_t(\theta)/\partial\theta_j$ and ι is an n-dimensional vector with every element equal to unity, then

$$d(\theta) = \Sigma_1^n[\partial l_t(\theta)/\partial\theta] = W(\theta)'\iota$$

and $W(\theta)'W(\theta)$ is the m by m matrix

$$\Sigma_1^n[(\partial l_t(\theta)/\partial\theta)(\partial l_t(\theta)/\partial\theta)'];$$

so that LM of equation (4.26) is asymptotically equivalent to

$$nR_w^2 = \iota'\hat{W}(\hat{W}'\hat{W})^{-1}\hat{W}'\iota,$$

where $\hat{W}$ denotes $W(\theta)$ evaluated at $\theta = \hat{\theta}$ and R_w^2 is the uncentred coefficient of determination of the least-squares regression of ι on $\hat{W}$. The nR_w^2 criterion is usually referred to as the *outer product gradient* (OPG) form of the LM test statistic.

Simplifications and special cases

Many checks for misspecification are simply tests of the hypothesis that s elements of θ equal zero. Without loss of generality, it can be assumed that the null model is obtained by setting the last s elements of θ equal to zero. If θ is partitioned as $(\theta_1', \theta_2')'$ where θ_1 is r by 1 and θ_2 is s by 1, then the hypothesis to be tested is

$$H_0: \theta_2 = 0 \tag{4.27}$$

which is clearly a special case of (4.2). The sub-vector θ_1 contains the nuisance parameters. The MLE vectors $\tilde{\theta}$ and $\hat{\theta}$ will be partitioned in the same way as θ with $\tilde{\theta}' = (\tilde{\theta}_1', \tilde{\theta}_2')$ and $\hat{\theta}' = (\hat{\theta}_1', 0')$, where $\hat{\theta}_2$ is a null vector since $\hat{\theta}$ must satisfy the parametric restrictions of (4.27).

In order to explore the simplifications resulting from restricting attention to constraints of the form (4.27), it will be useful to partition $d(\cdot)$ and $\mathscr{I}$ as follows:

$$d(\theta)' = [d_1(\theta)', d_2(\theta)'],$$

$$\mathscr{I} = \begin{bmatrix} \mathscr{I}_{11} & \mathscr{I}_{12} \\ \mathscr{I}_{21} & \mathscr{I}_{22} \end{bmatrix}$$

with

$$\mathscr{I}^{-1} = \begin{bmatrix} \mathscr{I}^{11} & \mathscr{I}^{12} \\ \mathscr{I}^{21} & \mathscr{I}^{22} \end{bmatrix},$$

where the suffix 1 denotes the set of nuisance parameters and the suffix 2 denotes the set of parameters under test.

The constrained MLE $\hat{\theta}$ is obtained by considering the first-order partial derivatives of the Lagrangian

$$\Lambda(\theta, \lambda) = l(\theta) + \lambda'\theta_2, \tag{4.28}$$

so that $\hat{\theta}$ and $\hat{\lambda}$ satisfy

$$\partial\Lambda(\hat{\theta}, \hat{\lambda})/\partial\theta_1 = d_1(\hat{\theta}) = 0$$
$$\partial\Lambda(\hat{\theta}, \hat{\lambda})/\partial\theta_2 = d_2(\hat{\theta}) + \hat{\lambda} = 0$$
$$\partial\Lambda(\hat{\theta}, \hat{\lambda})/\partial\lambda = \hat{\theta}_2 = 0.$$

The LR, W and LM statistics appropriate for testing $H_0: \theta_2 = 0$ are then

$$\text{LR} = 2[l(\tilde{\theta}_1, \tilde{\theta}_2) - l(\hat{\theta}_1, 0)] \tag{4.29}$$

$$\text{W} = \tilde{\theta}_2'[\tilde{\mathscr{I}}^{22}]^{-1}\tilde{\theta}_2 \tag{4.30}$$

and

$$\text{LM} = \hat{\lambda}'\hat{\mathscr{I}}^{22}\hat{\lambda} = d_2(\hat{\theta})'\hat{\mathscr{I}}^{22}d_2(\hat{\theta}), \tag{4.31}$$

where

$$\mathscr{I}^{22} = [\mathscr{I}_{22} - \mathscr{I}_{21}\mathscr{I}_{11}^{-1}\mathscr{I}_{12}]^{-1}.$$

In some econometric models, $\tilde{\theta}_1$ and $\tilde{\theta}_2$ are asymptotically independently distributed so that the information matrix is block diagonal and equations (4.30) and (4.31) can be further simplified. If $\mathscr{I}_{12}$ and $\mathscr{I}_{21}$ are set equal to null matrices of appropriate dimensions before the estimation of $\mathscr{I}$, then the W and LM statistics are given by

$$\text{W} = \tilde{\theta}_2'\tilde{\mathscr{I}}_{22}\tilde{\theta}_2 \qquad (4.32)$$

and

$$\text{LM} = \hat{\lambda}'\hat{\mathscr{I}}_{22}^{-1}\hat{\lambda} = d_2(\hat{\theta})'\hat{\mathscr{I}}_{22}^{-1}d_2(\hat{\theta}). \qquad (4.33)$$

Asymptotic power properties of LR, W and LM tests

The ability of a test to detect that $R\theta - r^0$ is not a null vector when H_0 is false is clearly of interest. If a test of H_0 is carried out with a fixed significance level, then the probability of rejecting false parametric constraints tends to unity as the sample size tends to infinity no matter which of the three procedures is employed. Using $\pi(\theta)$ to denote the limit as $n \to \infty$ of the probability of rejecting H_0, we have

$$\pi(\theta) = 1 \text{ if } (R\theta - r^0) \neq 0$$

for tests based upon LR, W and LM. (Procedures which have the property that $\pi(\theta) = 1$ if H_0 is false are known as *consistent tests*.) This result can be illustrated by considering the Wald statistic of (4.24) when the elements of $R\theta - r^0$ are not all equal to zero. The test statistic is

$$\text{W} = (R\tilde{\theta} - r^0)'[R.\tilde{\mathscr{I}}^{-1}R']^{-1}(R\tilde{\theta} - r^0)$$

and since $(R\tilde{\theta} - r^0)$ is $O_p(1)$, as opposed to its stochastic order of magnitude of $o_p(1)$ on H_0, the consistency of $\tilde{\theta}$ coupled with assumption (ix) on the asymptotic behaviour of $\mathscr{I}$ implies that W is $O_p(n)$. It follows that W will exceed any pre-set finite critical value for the $\chi^2(s)$ distribution with probability tending to unity as n tends to infinity (see Silvey, 1959, for a discussion of the consistency of the LR and LM procedures).

In order to obtain potentially useful measures of power with a fixed significance level, it is necessary to restrict the magnitude of the departure from the null hypothesis. More precisely, the elements of $(R\theta - r^0)$ must be small enough to ensure that LM, LR and W are $O_p(1)$ so that their asymptotic powers are less than unity. Alternative hypotheses which permit such small departures are known as *local alternatives* and have the property that they become closer and closer to the null hypothesis as the sample size tends to infinity. Local alternatives are not intended to have any physical significance. They are more properly regarded as artificial devices to be used in the hope of obtaining information from asymptotic theory about power in interesting regions.

If we continue to use the Wald criterion to illustrate general results, it is clear that using the sequence of local alternatives

$$H_n: R\theta - r^0 = [R\mathscr{I}^{-1}R']^{\frac{1}{2}}\eta, \tag{4.34}$$

where η is a fixed s-dimensional vector with finite non-zero elements, will lead to

$$(R\tilde{\theta} - r^0) = R(\tilde{\theta} - \theta) + [R\mathscr{I}^{-1}R']^{\frac{1}{2}}\eta,$$

or equivalently to

$$[R\mathscr{I}^{-1}R']^{-\frac{1}{2}}(R\tilde{\theta} - r^0) = [R\mathscr{I}^{-1}R']^{-\frac{1}{2}}R(\tilde{\theta} - \theta) + \eta. \tag{4.35}$$

The first term on the right-hand side of (4.35) converges in distribution to $N(0, I_s)$ whatever the value of the true parameter vector $\theta \in \Theta$. In particular, this term is asymptotically distributed as $N(0, I_s)$ for sequences of θ values satisfying H_n which approaches H_0 as $n \to \infty$ (the right-hand side of (4.34) being $O(n^{-\frac{1}{2}})$). Since η is a fixed vector, it follows that the left-hand side of (4.35) converges in distribution to $N(\eta, I_s)$ under H_n (see Cox and Hinkley, 1974, pp. 317–18, for a useful discussion of asymptotic behaviour under local alternatives). It also follows that the sum of the squared elements of the left-hand side of (4.35) will converge in distribution to a non-central chi-squared variable with s degrees of freedom and non-centrality parameter $\eta'\eta$. We can write this result more succinctly as

$$(R\tilde{\theta} - r^0)'[R\mathscr{I}^{-1}R']^{-1}(R\tilde{\theta} - r^0) \overset{a}{\sim} \chi^2(s, \eta'\eta) \tag{4.36}$$

under H_n. But the left-hand side of (4.36) is the W statistic of (4.24) with $\mathscr{J}^{-1}$ replaced by $\mathscr{I}^{-1}$. This substitution will not affect asymptotic properties, so that the W statistic converges in distribution to $\chi^2(s, \eta'\eta)$ under the specified sequence of local alternatives. It can be shown that the LR and LM statistics are also asymptotically distributed as $\chi^2(s, \eta'\eta)$ under H_n of (4.34); see Silvey (1959). Procedures whose test statistics have the same asymptotic distribution under the null hypothesis and all sequences of local alternatives are said to be *asymptotically equivalent tests*.

Although the strategy of considering only local alternatives does lead to LR, W and LM having asymptotic powers strictly less than unity, the asymptotic equivalence of the procedures implies that this approach does not provide any basis for choosing between them. It does, however, provide some information about the status of these three tests relative to other procedures. The LR, W and LM tests are in fact asymptotically most powerful against local alternatives.

It is possible to extend the above analysis by considering Edgeworth-type approximations to the distribution functions of asymptotically equivalent test statistics under local alternatives. Rothenberg (1983) has provided a valuable outline of this general approach and a summary of some results of interest to econometricians. Asymptotically equivalent tests sometimes have finite sample significance levels which differ substantially from the nominal size and are themselves quite dissimilar. In such circumstances, a simple comparison of rejection probabilities of the tests is of doubtful value. The first stage of the approach described by Rothenberg (1983) is, therefore, to use Edgeworth expansions of the null distributions in order to obtain modified (size-corrected) test statistics. The second stage is to employ a second Edgeworth expansion to approximate the power functions of the modified tests under a sequence of local alternatives. A general conclusion which emerges from the application of this method to various econometric problems is that no one modified test is uniformly superior to the other two procedures. Rothenberg (1983) also reports that power differences between size-adjusted tests are often quite small so that rankings by power may not have enormous practical importance. Indeed these power differences are frequently much smaller than the size corrections.

Rothenberg (1983) is careful to point out limitations of the Edgeworth series approach (e.g., the approximation may be poor when the test statistic has a markedly skewed distribution) and also mentions other approaches including Bahadur's (1960) 'approximate slope' method. His opinion, however, is that the Edgeworth approximations based upon local alternatives should be fairly accurate over the interesting range of intermediate power. If this is the case, then it would appear that it is important to check for differences between actual and nominal significance levels and to carry out modifications when necessary, but that after such modification there is possibly not much to be gained in terms of power by using one test rather than another.

The computational costs of the LR, W and LM tests

The LR test requires the calculation of both unrestricted and restricted MLEs, the W test uses only the unrestricted MLE, and the LM test involves the estimation of the restricted model alone. It follows that the computational costs of the three tests may be quite different.

If the calculation of the unrestricted estimator $\tilde{\theta}$ is simple relative to that of the constrained estimator $\hat{\theta}$, then, at first sight, the W test appears to be more attractive than the LR and LM procedures. For example, when the unrestricted model is a classical normal linear regression model and the null hypothesis imposes a set of non-linear constraints on θ, the estimator $\tilde{\theta}$ used to compute W is ordinary least squares (OLS) while $\hat{\theta}$, the estimator required for the calculation of LR and LM, must be derived by solving a non-linear optimization problem. (This kind of situation can arise in practice, as is demonstrated by Sargan's (1980) work on testing dynamic specification (also see Mizon, 1977).) However, problems can arise when the W test is used to test non-linear restrictions (see Section 2.7).

If the estimation of the null model is relatively simple, then the use of the LM principle is suggested. In the context of testing for errors of specification, the null model is the specification of interest whose adequacy is to be assessed, so that the constrained estimator $\hat{\theta}$ will be calculated. Moreover, the null model is usually obtained by setting some of the elements of θ equal to zero and, in such situations, $\hat{\theta}$ will be cheaper to compute than $\tilde{\theta}$. Accordingly, the LM approach is attractive when misspecification tests (sometimes referred to as diagnostic checks) are to be calculated.

There would, at first sight, appear to be little to justify the use of LR methods which require the calculation of both $\hat{\theta}$ and $\tilde{\theta}$. It has, however, been suggested that this feature does not represent an important weakness since the unrestricted estimate of $\tilde{\theta}$ will have to be calculated if the LM statistic is significant, and, if W is insignificant, $\hat{\theta}$ should be calculated in order to improve the precision of estimation. This argument is not entirely convincing. The significance of an LM statistic is evidence against the null model and not evidence in favour of the alternative, so that $\tilde{\theta}$ is not necessarily of value. The use of LR tests may be justified on other grounds. Estimation requirements may only form a part of the computational burden, and convenience of calculation may be of some interest. In some situations, the researcher may find that the LM and W tests are associated with very high (short-run) costs because available computer programmes do not readily permit their calculation, but $l(\tilde{\theta})$ and $l(\hat{\theta})$, the only quantities required for the LR test, can be obtained routinely. Further, the importance of computational costs should not be overestimated. The choice between procedures should also take proper account of any information available on the small sample behaviour of each test. Rothenberg (1983) points out that there is some evidence that in non-linear problems the LR test may be superior to LM and W as a result of its good performance in the central region of the power surface, that is, when the power is approximately 50 per cent.

1.5   Alternative approaches to testing parametric hypotheses

There are many ways to construct tests of the null hypothesis other than the LR, W and LM procedures. For example, if $\hat{\theta}$ is an estimator which is consistent, asymptotically normally distributed and inefficient relative to $\tilde{\theta}$ under local alternatives, then H_0 of (4.2) may be tested using the criterion

$$\dot{T} = (R\hat{\theta} - r^0)'[RV(\hat{\theta})R']^{-1}(R\hat{\theta} - r^0), \tag{5.1}$$

where $V(\hat{\theta})$ is a consistent estimator of the asymptotic covariance matrix of $\hat{\theta}$. The statistic $\dot{T}$ of (5.1) converges in distribution to $\chi^2(s)$ under H_0 (see Stroud, 1971) and so shares the limit null distribution of LR, W and LM. Under the sequence of local alternatives H_n of (4.34), $\dot{T}$ will be asymptotically distributed as non-central χ^2, but its non-centrality parameter will be less than $\eta'\eta$ and so its asymptotic local power will be smaller than that of the three asymptotically equivalent likelihood-based tests.

In the absence of evidence to the contrary, it seems reasonable to focus attention on tests which share the large sample properties of LR, W and LM if only to keep the list of procedures to be examined to a manageable length. Two types of tests meeting this requirement will be discussed below. We first consider procedures based upon a general theorem due to Durbin (1970). These tests involve the calculation of the restricted MLE $\hat{\theta}$ and are sometimes very closely related to the corresponding LM tests. The second type of procedure to be examined involves replacing maximum likelihood estimators in the so-called classical LR, W and LM tests by estimators which are asymptotically equivalent (at least under H_0 and H_n) but simpler to calculate.

In order to facilitate comparisons, we shall follow Durbin (1970) by assuming that the null hypothesis is of the form

$$H_0: \theta_2 = \theta_2^0, \tag{5.2}$$

where θ_2 is, as before, the sub-vector containing the last s elements of θ and θ_2^0 is some specified vector of constants. (This null is sufficiently general to generate a very large number of tests for misspecification). The fixed alternative hypothesis is $H_1: \theta_2 \neq \theta_2^0$ and, given assumption (ix) on the asymptotic order of magnitude of $\mathcal{I}$, it will be convenient to use

$$H_n: \theta_2 = \theta_2^0 + n^{-\frac{1}{2}}\delta \tag{5.3}$$

to denote a sequence of local alternatives, δ being a fixed s-dimensional vector with finite elements.

Durbin's test and related procedures

The approach proposed by Durbin (1970) can be summarized as follows:

(a) Obtain the constrained MLE $\hat{\theta}$ which has sub-vectors $\hat{\theta}_1$ and θ_2^0.
(b) Maximize the log-likelihood function $l(\theta)$ with respect to θ_2, conditional upon $\theta_1 = \hat{\theta}_1$, to obtain an estimator θ_2^*. The es-

timator θ_2^*, therefore, satisfies

$$\partial l(\hat{\theta}_1, \theta_2^*)/\partial\theta_2 = 0.[8] \tag{5.4}$$

(c)   Carry out a test of the joint significance of the elements of $(\theta_2^* - \theta_2^0)$. Values of an appropriate test statistic which exceed the pre-specified critical value suggest that the parametric restrictions of (5.2) are not consistent with the sample data.

It is clear that, for Durbin's method to be attractive relative to the LR approach, the solution of (5.4) for θ_2^* should be simple relative to that of $d(\tilde{\theta}) = 0$, the vector set of equations associated with the calculation of the unrestricted MLE. In order to derive a valid large sample test based upon $(\theta_2^* - \theta_2^0)$ and to show that such a test is asymptotically equivalent to LR, W and LM, it will be useful to consider the appropriate LM procedure and also a Taylor series expansion of $\partial l(\hat{\theta}_1, \theta_2^*)/\partial\theta_2$ about $\theta = \hat{\theta}$ under a sequence of local alternatives.

The Lagrangean for Durbin's problem can be written as

$$\Lambda(\theta, \lambda) = l(\theta) + \lambda'(\theta_2 - \theta_2^0), \tag{5.5}$$

so that, specializing previous results, we have

$$\partial l(\hat{\theta})/\partial\theta_1 = \hat{d}_1 = 0 \tag{5.6}$$

$$\partial l(\hat{\theta})/\partial\theta_2 + \hat{\lambda} = \hat{d}_2 + \hat{\lambda} = 0 \tag{5.7}$$

$$\hat{\theta}_2 - \theta_2^0 = 0, \tag{5.8}$$

where $\hat{d}_i$ denotes $\partial l(\theta)/\partial\theta_i$ evaluated at $\theta = \hat{\theta}$ $(i = 1, 2)$.

Next, under H_n of (5.3), the first-order condition of (5.4) can be linearized to yield

$$0 = d_2(\hat{\theta}_1, \theta_2^*) \stackrel{a}{=} \hat{d}_2 + \hat{D}_{22}(\theta_2^* - \theta_2^0), \tag{5.9}$$

where $\hat{D}_{22}$ denotes $\partial^2 l(\theta)/\partial\theta_2\partial\theta_2'$ evaluated at $\theta = \hat{\theta}$, $\hat{d}_2$ and $\hat{D}_{22}(\theta_2^* - \theta_2^0)$ are both $O_p(n^{\frac{1}{2}})$, and terms of $O_p(1)$ have not been shown. It follows that when $\theta_2 = \theta_2^0 + n^{-\frac{1}{2}}\delta$,

$$n^{\frac{1}{2}}(\theta_2^* - \theta_2^0) \stackrel{a}{=} -(n^{-1}\hat{D}_{22})^{-1}(n^{-\frac{1}{2}}\hat{d}_2). \tag{5.10}$$

Since $(n^{-1}\hat{D}_{22})$ tends to a finite non-singular matrix, the χ^2 test statistic based upon the right-hand side of (5.10) is equal to that based upon $n^{-\frac{1}{2}}\hat{d}_2$

---

[8] The notation of (5.4) along with that of some other equations in this section is, strictly speaking, incorrect because vectors should be taken as column vectors unless a transposition symbol is shown. The notation required to eliminate this inconsistency is, however, clumsy and, in any case, there should be no possibility of confusion or error.

which is, of course, the LM statistic. Consequently the test statistic provided by Durbin's method has the same limiting distribution as LM under H_n. The null hypothesis H_0 is a special case of H_n obtained by setting δ equal to a null vector, and so Durbin's test and LM have the same asymptotic distribution under the null and local alternatives. Durbin's procedure is, therefore, asymptotically equivalent to LM and hence also to LR and W.

The form of Durbin's test statistic can be derived by noting that equations (4.26) and (5.6) imply that the LM statistic for testing the parametric restriction $\theta_2 = \theta_2^0$ can be written as

$$\text{LM} = \hat{d}_2'\hat{\mathscr{I}}^{22}\hat{d}_2, \tag{5.11}$$

and that equation (5.10) yields the result that

$$(\theta_2^* - \theta_2^0) \stackrel{a}{=} \hat{\mathscr{I}}_{22}^{-1}\hat{d}_2,$$

or equivalently

$$\hat{d}_2 \stackrel{a}{=} \hat{\mathscr{I}}_{22}(\theta_2^* - \theta_2^0). \tag{5.12}$$

Combining equations (5.11) and (5.12) reveals that an appropriate form of Durbin's statistic is

$$
\begin{aligned}
T_D &= (\theta_2^* - \theta_2^0)'\hat{\mathscr{I}}_{22}\hat{\mathscr{I}}^{22}\hat{\mathscr{I}}_{22}(\theta_2^* - \theta_2^0) \\
&= (\theta_2^* - \theta_2^0)'\hat{\mathscr{I}}_{22}[\hat{\mathscr{I}}_{22} - \hat{\mathscr{I}}_{21}\hat{\mathscr{I}}_{11}^{-1}\hat{\mathscr{I}}_{12}]^{-1}\hat{\mathscr{I}}_{22}(\theta_2^* - \theta_2^0).
\end{aligned}
\tag{5.13}
$$

In the special case in which $\lim n^{-1}\mathscr{I}_{12}$ is a null matrix (which implies that $\tilde{\theta}_1$ and $\tilde{\theta}_2$ are asymptotically independently distributed), T_D may be reduced to the simpler form

$$(\theta_2^* - \theta_2^0)'\hat{\mathscr{I}}_{22}(\theta_2^* - \theta_2^0) \tag{5.14}$$

which is similar to the corresponding W statistic, $(\tilde{\theta}_2 - \theta_2^0)'\hat{\mathscr{I}}_{22}(\tilde{\theta}_2 - \theta_2^0)$.[9]

Durbin's (1970) theorem was generalized by Sargan and Mehta (1983) in order to permit greater flexibility in choosing which parameters to re-estimate. Sargan and Mehta consider a three-part division of the parameter vector

$$\theta' = (\theta_1', \theta_2', \theta_3')$$

with the null hypothesis $H_0: \theta_3 = \theta_3^0$. As in Durbin's (1970) approach, the

---

[9] Durbin (1970) describes tests of the general form (5.14) as 'naive' since they are based upon the belief that θ_2^* has the same asymptotic properties as the MLE of θ_2 when θ_1 is known. Replacing θ_1 by $\hat{\theta}_1$ is, however, only asymptotically irrelevant when $\lim n^{-1}\mathscr{I}_{12}$ is a null matrix.

first step is to obtain the restricted MLE

$$\hat{\theta}' = (\hat{\theta}'_1, \hat{\theta}'_2, \theta_3^{0\prime}),$$

but in the next stage $l(\theta)$ is maximized with respect to both θ_2 and θ_3 with only θ_1 being fixed at $\hat{\theta}_1$. If the maximizers are denoted by θ_2^* and θ_3^*, then the Sargan–Mehta statistic is a quadratic form in $(\theta_2^* - \hat{\theta}_2, \theta_3^* - \theta_3^0)$. The asymptotic equivalence of the Sargan–Mehta three-part division (TPD) test to LR, W and LM is straightforwardly established by expansions of first-order conditions. If

$$\theta^{*\prime} = (\hat{\theta}'_1, \theta_2^{*\prime}, \theta_3^{*\prime}),$$

then $d_3(\theta^*) = 0$ and so expanding this vector set of equations about $\theta = \hat{\theta}$ yields

$$0 = d_3(\theta^*) \stackrel{a}{=} \hat{d}_3 + \hat{D}_{32}(\theta_2^* - \hat{\theta}_2) + \hat{D}_{33}(\theta_3^* - \theta_3^0),$$

or equivalently

$$-\hat{D}_{32}(\theta_2^* - \hat{\theta}_2) - \hat{D}_{33}(\theta_3^* - \theta_3^0) \stackrel{a}{=} \hat{d}_3. \tag{5.15}$$

Equation (5.15) shows the connection between a set of linear combinations of the elements of $(\theta_2^* - \hat{\theta}_2, \theta_3^* - \theta_3^0)$ and the efficient score vector $\hat{d}_3$ used in the construction of the LM test of $\theta_3 = \theta_3^0$ (see Sargan and Mehta, 1983, for further details of the asymptotic theory of the TPD procedure).

Engle (1982a) also considers a three-part division of θ and proposes a test of the parametric restrictions $\theta_3 = \theta_3^0$. In the context of estimation based upon maximization of likelihoods, his procedure, which is appropriate when $\lim n^{-1}\mathscr{I}_{21}$ and $\lim n^{-1}\mathscr{I}_{23}$ are both null matrices, involves obtaining an estimator $\dot{\theta}_2$ which is root-n consistent for θ_2 under H_0.[10] A score test of $\theta_3 = \theta_3^0$ is then calculated with $\dot{\theta}_2$ being treated as if it were the true value.

In order to establish the asymptotic validity of Engle's (1982a) test, consider the Lagrangean

$$\Lambda(\theta_1, \theta_3, \lambda) = l(\theta_1, \dot{\theta}_2, \theta_3) + \lambda'(\theta_3 - \theta_3^0). \tag{5.16}$$

The constrained parameter estimates

$$\theta^+ = (\theta_1^+, \dot{\theta}_2, \theta_3^0)$$

and associated vector of multipliers λ^+ provided by the usual techniques satisfy $d_1^+ = 0$ and $\lambda^+ = -d_3^+$, where d_i^+ denotes $\partial l(\theta)/\partial \theta_i$ evaluated at $\theta = \theta^+$ ($i = 1, 3$).

---

[10] By 'root-n consistent,' we mean that $(\dot{\theta}_2 - \theta_2)$ is $O_p(n^{-\frac{1}{2}})$, which implies that plim $\dot{\theta}_2 = \theta_2$.

If $\hat{\theta}$ denotes the MLE when θ_1 and θ_2 are unrestricted and θ_3 is set equal to θ_3^0, then the conventional LM (score) test is based upon $\hat{\lambda} = -\hat{d}_3$, with $\hat{d}_1$ and $\hat{d}_2$ both being null vectors. In order to examine the relationship between d_3^+ and $\hat{d}_3$, and hence between Engle's procedure and the standard score test, we first expand d_1^+ about $\theta = \hat{\theta}$ assuming that H_0 is true. We then have

$$d_1^+ \overset{a}{=} \hat{d}_1 + \hat{D}_{11}(\theta_1^+ - \hat{\theta}_1) + \hat{D}_{12}(\dot{\theta}_2 - \hat{\theta}_2),$$

but $d_1^+ = \hat{d}_1 = 0$ and so

$$(\theta_1^+ - \hat{\theta}_1) \overset{a}{=} \hat{D}_{11}^{-1}\hat{D}_{12}(\dot{\theta}_2 - \hat{\theta}_2). \tag{5.17}$$

Under H_0, $\hat{\theta}_2 - \theta_2$ and $\dot{\theta}_2 - \theta_2$ are both $O_p(n^{-\frac{1}{2}})$ and hence their difference, $\hat{\theta}_2 - \dot{\theta}_2$, is at most $O_p(n^{-\frac{1}{2}})$. Moreover, the consistency of $\hat{\theta}$ on H_0 implies that $\hat{D}_{11}^{-1}\hat{D}_{12}$ and $D_{11}^{-1}D_{12}$ have a common probability limit. This common limit is a null matrix because plim $-\mathscr{I}^{-1}D = I$ and we are considering a case in which $\lim \mathscr{I}_{11}^{-1}\mathscr{I}_{12}$ is a null matrix. Equation (5.17), therefore, implies that $(\theta_1^+ - \hat{\theta}_1)$ is at most $o_p(n^{-\frac{1}{2}})$.

Next consider the expansion of d_3^+ about $\theta = \hat{\theta}$. If the null hypothesis is true, then

$$d_3^+ \overset{a}{=} \hat{d}_3 + \hat{D}_{31}(\theta_1^+ - \hat{\theta}_1) + \hat{D}_{32}(\dot{\theta}_2 - \hat{\theta}_2), \tag{5.18}$$

with $\hat{d}_3$ being $O_p(n^{\frac{1}{2}})$ and the other two terms on the right-hand side of (5.18) being $o_p(n^{\frac{1}{2}})$. Thus $d_3^+ \overset{a}{=} \hat{d}_3$ under H_0, and this result together with asymptotic block diagonality of n^{-1} times $\mathscr{I}$ and the consistency of $\dot{\theta}_2$ demonstrates that Engle's (1982a) theory is valid.

Engle's (1982a) procedure will be useful whenever obtaining $\hat{\theta}_1$ and $\hat{\theta}_2$ is appreciably more difficult than calculating a maximizer θ_1^+ conditional upon a fixed value of θ_2. The important econometric example of such a situation given by Engle (1982a) is the generalized regression model in which θ_1 contains the regression parameters and the elements of θ_2 determine the disturbance covariance matrix up to a constant of proportionality.

Two-step estimators and associated tests

As mentioned previously, there are close links between the theories of estimation and hypothesis testing. One area of estimation theory which has received considerable attention in econometrics is the development of procedures which share the asymptotic properties of MLEs; see, for example, the articles by Hausman (1975) and Hendry (1976). These estimators have usually been derived for cases in which the maximum likelihood estimation is thought, on grounds of computational cost, to be impractical. One important component of this computational cost is the solution of the first-order conditions for a local maximum of $l(\theta)$, and this task will be onerous when these conditions take the form of highly non-linear equations. An obvious route to computational saving is, therefore, to obtain an approximate solution based upon a linearization of the normal equations determining the MLEs. This approach has been discussed by Rothenberg and Leenders (1964) in the context of the estimation of simultaneous equation models, but is capable of more general application.

Rothenberg and Leenders (1964) assume that a first-stage estimator $\dot\theta$ is available such that $(\dot\theta - \theta)$ and $(\dot\theta - \tilde\theta)$ are both $O_p(n^{-\frac{1}{2}})$; so that $\dot\theta$ is consistent, but asymptotically inefficient. An asymptotically efficient estimator is then obtained without iterative calculations by examining the linearization of $d(\tilde\theta)$ (which is of course equal to a null vector) about $\theta = \dot\theta$.

Under regularity assumptions, we have

$$0 = d(\tilde\theta) \overset{a}{=} d(\dot\theta) + D(\dot\theta)(\tilde\theta - \dot\theta),$$

or more succinctly,

$$0 \overset{a}{=} \dot d + \dot D(\tilde\theta - \dot\theta). \tag{5.19}$$

It follows from equation (5.19) that the *linearized maximum likelihood estimator*

$$\tilde\theta = \dot\theta - \dot D^{-1} \dot d \tag{5.20}$$

has the same large sample distribution as $\tilde\theta$.

The calculations involved in the first step of obtaining $\tilde\theta$–that is to say, the computation of a suitable consistent estimate $\dot\theta$–will vary from case to case; for example, the method of moments will sometimes be useful. The second step as represented by (5.20) is to carry out a single iteration of the Newton–Raphson method for solving $d(\theta) = 0$ starting from $\theta = \dot\theta$. Alternative asymptotically equivalent two-step estimators could be obtained by other quadratically convergent non-linear optimization techniques since the first iterate of such schemes will differ from $\tilde\theta$ by $O_p(n^{-1})$ when $(\dot\theta - \tilde\theta)$ is $O_p(n^{-\frac{1}{2}})$. In particular, $-\dot D^{-1}$ could be replaced by any matrix G^{-1} such that $\text{plim}(-\dot D^{-1}G) = I_m$ without affecting the large sample behaviour of the two-step estimator of (5.20). Thus, for example, $-\dot D^{-1}$ could be replaced by the inverse of estimated information matrix, $\dot{\mathscr{I}}^{-1}$, in (5.20) and the estimator so derived would be the result of one iteration of the method of scoring with $\dot\theta$ as the initial value.

The calculation of $\tilde\theta$ is sufficient to enable a quasi-Wald test to be carried out based upon the criterion

$$W_2 = (\tilde\theta_2 - \theta_2^0)'[\tilde{\mathscr{I}}^{22}]^{-1}(\tilde\theta_2 - \theta_2^0), \tag{5.21}$$

where W_2 denotes a W statistic calculated using an asymptotically efficient two-step estimator. The computation of the corresponding approximations to LR and LM will, however, require the derivation of estimators which are asymptotically efficient under $H_0: \theta_2 = \theta_2^0$. If $\hat{\theta}$, like $\tilde{\theta}$, is difficult to obtain, then the Rothenberg–Leenders result can be modified to provide an appropriate two-step equivalent of the former estimator.

The constrained MLE $\hat{\theta}$ satisfies $\hat{d}_1 = 0$, and $\bar{\theta}' = (\dot{\theta}_1, \theta_2^0)$ differs from $\hat{\theta}$ by terms of $O_p(n^{-\frac{1}{2}})$ on the null hypothesis and local alternatives. Expanding $\hat{d}_1$ about $\theta = \bar{\theta}$, therefore, yields

$$0 = \hat{d}_1 \stackrel{a}{=} \bar{d}_1 + \bar{D}_{11}(\hat{\theta}_1 - \dot{\theta}_1), \tag{5.22}$$

so that the two-step estimator

$$\hat{\hat{\theta}}_1 = \dot{\theta}_1 - \bar{D}_{11}^{-1}\bar{d}_1$$

is asymptotically equivalent to $\hat{\theta}_1$ under H_n of (5.3). It follows that $\hat{\theta}$ in LR and LM can be replaced by $\hat{\hat{\theta}}' = (\hat{\hat{\theta}}_1, \theta_2^0)$ without changing the asymptotic properties of these tests under the null and a sequence of local alternatives.

The practical importance of two-step estimators should, however, not be overemphasized. With the increasing availability of powerful computers and programmes capable of solving complex estimation problems, there is less incentive to employ an approximation whose value might be sensitive to the choice of initial consistent estimate. This argument does not, however, imply that tests like W_2 of (5.21) will never be valuable alternatives to more conventional procedures.

The test statistic W_2 of (5.21) is also of some theoretical interest because it can be used to show how certain well-established statistical procedures can be interpreted as quasi-Wald tests. Using an obvious notation for the partitioned inverse of $\dot{D}$ and for the vector $\dot{d}$, we deduce from (5.20) that

$$\tilde{\theta}_2 = \dot{\theta}_2 - \dot{D}^{21}\dot{d}_1 - \dot{D}^{22}\dot{d}_2. \tag{5.23}$$

Now W_2 is based upon the difference between $\tilde{\theta}_2$ and θ_2^0. Under H_n, $\dot{\theta}_2$ can be set equal to θ_2^0, the value specified by the null hypothesis and, with this choice of $\dot{\theta}_2$, we can rewrite equation (5.23) as

$$(\tilde{\theta}_2 - \theta_2^0) = -(\dot{D}^{21}\dot{d}_1 + \dot{D}^{22}\dot{d}_2)$$

$$\stackrel{a}{=} (\dot{\mathscr{I}}^{21}\dot{d}_1 + \dot{\mathscr{I}}^{22}\dot{d}_2), \tag{5.24}$$

by using the assumption that plim $-D\mathscr{I}^{-1} = I_m$. Under H_n, $\dot{\theta}$ and $\tilde{\theta}$ have the same probability limit and so W_2 is asymptotically equivalent to the quasi-Wald procedure using

$$W_2^* = (\dot{\mathscr{I}}^{21}\dot{d}_1 + \dot{\mathscr{I}}^{22}\dot{d}_2)'[\dot{\mathscr{I}}^{22}]^{-1}(\dot{\mathscr{I}}^{21}\dot{d}_1 + \dot{\mathscr{I}}^{22}\dot{d}_2)$$

$$= (\dot{d}_2 - \dot{\mathscr{I}}_{21}\dot{\mathscr{I}}_{11}^{-1}\dot{d}_1)'\dot{\mathscr{I}}^{22}(\dot{d}_2 - \dot{\mathscr{I}}_{21}\dot{\mathscr{I}}_{11}^{-1}\dot{d}_1), \tag{5.25}$$

which is Neyman's (1959) $C(\alpha)$ test statistic.[11] It is certainly valid to use the constrained MLE $\hat{\theta}$ as the initial estimate $\dot{\theta}$ and, since $\hat{d}_1$ is a null vector, this choice will result in a much simpler expression for W_2^*, namely,

$$W_2^* = \hat{d}_2'.\hat{\mathscr{I}}^{22}\hat{d}_2$$

which is the familiar LM (score) statistic. Thus both the LM test and Neyman's (1959) $C(\alpha)$ procedure can be regarded as quasi-Wald tests based upon two-step estimators which are asymptotically equivalent to $\tilde{\theta}_2$ under H_n.

1.6   Testing when the null hypothesis is not in parametric form

As discussed in Section 1.2., it is possible to construct tests of a null hypothesis without specifying an alternative in the normal way.[12] Thus the adequacy of a model can be investigated without setting up a more general specification and testing a set of parametric restrictions, as in the analysis of Sections 1.4 and 1.5.

We are here concerned with general principles rather than individual pure significance tests developed for specific situations, such as the Box–Pierce (1970) Q statistic and White's (1980a) test for functional misspecification in regression analysis. The most well-known of such principles in econometrics are probably those due to Hausman (1978) and White (1982). The work by Newey (1985a) and Tauchen (1985) which extends the results of Hausman and White is also considered.

Hausman's specification test

As exposited in his influential article, Hausman's (1978) test involves the comparison of two estimators of the parameter vector of the null model being checked. These estimators are selected so that, when the null model is true, both are consistent and asymptotically normally distributed, one being asymptotically efficient and the other inefficient. It will be convenient to denote the parameter vector of the null model by θ_1, its asymptotically efficient estimator by $\hat{\theta}_1$, and the other estimator by $\dot{\theta}_1$. The estimator $\dot{\theta}_1$ is assumed by Hausman to be consistent when the null is

---

[11] Equation (5.25) has been derived using standard results on the inversion of partitioned matrices.

[12] As argued by Cox and Hinkley (1974, Section 3.1), there should be some idea about the nature of likely departures from the null, but such departures need not be characterized by constraints on parameters.

false.[13] The consistency of both $\hat{\theta}_1$ and $\dot{\theta}_1$ when the null hypothesis is true implies that

$$\text{plim}(\dot{\theta}_1 - \hat{\theta}_1) = 0$$

under H_0. Hausman bases his test upon the joint significance of the elements of the difference between the two estimators, namely, $\dot{\theta}_1 - \hat{\theta}_1$. (The symbol H_0 should now be read simply as the 'null hypothesis that the tentatively entertained model is correct' and it need not be identified with a set of parametric restrictions on a specified alternative model.)

Assuming that root-n norming is appropriate, we have

$$n^{\frac{1}{2}} \begin{bmatrix} \hat{\theta}_1 & -\theta_1 \\ \dot{\theta}_1 & -\theta_1 \end{bmatrix} \overset{a}{\sim} N(0, \Sigma) \tag{6.1}$$

under H_0. The variance–covariance matrix of the joint limiting distribution of (6.1) will, using an obvious notation, be partitioned as

$$\Sigma = \begin{bmatrix} \Sigma_{\wedge\wedge} & \Sigma_{\wedge\cdot} \\ \Sigma_{\cdot\wedge} & \Sigma_{\cdot\cdot} \end{bmatrix}, \tag{6.2}$$

so that the efficiency of $\hat{\theta}_1$ relative to $\dot{\theta}_1$ implies that $(\Sigma_{\cdot\cdot} - \Sigma_{\wedge\wedge})$ is a positive semi-definite matrix. The vector difference $n^{\frac{1}{2}}(\dot{\theta}_1 - \hat{\theta}_1)$ will converge in distribution to multivariate normality with a zero mean vector under H_0, so the large sample theory required to derive an appropriate χ^2 criterion reduces to the task of finding its covariance matrix. Hausman (1978) establishes that this matrix is simply the difference between the asymptotic covariance matrices of $n^{\frac{1}{2}}(\dot{\theta}_1 - \theta_1)$ and $n^{\frac{1}{2}}(\hat{\theta}_1 - \theta_1)$. This result can be obtained by considering the scalar $z'T_p$, where z is an arbitrary vector of finite constants and T_p is a weighted average of $\hat{\theta}_1$ and $\dot{\theta}_1$ defined by

$$T_p = p\hat{\theta}_1 + (1 - p)\dot{\theta}_1, \tag{6.3}$$

p being a scalar variable.

The asymptotic variance of $n^{\frac{1}{2}}z'(T_p - \theta)$ viewed as a function of p is then

$$v(p) = z'[p^2\Sigma_{\wedge\wedge} + (1 - p)^2\Sigma_{\cdot\cdot} + p(1 - p)(\Sigma_{\wedge\cdot} + \Sigma_{\cdot\wedge})]z.$$

The first-order condition for a minimum of $v(p)$ is, therefore,

$$0 = z'[2p\Sigma_{\wedge\wedge} - 2(1 - p)\Sigma_{\cdot\cdot} + (1 - 2p)(\Sigma_{\wedge\cdot} + \Sigma_{\cdot\wedge})]z. \tag{6.4}$$

Since $\hat{\theta}_1$ is asymptotically efficient, $v(p)$ must have a local minimum at

---

[13] This assumption is used to prove the consistency of the test when the misspecification implies that the probability limit of $\hat{\theta}_1$ does not equal θ_1, but, as will be shown below, a weaker condition will suffice.

$p = 1$ (corresponding to $T_p = \hat{\theta}_1$) and so from (6.4) we have

$$0 = z'[2\Sigma_{\wedge\wedge} - (\Sigma_{\wedge.} + \Sigma_{.\wedge})]z, \; \forall z$$

or equivalently

$$2\Sigma_{\wedge\wedge} = (\Sigma_{\wedge.} + \Sigma_{.\wedge}). \tag{6.5}$$

The asymptotic variance–covariance matrix of $n^{\frac{1}{2}}(\dot{\theta}_1 - \hat{\theta}_1)$ is

$$\Sigma_{\wedge\wedge} + \Sigma_{..} - (\Sigma_{\wedge.} + \Sigma_{.\wedge}),$$

which, by virtue of equation (6.5), reduces to $(\Sigma_{..} - \Sigma_{\wedge\wedge})$ as required.

Using $\dot{\Sigma}_{..}$ and $\hat{\Sigma}_{\wedge\wedge}$ to denote estimators of $\Sigma_{..}$ and $\Sigma_{\wedge\wedge}$ which are consistent under the null hypothesis of correct specification, the test statistic associated with Hausman's approach can be written as

$$H = n(\dot{\theta}_1 - \hat{\theta}_1)'[\dot{\Sigma}_{..} - \hat{\Sigma}_{\wedge\wedge}]^-(\dot{\theta}_1 - \hat{\theta}_1), \tag{6.6}$$

where $[\;]^-$ denotes a generalized inverse (g-inverse).[14] If the large sample distribution of $n^{\frac{1}{2}}(\dot{\theta}_1 - \hat{\theta}_1)$ is non-singular and the number of elements in θ_1 is r, then the g-inverse of (6.6) can be replaced by $[\dot{\Sigma}_{..} - \hat{\Sigma}_{\wedge\wedge}]^{-1}$ and the asymptotic null distribution of H will be $\chi^2(r)$.[15] Significantly large values of H are regarded as evidence that the null specification is not consistent with the data.

The simple form of the test statistic H of equation (6.6) has been important in establishing the popularity of Hausman's (1978) method in applied work. Equation (6.6) also throws light on the asymptotic power of H under an alternative hypothesis since the test statistic will be $O_p(n)$ whenever $(\dot{\theta}_1 - \hat{\theta}_1)$ is $O_p(1)$. In other words, Hausman's (1978) test will enjoy the property of consistency whenever $\dot{\theta}_1$ and $\hat{\theta}_1$ have different probability limits under the alternative.

In an attempt to compare Hausman's procedure to the LR, W and LM tests, Holly (1982) examines the application of the H test to the case considered by Durbin (1970) in which θ_1 is regarded as a sub-vector of a parameter vector $\theta' = (\theta'_1, \theta'_2)$ and the null hypothesis is assumed to consist of a set of s parameter restrictions $\theta_2 = \theta_2^0$. (It should be pointed out that

---

[14] A g-inverse of a matrix V is a matrix V^- such that $VV^-V = V$. Several important applications of Hausman's (1978) approach lead to singular distributions of $(\dot{\theta}_1 - \hat{\theta}_1)$ so that the use of g-inverses is sometimes unavoidable; see Rao and Mitra (1971) for a discussion of generalized inverses and their applications. Some large sample tests involving g-inverses will be considered in Section 5 of Chapter 3.

[15] If $(\Sigma_{..} - \Sigma_{\wedge\wedge})$ is singular, then H must be computed using (6.6), and its limit null distribution will be central χ^2, with degrees of freedom equal to the rank of $(\Sigma_{..} - \Sigma_{\wedge\wedge})$.

Hausman's procedure is much more widely applicable and that part of its appeal is that it is not necessary to specify a precise alternative with likelihood $L(\theta)$ satisfying the usual set of regularity conditions. For example, it can be used to test for the errors-in-variables problem without a detailed specification of the process generating the measurement errors.) Holly also assumes that estimation is based upon maximization of likelihoods with $\tilde{\theta}_1$, the appropriate subvector of the unrestricted MLE $\tilde{\theta}$, being used as the estimator which is consistent but asymptotically inefficient under the null hypothesis.[16] Holly's variant of Hausman's H test is, therefore, based upon the asymptotic distribution of the r-dimensional vector $(\tilde{\theta}_1 - \hat{\theta}_1)$ when $\theta_2 = \theta_2^0$; this modified H test is also discussed by Hausman and Taylor (1981).

As before, the expansion of first-order partial derivatives taken under a sequence of local alternatives $H_n: \theta_2 = \theta_2^0 + n^{-\frac{1}{2}}\delta$ will prove useful in deriving the required large sample distribution of $(\tilde{\theta}_1 - \hat{\theta}_1)$. Expanding the first r equations of the necessary conditions for an unrestricted local maximum of $l(\theta)$ about the constrained MLE $\hat{\theta}$ yields the following approximation which is valid under H_n:

$$0 = \tilde{d}_1 \overset{a}{=} \hat{d}_1 + \hat{D}_{11}(\tilde{\theta}_1 - \hat{\theta}_1) + \hat{D}_{12}(\tilde{\theta}_2 - \theta_2^0), \qquad (6.7)$$

but $\hat{d}_1$ is a null vector (see equation (5.6) above) and so we can rewrite (6.7) as

$$(\tilde{\theta}_1 - \hat{\theta}_1) \overset{a}{=} -\hat{D}_{11}^{-1}\hat{D}_{12}(\tilde{\theta}_2 - \theta_2^0)$$
$$\overset{a}{=} -\mathscr{I}_{11}^{-1}\mathscr{I}_{12}(\tilde{\theta}_2 - \theta_2^0).^{17} \qquad (6.8)$$

The limit of $-\mathscr{I}_{11}^{-1}\mathscr{I}_{12}$ is a finite r by s matrix which we will denote by B, so that

$$(\tilde{\theta}_1 - \hat{\theta}_1) \overset{a}{=} B(\tilde{\theta}_2 - \theta_2^0), \qquad (6.9)$$

under the sequence of local alternatives $\theta_2 = \theta_2^0 + n^{-\frac{1}{2}}\delta$. Equation (6.9) enables us to see the relationship between the modified H test and the W test based upon $(\tilde{\theta}_2 - \theta_2^0)$ and also shows that, under H_n,

$$n^{\frac{1}{2}}(\tilde{\theta}_1 - \hat{\theta}_1) \overset{a}{\sim} N(B\delta, \lim n[B\mathscr{I}^{22}B']) \qquad (6.10)$$

since

$$n^{\frac{1}{2}}(\tilde{\theta}_2 - \theta_2^0) \overset{a}{\sim} N(\delta, \lim n\mathscr{I}^{22})$$

---

[16] Since $\tilde{\theta}$ is consistent when $\theta_2 \neq \theta_2^0$, its sub-vector $\tilde{\theta}_1$ satisfies Hausman's (1978) condition that $\hat{\theta}_1$ should be compared to an estimator which is consistent under the alternative hypothesis as well as under the null.

[17] In deriving (6.8) we have used the consistency of $\hat{\theta}$ under H_n, the continuity of the elements of $D(\theta)$ and the assumption that $-\text{plim }\mathscr{I}^{-1}D(\theta) = I_m$.

under these conditions. The asymptotic variance–covariance matrix given in (6.10)–lim $n[\mathscr{I}_{11}^{-1}\mathscr{I}_{12}\mathscr{I}^{22}\mathscr{I}_{21}\mathscr{I}_{11}^{-1}]$–can also be obtained from Hausman's (1978) general result that it equals the difference between the corresponding matrices of the distributions of $n^{\frac{1}{2}}(\tilde{\theta}_1 - \theta_1)$ and $n^{\frac{1}{2}}(\hat{\theta}_1 - \theta_1)$. The asymptotic variance–covariance matrix of $n^{\frac{1}{2}}(\tilde{\theta}_1 - \theta_1)$ is $\lim(n\mathscr{I}^{11})$ while that of $n^{\frac{1}{2}}(\hat{\theta}_1 - \theta_1)$ can be derived from an expansion of $\hat{d}_1 = 0$ about the true parameter when H_0 is true.[18] Thus

$$0 = \hat{d}_1 \overset{a}{=} d_1 + D_{11}(\hat{\theta}_1 - \theta_1),$$

using $\hat{\theta}_2 = \theta_2 = \theta_2^0$ on H_0, or equivalently

$$n^{\frac{1}{2}}(\hat{\theta}_1 - \theta_1) \overset{a}{=} -(n^{-1}D_{11})^{-1}n^{-\frac{1}{2}}d_1$$
$$\overset{a}{=} (n^{-1}\mathscr{I}_{11})^{-1}n^{-\frac{1}{2}}d_1. \tag{6.11}$$

But $n^{-\frac{1}{2}}d_1 \overset{a}{\sim} N(0, \lim(n^{-1}\mathscr{I}_{11}))$ and so equation (6.11) implies that the asymptotic variance–covariance matrix of $n^{\frac{1}{2}}(\theta_1 - \theta_1)$ is $\lim(n^{-1}\mathscr{I}_{11})^{-1}$. Consequently, the formula for Holly's (1982) modification of the H test which corresponds to equation (6.6) is

$$(\tilde{\theta}_1 - \hat{\theta}_1)'[\mathscr{I}^{11} - \mathscr{I}_{11}^{-1}]^{-}(\tilde{\theta}_1 - \hat{\theta}_1), \tag{6.12}$$

where the g-inverse in (6.12) is evaluated using estimators which are consistent under H_0. (It is straightforward to verify that the matrix $(\mathscr{I}^{11} - \mathscr{I}_{11}^{-1})$ is equal to $\mathscr{I}_{11}^{-1}\mathscr{I}_{12}\mathscr{I}^{22}\mathscr{I}_{21}\mathscr{I}_{11}^{-1}$, which is the form used in equation (6.10).)

The derivation of further details of the large sample properties of the statistic of (6.12) and a comparison with those of LR, W and LM can usefully be based upon equations (6.9) and (6.10), the first of these equations showing that $(\tilde{\theta}_1 - \hat{\theta}_1)$ is asymptotically equivalent to a set of r linear combinations of the elements of $(\tilde{\theta}_2 - \theta_2^0)$. There are two important cases to be considered. First, suppose that r is greater than or equal to s and rank $(B) = s$. In this situation, the asymptotic distribution of $n^{\frac{1}{2}}(\tilde{\theta}_1 - \hat{\theta}_1)$ is singular when $r > s$ and a g-inverse form of the H statistic as given in equation (6.12) will be required. This difficulty is easily overcome since considering only a sub-set of s elements of $(\tilde{\theta}_1 - \hat{\theta}_1)$ corresponding to a non-singular transformation of $(\tilde{\theta}_2 - \theta_2^0)$ is equivalent to using a g-inverse. (This result is implied by Rao's, 1973, p. 27, remarks on the computation of g-inverses.) Further, as has been argued previously, the introduction of a non-singular linear transformation is irrelevant to the values of χ^2 statistics calculated as quadratic forms in normal variables.

---

[18] We need only consider the case in which H_0 is true because we seek to determine the asymptotic null distribution required for the construction of H.

Thus H is asymptotically equivalent to the W test and hence to the LR and LM procedures when rank $(B) = s$.

The second case to be considered is the one in which r is less than s and rank $(B) = r$. The appropriate H statistic is then

$$(\tilde{\theta}_1 - \hat{\theta}_1)'[B\mathscr{I}^{22}B']^{-1}(\tilde{\theta}_1 - \hat{\theta}_1)$$

which is seen from (6.10) to converge in distribution to χ^2 (r, ρ^2) under H_n, where the non-centrality parameter is given by

$$\rho^2 = \lim n^{-1}\delta'B'[B\mathscr{I}^{22}B']^{-1}B\delta. \tag{6.13}$$

The LR, W and LM statistics are, however, asymptotically distributed as $\chi^2(s, \mu^2)$, $s > r$, under the sequence of local alternatives, where the non-centrality parameter is given by

$$\mu^2 = \lim n^{-1}\delta'[\mathscr{I}^{22}]^{-1}\delta. \tag{6.14}$$

If δ_* and B_* are defined as $[\mathscr{I}^{22}]^{-\frac{1}{2}}\delta$ and $B[\mathscr{I}^{22}]^{\frac{1}{2}}$, respectively, then the non-centrality parameters of (6.13) and (6.14) can be written as

$$\mu^2 = \lim n^{-1}\delta'_*\delta_*$$

and

$$\rho^2 = \lim n^{-1}\delta'_*B'_*[B_*B'_*]^{-1}B_*\delta_*,$$

so that $(\mu^2 - \rho^2)$ is the limit of the residual variance from the least-squares regression of δ_* on B'_* and is, therefore, non-negative. It follows that μ^2 cannot be smaller than ρ^2.

To sum up, when rank(B) is r, $r < s$, we have, under H_n,

$$H \overset{a}{\sim} \chi^2(r, \rho^2)$$

and

$$\text{LR, W and LM} \overset{a}{\sim} \chi^2(s, \mu^2)$$

with r less than s and ρ^2 not greater than μ^2. As Holly (1982) points out, in this situation there is no universally valid ranking of the asymptotic local powers of the H test and the classical procedures, except of course that LR, W and LM are equally powerful. The relative local powers of the tests will depend upon the direction of the departure from H_0: $(\theta_2 - \theta_2^0) = 0$. When δ is such that $\rho^2 = \mu^2$, the H test will have greater asymptotic local power than LR, W and LM because r is smaller than s; see Das Gupta and Perlman (1974) and Holly (1982). If, on the other hand, δ is a non-null vector such that $B\delta = 0$, then ρ^2 will be zero and the asymptotic local power of H will only equal its size.[19]

---

[19] See Holly (1982) for further discussion of these results.

The result that the Hausman procedure can outperform LR, W and LM when $r < s$ is not in conflict with the earlier statement that the latter three tests are asymptotically the most powerful tests of $H_0: \theta_2 = \theta_2^0$ against all local alternatives. Consideration of equation (6.8) reveals that the null hypothesis underlying Hausman's test is

$$H_0^*: [\lim \mathscr{I}_{11}^{-1} \mathscr{I}_{12}](\theta_2 - \theta_2^0) = 0$$

and H_0^* is not equivalent to H_0 when $r < s$.

The result that the asymptotic local power of Hausman's test may only equal its size casts some doubt on its value as an omnibus test, but the practical significance of this problem should not be overstated in the context of Holly's model. For this problem to arise, the true parameter vector must satisfy H_0^* (which involves both θ_1 and θ_2 through the matrices $\mathscr{I}_{11}^{-1}$ and $\mathscr{I}_{12}$) and fail to satisfy H_0.

The relevance of the results for the case with $\text{rank}(B) = r$ to the problems of constructing tests for misspecification may, however, be limited. In such applications, r denotes the number of parameters in the model being tested and, in practice, often exceeds s, the number of parameters introduced when formulating the general model of the alternative hypothesis, that is, $r > s$. Consequently, with $\text{rank}(B) = s$, the H test is asymptotically equivalent to LR, W and LM.

More generally, it should be emphasized that Holly's results are derived for a very restricted version of Hausman's (1978) original procedure and only apply when the unrestricted MLE $\tilde{\theta}_1$ is used as the estimator which is asymptotically inefficient under the null and consistent under the alternative. The use of $\tilde{\theta}_1$ clearly conflicts with the aim of computing misspecification checks easily and inexpensively since the more complex alternative must be estimated.

Finally, it is sometimes suggested that Hausman's procedure can be interpreted as a score test. In a valuable review of work on Hausman's approach, Ruud (1984) points out that, in the context of Holly's (1982) framework,

$$d_1(\tilde{\theta}_1, \theta_2^0) \stackrel{a}{=} \hat{d}_1 + \hat{D}_{11}(\tilde{\theta}_1 - \hat{\theta}_1),$$

or, using $\hat{d}_1 = 0$,

$$d_1(\tilde{\theta}_1, \theta_2^0) \stackrel{a}{=} \hat{D}_{11}(\tilde{\theta}_1 - \hat{\theta}_1).$$

This relationship implies that the Hausman test based upon the estimator contrast $(\tilde{\theta}_1 - \hat{\theta}_1)$ is equivalent to a test of the joint significance of the elements of $d_1(\tilde{\theta}_1, \theta_2^0)$. The latter test is, however, not an LM/score test in the conventional sense because $d_1(\cdot)$ is the vector of first-order derivatives with respect to the nuisance parameters, and θ_1 is evaluated at $\tilde{\theta}_1$, rather than $\hat{\theta}_1$.

White's information matrix test

White (1982) observes that, when the model is correctly specified and standard regularity conditions are satisfied, the information matrix for a typical observation can be written in two equivalent ways, that is, as either

$$-E[\partial^2 l_t(\theta_1)/\partial\theta_1\partial\theta_1'] \qquad (6.15)$$

or

$$E[\{\partial l_t(\theta_1)/\partial\theta_1\}\cdot\{\partial l_t(\theta_1)/\partial\theta_1\}'], \qquad (6.16)$$

where for the sake of consistency of notation we use θ_1 to denote the r-dimensional parameter vector of the model of interest. (Note, however, that $l_t(\cdot)$ now denotes the log-likelihood under the null hypothesis of correct specification and not that for some more general model.) Expression (6.15) gives the information matrix in terms of a Hessian and (6.16) is the OPG version. Combining the equivalent forms of (6.15) and (6.16) yields the fundamental equation

$$E[\partial^2 l_t(\theta_1)/\partial\theta_1\partial\theta_1' + \partial l_t(\theta_1)/\partial\theta_1 \cdot \partial l_t(\theta_1)/\partial\theta_1'] = 0 \qquad (6.17)$$

or on summing over all observations

$$E[\Delta(\theta_1)] = 0,$$

where

$$\Delta(\theta_1) = \Sigma_1^n[\partial^2 l_t(\theta_1)/\partial\theta_1\partial\theta_1' + \partial l_t(\theta_1)/\partial\theta_1 \cdot \partial l_t(\theta_1)/\partial\theta_1']. \qquad (6.18)$$

The r by r random matrix $\Delta(\theta_1)$ of equation (6.18) is obviously unobservable because it depends upon the unknown parameter vector θ_1, but the MLE $\hat{\theta}_1$ is available as a substitute for θ_1.[20] White (1982), therefore, suggests that a test of model adequacy be based upon a consideration of the asymptotic distribution of $\Delta(\hat{\theta}_1)$. He shows that the elements of $n^{-\frac{1}{2}}\Delta(\hat{\theta}_1)$ are asymptotically normally distributed with zero means when the model is correctly specified and proposes an asymptotic χ^2 test of the joint significance of these elements.

Some of the r^2 elements of $\Delta(\hat{\theta}_1)$ can be ignored in the construction of the χ^2 criterion since, for example, the symmetry of $\Delta(\hat{\theta}_1)$ implies that there are at most $r(r + 1)/2$ distinct elements. At first sight, it might appear that a test could be based upon, say, the upper triangle of $\Delta(\hat{\theta}_1)$ to derive a χ^2 statistic with $r(r + 1)/2$ degrees of freedom. White (1982) points out, however, that in some cases the $r(r + 1)/2$ apparently distinct elements will not have a non-singular asymptotic normal distribution because some may be linear combinations of others or be identically zero. Also using all

---

[20] However, the estimator $\hat{\theta}_1$ is not regarded as a constrained MLE since no more general model containing the null has been specified.

of the available elements of $\Delta(\hat{\theta}_1)$ may lead to a test involving a χ^2 null distribution with a large number of degrees of freedom. In such situations, small sample null distributions may be poorly approximated by asymptotic results. It may, therefore, be useful to consider only a moderate number of the elements of $\Delta(\hat{\theta}_1)$; for example, one might test only the usable elements on the leading diagonal.[21]

In terms of power, White (1982) conjectures that his test will be consistent whenever the misspecification renders the usual maximum likelihood inference techniques invalid. If this conjecture is correct, then the information matrix test will be consistent against a wide range of alternatives and so will be attractive to applied workers who are uncertain about the precise form of the alternative they should employ.

As White (1982) does not specify an alternative hypothesis, it would appear at first sight that the notion of local asymptotic power has little relevance and that comparisons of the information matrix test with LR, W and LM will be difficult to make. Chesher (1983) has, however, provided an LM interpretation of White's procedure. In order to show that the information matrix test can be regarded as a score test, Chesher (1983) considers the alternative hypothesis that the parameter vector θ_1 of the model being examined is a continuous random variable with covariance matrix Ξ. Model adequacy is then assessed by investigating whether θ_1 can be assumed to be non-stochastic. Since θ_1 will be fixed if Ξ is a null matrix, the set of parametric restrictions to be tested can be written as $\theta_2 = 0$, where θ_2 contains the distinct elements of Ξ, and it can be shown that the appropriate score vector consists of the distinct elements of $\Delta(\hat{\theta}_1)$ (see Chesher, 1983, for details).

Although the alternative hypothesis used by Chesher (1983) may not be of great interest to economists who may regard significant values of the test statistic as evidence of some other misspecification, it does lead to a very simple method for calculating White's criterion. By using the OPG version of the LM procedure, Chesher shows that the information matrix test can be calculated as $\iota'\hat{W}(\hat{W}'\hat{W})^{-}\hat{W}'\iota$, where $\hat{W}$ is the matrix with tth row given by

$$\{\partial l_t(\hat{\theta}_1)/\partial\theta_1' : [\text{vech}(\partial^2 l_t(\hat{\theta}_1)/\partial\theta_1\partial\theta_1' + \partial l_t(\hat{\theta}_1)/\partial\theta_1 \cdot \partial l_t(\hat{\theta}_1)/\partial\theta_1']'\}$$

where vech$(\cdot)$ denotes the operation of column stacking the distinct elements of a symmetric matrix and, as before, $\iota = (1, 1, \ldots, 1)'$. This computational procedure has also been proposed by Lancaster (1984).

The application of the information matrix test to linear regression

---

[21] The use of a sub-set of indicators will be discussed in Chapter 4 in the context of the linear multiple regression model.

models is considered in Chapter 4, where its links with other procedures are discussed in some detail.

Moment condition tests

Newey (1985a) and Tauchen (1985) obtain a very wide class of tests by taking as their starting point a general function of the data and parameters which has zero expectation under the null hypothesis of correct specification. Let such a vector-valued function be denoted by $c_t(\theta_1)$ so that

$$E[c_t(\theta_1)] = 0, t = 1, \ldots, n, \qquad (6.19)$$

where, as usual, θ_1 is the parameter vector of the model under scrutiny, and the expectation in (6.19) is taken under the assumption that this model is correctly specified. If θ_1 were known, then it would be natural to base a test of the moment restriction (6.19) upon the corresponding sample average

$$\bar{c}(\theta_1) = n^{-1}\Sigma_1^n c_t(\theta_1).$$

The true value θ_1 is, however, unknown and Newey and Tauchen propose that it be replaced by its MLE $\hat{\theta}_1$ and the joint significance of the elements of

$$\bar{c}(\hat{\theta}_1) = n^{-1}\Sigma_1^n c_t(\hat{\theta}_1) \qquad (6.20)$$

be tested. Under appropriate regularity conditions, it can be shown that $n^{\frac{1}{2}}\bar{c}(\hat{\theta}_1)$ is asymptotically normally distributed with zero mean vector and finite covariance matrix when the model is correctly specified (for details, see Newey, 1985a; Tauchen, 1985). If the model is misspecified, then, in general, the Newey–Tauchen test will be consistent when $\text{plim}\,\bar{c}(\hat{\theta}_1) \neq 0$ under the true data process. Following Newey, we shall refer to $\bar{c}(\hat{\theta}_1)$ as a moment function and the associated significance test as an M test.

The M-test approach provides considerable unification of tests derived from MLE. For example, if no alternative model is specified and $l_t(\theta_1)$ denotes the log-likelihood for a typical observation under the null model, then White's information matrix test can be obtained by setting

$$c_t(\theta_1) = \text{vech}[\partial^2 l_t(\theta_1)/\partial\theta_1\partial\theta_1' + \partial l_t(\theta_1)/\partial\theta_1 \cdot \partial l_t(\theta_1)/\partial\theta_1']$$

with $\bar{c}(\hat{\theta}_1) = \text{vech}[n^{-1}\Delta(\hat{\theta}_1)]$; see equations (6.17) and (6.18) above. Moreover, many Hausman-type tests can be interpreted as M tests (see Newey, 1985a, pp. 1053–4).

The class of M tests also includes LM tests. Suppose that the null model is embedded in a more general model with parameter vector $\theta' = (\theta_1', \theta_2')$ with the former model being derived from the latter by imposing

$H_0: \theta_2 = \theta_2^0$, θ_2^0 being a specified vector of constants. The log-likelihood function for a typical observation on the alternative model will be written as $l_t(\theta)$ and the unrestricted and restricted MLE will, as usual, be denoted by $\tilde{\theta}' = (\tilde{\theta}_1', \tilde{\theta}_2')$ and $\hat{\theta}' = (\hat{\theta}_1', \theta_2^{0'})$, respectively. The LM test is equivalent to a test of the significance of

$$n^{-1}\hat{d}_2 = n^{-1}\Sigma_1^n \partial l_t(\hat{\theta}_1, \theta_2^0)/\partial\theta_2$$

since $(n^{-1}\hat{d})'[n^{-2}\hat{\mathcal{I}}]^{-1}(n^{-1}\hat{d}) = \hat{d}'.\hat{\mathcal{I}}^{-1}\hat{d}$. Also, when H_0 is true, the score satisfies

$$E[\partial l_t(\theta_1, \theta_2^0)/\partial\theta_2] = 0, \, t = 1, \ldots, n. \tag{6.21}$$

Hence the LM test is an M test with

$$c_t(\theta_1) = \partial l_t(\theta_1, \theta_2^0)/\partial\theta_2$$

since $n^{-1}\hat{d}_2$ is the moment function corresponding to the moment restriction of (6.21).

As well as generating LM tests from (6.21), the M-test approach can also be used to derive checks for misspecification from the moment restriction corresponding to differentiation with respect to elements of θ_1, that is, from

$$E[\partial l_t(\theta_1, \theta_2^0)/\partial\theta_1] = 0, \, t = 1, \ldots, n. \tag{6.22}$$

Moment restrictions (6.21) and (6.22) are both valid under H_0, but the vector $\partial l_t(\theta_1, \theta_2^0)/\partial\theta_1$ does not itself lead to a useful test because the corresponding moment function is

$$n^{-1}\Sigma_1^n \partial l_t(\hat{\theta})/\partial\theta_1 = n^{-1}\hat{d}_1$$

which equals zero for all samples. A test involving $\partial l_t(\theta_1, \theta_2^0)/\partial\theta_1$ can, however, be obtained if the econometric model includes exogenous variables. As pointed out by Newey (1985a), the expected values of the elements of $\partial l_t(\theta_1, \theta_2^0)/\partial\theta_1$ conditional upon such exogenous variables are all equal to zero when H_0 is true. Consequently functions of exogenous variables are uncorrelated with the score vector $\partial l_t(\theta_1, \theta_2^0)/\partial\theta_1$ under correct specification. M tests can, therefore, be derived using sample covariances between such exogenous functions and the score evaluated at the restricted MLE. M tests which are based upon functions that have conditional expectation equal to zero are termed CM tests by Newey. Thus, for example, CM tests can be obtained using moment restrictions of the form

$$E[F_t(\theta_1)\{\partial l_t(\theta_1, \theta_2^0)/\partial\theta_1\}] = 0, \tag{6.23}$$

where $F_t(\theta_1)$ is a matrix of functions of exogenous variables and θ_1 (see Newey, 1985a, pp. 1055–60). Provided regularity conditions are satisfied, different choices of the matrix $F_t(\theta_1)$ will affect the power of the CM test, but not its asymptotic validity.

CM tests are also available if testing is to be carried out in the absence of a precisely specified alternative. The moment restriction (6.23) is simply replaced by

$$E[F_t(\theta_1)\{\partial l_t(\theta_1)/\partial \theta_1\}] = 0,$$

where $l_t(\theta_1)$ denotes the log-likelihood function for an observation on the null model.

The theory of M and CM tests is attractive because it provides a unifying framework for developing tests for model misspecification after maximum likelihood estimation. As a practical issue, it is clearly desirable that the implementation of such tests should not be difficult, and Newey and Tauchen both propose simple general algorithms.

Newey (1985a) employs an OPG estimate of the asymptotic covariance matrix of $n^{\frac{1}{2}}\bar{c}(\hat{\theta})$ and proves that the test statistic can be calculated as n times the uncentred R^2 for the regression of a vector of ones on the regressor matrix with tth row $[\partial l_t(\hat{\theta})/\partial \theta', c_t(\hat{\theta})']$. Unfortunately, as is discussed at some length in subsequent chapters, tests based upon OPG estimates of covariance matrices tend to perform badly in finite samples with true null hypotheses being rejected too frequently; also see Orme (1987) for a discussion of this defect in the context of an information matrix test. Thus tests using the OPG covariance matrix estimate cannot be recommended for general use.

Tauchen (1985) suggests a different algorithm in which the researcher is required to estimate a set of artificial regression relationships by ordinary least squares. The set of regression relationships used in Tauchen's approach has the form

$$c_t(\hat{\theta}) = \gamma_0 + \Gamma[\partial l_t(\hat{\theta})/\partial \theta] + a_t, \ t = 1, \dots, n, \tag{6.24}$$

where γ_0 is a vector of intercept terms and Γ is a matrix of slope coefficients. The test of the significance of $n^{\frac{1}{2}}\bar{c}(\hat{\theta})$ is implemented as a test of the hypothesis that the intercept coefficients of γ_0 are all equal to zero. As noted by Tauchen (1985, p. 436), in the absence of degrees of freedom adjustments, the statistic derived from (6.24) will never be smaller than Newey's OPG variant. Consequently the arguments against the general use of Newey's algorithm apply a fortiori to Tauchen's procedure.

1.7   Summary and qualifications

We have discussed some of the advantages and disadvantages of both pure significance tests and tests based upon investigating the consistency of a set of parametric restrictions with the data. The majority of tests used in econometrics are probably of the latter type and accordingly can frequently be carried out using one of the likelihood-based approaches, namely the LR, W and LM principles. The asymptotic theory of the LR, W and LM tests has been outlined, as have the relationships between them. Provided that regularity conditions are satisfied and that any necessary adjustments to correct the significance levels are made, there seems to be little to choose between LR, W and LM tests on the grounds of statistical performance. It follows that if a test for misspecification is to be constructed, then the LM test is more attractive than LR and W since the latter procedures require the estimation of the more complex alternative containing the (null) model of interest.

The contributions of Hausman (1978) and White (1982) on testing for misspecification error in the absence of a precise alternative and an associated set of coefficient restrictions have also been discussed. Hausman's test may outperform LR, W and LM in some directions of departure from the null hypothesis of correct specification when it tests fewer restrictions than the classical tests, but in other situations it may be inferior to them. Also the original form of Hausman's (1978) test is more widely applicable than Holly's (1982) variant of it. The recent work by Newey (1985a) and Tauchen (1985) on deriving tests from moment conditions has also been considered.

The subsequent chapters are concerned with the application of the various general statistical procedures to the problem of testing for specification error in diverse types of econometric models. However, an important issue must be faced which at first sight seems to cast doubt on the usefulness of the classical testing procedures. The basic problem is that the null model may not be specified in sufficient detail to construct the likelihood function.

Economic theory is usually uninformative about the disturbance terms of econometric relationships and if an appeal is to be made only to asymptotic results on estimators and tests, it may not be necessary to specify the precise distribution of the disturbances; assumptions concerning variances, covariances and certain higher-order moments may suffice. In such cases, estimators are often derived by maximizing the likelihood which would be appropriate if the disturbances were jointly normally distributed (also termed Gaussian): such estimators are usually referred to as *quasi maximum likelihood estimators*.[22] Under appropriate conditions

---

[22] Gouriéroux, Monfort and Trognon (1982) consider a more general type of estimator based upon the maximization of a specified likelihood which need not be Gaussian. They refer to such procedures as 'pseudo-MLE' rather than the more conventional 'quasi MLE.'

on the true joint distribution of the disturbances, the large sample distribution of the quasi MLE will be as predicted by asymptotic theory based upon the false assumption of normality (see Schmidt, 1976, pp. 55–64, for an example in the context of least-squares regression).

The false assumption of normality is just one of a large number of possible specification errors and the effects of such errors on estimation and testing are clearly of considerable interest. The asymptotic validity of formulae for the distribution of quasi MLEs suggests that the test procedures described in this chapter may be robust to some misspecifications. A number of results have emerged from the analyses carried out so far on estimators and test statistics derived by maximizing the wrong likelihood, but our understanding is by no means complete.[23]

In view of the work of Chow (1981a, b, 1982) and the note of correction by White (1983a), it seems reasonable to concur with Pagan and Hall (1983) in their view that 'correct specification – at least up to the errors having no deterministic component – is a sine qua non of diagnostic tests.' Models which have a correct specification of the conditional mean, and hence offer the possibility of robust tests, are said by Domowitz and White (1982) to be *correct to first order*.

Engle (1982a) has considered the asymptotic distribution of quasi LM tests for models with non-normal errors which are correct to first order and have been estimated using a weighted least-squares approximation to quasi MLE.[24] He provides a set of regularity conditions in the spirit of Domowitz and White (1982) which are sufficient to ensure that the quasi-LM statistics will converge in distribution to χ^2 under the null, the degrees of freedom parameter being equal to the number of restrictions being tested. Related work by Burguete, Gallant and Souza (1982) establishes that, under fairly general regularity conditions, quasi LR, W and LM tests of linear restrictions will be asymptotically distributed as χ^2 under the null and non-central χ^2 under local alternatives (see Burguete et al., 1982, for

[23] Kent (1982) has provided results on the parametric models for which the LR test is robust, that is, for which the usual test statistic is asymptotically distributed as χ^2 with the assumed number of degrees of freedom, for all reasonable underlying true distributions. However, Kent's (1982) results are derived for the case of independently and identically distributed observations, and so are of limited applicability in econometric models for time-series data.

[24] Engle's (1982a) results would specialize to the case in which the disturbances were assumed to be uncorrelated and homoscedastic so that the quasi MLE would be obtained by ordinary least squares. Engle (1982a) also provides a theorem covering the case of instrumental variable estimation.

details).[25] It would, therefore, appear that the incorrect assumption of normality will often not invalidate the large sample tests described in this chapter. However, although the quasi-LR, W and LM tests may have the same large sample null distribution as the corresponding true tests, they will, in general, no longer enjoy the property of being locally asymptotically most powerful since they will be based upon maximization of the wrong likelihood.

Finally, note that it is possible to adjust the variance–covariance matrices appearing in the quadratic forms which determine the LM and W statistics, so that the associated adjusted tests are robust to some misspecifications arising from incorrect assumptions about the variances and covariances of the disturbances. The necessary generalizations of the standard LM and W tests are provided by Domowitz and White.[26] In the context of the problems that we shall be considering, the derivation of asymptotically valid misspecification robust tests requires that the model be correctly specified up to an additive uncorrelated error, and so the range of misspecifications against which the adjusted tests are robust is fairly limited (see Domowitz and White, 1982). Tests of the W and LM type which are robust against heteroscedasticity can be obtained by extending the work of White (1980b), and their application to regression models is considered in Chapter 4.

[25] Note, however, that it cannot be assumed that $E[\{\partial l(\theta)/\partial \theta\} . \{\partial l(\theta)/\partial \theta\}']$ equals $-E[\partial^2 l(\theta)/\partial \theta \partial \theta']$ when $l(\theta)$ is an incorrect log-likelihood function. Appropriate generalizations of standard formulae are given by Burguete et al. (1982).

[26] Domowitz and White (1982) show that, under appropriate conditions, their adjusted LM and W tests will converge in distribution to χ^2 when the null hypothesis is true. The LR test is, however, no longer asymptotically equivalent to these procedures.

CHAPTER 2

Inequalities between criteria for testing hypotheses in linear regression models

2.1   Introduction

Chapter 1 contained an examination of the relationships between the likelihood ratio (LR), Wald (W) and Lagrange multiplier (LM) tests in the context of fairly general statistical models. There is, however, a special case of econometric interest which merits attention because it leads to the systematic numerical inequality

$$W \geqslant LR \geqslant LM \tag{1.1}$$

among the sample values of test statistics.

This remarkable inequality is satisfied when testing linear restrictions on the parameters of a classical regression model with normally distributed errors, and its implications clearly deserve careful consideration. For example, if W, LR and LM are all compared to a common asymptotically valid critical value, then there is the possibility of conflict among the outcomes of the three asymptotically equivalent tests.[1]

This chapter proceeds as follows. In Section 2.2, it is shown that the three classical procedures lead to the same test statistic if the covariance matrix of the disturbances is known. While such knowledge is rarely available, the analysis of this simple case provides a useful stepping stone towards more realistic models and also highlights the effects of having to estimate the parameters of the error covariance matrix. These effects are examined in Section 2.3 and the inequality (1.1) is established, with the case of independent and homoscedastic disturbances being singled out for special comment. The implications of the inequality are discussed in Section 2.4.

While the classical normal regression model often provides a valuable starting point for analysis and permits the derivation of interesting finite sample results, its assumptions rule out many cases of considerable practical relevance. It is, therefore, natural to inquire whether the inequality still holds if one or more of these restrictive assumptions is

---

[1] If this common critical value is denoted by c, then, in view of the inequality (1.1), there can be no such conflict if either $W < c$ or $LM > c$.

43

relaxed. In particular, it seems useful to explore the consequences of allowing for lagged values of the dependent variable in the regressors, non-normal disturbances, and non-linear parameter restrictions. These various extensions of the basic framework are discussed in Sections 2.5, 2.6 and 2.7, respectively. Section 2.8 contains a summary and some concluding remarks.

2.2   Testing linear restrictions with known error covariance matrix

Suppose that the unrestricted linear regression model is written as

$$y = X\beta + u, \tag{2.1}$$

where y and u are n-dimensional stochastic vectors, X is an n by k non-stochastic matrix with rank equal to k, and β is the unknown k-dimensional parameter vector. The disturbances are assumed to be jointly normally distributed with $u \sim N(0, \Omega)$, Ω being a known symmetric positive definite matrix. The null hypothesis to be tested consists of $s(<k)$ independent linear restrictions of the form

$$R\beta = r, \tag{2.2}$$

where R is a known s by k matrix and r is a known s-dimensional vector. It will be assumed that restrictions which can be written as (2.2) will be tested in this form, rather than using some equivalent non-linear representation. The importance of this assumption will be discussed in Section 2.7.

The linear regression equation (2.1) may at first sight appear to be less general than the multivariate regression model used by Berndt and Savin (1977) in their influential article on conflicts between the classical tests criteria, but this is not the case. As noted by Breusch (1979), equation (2.1) can be interpreted as the vectorized form of a set of seemingly unrelated regression equations (SURE) and so actually has the Berndt–Savin model as the special case obtained by using the same set of regressors in every equation of a SURE system.

The log-likelihood function, score vector and information matrix for the regression model of (2.1) are then

$$l(\beta) = \text{cnst} + \tfrac{1}{2}\ln|\Omega^{-1}| - \tfrac{1}{2}(y - X\beta)'\Omega^{-1}(y - X\beta), \tag{2.3}$$

$$d(\beta) = X'\Omega^{-1}(y - X\beta) \tag{2.4}$$

and

$$\mathscr{I} = (X'\Omega^{-1}X), \tag{2.5}$$

respectively. The term in $|\Omega^{-1}|$ is a constant, but is shown explicitly in (2.3) to simplify extension to the case in which Ω is not known. The unrestricted MLE $\tilde{\beta}$ (which forms the basis of the W test) satisfies

$$d(\tilde{\beta}) = X'\Omega^{-1}(y - X\tilde{\beta}) = 0$$

and so is the generalized least-squares (GLS) estimator

$$\tilde{\beta} = (X'\Omega^{-1}X)^{-1}X'\Omega^{-1}y \tag{2.6}$$

with associated residual vector

$$\tilde{u} = y - X\tilde{\beta}$$

and maximized log-likelihood

$$l(\tilde{\beta}) = \text{cnst} + \tfrac{1}{2}\ln|\Omega^{-1}| - \tfrac{1}{2}\tilde{u}'\Omega^{-1}\tilde{u}. \tag{2.7}$$

The restricted MLE $\hat{\beta}$ (which is required for the LM and LR tests) is obtained by maximizing $l(\beta)$ subject to $R\beta - r = 0$ and so it is useful to consider the Lagrangean

$$\Lambda(\beta,\ \lambda) = l(\beta) + \lambda'(R\beta - r),$$

where λ is the s-dimensional vector of multipliers. The restricted MLE $\hat{\beta}$ is then obtained by solving

$$X'\Omega^{-1}(y - X\hat{\beta}) + R'\hat{\lambda} = 0 \tag{2.8}$$

and

$$R\hat{\beta} - r = 0, \tag{2.9}$$

where $\hat{\lambda}$ denotes the vector of multipliers whose significance is tested in the LM/score procedure.

Equation (2.8) yields a relationship between the restricted and unrestricted estimators of β, namely,

$$\hat{\beta} = \tilde{\beta} + (X'\Omega^{-1}X)^{-1}R'\hat{\lambda}, \tag{2.10}$$

so that, using $R\hat{\beta} - r = 0$, it can be deduced that

$$\hat{\lambda} = [R(X'\Omega^{-1}X)^{-1}R']^{-1}(r - R\tilde{\beta})$$
$$= -[R(X'\Omega^{-1}X)^{-1}R']^{-1}(R\tilde{\beta} - r), \tag{2.11}$$

which can be combined with (2.10) to obtain an expression for $\hat{\beta}$. The residual vector from constrained estimation, that is, $y - X\hat{\beta}$, will be denoted by $\hat{u}$, and the restricted maximum of $l(\beta)$ can then be written as

$$l(\hat{\beta}) = \text{cnst} + \tfrac{1}{2}\ln|\Omega^{-1}| - \tfrac{1}{2}\hat{u}'\Omega^{-1}\hat{u}. \tag{2.12}$$

The three classical test criteria for the null hypothesis

$H_0: R\beta - r = 0$ are then given by the following expressions

$$LM = d(\hat{\beta})' \mathscr{I}^{-1} d(\hat{\beta})$$

$$= \hat{u}'\Omega^{-1}X[X'\Omega^{-1}X]^{-1}X'\Omega^{-1}\hat{u}$$

$$= \hat{\lambda}'R[X'\Omega^{-1}X]^{-1}R'\hat{\lambda}; \tag{2.13}$$

$$W = [R\tilde{\beta} - r]'[R(X'\Omega^{-1}X)^{-1}R']^{-1}[R\tilde{\beta} - r] \tag{2.14}$$

$$= LM \text{ (using equations (2.11) and (2.13));}$$

and

$$LR = -2(l(\hat{\beta}) - l(\tilde{\beta}))$$

$$= \hat{u}'\Omega^{-1}\hat{u} - \tilde{u}'\Omega^{-1}\tilde{u}, \tag{2.15}$$

from equations (2.7) and (2.12).

As it has been shown that $W = LM$, it only remains to prove that $LR = LM$. Equation (2.10) which links $\hat{\beta}$ and $\tilde{\beta}$ implies that

$$\Omega^{-\frac{1}{2}}\hat{u} = \Omega^{-\frac{1}{2}}(y - X\hat{\beta})$$

$$= \Omega^{-\frac{1}{2}}[(y - X\tilde{\beta}) - X(X'\Omega^{-1}X)^{-1}R'\hat{\lambda}],$$

whence (using $X'\Omega^{-1}\tilde{u} = 0$) we have

$$\hat{u}'\Omega^{-1}\hat{u} = \tilde{u}'\Omega^{-1}\tilde{u} + \hat{\lambda}'R[X'\Omega^{-1}X]^{-1}R'\hat{\lambda}$$

$$= \tilde{u}'\Omega^{-1}\tilde{u} + LM,$$

or equivalently

$$LM = \hat{u}'\Omega^{-1}\hat{u} - \tilde{u}'\Omega^{-1}\tilde{u} = LR,$$

which is the required result.

To sum up, if a set of linear restrictions is to be tested in the context of a classical regression model with known error covariance matrix, then the LR, W and LM principles lead to exactly the same test statistic. Moreover, since $(R\tilde{\beta} - r) \sim N(0, R(X'\Omega^{-1}X)^{-1}R')$ when H_0 is true and Ω is known, the null distribution of this common test statistic is $\chi^2(s)$ in finite samples, so that the asymptotic tests are valid for all $n \geqslant k$.

2.3   Testing linear restrictions with unknown error covariance matrix

It will rarely be the case that Ω, the covariance matrix of the disturbances, is known, and this assumption will now be relaxed. In order to proceed within the framework of maximum likelihood estimation, it will be supposed that the elements of Ω are smooth functions of the elements of a

p-dimensional parameter vector α. If θ denotes the full parameter vector, that is, $\theta' = (\alpha', \beta')$, then the log-likelihood function can be written as

$$l(\theta) = \text{cnst} + \ln|\Omega^{-1}(\alpha)| - \tfrac{1}{2}(y - X\beta)'[\Omega(\alpha)]^{-1}(y - X\beta),$$

with the null hypothesis being, as before, $H_0: R\beta - r = 0$. It is assumed that the vectors α and β are unrelated and can vary independently.[2] This assumption combined with standard regularity conditions implies that the information matrix is block diagonal with plim $n^{-1}\partial^2 l(\theta)/\partial\alpha\partial\beta' = 0$, a p by k null matrix.[3] This block diagonality ensures that simple modifications of the LM and W tests of the previous section can be employed. (See the discussion of simplifications and special cases provided in Section 1.4 and, in particular, equations (4.32) and (4.33) of Chapter 1.)

Let the restricted and unrestricted maximizers of $l(\theta)$ be denoted by $\hat{\theta}' = (\hat{\alpha}', \hat{\beta}')$ and $\tilde{\theta}' = (\tilde{\alpha}', \tilde{\beta}')$, respectively.[4] Also it will be useful to define $\hat{\Omega} = \Omega(\hat{\alpha})$, $\tilde{\Omega} = \Omega(\tilde{\alpha})$, $\hat{\mathscr{I}} = \mathscr{I}(\hat{\theta})$ and $\tilde{\mathscr{I}} = \mathscr{I}(\tilde{\theta})$. The LM and W statistics for testing H_0 can be shown to be the following generalizations of (2.13) and (2.14):

$$\text{LM} = \hat{u}'\hat{\Omega}^{-1}X[X'\hat{\Omega}^{-1}X]^{-1}X'\hat{\Omega}^{-1}\hat{u}; \tag{3.1}$$

and

$$\text{W} = [R\tilde{\beta} - r]'[R(X'\tilde{\Omega}^{-1}X)^{-1}R']^{-1}[R\tilde{\beta} - r]. \tag{3.2}$$

(Note that the LM and W statistics involve different estimates of Ω.) The corresponding LR statistic is

$$\text{LR} = -2[l(\hat{\alpha}, \hat{\beta}) - l(\tilde{\alpha}, \tilde{\beta})]. \tag{3.3}$$

It will now be shown that the statistics defined by (3.1), (3.2) and (3.3) satisfy the inequality

$$\text{W} \geqslant \text{LR} \geqslant \text{LM}.$$

The inequality will be established using an indirect proof given by Breusch (1979). The basic idea is to reinterpret the LM and W statistics of (3.1) and (3.2) in such a way that the results of Section 2.2 can be applied. It

---

[2] This assumption rules out one or two cases of econometric interest, e.g., heteroscedastic disturbances with variances proportional to the squares of the expected values of the dependent variable.

[3] Rothenberg (1984) gives the regularity conditions required to justify the application of conventional asymptotic theory to models of the type considered here. Note, however, that Rothenberg uses Ω to denote the inverse of the error covariance matrix.

[4] The estimators $\hat{\beta}$ and $\tilde{\beta}$ are, of course, no longer defined by equations contained in the preceding section.

has already been pointed out that the LM and W statistics use different estimates of Ω and it is now useful to regard the associated estimators $\hat{\beta}$ and $\tilde{\beta}$ as conditional maximizers. The definitions of the restricted and unrestricted MLEs $\hat{\theta}$ and $\tilde{\theta}$ imply that $\hat{\beta}$ maximizes the function $l(\hat{\alpha}, \beta)$ subject to $R\beta - r = 0$ and that $\tilde{\beta}$ is the unrestricted maximizer of $l(\tilde{\alpha}, \beta)$. The results of Section 2.2 for tests using a common value of Ω can then be used to deduce that the LM statistic of (3.1) equals the LR-type statistic

$$\text{LR}(\hat{\alpha}) = -2[l(\hat{\alpha}, \hat{\beta}) - l(\hat{\alpha}, \hat{\beta}_u)], \tag{3.4}$$

where $\hat{\beta}_u$ denotes the unrestricted maximizer of $l(\hat{\alpha}, \beta)$; and the W statistic of (3.2) is equal to

$$\text{LR}(\tilde{\alpha}) = -2[l(\tilde{\alpha}, \tilde{\beta}_r) - l(\tilde{\alpha}, \tilde{\beta})], \tag{3.5}$$

where $\tilde{\beta}_r$ maximizes $l(\tilde{\alpha}, \beta)$ subject to $R\beta - r = 0$.

The inequality between LM, LR and W can now be derived by comparing the LR-type criteria of (3.4) and (3.5) with the actual LR statistic of (3.3). More precisely, we have

$$\text{LR} - \text{LM} = \text{LR} - \text{LR}(\hat{\alpha})$$

$$= 2[l(\tilde{\alpha}, \tilde{\beta}) - l(\hat{\alpha}, \hat{\beta}_u)],$$

which must be non-negative since $\tilde{\theta}' = (\tilde{\alpha}', \tilde{\beta}')$ is the unrestricted MLE, and

$$\text{W} - \text{LR} = \text{LR}(\tilde{\alpha}) - \text{LR}$$

$$= 2[l(\hat{\alpha}, \hat{\beta}) - l(\tilde{\alpha}, \tilde{\beta}_r)],$$

which is non-negative since $R\tilde{\beta}_r - r = 0$ and $\hat{\theta}' = (\hat{\alpha}', \hat{\beta}')$ is the restricted MLE. Consequently, if the parameters of the error covariance matrix are unknown and are estimated jointly with the regression parameters, there is a systematic inequality relationship

$$\text{W} \geqslant \text{LR} \geqslant \text{LM}$$

between the values of the test statistics when testing restrictions of the form $R\beta - r = 0$.

If the attention is confined to asymptotic relationships under a sequence of local alternatives of the form $H_n: R\beta - r = \delta/\sqrt{n}$, $\delta'\delta < \infty$, then the expressions for $\text{LR}(\hat{\alpha})$, $\text{LR}(\tilde{\alpha})$ and LR given above can be used to derive another interesting result concerning LM, W and LR. Rothenberg (1984) considers Taylor series expansions and shows that, under H_n,

$$\text{LR} = (\text{W} + \text{LM})/2 + o_p(n^{-1});$$

that is, the LR statistic is approximately equal to the average of the other two statistics when the sample size is large.

Further results can be obtained if the covariance matrix is restricted to be proportional to the n by n identity matrix, that is, $\Omega = \sigma^2 I$. Since it is frequently assumed that the disturbances of a regression equation are independent and homoscedastic, this special case merits discussion.

Independent and homoscedastic disturbances

If the covariance matrix Ω is of the form $\sigma^2 I$, then the disturbances are independent $N(0, \sigma^2)$ variates and the log-likelihood is

$$l(\theta) = -n/2 \ln(2\pi) - n/2 \ln(\sigma^2)$$
$$-\tfrac{1}{2}(y - X\beta)'(y - X\beta)/\sigma^2, \tag{3.6}$$

where $\theta' = (\sigma^2, \beta')$. The other ingredients of classical inference are the score vector and the information matrix. The first-order partial derivatives of $l(\theta)$ are given by

$$\partial l(\theta)/\partial \sigma^2 = n/(2\sigma^4)[(y - X\beta)'(y - X\beta)/n - \sigma^2] \tag{3.7}$$

and

$$\partial l(\theta)/\partial \beta = X'(y - X\beta)/\sigma^2. \tag{3.8}$$

The information matrix can be shown to be

$$\mathscr{I}(\theta) = \begin{bmatrix} n/(2\sigma^4) & 0' \\ 0 & \sigma^{-2}(X'X) \end{bmatrix}, \tag{3.9}$$

and is block diagonal and independent of β.

Expressions for the unrestricted MLE $\tilde{\theta}' = (\tilde{\sigma}^2, \tilde{\beta}')$ can be derived by solving the first-order conditions $\partial l(\tilde{\theta})/\partial \sigma^2 = 0$ and $\partial l(\tilde{\theta})/\partial \beta = 0$. Equation (3.8) yields

$$\tilde{\beta} = (X'X)^{-1}X'y,$$

so that the unrestricted MLE is the ordinary least-squares (OLS) estimator. If $\tilde{u}$ denotes the OLS residual $y - X\tilde{\beta}$, then equation (3.7) implies that

$$\tilde{\sigma}^2 = n^{-1}\tilde{u}'\tilde{u}.$$

Substitution of $\tilde{\theta}$ for θ in (3.6) then gives the unrestricted maximum of $l(\theta)$ as

$$l(\tilde{\theta}) = -n/2[\ln(2\pi) + 1] - n/2 \ln \tilde{\sigma}^2.$$

Turning to the derivation of the restricted MLE $\hat{\theta}' = (\hat{\sigma}^2, \hat{\beta}')$, it will, as usual, be useful to set up a Lagrangian function. A suitable function is

$$\Lambda(\theta, \lambda) = l(\theta) + \lambda'(R\beta - r). \tag{3.10}$$

The equations to be solved are $\partial \Lambda(\hat{\theta}, \hat{\lambda})/\partial \sigma^2 = 0$, $\partial \Lambda(\hat{\theta}, \hat{\lambda})/\partial \beta = 0$ and $\partial \Lambda(\hat{\theta}, \hat{\lambda})/\partial \lambda = 0$ which, in view of (3.7), (3.8) and (3.10), are equivalent to

$$n^{-1}\hat{u}'\hat{u} - \hat{\sigma}^2 = 0 \tag{3.11}$$

$$\hat{\sigma}^{-2}X'(y - X\hat{\beta}) + R'\hat{\lambda} = 0 \tag{3.12}$$

$$R\hat{\beta} - r = 0, \tag{3.13}$$

where $\hat{u}$ denotes the residual vector from restricted estimation, that is, $\hat{u} = y - X\hat{\beta}$. Equation (3.12) can be used to determine the vector of estimated multipliers. A little manipulation yields

$$\hat{\lambda} = -\hat{\sigma}^{-2}[R(X'X)^{-1}R']^{-1}[R\hat{\beta} - r],$$

which could be substituted to obtain an expression for $\hat{\beta}$. The restricted maximum of $l(\theta)$ is, using (3.7) and (3.11), given by

$$l(\hat{\theta}) = -n/2[\ln(2\pi) + 1] - n/2 \ln \hat{\sigma}^2,$$

where $\hat{\sigma}^2 = n^{-1}\hat{u}'\hat{u}$.

The above results enable us to write the following equations for the LM, LR and W statistics:

$$\begin{aligned} \text{LM} &= \hat{\sigma}^2 \hat{\lambda}' R(X'X)^{-1}R'\hat{\lambda} \\ &= \hat{\sigma}^{-2}(R\hat{\beta} - r)'[R(X'X)^{-1}R']^{-1}(R\hat{\beta} - r); \\ \text{LR} &= -2[l(\hat{\theta}) - l(\tilde{\theta})] \\ &= n \ln(\hat{\sigma}^2/\tilde{\sigma}^2); \end{aligned}$$

and

$$W = \tilde{\sigma}^{-2}(R\tilde{\beta} - r)'[R(X'X)^{-1}R']^{-1}(R\tilde{\beta} - r).$$

It is now useful to note that it can be shown that

$$(R\tilde{\beta} - r)'[R(X'X)^{-1}R']^{-1}(R\tilde{\beta} - r) = n(\hat{\sigma}^2 - \tilde{\sigma}^2)$$

(see, for example, Schmidt, 1976, p. 26). Consequently, the test criteria can be rewritten as

$$\text{LM} = n(\hat{\sigma}^2 - \tilde{\sigma}^2)/\hat{\sigma}^2,$$

$$\text{LR} = n \ln(\hat{\sigma}^2/\tilde{\sigma}^2),$$

and

$$W = n(\hat{\sigma}^2 - \tilde{\sigma}^2)/\tilde{\sigma}^2.$$

All three test principles therefore lead to a comparison of restricted and unrestricted estimates of σ^2. Moreover, in contrast to the case in which Ω is not proportional to an identity matrix, the test statistics are simple functions of each other. Evans and Savin (1983) point out that the LM and LR statistics can be expressed as the following functions of the W statistic:

$$LM = W/(1 + W/n);$$

and

$$LR = n \ln(1 + W/n).$$

Consequently, for small values of W/n, a second-order Taylor series approximation gives

$$W - LR \approx LR - LM \approx W^2/2n^2$$

which implies the result

$$LR = (W + LM)/2 + o_p(n^{-1})$$

derived by Rothenberg (1984) for the more general model in which Ω is not of the form $\sigma^2 I$.

An alternative way to show that the classical criteria are functions of each other when $\Omega = \sigma^2 I$ is to write each of them as a function of the familiar F statistic. As well as having some interest in its own right, this device will be useful in subsequent discussions of the implications of the inequality $W \geqslant LR \geqslant LM$. The F test of $H_0: R\beta - r = 0$ is based upon

$$F = \frac{(\hat{u}'\hat{u} - \tilde{u}'\tilde{u})}{\tilde{u}'\tilde{u}} \cdot \frac{(n - k)}{s}$$

$$= \frac{(\hat{\sigma}^2 - \tilde{\sigma}^2)}{\tilde{\sigma}^2} \cdot \frac{(n - k)}{s},$$

which is distributed as central $F(s, n - k)$ under H_0. Combining this expression with those for LM, LR and W yields the following:

$$LM = ns/[(n - k)F^{-1} + s]; \tag{3.14}$$

$$LR = n \ln \left(1 + \left(\frac{s}{n - k} \right) F \right); \tag{3.15}$$

and

$$W = nsF/(n - k). \tag{3.16}$$

Each of the classical test statistics is, therefore, a different function of the F statistic and so has a different finite sample distribution. The implications of these results and those obtained for a general error covariance matrix are examined next.

2.4   Implications of the inequality

The inequality $W \geqslant LR \geqslant LM$ applies under the null hypothesis and so the finite sample significance levels of the three tests must be different if a common critical value is employed. Hence the inequality cannot by itself lead to any conclusion about the relative powers of the W, LR and LM tests. A detailed examination of the implications of the inequality has been provided by Evans and Savin (1982) for the case in which the disturbances are $NID(0, \sigma^2)$ variates.

Models with independent and homoscedastic errors

Evans and Savin exploit the fact that the W, LR and LM statistics can all be written as functions of the F statistic when the error covariance matrix Ω takes the form $\sigma^2 I$, σ^2 unknown (see equations (3.14) to (3.16) above). As previously observed, this result implies that each test statistic has a different exact distribution and hence a different critical value for any common significance level. If $F_\varepsilon(s, n - k)$ denotes the upper ε significance point of a central $F(s, n - k)$ distribution, that is,

$$\text{prob}(F(s, n - k) > F_\varepsilon(s, n - k)) = \varepsilon,$$

then the exact critical values for LM, LR and W are determined by equations (3.14) to (3.16) and are

$$z_{LM} = ns/[(n - k)F_\varepsilon(s, n - k)^{-1} + s],$$

$$z_{LR} = n \ln \left(1 + \left(\frac{s}{n - k}\right) F_\varepsilon(s, n - k)\right),$$

and

$$z_W = nsF_\varepsilon(s, n - k)/(n - k),$$

respectively. If these exact critical values are used, then the associated tests are referred to as exact tests. The significance levels of the exact tests are correct since, for example,

$$\text{prob}(W > z_W) = \text{prob}(nsF/(n - k) > nsF_\varepsilon(s, n - k)/(n - k))$$

$$= \text{prob}(F > F_\varepsilon(s, n - k))$$

$$= \varepsilon \text{ when } H_0 \text{ is true.}$$

In addition to providing exact critical values, the equations which define each of the classical criteria as a function of the F statistic also imply that the exact tests based upon W, LR and LM must be equivalent since each has the power function of the F test. (This power function can be derived from the appropriate non-central F distribution.) Consequently there is no possibility of conflict if the exact tests are used; the outcomes of the exact tests will all be the same as that of the F test of H_0.

It is, however, sometimes the case that tests are based upon the asymptotic distributions of the W, LR and LM statistics. If the s linear restrictions of $R\beta - r = 0$ are valid, then the W, LR and LM statistics are all asymptotically distributed as central $\chi^2(s)$. Valid large sample tests with nominal significance level ε can, therefore, be obtained by comparing values of these three statistics to z, the upper ε significance point of the $\chi^2(s)$ distribution, defined by

$$\text{prob}(\chi^2(s) > z) = \varepsilon.$$

Evans and Savin refer to tests based upon z as large sample tests.

In contrast to the exact tests, large sample tests can produce conflicting outcomes. The asymptotically valid critical value z cannot equal all three different exact critical values and may not be close to any of them. The inequality $W \geqslant LR \geqslant LM$ obviously implies that

$$\text{prob}(W > z) \geqslant \text{prob}(LR > z) \geqslant \text{prob}(LM > z),$$

and so there is an inequality between the true significance levels of the large sample tests. The true powers of the large sample tests will also differ and conflicting outcomes will occur if

$$W > z > LR \geqslant LM$$

or

$$W \geqslant LR > z > LM.$$

If asymptotic theory provides a poor approximation to actual behaviour, then the probability of such conflicts may be large.

The probabilities of conflict and the differences between the true powers of large sample tests are investigated by Evans and Savin (1982, pp. 741–2). The expressions for W, LR and LM in terms of F again provide the key to the analysis. Suppose that, under some alternative hypothesis with $R\beta - r \neq 0$, the F statistic is distributed as non-central F with non-centrality parameter μ, that is, $F \sim F(s, n - k, \mu)$, then equations (3.14) to (3.16) can be used to calculate the true powers of the large sample tests. For example, the true power of the large sample W test is

$$\text{prob}(W > z) = \text{prob}(nsF/(n - k) > z)$$

$$= \text{prob}(F > z(n - k)/ns)$$

$$= \text{prob}(F(s, n - k, \mu) > z(n - k)/ns)$$

which can be calculated for specified values of (s, n, k, μ, z). The true significance levels of the large sample tests in different situations can, of course, be determined by varying (s, n, k, z) with the non-centrality parameter μ set equal to zero.

Evans and Savin evaluate rejection probabilities and probabilities of conflict for a number of cases. They find that the true significance levels can differ substantially from the nominal values. For a nominal significance level of 5 per cent, the ranges of true significance levels are as follows:

W: 7.5 to 21.8 per cent

LR: 6.4 to 11.0 per cent

LM: 2.4 to 8.2 per cent.

These results indicate that asymptotic theory cannot be relied upon to give a good approximation. In several cases, the approximation is so poor that there are marked differences between the powers of the large sample tests and the exact F test.

As a result of these differences between significance levels and powers, there is sometimes a high probability of conflict. The ranges of calculated probabilities of conflict are

H_0 true: 0.9 to 19.4 per cent

H_0 false: 0.0 to 37.3 per cent.

While it may be unwise to attach too much weight to cases in which the quality of the asymptotic approximation is very poor and the probability of conflict is high, the results provided by Evans and Savin clearly show that asymptotically valid procedures may require modifications to improve their small sample behaviour. One quite common modification is to use degrees-of-freedom-adjusted estimates of variances. This device leads to the following expressions for modified W and LM statistics:

$$W_* = (R\tilde{\beta} - r)'[R(X'X)^{-1}R']^{-1}(R\tilde{\beta} - r)/\tilde{s}^2$$

and

$$LM_* = \hat{s}^2\hat{\lambda}'R(X'X)^{-1}R'\hat{\lambda},$$

where $\tilde{s}^2 = (n - k)^{-1}\tilde{u}'\tilde{u}$ and $\hat{s}^2 = (n - k + s)^{-1}\hat{u}'\hat{u}$. Evans and Savin consider W_* and LM_* along with the modified LR statistic

$$LR_e = (n - k - 1 + s/2)\ln(\hat{u}'\hat{u}/\tilde{u}'\tilde{u}),$$

which is an Edgeworth-corrected form with a significance level which is correct to order n^{-1}. The differences in the adjustments to the W, LR and LM statistics imply that the modified statistics will not satisfy the inequality.

Evans and Savin examine the performances of these modified procedures. They find that, even though the actual significance levels of W_* and LM_* are closer to the nominal value, the differences between the power functions of these two modified tests and the exact test based upon F can still be substantial. Further there is still a high probability of conflict when $s/(n - k)$ is large. The behaviour of the third modified test, namely LR_e, is, however, excellent and its rejection probabilities are very similar to those of the exact test.

In view of the good performance of the LR_e test, Evans and Savin (1982, pp. 745–6) derive the corresponding Edgeworth size-corrected W_* and LM_* tests. It is found that, over a wide range of cases, these size-corrected tests behave well and that the probabilities of conflict are of no practical importance.

The results reported by Evans and Savin are interesting and indicate the potential value of Edgeworth size-corrected tests when asymptotic theory provides an inadequate approximation. These results, however, are derived for a framework within which the large sample tests have little appeal and a researcher would normally turn to the exact F test (which is equivalent to the exact forms of the W, LR and LM tests). Some more general results have been obtained for the case in which the disturbances are not assumed to be independent and homoscedastic, and the F test is inappropriate.

Models with general error covariance matrix

Rothenberg (1984) examines the case of a general error covariance matrix and derives Edgeworth corrections for critical regions so that the adjusted tests have the same significance level to order n^{-1}. He finds that if the null hypothesis consists of only one linear restriction, that is, $s = 1$, then the size-corrected tests have the same approximate local power function. For the more general case in which several linear restrictions are to be tested, correcting the critical values will probably remove much of the difference between tests. However, the tests are not functions of each other when $s > 1$. Hence, even after size corrections have been made, the power functions may cross and there is the possibility of conflicting outcomes. The intersection of power functions also implies that no one of these tests is uniformly more powerful than the others, and it is not clear how to make the choice between them.

Testing for misspecification

It is shown in Chapter 4 that many checks of the adequacy of a linear regression model

$$y = X_1\beta_1 + u \tag{4.1}$$

can be implemented as tests of $\beta_2 = 0$ in the augmented model

$$y = X_1\beta_1 + X_2\beta_2 + u, \tag{4.2}$$

where X_2 is an n by s matrix of variables introduced to detect specification errors. Relationships like (4.2) will be referred to as test models and the regressors of matrices like X_2 will be referred to as test variables. The restrictions of $\beta_2 = 0$ are clearly included in the general class considered in this chapter. Hence, provided that the assumptions of the classical normal regression model apply to the test model (4.2), the earlier discussion of the inequality $W \geqslant LR \geqslant LM$ and its implications will be relevant to tests for misspecification.

It must, however, be acknowledged that, in practice, the classical assumptions will sometimes be inappropriate for the original (null) model and/or the test model. For example, there is little reason to suppose that the disturbances of the regression model under scrutiny will be jointly normally distributed. Also the regressors of such models may include lagged values of the dependent variable, and the matrix X_1 cannot be regarded as non-stochastic in such cases. Moreover, even if X_1 can be taken as fixed in repeated sampling, the matrix of test variables X_2 will often include stochastic variables constructed from the regression of y on X_1 alone (see Chapter 4). When the test variables are constructed in this way, the augmented model (4.2) should be interpreted as an algorithm for the computation of a test statistic and not as a potentially valid characterization of the data process. Consequently comparisons of power functions of tests in such cases should be based not on the augmented regression model, but on the alternative hypothesis from which it was derived (see Chapter 3 for a general discussion of the relationship between alternative hypotheses and their associated test variables, and Chapter 4 for several examples in the context of testing for specification errors in regression analysis).

It would be inappropriate at this stage to examine the consequences of adding test variables to the original specification, rather than using the underlying alternative model, but the implications of relaxing some of the assumptions of the classical normal regression model will be considered. The topics to be discussed have considerable practical relevance and are as follows: lagged dependent variables in the regressor set; non-normality of the disturbances; and non-linear restrictions.

2.5   Models with lagged dependent variables

It will now be assumed that the regressors of the linear model

$$y = X\beta + u$$

contain lagged dependent variables. This model can then be regarded as a stochastic difference equation, and it will be assumed that the coefficients of the lagged dependent variables satisfy stability conditions. One new difficulty that must be considered in a likelihood-based approach to inference is the treatment of relevant pre-sample values of the dependent variable. In order to simplify the analysis, these pre-sample values are assumed to be known constants. This strategy involves some asymmetry in the treatment of values of the dependent variable, but its consequences are asymptotically negligible.

The disturbances are assumed to be independent $N(0, \sigma^2)$ variates; that is, the covariance matrix $\Omega(\alpha) = E(uu')$ is restricted to be proportional to the n by n identity matrix. One reason for imposing this restriction is that the natural generalization in dynamic models would be to allow the form of $\Omega(\alpha)$ to be determined by some error autocorrelation scheme. However, if error autocorrelation and lagged dependent variables were jointly present, the MLEs of α and β would, in general, be asymptotically correlated, so that the information matrix would not be block diagonal and the expressions for the W and LM given above would be invalid. Savin (1976, Section 7) compares the invalid W test with the correct large sample test for a simple case with a single lag and first-order autoregressive disturbances. He proves that the inappropriate W statistic is never smaller than the correct form and also gives an example to show that the inequality $W \geqslant LR \geqslant LM$ is not satisfied (see Savin, 1976, Section 8).

If attention is restricted to the case of $\text{NID}(0, \sigma^2)$ disturbances, then the information matrix can be shown to be

$$\mathscr{I}(\theta) = \begin{bmatrix} n/(2\sigma^4) & 0' \\ 0 & \sigma^{-2}E(X'X) \end{bmatrix}, \quad \theta' = (\sigma^2, \beta'),$$

where the matrix $E(X'X)$ is a function of the fixed regressors of the model and the elements of the parameter vector θ. The matrix $\mathscr{I}(\theta)$ must, of course, be estimated when constructing the W and LM tests. Consequently, carrying out either of these tests of $H_0: R\beta - r = 0$ involves making a decision about how to estimate $E(X'X)$. Evans and Savin (1983) point out that $E(X'X)$ can be replaced by the sample cross-product matrix $X'X$, or be estimated by replacing θ in the analytic expression for $E(X'X)$ by $\tilde{\theta}$ for the W test and by $\hat{\theta}$ for the LM test (see Evans and Savin, 1983, Section 4, for an example).

It seems reasonable to suppose that, in practice, $E(X'X)$ will usually be replaced by its sample analogue $X'X$. If this method is adopted, the W, LR and LM statistics are calculated exactly as they are when all regressors are fixed in repeated sampling. Consequently the inequality $W \geqslant LR \geqslant LM$ is satisfied and the three test statistics are all functions of the F statistic. If the exact critical value of the F test were known, then it would be possible to derive exact versions of the W, LR and LM tests. These exact tests would be equivalent, having the same critical region in the original n-dimensional sample space and the same power function. There would, therefore, be no possibility of conflict in the outcomes of exact tests. Unfortunately, these properties are of little real interest because the exact critical value of the F statistic cannot be readily found when the regressors include lagged values of the dependent variable. In contrast to the case of a classical regression model with fixed regressors, the distribution of F will not be $F(s, n - k)$ under H_0.

Since the small sample distribution of F is not easily obtained, it seems inevitable that, in empirical work, tests will have to be based upon asymptotic theory with W, LR and LM being compared to z, a pre-specified upper significance point of the $\chi^2(s)$ distribution. The actual significance levels of these large sample tests will not be the same and may differ substantially from the nominal value. Further, the true powers of the large sample tests will not be equal and there will be the possibility of conflicting outcomes.

If the second approach to the estimation of $E(X'X)$ is adopted with this matrix being viewed as a function of the non-stochastic regressors and the elements of θ, then the previous remarks on the inequality do not apply. The W test will be based upon the unrestricted MLE $\tilde{\theta}$ while the restricted MLE $\hat{\theta}$ will be used for the LM test. The W and LM statistics derived in this way will not be functions of the conventional F statistic and will not satisfy the inequality. Even if exact versions of these tests were obtained, there would still be a probability of conflict because they are not equivalent.

In order to illustrate some of the general issues related to the two approaches to the estimation of $E(X'X)$, Evans and Savin (1983) consider the following simple dynamic model

$$y_t = \xi + \beta y_{t-1} + u_t, \quad |\beta| < 1, \quad t = 1, \ldots, n, \tag{5.1}$$

where y_0 is a known constant and the disturbances u_t are NID $(0, \sigma^2)$ variates. The null hypothesis discussed by Evans and Savin consists of the single restriction $\beta = \beta_0$, where β_0 is a specified constant which is less than unity in absolute value, and the alternative hypothesis is $\beta \neq \beta_0$. The power functions of the LR procedure and alternative forms of the W and

LM tests are examined, as is the probability of conflict. Evans and Savin find that the quality of the approximation derived from standard asymptotic theory and the probability of conflict both depend upon the size of β. As might be expected, large sample tests are good approximations to exact tests when testing $H_0: \beta = 0$, but are very poor approximations in the case $H_0: \beta = 0.95$. Overall, when the root of the difference equation (5.1) is close to unity, the true significance level of each test can differ substantially from the common nominal value and the probability of conflict can be high. Evans and Savin observe that, loosely speaking, the less stable the model the higher the probability of conflict. These results indicate that when the root is not much smaller than unity, the large sample critical value z requires some adjustment to achieve a test whose size is close to the nominal value. As in the case of the static regression model, differences in adjustments will imply that the inequality is no longer satisfied even when $E(X'X)$ is estimated by $X'X$.

2.6   Models with non-normal disturbances

If the familiar framework of the multivariate normal distribution is abandoned, then there is little reason to suppose that the results above will still be valid. Least-squares estimators will, in general, no longer correspond to maximum likelihood procedures and the inequality cannot be expected to be satisfied. A simple example can be used to illustrate these points.

Let $y_1, y_2, \ldots, y_n$ be a sequence of independent Bernoulli variates with

$$\text{prob}(y_t = 1) = \theta, \qquad 0 < \theta < 1,$$

and

$$\text{prob}(y_t = 0) = (1 - \theta), \quad t = 1, 2, \ldots, n.$$

The null hypothesis will be taken to be $H_0: \theta = \theta_0$, θ_0 being a specified constant between zero and unity, with the alternative hypothesis being $\theta \neq \theta_0$. The log-likelihood, score and information measure for this example are

$$l(\theta) = \sum_t [y_t \log \theta + (1 - y_t) \log (1 - \theta)],$$

$$d(\theta) = \sum_t (y_t - \theta)/[\theta(1 - \theta)],$$

and

$$\mathscr{I}(\theta) = n/[\theta(1 - \theta)],$$

respectively. The unrestricted MLE is $\tilde{\theta} = n^{-1}\Sigma y_t$ and so the W statistic for H_0 is

$$W = n(\tilde{\theta} - \theta_0)^2/[\tilde{\theta}(1 - \tilde{\theta})]. \tag{6.1}$$

The LM statistic is $d(\theta_0)' \mathscr{I}(\theta_0)^{-1} d(\theta_0)$ which, using

$$d(\theta) = \sum_t (y_t - \theta)/[\theta(1 - \theta)]$$

$$= n(\tilde{\theta} - \theta)/[\theta(1 - \theta)],$$

can easily be shown to be

$$LM = n(\tilde{\theta} - \theta_0)^2/[\theta_0(1 - \theta_0)]. \tag{6.2}$$

A comparison of expressions (6.1) and (6.2) reveals that the relative magnitudes of LM and W depend upon the denominators of the test statistics. For example, if $\theta_0 = 0.1$, then $W < LM$ if $0.1 < \tilde{\theta} < 0.9$, while if $\theta_0 = 0.5$, then $W \geqslant LM$, since $\theta(1 - \theta)$ has its maximum at $\theta = 0.5$.

The fact that the inequality is not robust to non-normality can also be demonstrated using a model which has several of the features of the one discussed in previous sections of this chapter. Ullah and Zinde-Walsh (1984) consider the problem of testing the linear restrictions of $H_0: R\beta = r$ against $R\beta \neq r$ in the context of the regression model

$$y = X\beta + u,$$

where the regressor matrix is fixed and has full column rank. The distribution of the elements of u is assumed by Ullah and Zinde-Walsh to be multivariate Student-t, rather than multivariate normal. Thus the joint density of the disturbances can be written as

$$p(u) = [c/\sigma^n]/[\gamma + (u'u/\sigma^2)]^{(n+\gamma)/2}, \tag{6.3}$$

where c is the normalizing constant

$$c = \gamma^{\gamma/2}\Gamma[(n + \gamma)/2]/\pi^{n/2}\Gamma(\gamma/2),$$

and γ is the degrees-of-freedom parameter, $\gamma > 0$.

The linear regression model with multivariate Student-t errors has been discussed by Zellner (1976). Zellner points out that the p.d.f. $p(u)$ of (6.3) is symmetric about the origin, which is also the modal value. The mean vector and covariance matrix of the disturbance vector u are given by

$$E(u) = 0 \text{ for } \gamma > 1$$

and

$$V(u) = [(\gamma\sigma^2)/(\gamma - 2)]I_n \text{ for } \gamma > 2.$$

Since $V(u)$ is proportional to the n by n identity matrix, the disturbances are uncorrelated. It is, however, worth noting that they are not independently distributed. Also the multivariate Student-t distribution includes the multivariate Cauchy distribution and the $N(0, \sigma^2 I_n)$ distribution as special cases: the former being obtained when $\gamma = 1$ and the latter being approached as $\gamma \to \infty$.

In order to develop likelihood-based tests of H_0, Ullah and Zinde-Walsh assume that the degrees of freedom parameter γ is a known constant and is larger than 2. If γ were treated as an unknown constant to be estimated jointly with σ^2 and β, then the MLE method would break down (see Zellner, 1976, p. 402). Under the assumption of known γ, the log-likelihood function is

$$l(\theta) = c^* - \frac{n}{2} \ln \sigma^2 - \left(\frac{n+\gamma}{2}\right) \ln \left(\gamma + \frac{S(\beta)}{\sigma^2}\right), \tag{6.4}$$

where c^* is independent of the unknown parameters, $\theta' = (\sigma^2, \beta')$, and $S(\beta)$ denotes the sum of squares function $(y - X\beta)'(y - X\beta)$.

Ullah and Zinde-Walsh (1984) relate their results to those of, for example, Evans and Savin (1982) on the relationships between criteria in the classical normal regression model. In contrast to the inequality $W \geqslant LR \geqslant LM$, the findings of Ullah and Zinde-Walsh lead to the weaker relationship

$$W_t \geqslant \lambda LR_t \geqslant \lambda^2 LM_t,$$

where $\lambda = (n + \gamma)/(n + \gamma + 2) < 1$ and a subscript t denotes a test derived using the log-likelihood of (6.4). Thus the usual inequality is not satisfied when the errors are multivariate Student-t (see Ullah and Zinde-Walsh, 1984, for further discussion, and the papers by Ullah and Zinde-Walsh, 1985, and Zinde-Walsh and Ullah, 1987, for generalizations).

2.7   Models with non-linear restrictions

Suppose now that the null hypothesis to be tested consists of s non-linear restrictions on the regression coefficient vector β of the model

$$y = X\beta + u,$$

where the n by k matrix X is fixed and has full column rank, and s is less than k. Also suppose that the disturbances of this model have an $N(0, \Omega(\alpha))$ distribution of the type discussed in Section 2.3. The restrictions will be written in constraint equation form as

$$g(\beta) = 0. \tag{7.1}$$

In order to make use of standard results on estimation and inference, it is assumed that the elements of $g(\beta)$ are continuous and possess partial derivatives of at least the second order with the s by k matrix of first-order derivatives $G(\beta) = \partial g(\beta)/\partial \beta$ having full row rank in a neighbourhood of the true value of β.

The null hypothesis $H_0: g(\beta) = 0$ is to be tested against $H_1: g(\beta) \neq 0$ by means of the classical likelihood-based procedures, and the purpose of this section is to consider whether or not any systematic relationship exists between the test statistics W, LR and LM. The log-likelihood function is given by

$$l(\theta) = \text{cnst} - \tfrac{1}{2}\ln|\Omega(\alpha)| - \tfrac{1}{2}(y - X\beta)'[\Omega(\alpha)]^{-1}(y - X\beta), \qquad (7.2)$$

and, as in Section 2.3, the unrestricted MLE will be denoted by $\tilde{\theta}' = (\tilde{\alpha}', \tilde{\beta}')$ and the restricted MLE by $\hat{\theta}' = (\hat{\alpha}', \hat{\beta}')$. The latter estimator can be derived using the Lagrangean function

$$\Lambda(\theta, \lambda) = l(\theta) + \lambda'g(\beta)$$

by solving the non-linear equations

$$\partial\Lambda(\hat{\theta}, \hat{\lambda})/\partial\alpha = \partial l(\hat{\theta})/\partial\alpha = 0,$$

$$\partial\Lambda(\hat{\theta}, \hat{\lambda})/\partial\beta = \partial l(\hat{\theta})/\partial\beta + G(\hat{\beta})'\hat{\lambda} = 0,$$

and

$$\partial\Lambda(\hat{\theta}, \hat{\lambda})/\partial\lambda = g(\hat{\beta}) = 0,$$

where $\hat{\lambda}$ is the s-dimensional vector of multipliers to be tested for significance in the LM procedure.

The information matrix is block diagonal with $E(\partial^2 l(\theta)/\partial\alpha\partial\beta') = 0$ and so the variability of MLEs of α can be ignored when constructing W and LM tests of $H_0: g(\beta) = 0$. The test statistics can, therefore, be written as

$$W = g(\hat{\beta})'[G(\hat{\beta})(X'\tilde{\Omega}^{-1}X)^{-1}G(\hat{\beta})']^{-1}g(\hat{\beta}), \qquad (7.3)$$

$$LR = -2[l(\hat{\theta}) - l(\tilde{\theta})], \qquad (7.4)$$

and

$$LM = \hat{u}'\hat{\Omega}^{-1}X(X'\hat{\Omega}^{-1}X)^{-1}X'\hat{\Omega}^{-1}\hat{u}, \qquad (7.5)$$

where $\tilde{\Omega} = \Omega(\tilde{\alpha})$, $\hat{\Omega} = \Omega(\hat{\alpha})$ and $\hat{u} = y - X\hat{\beta}$; these formulae are generalizations of the corresponding equations for the case of linear restrictions (see equations (3.1) to (3.3) of this chapter).

Breusch (1979, p. 206) outlines a simple modification of his treatment of the linear restrictions case that leads to the interesting result that $LR \geqslant LM$. This modification is based upon Breusch's interpretation of the

LM test as a conditional LR test. The estimator $\hat{\beta}$ can be regarded as the restricted conditional MLE when α is set equal to $\hat{\alpha}$; that is, it can be obtained by solving the optimization problem

$$\underset{\beta}{\text{maximize}}\ l(\hat{\alpha}, \beta)$$

subject to $g(\beta) = 0$.

Using (7.2), the restricted maximum of the conditional log-likelihood function $l(\hat{\alpha}, \beta)$ is given by

$$\kappa(\hat{\alpha}) - \tfrac{1}{2}\hat{u}'\hat{\Omega}^{-1}\hat{u} = l(\hat{\theta}), \tag{7.6}$$

where

$$\kappa(\hat{\alpha}) = \text{cnst} - \tfrac{1}{2}\ln|\hat{\Omega}| \text{ and } \hat{u} = y - X\hat{\beta}.$$

The unrestricted maximizer of the conditional log-likelihood function $l(\hat{\alpha}, \beta)$ is the GLS-type estimator

$$\hat{\beta}_u = (X'\hat{\Omega}^{-1}X)^{-1}X'\hat{\Omega}^{-1}y.$$

If e denotes the residual $y - X\hat{\beta}_u$, then the unrestricted maximized conditional log-likelihood is

$$\kappa(\hat{\alpha}) - \tfrac{1}{2}e'\hat{\Omega}^{-1}e = l(\hat{\alpha}, \hat{\beta}_u). \tag{7.7}$$

It will be useful to note that $X'\hat{\Omega}^{-1}e = 0$.

Equations (7.6) and (7.7) imply that the conditional likelihood ratio test of H_0 with $\alpha = \hat{\alpha}$ is given by

$$\begin{aligned} \text{CLR} &= -2[l(\hat{\theta}) - l(\hat{\alpha}, \hat{\beta}_u)] \\ &= \hat{u}'\hat{\Omega}^{-1}\hat{u} - e'\hat{\Omega}^{-1}e \\ &= (\hat{\beta}_u - \hat{\beta})'(X'\hat{\Omega}^{-1}X)(\hat{\beta}_u - \hat{\beta}), \end{aligned} \tag{7.8}$$

using $\hat{u} = y - X\hat{\beta} = e + X(\hat{\beta}_u - \hat{\beta})$ and $X'\hat{\Omega}^{-1}e = 0$.

It is easily verified that

$$(\hat{\beta}_u - \hat{\beta}) = (X'\hat{\Omega}^{-1}X)^{-1}X'\hat{\Omega}^{-1}\hat{u},$$

so that substitution in (7.8) yields

$$\text{CLR} = \hat{u}'\hat{\Omega}^{-1}X(X'\hat{\Omega}^{-1}X)^{-1}X'\hat{\Omega}^{-1}\hat{u} = \text{LM}.$$

Further the definition of $\tilde{\theta}$ ensures that $l(\tilde{\theta}) \geqslant l(\hat{\alpha}, \hat{\beta}_u)$ and so

$$\begin{aligned} \text{LR} - \text{LM} &= \text{LR} - \text{CLR} \\ &= 2[l(\tilde{\theta}) - l(\hat{\alpha}, \hat{\beta}_u)] \end{aligned}$$

is non-negative. It follows that the inequality LR $\geqslant$ LM is satisfied when testing non-linear restrictions on the parameter vector β of a classical normal regression model.

Having demonstrated that part of the inequality W $\geqslant$ LR $\geqslant$ LM holds in the more general case examined in this section, it remains to investigate whether W $\geqslant$ LR for tests of non-linear restrictions. Clearly, if numerical examples can be found with LR $>$ W, then this is sufficient evidence to prove that the full inequality relationship is not satisfied.[5] A Monte Carlo study by Mizon and Hendry (1980) provides such evidence.

Mizon and Hendry (1980) carry out simulation experiments to investigate the small sample performance of LR and W tests of non-linear restrictions associated with testing the assumption that the errors of a regression model are autoregressive. In order to illustrate how such non-linear restrictions arise, suppose that

$$y_t = \beta_1 x_t + \beta_2 y_{t-1} + \beta_3 x_{t-1} + u_t, \quad t = 1, \ldots, n,$$

where $\beta_1 \neq 0, |\beta_2| < 1$ and the disturbances u_t are NID$(0, \sigma^2)$ variates. This dynamic model can be written as a static relationship

$$y_t = \beta_1 x_t + \varepsilon_t$$

with autoregressive errors

$$\varepsilon_t = \beta_2 \varepsilon_{t-1} + u_t$$

if its parameters satisfy the non-linear restriction of

$$H_0: g_1(\beta_1, \beta_2, \beta_3) = \beta_1 \beta_2 + \beta_3 = 0.[6]$$

After studying a number of cases, Mizon and Hendry (1980, p. 39) report that the average significance levels of the asymptotically equivalent W and LR tests are 4 per cent and 9 per cent, respectively. These results are obviously inconsistent with the conjectured inequality W $\geqslant$ LR. Indeed, in one case the estimated significance level of the LR test is 16 per cent while the W test never leads to the rejection of the null hypothesis (see case (ii) of Table VII of Mizon and Hendry, 1980, p. 39). It follows that, although LR $\geqslant$ LM, the inequality W $\geqslant$ LR $\geqslant$ LM is not, in general, satisfied when the parametric restrictions to be tested are non-linear.

It should also be noted that there is an important difficulty associated

---

[5] Mizon (1977b) finds cases with LR $>$ W when testing linear restrictions on the parameters of non-linear models, thus establishing that the inequality does not apply in this generalization of the classical regression model.

[6] See Rothenberg (1973, pp. 27–9) for a more detailed discussion of this example.

with comparing the W statistic to the other two statistics. There are many mathematically equivalent ways of expressing a set of non-linear restrictions. In the simple example above, the restriction implied by the autoregressive error hypothesis was written as

$$g(\beta_1, \beta_2, \beta_3) = \beta_1\beta_2 + \beta_3 = 0,$$

but this expression could be replaced by any algebraically equivalent form, for example,

$$g_1^*(\beta_1, \beta_2, \beta_3) = \beta_2 + (\beta_3/\beta_1) = 0.$$

Unlike LM and LR, the sample value of the W statistic is not invariant with respect to such essentially irrelevant changes in the formulation of the null hypothesis.

This undesirable feature of the W test reflects the fact that it is derived from a linear approximation to the constraint vector evaluated at $\beta = \tilde{\beta}$, and different ways of expressing the restrictions lead to differences in the linearization. Provided regularity conditions are satisfied, such variations in the W statistic will be asymptotically negligible, but they may be important in finite samples.

Gregory and Veall (1985) provide Monte Carlo evidence that highlights the potential small sample importance of differences in the functional form of the non-linear restrictions to be tested. They consider a classical normal regression model

$$y_t = \beta_1 x_{t1} + \beta_2 x_{t2} + \beta_3 + u_t, \ u_t \text{NID}(0, \sigma^2),$$

where NID denotes normally and independently distributed. The two mathematically equivalent hypotheses to be tested are

$$\text{H}_0^A: g^A(\beta_1, \beta_2) = \beta_1 - (1/\beta_2) = 0$$

and

$$\text{H}_0^B: g^B(\beta_1, \beta_2) = \beta_1\beta_2 - 1 = 0.$$

The general form of the W statistic is

$$\text{W} = g(\tilde{\beta})'[G(\tilde{\beta})\tilde{V}(\tilde{\beta})G(\tilde{\beta})']^{-1}g(\tilde{\beta}),$$

where $\tilde{\beta}$ is the OLS estimator and $\tilde{V}(\tilde{\beta})$ is the usual estimator of its covariance matrix. Substitution of the two specific forms under consideration yields the following expressions for the test statistics:

$$\text{W}^A = (\tilde{\beta}_1\tilde{\beta}_2 - 1)^2/(\tilde{\beta}_2^2\tilde{v}_{11} + 2\tilde{v}_{12} + \tilde{\beta}_2^{-2}\tilde{v}_{22}), \tag{7.9}$$

and

$$\text{W}^B = (\tilde{\beta}_1\tilde{\beta}_2 - 1)^2/(\tilde{\beta}_2^2\tilde{v}_{11} + 2\tilde{\beta}_1\tilde{\beta}_2\tilde{v}_{12} + \tilde{\beta}_1^2\tilde{v}_{22}), \tag{7.10}$$

where the $\tilde{v}_{ij}$ are elements of $\tilde{V}(\tilde{\beta})$, $i, j = 1, 2$. The test statistics W^A and W^B are clearly not identical, although, under the equivalent null hypotheses,

$$\text{plim } \tilde{\beta}_1 \tilde{\beta}_2 = 1 \text{ and plim } \tilde{\beta}_1^2 = \text{plim } \tilde{\beta}_2^{-2},$$

so that they have the same asymptotic null distribution (the central $\chi^2(1)$ distribution).

The Monte Carlo results reported by Gregory and Veall reveal that there can be substantial differences between W^A and W^B in finite samples. The W^A variant performs quite poorly with a marked tendency to reject a true null hypothesis too frequently. The W^B form is much better behaved in this respect, and Gregory and Veall conclude that there is possibly some advantage in testing non-linear restrictions in multiplicative form, as opposed to ratio form.

In previous sections, it was assumed that if parameter restrictions could be expressed as $R\beta = r$ then they would be tested in this form. Linear restrictions, however, often have equivalent non-linear representations and the inequality $W \geqslant LR \geqslant LM$ need not be satisfied if such a representation is used as the basis for calculating test statistics. If the restrictions of $R\beta = r$ were tested in a number of equivalent non-linear forms, then the LR and LM statistics would be unchanged, but the variations in the W statistic could be substantial. Lafontaine and White (1986, Section 2) provide an example for the case in which there is a single restriction which sets one regression coefficient equal to unity, and the set of non-linear representations is derived from exponent transformations.

2.8   Summary and conclusions

Most of the discussion in this chapter has been concerned with the problem of testing linear restrictions in linear regression models with fixed regressors and normally distributed disturbances. If the covariance matrix of the disturbances is known, then the three likelihood-based tests have the same numerical value, that is, $W = LR = LM$. If, on the other hand, this covariance matrix depends upon a parameter vector that is estimated jointly with the regression parameters, then, provided the unrestricted MLEs of these two sets of parameters are asymptotically uncorrelated, the inequality $W \geqslant LR \geqslant LM$ is satisfied. This remarkable inequality, therefore, applies to regression models with specified forms of autocorrelation or heteroscedasticity.

The special case in which the errors are $NID(0, \sigma^2)$ variates has been singled out for discussion. In this case, the three classical test criteria can be expressed as functions of each other, or as different functions of the conventional F statistic for the hypothesis-testing problem under consideration.

The possibilities of extending the inequality to more general problems has also received attention. As a rule, the inequality does not apply if the errors are non-normal or the restrictions are non-linear, although in the latter case it has been established that $LR \geqslant LM$. The case of models with lagged dependent variables in the regressor set has also been discussed and the inequality shown to be satisfied when the errors are $NID(0, \sigma^2)$, provided that the sample cross-product matrix $X'X$ is used to estimate $E(X'X)$ in the information matrix.

These findings cover the form and range of applicability of the inequality $W \geqslant LR \geqslant LM$. It is, of course, extremely important to examine the consequences of this inequality for inference in regression analysis. A researcher dealing with a model in which the inequality is satisfied can select the statistic most likely to be greater than (or less than) a critical value. This implication has led to some unease about the possibility of introducing prejudice when testing hypotheses in empirical work. There are, however, many ways in which econometric methods and the data can be abused (e.g., the selection of the significance level on the basis of the calculated test statistics, the choice of sample period, etc.), and it seems more fruitful to focus on the genuine statistical implications of the inequality.

It has been emphasised that, when it is applicable, the inequality is satisfied under both the null and alternative hypotheses. Consequently, if large sample tests are derived by comparing W, LR and LM to z, a critical value from their common χ^2 asymptotic null distribution, then

$$\text{prob}(W > z) \geqslant \text{prob}(LR > z) \geqslant \text{prob}(LM > z)$$

whether or not H_0 is true. It follows that the inequality does not imply anything about the relative merits of these tests as measured by powers for a common significance level.

The inequality does, however, imply that there is the possibility of conflict among the outcomes of large sample tests. The probability of conflict may be substantial if asymptotic theory provides a poor approximation to the small sample behaviour of the W, LR and LM statistics. In such cases, some modification of large sample theory is required. There is some evidence to suggest that Edgeworth correction factors may be useful. If Edgeworth size-corrected tests are employed, it appears that the differences between them may be small and the probability of conflict may be of no practical importance.

There is, of course, no need to resort to large sample tests if the disturbances are NID$(0, \sigma^2)$ variates. In this special case, the statistics W, LR and LM are all monotonic functions of the familiar F statistic, so that exact tests based upon W, LR and LM are all equivalent to the F test. There is, therefore, no possibility of conflict among the exact versions of the W, LR and LM tests.

CHAPTER 3

The Lagrange multiplier test and testing for misspecification: an extended analysis

3.1   Introduction

The LM principle deserves special consideration when discussing tests for misspecification because, unlike the asymptotically equivalent W and LR methods, it does not require the estimation of the more complex alternative in which the original model of interest has been embedded. The purpose of this chapter is to provide a detailed analysis of LM tests in the context of detecting specification errors and deciding how to respond to significant evidence of model inadequacy.

In Section 3.2, it is shown that several alternatives can lead to the same value of the LM statistic for a given null specification. Consequently, only a class of alternative hypotheses need be selected in order to determine the form of the LM statistic. The members of such a class will, however, correspond to quite different types of specification. It is, therefore, natural to ask whether the LM test based upon the selection of the correct class of alternative hypotheses is inferior to the LR and W tests when the latter tests are derived using the correct member of this class. This issue is examined, and some Monte Carlo evidence on the relative performance of the LM test is summarized.

The techniques used to derive the set of alternatives which share the same LM test of the null model can also be used to derive a flexible and easily implemented scheme for calculating test statistics. It is shown in Section 3.2 that LM checks for misspecification can often be calculated as simple tests for omitted variables. This result provides a very general and extremely convenient approach to the derivation of tests for errors of specification which is easily extended to permit the testing of more than one hypothesis. This feature is useful because it is becoming increasingly common for applied workers to check for more than one kind of misspecification; for example, estimated regression equations are often accompanied by tests for parameter stability and autocorrelated disturbances. In such cases, researchers must decide whether to carry out a joint test or a set of separate tests for each of the specification errors being entertained.

69

Section 3.3 covers the methods that can be used to carry out joint tests for combinations of misspecifications and the relationships between joint tests and the procedure induced by separate tests. The important problem of diagnosing the causes of significant values of test statistics is also examined in this section, and some arguments based upon asymptotic theory are put forward.

One difficulty in relying upon asymptotic theory is that terms that are asymptotically negligible sometimes turn out to be important for sample sizes of the magnitude encountered in empirical work. The choice of the estimator of the information matrix is particularly important in this context. Any consistent estimator will lead to an asymptotically valid LM test, and several candidates have been proposed. Section 3.4 deals with the relative merits of these different estimators in various types of statistical model.

Sections 3.2 to 3.4 are based upon the assumption that the regularity conditions set out in Chapter 1 are satisfied. Although these conditions are sufficiently general to cover most cases of econometric interest, certain non-standard cases, such as singular information matrices, merit discussion. Section 3.5 contains such a discussion and extends the analysis of Chapter 1 to consider various problems associated with tests for misspecification, with the role of LM procedures receiving special attention. As in Chapter 1, the notation in this chapter is often simplified by not showing the dependence of the score and the information matrix on the sample size n and the parameter vector θ. Also, NID is used to denote normally and independently distributed.

3.2   Alternative hypotheses leading to the same Lagrange multiplier statistic

One of the theoretical insights provided by the LM approach is that the same classical test may be appropriate for a number of different alternative hypotheses. Of course, the form of the LM statistic, for example, is not completely insensitive to the choice of alternative hypothesis. Alternative models requiring different numbers of parametric restrictions to yield the null model could not share the same LM statistic. In order to define the class of alternative models for which a given test statistic is appropriate, consider a general alternative written as

$$g(y_t, x_t, F_{t-1}; \theta) = u_t, \quad u_t \text{NID}(0, \Sigma_t(\theta)), \tag{2.1}$$

where y_t denotes a vector of observations on endogenous variables, x_t is a vector of exogenous variables, F_{t-1} is a vector of past values of y_t and x_t, and θ is the unknown parameter vector.[1] The vectors $g(\cdot)$ and u_t are both M-dimensional and $\Sigma_t(\theta)$, which can vary from one observation to another, is non-singular. Pre-multiplying both sides of equation (2.1) by $[\Sigma_t(\theta)]^{-\frac{1}{2}}$ yields

$$f(y_t, x_t, F_{t-1}; \theta) = \varepsilon_t, \quad \varepsilon_t \mathrm{NID}(0, I_M), \tag{2.2}$$

where $f(\cdot) \equiv [\Sigma_t(\theta)]^{-\frac{1}{2}}g(\cdot)$ and $\varepsilon_t \equiv [\Sigma_t(\theta)]^{-\frac{1}{2}}u_t$. If the parameter vector is partitioned as $\theta' = (\theta'_1, \theta'_2)$, then it will be assumed that the null model to be tested is obtained by imposing the s restrictions $\theta_2 = \theta_2^0$ on (2.2).

The log-likelihood for a single observation on (2.2) is

$$l_t(\theta) = \mathrm{cnst} - \tfrac{1}{2}\varepsilon_t(\theta)'\varepsilon_t(\theta) + \ln\|\partial\varepsilon_t(\theta)/\partial y_t\|, \tag{2.3}$$

where $\varepsilon_t(\theta)$ is defined as a function of the data y_t and the parameter vector θ by (2.2). The LM test of the null hypothesis $H_0: \theta_2 = \theta_2^0$ will be recalled to be an asymptotically valid check of the joint significance of the elements of $\hat{d}_2 = \Sigma_1^n[\partial l_t(\hat{\theta})/\partial\theta_2]$, where $\hat{\theta}$ is the constrained MLE with sub-vectors $\hat{\theta}_1$ and θ_2^0. The contribution of a single observation to $\hat{d}_2$ is, using equation (2.3), given by

$$\partial l_t(\hat{\theta})/\partial\theta_2 = \{-[\partial\varepsilon_t(\theta)/\partial\theta_2]'\varepsilon_t(\theta) + \partial(\ln\|\partial\varepsilon_t(\theta)/\partial y_t\|)/\partial\theta_2\}_{\theta=\hat{\theta}}. \tag{2.4}$$

Now $\hat{\theta}_1$ is the MLE of the parameter vector of the null model and $\varepsilon_t(\hat{\theta})$ is the associated residual. It is, therefore, clear from (2.4) that the choice of alternative affects $\hat{d}_2$ (and hence the LM test) through $\partial\varepsilon_t(\theta)/\partial\theta_2$ and $\partial(\ln\|\partial\varepsilon_t(\theta)/\partial y_t\|)/\partial\theta_2$ evaluated at $\theta = \hat{\theta}$.

Consider the vector

$$\varepsilon_t^*(\theta) = \varepsilon_t(\theta_1, \theta_2^0) + [\partial\varepsilon_t(\theta_1, \theta_2^0)/\partial\theta_2]'(\theta_2 - \theta_2^0), \tag{2.5}$$

which is obtained by linearizing $\varepsilon_t(\theta)$ about $\theta_2 = \theta_2^0$.[2] It is straightforward to verify that $\varepsilon_t^*(\theta)$ has the following properties:

(i) $\varepsilon_t^*(\theta_1, \theta_2 = \theta_2^0) = \varepsilon_t(\theta_1, \theta_2 = \theta_2^0)$

so that imposing the restrictions of H_0 on the alternative models corresponding to $\varepsilon_t^*(\theta)$ and $\varepsilon_t(\theta)$ yields the same null model, and hence these alternatives share the same constrained MLE $\hat{\theta}$ and residual vector, that is, $\varepsilon_t^*(\hat{\theta}) = \varepsilon_t(\hat{\theta})$;

(ii) $\partial\varepsilon_t^*(\hat{\theta})/\partial\theta_2 = \partial\varepsilon_t(\hat{\theta})/\partial\theta_2$,

a result that follows from differentiation of (2.5); and

---

[1] The vector x_t is defined to include any exogenous variables appearing in the elements of the matrix $\Sigma_t(\theta)$.

[2] It is again convenient to violate the usual rules of notation and to write, e.g., $\varepsilon_t(\theta_1, \theta_2^0)$ even though θ_1 and θ_2^0 are column vectors.

(iii) $\partial \ln(\|\partial \varepsilon_t^*(\theta)/\partial y_t\|)/\partial \theta_2 = \partial \ln(\|\partial \varepsilon_t(\theta)/\partial y_t\|)/\partial \theta_2,$

when $\theta = \hat{\theta}$, which is a consequence of the fact that $\varepsilon_t(\theta)$ and $\varepsilon_t^*(\theta)$ differ by terms involving second and higher powers of the elements of $\theta_2 - \theta_2^0$.

It follows that when testing the adequacy of the null model represented by $\varepsilon_t(\theta_1, \theta_2^0)$, the choice between the alternatives of $\varepsilon_t(\theta)$ and $\varepsilon_t^*(\theta)$ is irrelevant as far as the value of the LM criterion $\hat{d}_2$ is concerned.[3] Thus, provided a common consistent estimator of the information matrix is employed, the sample value of the LM statistic will be the same whether the alternative is characterized by $\varepsilon_t(\theta)$ or $\varepsilon_t^*(\theta)$. Since $\varepsilon_t^*(\theta)$ of (2.5) is derived as a local approximation to $\varepsilon_t(\theta)$ by linearization about $\theta_2 = \theta_2^0$, it seems natural to refer to the models underlying $\varepsilon_t(\theta)$ and $\varepsilon_t^*(\theta)$ as *locally equivalent alternatives* (LEAs) with respect to the null hypothesis $\theta_2 = \theta_2^0$. The LR and W statistics for LEAs will be asymptotically equivalent, but not algebraically equal.

The linearization of $\varepsilon_t(\theta)$ about $\theta_2 = \theta_2^0$ can be motivated by observing that the relationship of asymptotic equivalence – for example, as between the LR, W and LM procedures under standard conditions – is based upon an examination of the behaviour of tests under a sequence of local alternatives. An appropriate sequence of local alternatives can be written as $H_n: \theta_2 = \theta_2^0 + n^{-\frac{1}{2}}\eta, \eta'\eta < \infty.$[4] Expanding $\varepsilon_t(\theta)$ about $\theta_2 = \theta_2^0$ in a Taylor series and ignoring second- and higher-order terms in the elements of $(\theta_2 - \theta_2^0)$ is, therefore, equivalent to dropping terms with coefficients which are $o(n^{-\frac{1}{2}})$ under H_n. The omission of such terms is asymptotically valid because they have no effect on the non-centrality parameter of the relevant non-central χ^2 distribution.

An example

In order to illustrate that alternatives that appear to be quite different can lead to the same LM test statistic, consider a case in which the null model is the semi-log regression

$$y_t = \beta_1 + \beta_2 \ln x_t + u_t, \ u_t\,\text{NID}(0, \sigma^2), \tag{2.6}$$

and the alternative corresponding to (2.1) is the Box–Cox regression model

$$y_t = \beta_1 + \beta_2 T(x_t, \gamma) + u_t, \ u_t\,\text{NID}(0, \sigma^2), \tag{2.7}$$

---

[3] This result can be extended by considering linearizations of $\varepsilon_t(\theta)$ about sub-sets of the elements of θ_2^0.

[4] It is convenient to make the usual assumption that the information matrix has elements of $O(n)$, and so to consider deviations from the null value which are $O(n^{-\frac{1}{2}})$.

where

$$T(x_t, \gamma) = (x_t^\gamma - 1)/\gamma, \; \gamma \neq 0$$

$$= \ln x_t, \quad \gamma = 0,$$

and the sequence $\{x_1, \ldots, x_n\}$ is fixed in repeated sampling. In terms of previous notation, we have

$$\theta_1' = (\beta_1, \beta_2, \sigma^2)$$

$$\theta_2 = \gamma$$

$$\theta_2^0 = 0$$

and

$$\varepsilon_t(\theta) = [y_t - \beta_1 - \beta_2 T(x_t, \gamma)]/\sigma. \tag{2.8}$$

Since $\partial T(x_t, \gamma = 0)/\partial \gamma = \frac{1}{2}(\ln x_t)^2$, the partial derivative of $\varepsilon_t(\theta)$ of (2.8) with respect to γ is $-(\beta_2/2\sigma)(\ln x_t)^2$ when $\gamma = 0$, so that the expression corresponding to (2.5) is

$$[y_t - \beta_1 - \beta_2 \ln x_t]/\sigma - [\beta_3(\ln x_t)^2]/\sigma, \tag{2.9}$$

where $\beta_3 \equiv (\beta_2/2)\gamma$. Thus, despite the fact that the alternatives of

$$y_t = \beta_1 + \beta_2 T(x_t, \gamma) + u_t, \; u_t \text{NID}(0, \sigma^2) \tag{2.7}$$

and

$$y_t = \beta_1 + \beta_2 \ln x_t + \beta_3(\ln x_t)^2 + u_t, \; u_t \text{NID}(0, \sigma^2) \tag{2.10}$$

are apparently dissimilar, they lead to asymptotically equivalent LR, W and LM tests of the semi-log model of (2.6).

Small sample power

Asymptotic equivalence need not be associated with similar small sample performance, and it might be conjectured that the LM test was, owing to its insensitivity to certain variations in the alternative, inferior to LR and W procedures calculated for the correct alternative hypothesis. The connection between small sample power and the amount of information about the alternative employed must usually be investigated by Monte Carlo methods because finite sample distributions are difficult to derive. Godfrey (1981) has reported on some experiments in which LM and LR tests for autocorrelation and functional form are compared, and Bera (1982) provides evidence for heteroscedasticity tests. Both researchers find that, despite its lack of sensitivity to the precise specification of the alternative, the LM procedure is by no means markedly inferior to the LR test based upon the true data generating process. They also find that the LR tests derived for LEAs have similar power properties.

Computational costs

It should also be noted that the asymptotic equivalence of LR, W and LM tests derived for LEAs certainly does not imply that the computational costs of the various tests will be similar. For example, compare the simplicity of a W-type '*t*-test' of $\beta_3 = 0$ in (2.10) with the complexity of the corresponding W-test of $\gamma = 0$ in (2.7). A particularly useful computational device can be obtained by constructing an artificial model which can be regarded as locally equivalent to (2.1) when the null hypothesis is $H_0: \theta_2 = \theta_2^0$. This artificial model is derived by replacing the M by s matrix of derivatives $\partial \varepsilon_t(\theta_1, \theta_2^0)/\partial \theta_2$ in equation (2.5) by $\partial \varepsilon_t(\hat{\theta})/\partial \theta_2$. The difference between $\partial \varepsilon_t(\theta_1, \theta_2^0)/\partial \theta_2$ and $\partial \varepsilon_t(\hat{\theta})/\partial \theta_2$ is a matrix in which the elements are linear combinations of the elements of $(\hat{\theta}_1 - \theta_1)$ and the weights of these combinations are second-order derivatives evaluated at points between $\hat{\theta}$ and (θ_1, θ_2^0). Provided attention is confined to behaviour under the null and local alternatives, the term $(\hat{\theta}_1 - \theta_1)$ will be $o_p(1)$, and so the difference between the two matrices will be asymptotically negligible.

Therefore, if we approximate $\varepsilon_t(\theta)$ by

$$\varepsilon_t^+(\theta) = \varepsilon_t(\theta_1, \theta_2^0) + [\partial \varepsilon_t(\hat{\theta})/\partial \theta_2]'(\theta_2 - \theta_2^0), \qquad (2.11)$$

then $\varepsilon_t^+(\theta)$ can be interpreted as providing an algorithm for computing tests of H_0 with the same large-sample properties (under H_n) as those derived by using $\varepsilon_t(\theta)$ or $\varepsilon_t^*(\theta)$. (The LM test of $\theta_2 = \theta_2^0$ will take on the same sample value whichever formulation is employed if a common estimate of the information matrix is used.)

The appeal of the artificial alternative associated with $\varepsilon_t^+(\theta)$ arises from the fact that it differs from the null model by the addition of a linear combination of test variables corresponding to $\partial \varepsilon_t(\hat{\theta})/\partial \theta_2$. It follows that the adoption of the LEA of (2.11) reduces the task of checking model specification to the familiar problem of testing for omitted variables.[5] This approach is especially attractive when the null specification is a linear regression model with i.i.d. $(0, \sigma^2)$ disturbances since it is then only necessary to apply an asymptotically valid F-type test of $\delta = 0$ in the context of the alternative

$$y_t = x_t'\beta + [\partial \varepsilon_t(\hat{\theta})/\partial \theta_2]'\delta + u_t. \qquad (2.12)$$

The test variables included in augmented models like (2.12) will depend upon the specification of the alternative, but require only the estimation of the null model for their construction. It should also be noted that there is no compelling reason to use the LM principle to test $\delta = 0$ in augmented

[5] See Engle (1982a) and Pagan (1984) for important discussions of testing by adding variables.

models: it would clearly be quite convenient to use W or LR tests when the $\varepsilon_t^+(\theta)$ approximation leads to models like (2.12).

Summary

The results of this section may be summarized as follows.

(i) An LR, W or LM test of a given null model is asymptotically optimal for a class of alternatives: members of this class have been termed LEAs. It follows that the advice "accept the alternative if the null is rejected" is not only dangerous, but is meaningless in the sense that many different alternatives would have resulted in the same test (or an asymptotically equivalent test) being carried out.

(ii) Checks for misspecification derived by embedding the null model in a more complex specification can be carried out as tests of the joint significance of an appropriate set of test variables. The form of the test variables will vary from one class of LEAs to another, but their construction requires only the estimation of the null model.

The above results do not imply that the choice of alternative is irrelevant. For a given unknown true data generation process, the probability of rejecting an inadequate null specification will vary with the selected alternative. The choice of alternative should, therefore, be based on careful consideration and evaluation of information about potential misspecifications.

3.3 Testing against several types of misspecification

It is not difficult to find examples of empirical work in which the selected alternative as represented by (2.1) differs from the null model only by the presence of a single generalization; for example, the assumption of independent disturbances might be replaced by the alternative hypothesis of some specified autocorrelation scheme. Modelling complex economic processes is, however, likely to lead to several types of error, so that it may often be useful to test for more than one kind of misspecification. Applied workers have sometimes recognized this problem and have reported the values of several test statistics, each of which is designed for a different alternative. The advantages and disadvantages of using such collections of separate tests as opposed to an appropriate joint test were discussed in general terms in Chapter 1, where it was argued that the overall significance level of a group of tests would often be difficult to determine and that the sample values of the individual statistics might be of very limited value in guiding respecification. Consequently, it was suggested that joint tests were worthy of consideration.[6]

It would be possible to form a super-model which included all the individual alternatives (and hence the null) as special cases. The standard LM test would then be obtained by evaluating the relevant partial derivatives of the log-likelihood for the super-model at the constrained MLE. The LEA approach of Section 3.2, however, provides a simpler framework for constructing joint tests. Suppose that there are q separate alternatives under consideration, none of which is a special case of the others. (If one alternative were nested in another, then there would be redundant restrictions in the parametric hypothesis defining the null model.) The corresponding partition of the vectors θ_2 and θ_2^0 will be written as

$$\theta_2' = (\theta_{21}', \ldots, \theta_{2q}')$$

and

$$\theta_2^{0'} = (\theta_{21}^{0'}, \ldots, \theta_{2q}^{0'}),$$

where it assumed that there is functional independence between the elements of θ_{2i} and those of θ_{2j} whenever i does not equal j. This assumption is quite plausible since, for example, there is no reason to suppose that the parameters of an autocorrelation alternative are functions of the coefficients of a selected heteroscedasticity scheme. The vector $\varepsilon_t^+(\theta)$ of (2.11) can, therefore, be written as

$$\varepsilon_t^+(\theta) = \varepsilon_t(\theta_1, \theta_2^0) + \Sigma_{j=1}^q [\partial \varepsilon_t(\hat{\theta})/\partial \theta_{2j}]'(\theta_{2j} - \theta_{2j}^0), \tag{3.1}$$

but $[\partial \varepsilon_t(\hat{\theta})/\partial \theta_{2j}]$ is just the set of variables added to the null model to yield a LEA when testing against the jth alternative alone. Thus joint tests against many combinations of misspecification can be calculated using the LEA derived by evaluating the matrix $[\partial \varepsilon_t(\hat{\theta})/\partial \theta_{2j}]$ for each of the q separate alternatives and then using (3.1). There is no need to consider the complicated log-likelihood function for a super-model incorporating all alternatives. It is important to note that this result does not imply that it is generally valid to add the q individual test statistics together in order to obtain an overall test.

These points can be illustrated using the following example. Suppose that the null model is

$$M_0: y_t = u_t, \quad u_t \text{NID}(0, 1), \tag{3.2}$$

---

[6] The value of separate tests in identifying the particular kinds of misspecification present in a null model is discussed in greater detail later in this section.

and there are two separate alternatives

$$\mathrm{M}_i: y_t = x_{ti}\beta_i + x_{ti}^2\beta_i^2 + u_t,\ u_t\,\mathrm{NID}(0,\,1),\ i = 1,\,2, \tag{3.3}$$

with corresponding null hypotheses $\mathrm{H}_{0,i}: \beta_i = 0,\ i = 1,\,2$. A super-model containing both M_1 and M_2 of (3.3) is then

$$\mathrm{M}_s: y_t = x_{t1}\beta_1 + x_{t2}\beta_2 + x_{t1}^2\beta_1^2 + x_{t2}^2\beta_2^2 + u_t,\ u_t\,\mathrm{NID}(0,\,1), \tag{3.4}$$

with M_0 being obtained by imposing the two restrictions $\beta_1 = \beta_2 = 0$. The LEAs for the individual alternatives of (3.3) are

$$y_t = x_{ti}\beta_i + u_t,\ u_t\,\mathrm{NID}(0,\,1),\ i = 1,\,2, \tag{3.5}$$

since β_i^2 is $\mathrm{O}(n^{-1})$ when β_i is $\mathrm{O}(n^{-\frac{1}{2}})$. An LR, W or LM test of $\beta_i = 0$ in (3.5) will be asymptotically distributed as $\chi^2(1)$ when M_0 is true ($i = 1,\,2$). The LEA for the super-model M_s is formed using (3.1) with the two $[\partial\varepsilon_t(\hat\theta)/\partial\theta_{2j}]$ terms being x_{t1} and x_{t2}, and so can be written as

$$y_t = x_{t1}\beta_1 + x_{t2}\beta_2 + u_t,\ u_t\,\mathrm{NID}(0,\,1). \tag{3.6}$$

The application of one of the classical principles – namely, LR, W and LM – to testing $\beta_1 = \beta_2 = 0$ in (3.6) yields a statistic which is asymptotically distributed as $\chi^2(2)$ under the null. The sum of the two $\chi^2(1)$ statistics associated with the separate tests of $\beta_1 = 0$ and $\beta_2 = 0$ will, however, only be distributed as $\chi^2(2)$ if the two individual test statistics are asymptotically independently distributed. Thus, in this example, it is only valid to add up the individual test statistics if

$$\lim n^{-1}\sum_t x_{t1}x_{t2} = 0.$$

More generally, if the q individual χ^2 test criteria are asymptotically independently distributed under the null, then it will be valid to evaluate the corresponding joint test as their sum, and it will also be possible to evaluate the large sample significance level of the induced test of $\mathrm{H}_0: \theta_2 = \theta_2^0$ based upon the set of q separate tests. For example, if the nominal size of the test against the jth alternative alone is denoted by α_j, then the nominal size of the induced test of $\theta_2 = \theta_2^0$ is $1 - \Pi_{j=1}^q(1 - \alpha_j)$ when the q test statistics are independently distributed under the null.[7] It is, therefore, of some interest to investigate the conditions under which individual test statistics are independent and so can be added together to form a valid joint test.

[7] If, on the other hand, the test statistics for $\theta_{2j} = \theta_{2j}^0$ ($j = 1,\,2,\,\ldots,\,q$) are not independent, then the overall size of the induced test is difficult to determine, but will be between the maximum of $\alpha_1,\,\alpha_2,\,\ldots,\,\alpha_q$ and the sum of these individual significance levels.

Asymptotic independence of test statistics

Consider the general expression for the LM statistic in its efficient score form, that is,

$$\text{LM} = \hat{d}'.\hat{\mathscr{I}}^{-1}\hat{d}, \tag{3.7}$$

where $\hat{\mathscr{I}}$ is some estimator of the information matrix $\mathscr{I}$ which has the property that plim $\hat{\mathscr{I}} I^{-1} = I$. For situations of the type considered here in which the constraint set is $\theta_2 = \theta_2^0$, the elements of $\hat{d}$ corresponding to the parameters of θ_1 are all zero and (3.7) reduces to

$$\text{LM} = \hat{d}_2'.\hat{\mathscr{I}}^{22}\hat{d}_2 = \hat{d}_2'[\hat{\mathscr{I}}_{22} - \hat{\mathscr{I}}_{21}\hat{\mathscr{I}}_{11}^{-1}\hat{\mathscr{I}}_{12}]^{-1}\hat{d}_2, \tag{3.8}$$

where $\hat{\mathscr{I}}^{22}$ denotes the appropriate sub-matrix of $\hat{\mathscr{I}}^{-1}$. The statistic LM will clearly be equal to the sum of the q individual tests if $\hat{\mathscr{I}}^{22}$ is block diagonal with each of the q diagonal blocks corresponding to a different type of misspecification.[8] If the LM test of $\theta_2 = \theta_2^0$ can be expressed as the sum of the LM tests for the q separate misspecifications, then, as Bera (1982) points out, a similar decomposition will be valid for tests based upon the LR and W principles. This result follows from the fact that, when the null model is true, the differences between LR, W and LM tests of the same set of restrictions are asymptotically negligible whether these tests are derived for a particular alternative or the super-model.

The conditions for the validity of the decomposition of the joint test can often be easily checked when the null model is a linear regression and the test is derived by means of the $\varepsilon_t^+(\theta)$ type of LEA. For example, let the null model be

$$y_t = x_t'\beta + u_t, \; u_t \, \text{NID}(0, \sigma^2), \tag{3.9}$$

with the LEA for a super-model allowing for two types of misspecification in (3.9) being written as

$$y_t = x_t'\beta + w_t'\alpha + z_t'\gamma + u_t, \; u_t \, \text{NID}(0, \sigma^2), \tag{3.10}$$

where w_t and z_t denote vectors of test variables for the two specification errors under consideration.[9] Using an obvious matrix–vector notation, n

---

[8] Strictly speaking, it is the probability limit of $(n.\hat{\mathscr{I}}^{22})$ which must be block diagonal on the null to justify the adding-up method, rather than a particular sample value.

[9] There is really no need to assume normality of the disturbances u_t because attention will be confined to large sample behaviour under the null hypothesis and the asymptotic normality of the OLS estimators can be established under much weaker assumptions about the u_t. Procedures derived from the Gaussian log-likelihood can, therefore, be regarded as, e.g., quasi-LM tests.

observations on (3.10) can be represented by, say,

$$y = X\beta + W\alpha + Z\gamma + u = R\psi + u. \tag{3.11}$$

Assuming that it is asymptotically valid to apply standard least-squares theory to (3.11) when $\alpha = 0$ and $\gamma = 0$, and that $R'R$ is $O_p(n)$, the condition for the valid decomposition of the LM test of $H_0: \{\alpha = 0$ and $\gamma = 0\}$ is

$$\text{plim } n^{-1}W'[I - X(X'X)^{-1}X']Z = 0, \tag{3.12}$$

which implies the asymptotic independence of the OLS estimators of α and γ. The following conditions guarantee that (3.12) is satisfied and are frequently valuable in examining tests of regression models:

(i)   plim $n^{-1}(W'Z) = 0$ and
(ii) either plim $n^{-1}(W'X) = 0$ or plim $n^{-1}(Z'X) = 0$.

Note that it is not sufficient for W and Z to be asymptotically uncorrelated and that the "either ... or ..." nature of (ii) implies that it is not necessary for both sets of test variables to be asymptotically orthogonal to the regressors of the null model.

Behaviour of test statistics when the model is misspecified

It is worth stressing that the asymptotic independence of tests we have been discussing holds when the null model is true and that no consideration has been given to the behaviour of tests under some other data generation process. In general, the asymptotic distributions of test statistics will not be robust to the presence of misspecifications for which they were not designed.[10] The extent of this lack of robustness has important implications for the usefulness of separate tests in identifying the source (or sources) of model misspecification.

In order to gain some insight into the problems involved in discovering the causes of model rejection, consider a situation in which a null model is to be tested against $q > 1$ separate alternatives by means of test statistics T_i, $i = 1, 2, \ldots, q$. It is assumed that each statistic is $O_p(1)$ under the null model and is $O_p(n)$ under the alternative for which it was derived. Suppose that the null model is false and that the true data-generating process is the super-model implied by the first $q_1(q_1 < q)$ separate alternatives. It seems reasonable to assume that, in this case, T_i is $O_p(n)$ for $i = 1, 2, \ldots, q_1$; in other words, the presence of the other $(q_1 - 1)$ misspecifications will not make a test for a single error inconsistent.[11] If T_j, some $j > q_1$, is also

---

[10] Some specific cases will be considered in Chapter 4 in the context of testing the specification of regression models.

[11] It is, of course, possible that combinations of misspecifications may lead to low small sample power of separate tests in some parts of the parameter space, and hence to a poor induced test of H_0.

$O_p(n)$, then the probability of correctly accepting the absence of the jth type of misspecification tends to zero as $n \to \infty$ for all finite critical values. In this situation, it might, therefore, be conjectured that a researcher testing by induction and looking at individual test outcomes might over-parameterize the model when attempting to correct the errors present in the original null specification. On the other hand, if T_j is $O_p(1)$ for all $j > q_1$, then the probability of incorrectly accepting the presence of the jth type of error will not tend to unity with the sample size. The asymptotic limit of this probability will, in general, be difficult to derive, but it will equal the nominal significance level in those (very) special cases in which a test statistic has the same distribution under the false null and the true data generation process.

Large-sample theory therefore prompts the conjecture that a multiple comparison procedure involving the consideration of the q separate tests is more likely to be helpful in respecifying rejected null models if test statistics for alternatives not contained in the true model are $O_p(1)$.[12] This conjecture is, however, based upon the assumption that the super-model contains (an adequate approximation to) the true data process. Alternative hypotheses in econometrics are, however, sometimes selected to obtain simple tests that are thought to be powerful against other more vaguely specified alternatives (e.g., see Desai's, 1974, work, in which the Durbin–Watson statistic is used to test for incorrect pooling, rather than for first-order autoregressive errors).[13] Since there can be no guarantee that the set of alternatives being considered is sufficiently rich to include an adequate specification, the ability of the corresponding test statistics to point clearly towards better models should not be overestimated.

3.4   Alternative forms of the Lagrange multiplier statistic

In the discussion of Section 3.2, it was stressed that the sample value of the LM statistic would be the same for all alternative hypotheses that were locally equivalent with respect to the null model, provided that a common consistent estimate of the information matrix $\mathscr{I}$ was used. Several alternative consistent estimates of $\mathscr{I}$ have been proposed in the literature. It is important to examine these estimates and to evaluate the existing evidence on their relative merits because they differ in their computational costs and will not all lead to the same value of the LM statistic in finite

---

[12] Bera and Jarque (1982) provide some Monte Carlo evidence on the usefulness of a multiple comparison procedure.

[13] The Durbin–Watson test appears to be regarded as a very general procedure and has also been used after ordering of data to check for incorrect functional form.

samples. The null hypothesis is assumed to take the form $\theta_2 = \theta_2^0$ and the information matrix is assumed to be $O(n)$.

Provided the expected value of $D(\theta) = \partial^2 l(\theta)/\partial\theta\partial\theta'$ can be obtained, the matrix $-E[D(\theta)]$ evaluated at $\theta = \hat\theta$ can be employed to estimate $\mathcal{I}$. It is, however, valid to omit the operation of taking expectations and to estimate $\mathcal{I}$ by $-D(\theta)$ evaluated at $\theta = \hat\theta$. In the terminology of Efron and Hinkley (1978), the estimated variance–covariance matrix of the score vector is in the first case derived from the 'expected Fisher information,' while the second approach uses the 'observed Fisher information.' The estimate $-D(\hat\theta)$ has been recommended by Efron and Hinkley (1978) on the grounds that it is closer to the data than the corresponding expected information estimate. The latter estimate obviously requires that expectations be obtained, and on occasion may fail to be positive definite, implying that the associated test is sometimes unavailable owing to sampling fluctuations; an econometric example of this phenomenon is provided by Durbin's (1970) h test.[14]

In some cases, the second-order partial derivatives may be difficult to calculate, so that tests based upon either the Hessian $D(\theta)$ or its expected value are unattractive. It is, therefore, worth considering an estimate of $\mathcal{I}$ which is derived from the fundamental information matrix equality

$$-E[D(\theta)] = \sum_t E[\partial l_t(\theta)/\partial\theta][\partial l_t(\theta)/\partial\theta]'$$

and requires only first-order partial differentiation. This estimate is

$$\sum_t [\partial l_t(\hat\theta)/\partial\theta][\partial l_t(\hat\theta)/\partial\theta]' \tag{4.1}$$

(see Berndt, Hall, Hall and Hausman, 1974, for a discussion of the uses of this estimate in estimation and inference in non-linear simultaneous equation models). As shown in Section 1.4, using the estimate of (4.1) leads to the following expression for the test statistic,

$$\begin{aligned}
\text{LM} &= \sum_t [\partial l_t(\hat\theta)/\partial\theta]' \left\{ \sum_t [\partial l_t(\hat\theta)/\partial\theta][\partial l_t(\hat\theta)/\partial\theta]' \right\}^{-1} \sum_t [\partial l_t(\hat\theta)/\partial\theta] \\
&= \iota'\hat W(\hat W'\hat W)^{-1}\hat W'\iota,
\end{aligned} \tag{4.2}$$

where ι is the n-dimensional vector with every element equal to unity and $\hat W$ is a matrix whose n rows consist of the vectors $(\partial l_t(\hat\theta)/\partial\theta)'$. Expression (4.2) can be interpreted as n times the *uncentred* coefficient of determination for the OLS regression of ι on $\hat W$, but, as pointed out by Davidson and

---

[14] This problem may also arise when the estimate $-D(\hat\theta)$ is used with some asymptotically negligible elements set equal to zero.

MacKinnon (1983), regression programmes usually compute *centred* R^2 statistics. If LM of (4.2) is to be calculated as a by-product of the regression of ι on $\hat{W}$, it will, therefore, be more convenient to evaluate it as (n-SSR), where SSR is the sum of the squared residuals obtained in this regression. This variant of the LM procedure is very simple to calculate and is usually referred to as the "outer product of the gradient" (OPG) form of the LM test.

Small sample performance of the OPG variant

The OPG form has been criticized by Davidson and MacKinnon (1983) on the grounds that equation (4.1) often provides an inefficient estimator of the information matrix. They conjecture that this inefficiency will tend to result in relatively poor small sample properties. The argument concerning the inefficiency of the OPG estimate of the information matrix can be illustrated by considering the problem of testing $\beta = 0$ in the regression model

$$y_t = \beta x_t + u_t, \, u_t \text{NID}(0, 1), \, t = 1, \ldots, n, \tag{4.3}$$

where the regressor is fixed in repeated sampling. The log-likelihood for a single observation is then

$$l_t(\beta) = \text{cnst} - [y_t - \beta x_t]^2/2$$

and $\mathscr{I}$ is $\Sigma_t x_t^2$. Evaluation of second-order derivatives to estimate the information measure leads to the unbiased zero variance estimator $\Sigma_t x_t^2$, whereas the OPG estimator of $\mathscr{I}$ is, under $\beta = 0$,

$$\sum_t x_t^2 + \sum_t [x_t^2(u_t^2 - 1)],$$

which is also unbiased but has variance equal to $2 \sum x_t^4$.

The conjecture regarding the implications for small sample performance can, in general, only be investigated by means of Monte Carlo studies. Some Monte Carlo experiments involving LM tests of linear and log-linear specifications of regression equations led Davidson and MacKinnon (1983) to conclude that the OPG variant is inferior to an alternative form which they refer to as the Double Length Regression (DLR) test.

The DLR variant of the LM test

The DLR test can be applied when the alternative model can be written as

$$f_t(y_t, Y_{t-1}, \theta) = \varepsilon_t, \, \varepsilon_t \text{NID}(0, 1), \tag{4.4}$$

where y_t is the dependent variable, Y_{t-1} denotes its lagged values, θ is the parameter vector and the jacobian of the transformation from the y's to the ε's is lower triangular.[15] Provided the ε_t's are independently and normally distributed, it can be shown that

$$l_t(\theta) = \text{cnst} - \tfrac{1}{2}f_t(\theta)^2 + j_t(\theta), \tag{4.5}$$

where $j_t(\theta)$ denotes $\ln|\partial f_t(y_t, Y_{t-1}, \theta)/\partial y_t|$, $t = 1, 2, \ldots, n$, and that the information matrix is given by

$$\mathscr{I}(\theta) = E[F'F + J'J], \tag{4.6}$$

where the n rows of F and J are the derivatives $\partial f_t(\theta)/\partial\theta'$ and $\partial j_t(\theta)/\partial\theta'$, respectively. If $f(\theta)$ denotes the n-dimensional vector with typical element $f_t(\theta)$, then the gradient vector $\partial l(\theta)/\partial\theta$ is

$$d(\theta) = -F'f + J'\iota,$$

so that the use of (4.6) in constructing an LM statistic leads to the expression

$$[-\hat{f}'\hat{F} + \iota'\hat{J}][\hat{F}'\hat{F} + \hat{J}'\hat{J}]^{-1}[-\hat{F}'\hat{f} + \hat{J}'\iota], \tag{4.7}$$

where $\hat{}$ denotes evaluation at the constrained maximum likelihood estimator $\hat{\theta}$. The statistic of (4.7) is, however, simply the explained sum of squares for the OLS estimation of the linear regression model

$$\begin{bmatrix} \hat{f} \\ \iota \end{bmatrix} = \begin{bmatrix} -\hat{F} \\ \hat{J} \end{bmatrix} b + residuals, \tag{4.8}$$

which has $2n$ observations and is accordingly termed a 'double length' model.

Employing the DLR approach in the example of (4.3) would lead to the use of the true information $\Sigma_t x_t^2$ (as opposed to an unbiased estimator of this quantity) because the terms involving jacobians vanish, and $\partial f_t(\theta)/\partial\theta$ equals $-x_t$.

If a choice is to be made between the OPG and DLR variants, then the available Monte Carlo evidence as reported by Bera and McKenzie (1986) and Davidson and MacKinnon (1983) suggests that the latter form of the LM statistic should be used. The OPG test is, however, more widely applicable than the DLR test; for example, it can be used in the context of general systems of non-linear simultaneous equations and in limited dependent variable models. In some cases, therefore, the Davidson–

---

[15] The assumption that the disturbances ε_t have common unit variance is unimportant since variance parameters can form a sub-vector of θ. The presence of the subscript t on $f(\cdot)$ allows for the presence of exogenous variables.

MacKinnon procedure will not be available as an alternative to the OPG test. Further, the DLR test may be sensitive to violation of the normality assumption. This assumption is often regarded simply as a convenient basis for generating asymptotically well-behaved quasi-LM tests (see Burguete et al., 1982) but it is more important for the DLR method because the fundamental result that the information matrix equals $E[F'F + J'J]$ is derived using properties of the normal distribution. Consequently, if the errors are non-normal, the DLR test may be invalid and lead to incorrect asymptotic significance levels.

The results of Davidson and MacKinnon can be specialized to the case in which

$$y_t = g_t(Y_{t-1}; \theta) + u_t, \; u_t \text{NID}(0, \sigma^2), \tag{4.9}$$

and the elements of θ and σ^2 are functionally independent. Since (4.9) is sufficiently general to cover linear and non-linear regression models, it is clearly of considerable econometric interest. Exploiting the block diagonality of the information matrix between σ^2 and θ, and also the fact that the jacobian term vanishes from (4.5), it can be shown that a valid LM test can be calculated as the explained sum of squares associated with the OLS estimation of the artificial model

$$\hat{\sigma}^{-1}\hat{u} = (\hat{\sigma}^{-1}\hat{G})b + residual$$

$$= \hat{G}c + residual, \; c = \hat{\sigma}^{-1}b, \tag{4.10}$$

where $\hat{u}$ denotes the residual vector with typical element $y_t - g_t(\hat{\theta})$, $\hat{\sigma}^2 = n^{-1}\hat{u}'\hat{u}$, and $\hat{G}$ denotes the matrix whose n rows consist of the derivative vectors $\partial g_t(\hat{\theta})/\partial\theta$. This explained sum of squares is

$$\hat{\sigma}^{-2}\hat{u}'\hat{G}(\hat{G}'\hat{G})^{-1}\hat{G}'\hat{u} = n[\hat{u}'\hat{G}(\hat{G}'\hat{G})^{-1}\hat{G}'\hat{u}]/\hat{u}'\hat{u}, \tag{4.11}$$

which is simply n times the R^2 of the regression of $\hat{u}$ on $\hat{G}$. The LM statistic of (4.11) is robust to non-normality (see Burguete et al., 1982, for details). Further, it is asymptotically equivalent to the W, LR and LM tests of $\theta_2 - \theta_2^0 = 0$ in the context of the LEA specification

$$y_t = g_t(\theta_1, \theta_2^0) + [\partial g_t(\hat{\theta}_1, \theta_2^0)/\partial\theta_2]'(\theta_2 - \theta_2^0) + u_t.$$

The small-sample behaviour of autocorrelation tests based upon the general form (4.11) has been studied by Godfrey (1979a) and Mizon and Hendry (1980); these authors report quite favourable results.

3.5   Non-standard cases

Chapter 1 contained a discussion of the LM principle and its relationships to other approaches to hypothesis testing. However, the results presented there were based upon the assumption that the regularity conditions of Section 1.4 were satisfied. This assumption is invalid for certain models and null hypotheses. Consequently, some extensions of the analysis of Chapter 1 are required. This section covers some of the non-standard cases that may arise in the context of testing for misspecification.

Two general types of non-standard situation are examined. The first of these involves the breakdown of the assumption that the information matrix $\mathscr{I}$ is non-singular, and the second consists of problems involving testing on the boundary of the parameter space.

3.5.1 *Singular information matrices*

The standard form of the LM statistic – namely, $\hat{d}'\hat{\mathscr{I}}^{-1}\hat{d}$ – is based upon the result that the quadratic form $\hat{d}'\mathscr{I}^{-1}\hat{d}$ is asymptotically distributed as χ^2 when the null hypothesis is true. This result clearly cannot be applied if $\mathscr{I}$ is singular. The possibility of singularity (under the alternative hypothesis and/or the null hypothesis) was recognized by Silvey (1959). Silvey pointed out that singularity of $\mathscr{I}$ would sometimes occur as a result of a desire to maintain symmetry in the model's parameterization. The 'dummy variable' trap provides a familiar example: if all four quarterly shift dummies are included with an intercept term in a regression equation, there will be a problem of under-identification with $\mathscr{I}$ being singular. One obvious solution in such cases is to reparameterize and sacrifice symmetry, for example, to omit one of the dummy variables of the previous example.

Aitchison and Silvey (1960), however, regard the introduction of asymmetry via reparameterization as undesirable. They advocate an alternative general procedure derived by Silvey (1959). Silvey's approach can be outlined as follows. Suppose that the parameter vector θ contains m elements and there are a total of $(r + s) < m$ restrictions of the form

$$h_i(\theta) = 0, \qquad i = 1, \ldots, (r + s),$$

where the functions $h_i(\theta)$ are continuous. In the absence of a priori restrictions, θ is not identified and the information matrix $\mathscr{I}$ is singular.

Silvey assumes that r of the restrictions $h_i(\theta) = 0$ are sufficient to make θ identified, so that the remaining s restrictions make up the null hypothesis to be tested. Without loss of generality, suppose the first r restrictions ensure identifiability. Let $H(\theta)$ denote the $(r + s)$ by m jacobian matrix with typical element $\partial h_i(\theta)/\partial\theta_j$ and write this matrix in partitioned form as

$$H(\theta)' = [H_1(\theta)', H_2(\theta)'],$$

where $H_1(\theta)$ is r by m and $H_2(\theta)$ is s by m. The matrix $[\mathscr{I} + H_1(\theta)'H_1(\theta)]$ will then normally be non-singular, and Silvey's (1959) modified LM statistic is defined by

$$\text{LM}^* = \hat{d}'[\hat{\mathscr{I}} + H_1(\hat{\theta})'H_1(\hat{\theta})]^{-1}\hat{d}. \tag{5.1}$$

Thus the only modification required when calculating the test statistic LM* is to replace the usual estimate of $\mathscr{I}$ by an estimate of $[\mathscr{I} + H_1(\theta)'H_1(\theta)]$. Silvey points out that sample values LM* should be compared to critical values of the $\chi^2(s)$ distribution, rather than the $\chi^2(r + s)$ distribution, because the null hypothesis consists only of the last s restrictions.

Several authors (e.g., Poskitt and Tremayne, 1981), have pointed out that $[\mathscr{I} + H_1(\theta)'H_1(\theta)]^{-1}$ is a generalized inverse (g-inverse) of $\mathscr{I}$.[16] Consequently, Silvey's modified LM criterion for models with singular information matrices can be obtained from the general expression

$$\text{LM}^* = \hat{d}'\hat{\mathscr{I}}^-\hat{d}, \tag{5.2}$$

where $\hat{\mathscr{I}}^-$ denotes a g-inverse of $\hat{\mathscr{I}}$.

Since g-inverses are not unique, it is natural to consider the dependence of LM* on the choice of $\hat{\mathscr{I}}^-$ in (5.2). Breusch (1986) points out that LM* is invariant to the choice of g-inverse if and only if $\text{rank}(\hat{\mathscr{I}}, \hat{d}) = \text{rank}(\hat{\mathscr{I}})$. He argues that this condition will be met with probability one under the null hypothesis in any problem that satisfies standard assumptions, except that $\mathscr{I}$ is singular, and also provides some econometric examples.

It is often easy to identify a direct approach involving a standard LM test which is equivalent to the g-inverse procedure. Such direct tests can cast light upon the sensitivity of the modified statistic LM* to the choice of g-inverse and simplify implementation. Consider, for example, a classical regression model

$$y = X\beta + u, \quad u' = (u_1, \ldots, u_n), \tag{5.3}$$

with X being non-stochastic and of full column rank, and the disturbances u_t being $N(0, \sigma_u^2)$ variates. The null hypothesis is that the disturbances are independent and the alternative hypothesis is that they are generated by the mixed autoregressive-moving average ARMA (p, q) scheme

$$u_t - \rho_1 u_{t-1} - \cdots - \rho_p u_{t-p}$$
$$= \varepsilon_t + \mu_1\varepsilon_{t-1} + \cdots + \mu_q\varepsilon_{t-q}, \quad \varepsilon_t\text{NID}(0, \sigma_\varepsilon^2). \tag{5.4}$$

If $\rho_1 = \cdots = \rho_p = \mu_1 = \cdots = \mu_q = 0$, then the errors u_t are independent, but it is straightforward to verify that the information matrix for the

---

[16] A g-inverse of a matrix V is a matrix V^- such that $VV^-V = V$. Rao and Mitra (1971) provide a detailed discussion of such matrices and their applications.

alternative of (5.3) and (5.4) is singular when these restrictions hold. The problem is, therefore, non-standard. The vector of estimated multipliers relevant to testing $\rho_1 = \cdots = \rho_p = \mu_1 = \cdots = \mu_q = 0$ is shown by Godfrey (1978c) to be

$$\hat{\lambda}' = (r_1, r_2, \ldots, r_p, r_1, r_2, \ldots, r_q),$$

where $r_i = \Sigma \hat{u}_t \hat{u}_{t-i} / \Sigma \hat{u}_t^2$ and $\hat{u}_t$ is a typical OLS residual; that is, the r_i are estimated autocorrelations. Under the assumption of independence, $\sqrt{n}\hat{\lambda}$ is asymptotically normally distributed with zero mean vector and a singular covariance matrix – this singularity reflects the duplication of elements of $\hat{\lambda}$.

The obvious solution is to delete redundant terms of $\hat{\lambda}$ and to construct a test of the significance of $(r_1, r_2, \ldots, r_s)$, $s = \max(p, q)$. This strategy corresponds to Silvey's procedure with $r = \min(p, q)$ restrictions being imposed on the error model (5.4) to achieve identification under the null hypothesis. Two valid sets of identifying restrictions are $\{\rho_1 = \cdots = \rho_r = 0\}$ and $\{\mu_1 = \cdots = \mu_r = 0\}$. However, the imposition of any such set of r-identifying restrictions will be equivalent to a direct test based upon $(r_1, r_2, \ldots, r_s)$ and so the choice of g-inverse is irrelevant. The use of a common estimate of the covariance matrix of $(r_1, r_2, \ldots, r_s)$ will ensure numerical equality of test statistics against all suitable alternatives derived by imposing $\min(p, q)$ zero restrictions on the ARMA model of (5.4).

In general, it will often be possible to identify and eliminate redundant terms without difficulty. This simple strategy is, of course, equivalent to the use of a g-inverse of the information matrix. A different approach is required, however, if the singularity of the information matrix is caused by one or more nuisance parameters vanishing under the null hypothesis. This problem is considered next.

Testing when a nuisance parameter is present only under the alternative hypothesis

In discussing the problems associated with testing hypotheses when some nuisance parameters only enter the likelihood function under the alternative, it is convenient to focus on some simple examples. The first of these examples is a simplified version of a model considered by Engle (1984, p. 823):

$$y_t = \theta_1 x_t + \theta_1 \theta_2 z_t + u_t, \quad t = 1, \ldots, n, \tag{5.5}$$

where the regressors are non-stochastic variables and the disturbances u_t are NID(0, 1). The null hypothesis is $H_0: \theta_1 = 0$ and θ_2 is obviously not present when H_0 is imposed.

The score vector for the model of (5.5) has as its two elements

$$\partial l(\theta_1, \theta_2)/\partial \theta_1 = \sum_t [x_t + \theta_2 z_t] u_t$$

and

$$\partial l(\theta_1, \theta_2)/\partial \theta_2 = \theta_1 \sum_t z_t u_t,$$

so that, if $\theta_1 = 0$, we have

$$\partial l(0, \theta_2)/\partial \theta_1 = \sum_t [x_t + \theta_2 z_t] y_t$$

and

$$\partial l(0, \theta_2)/\partial \theta_2 = 0.$$

The information matrix is

$$\mathscr{I}(\theta_1, \theta_2) = \begin{bmatrix} \sum_t (x_t + \theta_2 z_t)^2 & \theta_1 \sum_t z_t(x_t + \theta_2 z_t) \\ \theta_1 \sum_t z_t(x_t + \theta_2 z_t) & \theta_1^2 \sum_t z_t^2 \end{bmatrix}$$

and the imposition of H_0 yields the singular matrix

$$\mathscr{I}(0, \theta_2) = \begin{bmatrix} \sum_t (x_t + \theta_2 z_t)^2 & 0 \\ 0 & 0 \end{bmatrix}.$$

Davies (1977, 1987) suggests that, in this kind of situation, the LM statistic for H_0 should be treated as a function of the underidentified nuisance parameters and the test based upon the maximum of this function.[17] The asymptotic distribution of this maximum will not be the standard central χ^2 with degrees of freedom equal to the number of restrictions imposed by H_0, but Davies provides an upper bound for the significance level of his procedure.

Applying the technique proposed by Davies to the model of (5.5) with $H_0: \theta_1 = 0$ leads to the maximization of

$$\text{LM}(\theta_2) = \left[\sum_t (x_t + \theta_2 z_t) y_t \right]^2 \bigg/ \sum_t (x_t + \theta_2 z_t)^2$$

---

[17] This approach can be justified by appeal to Roy's (1953) union-intersection principle.

with respect to θ_2. This optimization problem is equivalent to finding the value of θ_2 which maximizes

$$R^2(\theta_2) = \left[\sum_t (x_t + \theta_2 z_t) y_t\right]^2 \bigg/ \left[\sum_t (x_t + \theta_2 z_t)^2 \sum_t y_t^2\right],$$

the uncentred R^2 statistic from the regression of y_t on $(x_t + \theta_2 z_t)$. If we reparameterize and write (5.5) as

$$y_t = \beta_1 x_t + \beta_2 z_t + u_t, \; \beta_1 = \theta_1, \; \beta_2 = \theta_1 \theta_2, \qquad (5.6)$$

then the required maximizer θ_2^* is just the ratio $\hat\beta_2/\hat\beta_1$, where $\hat\beta_1$ and $\hat\beta_2$ are the OLS parameter estimates for (5.6). It follows that $\text{LM}(\theta_2^*)$, the maximized $\text{LM}(\theta_2)$ statistic, is the explained sum of squares for the OLS regression of y_t on x_t and z_t. The distribution of $\text{LM}(\theta_2^*)$, under H_0, is therefore $\chi^2(2)$.

The above example has several noteworthy features. First, the application of the procedure proposed by Davies (1977, 1987) has led to the standard two-degrees-of-freedom test derived by reparameterization and writing the model as the linear regression (5.6). Second, the significance level of the $\text{LM}(\theta_2^*)$ test can be determined, and there is no need to rely upon the upper bound provided by Davies. Unfortunately, in other cases, Davies's approach does not lead to such convenient procedures.

In order to illustrate some potential difficulties, consider the following simplification of Engle's (1984) second example:

$$y_t = \beta x_t^\alpha + u_t, \; t = 1, \dots, n, \qquad (5.7)$$

where x_t is non-stochastic and the errors u_t are NID$(0, 1)$. The null hypothesis is $H_0: \beta = 0$ and unless α is given a priori, the information matrix will be singular under H_0. The criterion to be maximized in the solution proposed by Davies is readily shown to be

$$\text{LM}(\alpha) = \left[\sum_t x_t^\alpha y_t\right]^2 \bigg/ \sum_t x_t^{2\alpha}.$$

Determining the maximizing value of α will require the solution of a non-linear first-order condition, and no explicit solution can be obtained. However, approximate methods are available.

Suppose that α is known to be in the range $[\alpha_L, \alpha_U]$, α_L and α_U being given constants. A grid-search technique could be used with $\text{LM}(\alpha)$ being evaluated at a number of points in $[\alpha_L, \alpha_U]$. A Davies-type test could then be based upon the maximum of the values obtained in the grid-search. Since the maximum of a set of dependent $\chi^2(1)$ variates is not itself $\chi^2(1)$, there will be the difficulty of assessing the significance level of this approximation to the procedure described by Davies Bonferroni's inequality could be used – for example, if 10 statistics were calculated and their maximum compared to the 1 percent critical point for a $\chi^2(1)$ distribution, then the significance level would be at most 10 per cent.[18]

Difficulties obviously become more serious when several nuisance parameters vanish under the null hypothesis and there is no analytically tractable solution to Davies's maximization problem. A multidimensional grid-search could be attempted, but would involve a trade-off between the computational cost of evaluation at a large number of points and the likely quality of the approximation to the true maximum of the LM statistic. It may therefore be useful to consider a simpler solution to this problem.

Since the difficulty arises because the likelihood function is independent of some nuisance parameters when the null hypothesis is true, any number of asymptotically valid tests can be obtained by fixing the values of these parameters at the start. Returning to the example of (5.7), if α is set equal to some constant α_0, then when $\beta = 0$ the statistic $LM(\alpha_0)$ is $\chi^2(1)$ whatever the choice of α_0. The value of α_0 will, of course, influence the small sample power of this simple test, but there is no reason to suppose that it will always be inferior to a Davies-type procedure.

Relative powers are more easily compared in the framework of equation (5.5) with $H_0: \theta_1 = 0$. If θ_2 in (5.5) is set equal to zero, then the associated $LM(0)$ procedure tests $\theta_1 = 0$ in the regression model

$$y_t = \theta_1 x_t + u_t, \ t = 1, \ldots, n.$$

It will be recalled that the Davies test $LM(\theta_2^*)$ is equivalent to a test of $\beta_1 = \beta_2 = 0$ in

$$y_t = \beta_1 x_t + \beta_2 z_t + u_t, \ t = 1, \ldots, n.$$

Standard regression theory implies there is no generally valid ranking of the powers of the two tests if $\theta_1 \neq 0$ and $\theta_2 \neq 0$. For some values of (θ_1, θ_2) and the regressor covariance matrix, the simple procedure will be inferior, but for other cases the $LM(\theta_2^*)$ test suggested by Davies will have lower power.

The two examples above have served to simplify the exposition and to illustrate certain important problems. Examples of real econometric interest are given by Engle (1984). In particular, Engle refers to Watson's (1982) unpublished work on testing for regression parameter constancy in the context of the alternative model:

$$y_t = x_t \beta_t + z_t \gamma + u_t,$$

---

[18] Sidák's inequality gives a slightly smaller upper bound of about 9.6 per cent. Alternatively, the bound given by Davies (1977, equation 6.1) could be employed.

$$\beta_t = \rho\beta_{t-1} + \varepsilon_t,$$

$$\begin{bmatrix} u_t \\ \varepsilon_t \end{bmatrix} \sim N\left(\begin{bmatrix} 0 \\ 0 \end{bmatrix}, \begin{bmatrix} \sigma_u^2 & 0 \\ 0 & \sigma_\varepsilon^2 \end{bmatrix} \right).$$

The null hypothesis is $\sigma_\varepsilon^2 = 0$, but imposing this restriction renders ρ underidentified, and Watson employs an approximation to Davies's method. Watson and Engle (1985) give Monte Carlo evidence on the power and size of a Davies-type test.

Identically zero scores

As well as being caused by redundant parameters and nuisance parameters that vanish under the null hypothesis, singularity of the information matrix may also occur as a result of the score vector being identically zero. This type of singularity is not merely a mathematical curiosity of little practical relevance: Lee and Chesher (1986) provide some econometric examples, such as testing for selectivity bias, in which the efficient score is identically zero.

If $\hat{d} = 0$ for all samples, then it is clearly not sufficient to turn to Silvey's g-inverse approach, and other procedures are required. Lee and Chesher show that reparameterization of the model sometimes provides a solution to the problem, but that this method may not always prevent the breakdown of the LM test. In order to derive a more generally applicable procedure, Lee and Chesher extend the LM test based upon the first-order partial derivatives and propose a class of extremum tests involving the consideration of higher-order derivatives. The extremum test principle is illustrated by applying it to the problems of testing for selectivity bias and for efficiency in stochastic frontier production function models (see Lee and Chesher, 1986, Section 5).

A simple model discussed by Cox and Hinkley (1974, pp. 117–18) can be used to provide examples of problems and solutions. Let $z_1, z_2, \ldots, z_n$ be positive constants and $y_1, y_2, \ldots, y_n$ be independently normally distributed variates with $E(y_i) = 0$ and $\text{Var}(y_i) = 1 + \theta^2 z_i$, $i = 1, 2, \ldots, n$. The problem is to construct an LM test of $H_0: \theta = 0$. The log-likelihood function is

$$l(\theta) = -\tfrac{1}{2}\Sigma_1^n \ln(1 + \theta^2 z_i) - \tfrac{1}{2}\Sigma_1^n y_i^2/(1 + \theta^2 z_i),$$

so that its first derivative is

$$d(\theta) = -\theta\{\Sigma_1^n z_i/(1 + \theta^2 z_i) - \Sigma_1^n z_i y_i^2/(1 + \theta^2 z_i)^2\},$$

which equals zero under H_0 whatever the data, as does the information measure $\mathscr{I}$.

In order to illustrate the extremum test approach, consider the second-order derivative of $l(\theta)$ evaluated at $\theta = 0$, that is,

$$d^2l(0)/d\theta^2 = \Sigma_1^n z_i(y_i^2 - 1).$$

Under H_0, $d^2l(0)/d\theta^2$ is asymptotically normally distributed with zero mean and variance $2\Sigma_1^n z_i^2$. It follows that an extremum test can be based upon the statistic

$$\tfrac{1}{2}[\Sigma z_i(y_i^2 - 1)]^2/\Sigma_1^n z_i^2,$$

which is asymptotically distributed as $\chi^2(1)$ when $H_0: \theta = 0$ is true. Cox and Hinkley point out that the same test can be obtained by adopting a reparameterization.

Let the model be reparameterized by introducing $\psi = \theta^2$, so that the null hypothesis is now $H_0^*: \psi = 0$. Since ψ equals θ^2, the former parameter is non-negative and its parameter space can be written as $\Psi = \{\psi: \psi \geqslant 0\}$. The null hypothesis $\psi = 0$, therefore, forces a solution on the boundary of the parameter space. For the moment, this point will be ignored and a standard LM test of H_0^* will be derived. The log-likelihood for the reparameterized model is

$$g(\psi) = -\tfrac{1}{2}\Sigma_1^n \ln(1 + \psi z_i) - \tfrac{1}{2}\Sigma_1^n y_i^2/(1 + \psi z_i),$$

so that the efficient score is

$$dg(0)/d\psi = \tfrac{1}{2}\Sigma_1^n z_i(y_i^2 - 1)$$
$$= \tfrac{1}{2}d^2l(0)/d\theta^2.$$

It follows that the LM test of $H_0^*: \psi = 0$ is equivalent to the extremum test of $H_0: \theta = 0$.

In addition to illustrating the usefulness of extremum tests and reparameterization, the example above also indicates that null hypotheses may restrict parameters to be on a boundary of the parameter space. The difficulties that arise in such situations are discussed next.

3.5.2   *Testing on a boundary of the parameter space*

The first regularity condition given in Section 1.4 was that the true parameter value should be an interior point of the parameter space Θ. In some situations, however, parameters are subject to inequality restrictions and the null hypothesis forces one or more parameters to be on a boundary. For example, in some econometric applications (such as the error components model discussed by Breusch and Pagan, 1980, pp. 245–7), the assumption that intrinsically non-negative variance terms equal zero is to be tested. The implications of parameters being placed on the boundary by the null hypothesis, therefore, merit investigation.

The fact that the standard asymptotic theory of classical tests outlined in Chapter 1 will not be applicable in boundary situations can be illustrated by the following example. Suppose that there is a simple random sample $x_1, x_2, \ldots, x_n$ from the $N(\theta, 1)$ distribution with parameter space $\Theta = \{\theta : \theta \geqslant 0\}$ and $H_0 : \theta = 0$ is to be tested against $H_1 : \theta > 0$. The conventional components of likelihood-based inference are then the log-likelihood function

$$l(\theta) = \text{cnst} - \tfrac{1}{2} \sum_{i=1}^{n} (x_i - \theta)^2,$$

its derivative

$$d(\theta) = \sum_{i=1}^{n} (x_i - \theta) = n(\bar{x} - \theta),$$

and the information measure

$$\mathscr{I} = n.$$

The LM test of $H_0 : \theta = 0$ is, in view of the above,

$$\text{LM} = n\bar{x}^2,$$

and since $\bar{x} \sim N(0, n^{-1})$ under H_0, the LM statistic has the $\chi^2(1)$ null distribution predicted by standard theory. It might be argued that the LM procedure is deficient because it fails to take into account the one-sided nature of the alternative hypothesis, but this is easily rectified. All that needs to be done is to work with $\sqrt{n}\bar{x}$ and to have the critical region in the right-hand tail of the $N(0, 1)$ distribution. In this example, therefore, the boundary situation causes no real problems for the LM principle.

Turning now to the W and LR tests of $H_0 : \theta = 0$, it is necessary to obtain the unrestricted MLE, that is, the value of θ in Θ which maximizes $l(\theta)$. If this unrestricted estimator is denoted by $\tilde{\theta}$, then the forms of $l(\theta)$ and $d(\theta)$ imply that

$$\tilde{\theta} = \max(0, \bar{x}).$$

Further since, under H_0, $\bar{x}$ is $N(0, n^{-1})$,

$$\text{prob}(\tilde{\theta} = \bar{x}) = \text{prob}(\tilde{\theta} = 0) = 0.5$$

when the null hypothesis is true. As $\mathscr{I} = n$, the conventional W statistic for the problem under consideration is $n\tilde{\theta}^2$. If $\theta = 0$ then $n\bar{x}^2$ is $\chi^2(1)$ and so $n\tilde{\theta}^2$ is a random variable equal to zero half of the time and to a $\chi^2(1)$ variable the other half. Thus, in this boundary situation, the W test statistic has a mixture of chi-squared distributions of the general form

$$\sum_{i=0}^{s} w(i)\chi^2(i),$$

where $s = 1$, the $w(i)$ are probability weights and $\chi^2(0)$ denotes the unit probability mass at the origin. Clearly standard theory does not apply.

The restricted and unrestricted maxima of $l(\theta)$ are given by

$$l(0) = \text{cnst} - \tfrac{1}{2} \sum_{i=1}^{n} x_i^2$$

and

$$l(\tilde\theta) = \text{cnst} - \tfrac{1}{2} \sum_{i=1}^{n} (x_i - \tilde\theta)^2,$$

respectively, so that the likelihood ratio statistic is

$$LR = (2n\bar{x}\tilde\theta - n\tilde\theta^2)$$

$$= n\bar{x}^2 \text{ when } \bar{x} \geqslant 0$$

$$= 0 \text{ when } \bar{x} < 0;$$

that is, $LR = W$. Hence, unlike the LM criterion, the two test statistics which require the estimation of the unrestricted model are not distributed as $\chi^2(1)$ under H_0.

The fact that the properties of the LM test are not altered is encouraging in so far as our principal concern is with the construction of checks for misspecification and it has been argued that LM tests are particularly suitable for this purpose. The model used to derive these results is, however, extremely simple and so it is necessary to discuss whether or not similar results apply to more general cases.

General discussions of maximum likelihood estimation and asymptotic tests in boundary situations have been provided by Chernoff (1954), Moran (1971a, b) and Chant (1974). The results obtained by these authors may be summarized as follows. As before, the m-dimensional parameter vector will be partitioned as $\theta' = (\theta_1', \theta_2')$, and the null hypothesis will be taken to be a set of s restrictions written as $H_0: \theta_2 = 0$. The assumptions of Moran (1971a, b) and Chant (1974) will be adopted. In particular, the true parameter value will be assumed to be in Θ^*, a subset of Euclidean space, given by

$$-\infty < \theta_i < \infty, \, i = 1, \ldots, (m - s) \tag{5.8}$$

$$0 \leqslant \theta_i < a_i, \, 0 < a_i, \, i = (m - s + 1), \ldots, m, \tag{5.9}$$

where θ_i denotes an element of θ.

The MLE $\tilde{\theta}$ is the value of θ in Θ^* maximizing $l(\theta)$ and satisfies

$$\partial l(\tilde{\theta})/\partial\theta_i = 0, \ i = 1, \ldots, (m - s) \tag{5.10}$$

$$\partial l(\tilde{\theta})/\partial\theta_i \leqslant 0, \ i = (m - s + 1), \ldots, m, \tag{5.11}$$

where the derivative of (5.11) is taken to the right if $\tilde{\theta}_i = 0$ and is an equality if $\tilde{\theta}_i > 0$, $i = (m - s + 1), \ldots, m$. If $l(\theta)$ is maximized without imposing the restriction that the estimate should be in Θ^*, then we obtain what Moran (1971b, p. 449) calls the 'pseudo-MLE.' The pseudo-MLE will be denoted by $\bar{\theta}$ and satisfies the first-order conditions of conventional theory; that is,

$$\partial l(\bar{\theta})/\partial\theta_i = 0, \ i = 1, \ldots, m.$$

If $l(\theta)$ is maximized subject to the constraints of H_0 (so that θ_2 is set equal to a null vector and the inequalities of (5.9) are irrelevant) then the restricted MLE $\hat{\theta}' = (\hat{\theta}_1', 0')$ is obtained with

$$\partial l(\hat{\theta})/\partial\theta_i = 0, \ i = 1, \ldots, (m - s),$$

and the quantities $\partial l(\hat{\theta})/\partial\theta_i$, $i = (m - s + 1), \ldots, m$, are to be assessed for joint (asymptotic) significance in the LM test of H_0.

One important general result which emerges from the analyses of Chernoff, Moran and Chant is that the W and LR tests of H_0 will not have their usual asymptotic properties. This breakdown of conventional theory reflects the fact that these tests involve the MLE $\tilde{\theta}$. In the standard case in which the true value is interior to an open set in the parameter space, the MLE for the alternative model is asymptotically normally distributed and this result is crucial to the classical theory of W and LR procedures. In the case under consideration, however, the estimator $\tilde{\theta}$ must lie in Θ^* so that its last s elements will satisfy the conditions

$$0 \leqslant \tilde{\theta}_i < a_i, \ 0 < a_i, \ i = (m - s + 1), \ldots, m,$$

which are inconsistent with normality under H_0.

In contrast, the LM test based upon $\hat{\theta}$ (and not involving $\tilde{\theta}$) is not affected by the fact that θ lies on a boundary when H_0 is true. More generally, asymptotically optimal $C(\alpha)$ tests (which include the LM procedure as a special case) do not require additional investigation in boundary situations (see Moran, 1971b, p. 445; Chant, 1974, p. 296). Further, the LM test of H_0 is asymptotically equivalent to the pseudo-LR and pseudo-W tests derived using $\bar{\theta}$, rather than $\tilde{\theta}$.[19] This equivalence is

[19] In an article dealing with testing linear restrictions in regression models, Gouriéroux, Holly and Monfort (1982) propose a Kuhn–Tucker multiplier test which is asymptotically equivalent to the LR and W tests based upon $\bar{\theta}$.

possible because $\bar{\theta}$ is not restricted to be in Θ^*. Ignoring the inequality restrictions on the model's parameters removes the difficulties of non-normal asymptotic distributions of estimators that invalidate the standard large sample theory of LR and W tests.[20]

Although, in general, the LR, W and LM are not asymptotically equivalent, a relationship between these tests can be obtained when only one restriction is imposed by H_0. In the special case $s = 1$, the last element of θ is subject to the inequality $0 \leqslant \theta_m < a_m$ and $H_0: \theta_m = 0$ is to be tested. The results of Section 1.5 concerning the interpretation of the LM test as a W-type test using a two-step estimator imply that the efficient score satisfies

$$\hat{d}_m = \partial l(\hat{\theta})/\partial \theta_m = \theta_m^* / \hat{\mathscr{I}}^{mm},$$

where θ_m^* is asymptotically equivalent to $\bar{\theta}_m$ under H_0 and local alternatives, and $\hat{\mathscr{I}}^{mm}$ is the (m, m) element of $\hat{\mathscr{I}}^{-1}$. Since it is being assumed that $\mathscr{I}$ is positive definite, an appropriate asymptotically valid one-sided test of H_0 is easily constructed with H_0 being rejected if $\hat{d}_m$ is significantly positive. This one-sided LM test will have the same asymptotic rejection region as the LR and W tests of the single restriction $\theta_m = 0$. If, however, the null hypothesis specifies the values of two or more parameters, then this asymptotic equivalence is lost.[21]

As the LR, W and LM tests are not, in general, asymptotically equivalent, consideration must be given to the problem of choosing between them. The LM procedure and tests based upon pseudo-MLEs do not take into account the inequality restrictions on θ_2, and so can be expected to be less powerful than the LR and W tests which do incorporate this information (via the MLE $\bar{\theta}$). There is, however, some support for LM (and asymptotically equivalent) tests. First, the determination of the appropriate critical regions for the LR and W tests will pose considerable practical difficulties. Second, if the test of $H_0: \theta_2 = 0$ is being used as a check of model adequacy, it seems unwise to insist on imposing inequality restrictions because of the likely uncertainty about the nature of specification errors. (These arguments are put forward by Pagan and Hall, 1983, p. 180, in the context of testing for heteroscedasticity and random parameter variation.)

---

[20] In practice, a priori inequality restrictions on parameters (e.g., a marginal propensity to consume) are often ignored. Rothenberg (1973, Chapter 3) discusses the value of inexact prior information in estimation.

[21] Asymptotic equivalence no longer obtains even if only one parameter is on the edge of the parameter space; see Chant (1974).

Some regression model examples

The general findings which have been outlined above can be illustrated in the context of the linear regression model examined by Gouriéroux, Holly and Monfort (1982). Consider the model

$$y = X\beta + u, \, u \sim N(0, \sigma^2 I), \tag{5.12}$$

where, as usual, y and u are n-dimensional, X is a non-stochastic n by k matrix of full column rank, and β is the k-dimensional vector of unknown parameters. Let $\theta' = (\sigma^2, \beta')$. Suppose that β is partitioned according to $\beta' = (\beta'_1, \beta'_2)$, where β_i is k_i by $1(i = 1, 2)$. The elements of β_1 are unrestricted, but those of β_2 must be non-negative. The null hypothesis is $H_0: \beta_2 = 0$ which forces the parameter point to be on a boundary.

It will be useful to rewrite (5.12) as

$$y = X_1\beta_1 + X_2\beta_2 + u \tag{5.13}$$

with $\beta_2 \geqslant 0$ and $H_0: \beta_2 = 0$. The MLE (which satisfies the a priori inequality restrictions) will be denoted by $\tilde{\beta}' = (\tilde{\beta}'_1, \tilde{\beta}'_2)$ and is obtained by solving the optimization problem:

$$\underset{\beta_1, \beta_2}{\text{minimize}} \, (y - X_1\beta_1 - X_2\beta_2)'(y - X_1\beta_1 - X_2\beta_2)$$

subject to $\beta_2 \geqslant 0$. (Judge and Takayama, 1966, and Liew, 1976, discuss such constrained least-squares estimators.) The pseudo-MLE is the familiar OLS estimator

$$\bar{\beta} = (X'X)^{-1}X'y.$$

Minimizing the residual sum of squares subject to the restrictions of $H_0: \beta_2 = 0$ yields the restricted MLE $\hat{\beta}' = (\hat{\beta}'_1, 0')$ with

$$\hat{\beta}_1 = (X'_1 X_1)^{-1} X'_1 y.$$

Now the pseudo-MLE of β_2, namely, $\bar{\beta}_2$, is a non-singular transformation of the score vector $\partial l(\hat{\theta})/\partial \beta_2$ since

$$\bar{\beta}_2 = (X'_2 M_1 X_2)^{-1} X'_2 (y - X_1 \hat{\beta}_1)$$

and $\partial l(\hat{\theta})/\partial \beta_2$ is proportional to $X'_2(y - X_1\hat{\beta}_1)$, M_1 being the projection matrix $I - X_1(X'_1 X_1)^{-1} X'_1$. It follows that the pseudo-W test will be equivalent to the LM test. Further, under H_0,

$$X'_2(y - X_1\hat{\beta}_1) = X'_2 M_1 u \sim N(0, \sigma^2(X'_2 M_1 X_2)),$$

and so, for example, an asymptotically valid pseudo-W test of H_0 can be derived by treating

$$\bar{\beta}_2'(X_2'M_1X_2)\bar{\beta}_2/\dot{\sigma}^2$$

as a $\chi^2(k_2)$ variate, $\dot{\sigma}^2$ being a consistent estimator of σ^2. (If σ^2 were known, then the pseudo-LR and W tests would be exactly equivalent to the LM procedure.) To sum up, LM-, LR- and W-type procedures based upon OLS results remain valid despite the fact that H_0 puts β on a boundary of the parameter space.

In contrast, asymptotic tests constructed from the MLE $\tilde{\theta}' = (\tilde{\sigma}^2, \tilde{\beta}')$ will not possess conventional properties when H_0 is true because $\tilde{\beta}_2$ is forced to be non-negative and so $\tilde{\beta}$ does not have a multivariate normal distribution. As in the previous simpler example, the LR and W tests derived using $\tilde{\beta}$ have, under H_0, the same asymptotic distribution which is a mixture of chi-squared distributions of the form $\Sigma_0^s w(i)\chi^2(i)$ with $s = k_2$; see Gouriéroux, Holly and Monfort (1982, Section 5).

Consider next the special case in which there is a single parametric restriction, and, in order to simplify the exposition, assume that the variance term σ^2 is known. It is also known that β_k, the last element of β, is non-negative and the null hypothesis is that this coefficient equals zero.[22] The MLE $\tilde{\beta}_k$ is given by $\max(\bar{\beta}_k, 0)$, where $\bar{\beta}_k$ is the OLS estimator of β_k. If the usual t-statistic, $\bar{\beta}_k/SE(\bar{\beta}_k)$, is denoted by t_k, then the W-criterion based upon $\bar{\beta}_k$ is

$$W = t_k^2 \text{ if } t_k \geqslant 0$$

$$= 0 \text{ otherwise.}$$

If $H_0: \beta_k = 0$ is true, then t_k is distributed as $N(0, 1)$ and so W will be distributed as $\frac{1}{2}\chi^2(0) + \frac{1}{2}\chi^2(1)$. Consequently the critical region for a significance level of ε is $\{W > c\}$, where c is the constant such that $\text{prob}(\chi^2(1) > c) = 2\varepsilon$. This critical region is equivalent to $\{t > \sqrt{c}\}$ which is that of the usual one-sided U.M.P. test. A two-sided LM test would use the critical region $\{|t| > \sqrt{d}\}$, where d is the constant such that $\text{prob}(\chi^2(1) > d) = \varepsilon$.[23]

Modifying the LM test of $\beta_k = 0$ to allow for the nature of the alternative hypothesis $H_1: \beta_k > 0$ leads to exactly the same rejection region as W and LR, that is, $\{t > \sqrt{c}\}$. Finally, if the variance parameter σ^2 is unknown, these equivalences will only apply asymptotically.

[22] This example is a special case of the model discussed by Gouriéroux et al. (1982, Section 4.1).

[23] An example of a two-sided LM test being applied when the parameter under scrutiny is intrinsically non-negative is provided by the liquidity trap test described by Breusch and Pagan (1980, Section 3.1, p. 243).

3.6   Conclusions

It has been shown that the LR, W and LM tests of a null model against a specified alternative are not only asymptotically equivalent to each other, but are also asymptotically equivalent to the LR, W and LM tests derived for other quite different alternatives. The alternatives which led to asymptotically equivalent tests of a null model were termed 'locally equivalent alternatives' (LEAs) because their general form was obtained by considering a linearization of an alternative model under a sequence of local alternatives. The available Monte Carlo evidence suggests that small sample power is not greatly affected by selecting an incorrect alternative which is locally equivalent to the true data process. This result supports the use of LEAs to simplify the calculation of test statistics.

One especially useful form of LEA can be obtained by adding a set of test variables to the original (null) specification. Many checks for misspecification can be implemented as tests for omitted variables using such LEAs. Moreover there is no need to construct the log-likelihood function for a complicated super-model if several different types of misspecification error are being considered. It is instead only necessary to determine the set of test variables for each of the misspecifications in isolation and then to add all the variables to the null model, after eliminating any redundant terms. A check of the significance of the complete set of test variables then provides the required test of the null model against the super-model under the reasonable assumption that the parameters characterizing the separate misspecifications are functionally independent.

Assuming that the LM principle is to be used to check for misspecification, it is necessary to decide upon the precise form of the score statistic. The Monte Carlo results on the effects of varying the estimate of the information matrix reported so far suggest that the OPG form is to be avoided if at all possible. If the model is such that the DLR method cannot be employed, then the second-order derivatives of the log-likelihood function should be calculated. It is not clear that it is worth obtaining the expected values of these derivatives under the null hypothesis.

Finally, the behaviour of the classical asymptotic tests under non-standard conditions has been considered. It was shown that the LM test can be modified to take into account singularity of the information matrix and that it is applicable to testing hypotheses that place the parameter value on a boundary of the parameter space.

CHAPTER 4

Tests for misspecification of regression equations

4.1   Introduction

Chapters 1 and 3 were devoted to fairly general discussions of test procedures. This chapter is concerned with the application of these methods to the problem of evaluating the adequacy of regression models. The number of possible misspecifications that could be made when formulating a regression model is very large, but most of those usually considered fall into one of the following categories:

(i)   omitted variables (OV)
(ii)   incorrect functional form
(iii) autocorrelation
(iv)   heteroscedasticity
(v)   lack of regression parameter constancy
(vi)   non-normality of disturbances
(vii) invalid assumptions about the exogeneity of one or more regressors.

Although much of this chapter is taken up with a detailed account of parametric tests designed for alternative hypotheses included in (i) to (vii), some results on pure significance checks for regression models are also considered. Indeed, one point made is that such general checks can often be interpreted as classical tests for some specific specification error.[1] Appropriate tests are discussed for each of the problems considered, and where possible a unifying theme (often based upon the LM principle) is provided, along with a summary of relevant Monte Carlo evidence.

The next section deals with testing for omitted variables and is particularly important because many checks for different types of misspec-

---

[1] Such reinterpretation of general checks is presented to show how their implementation can be simplified. These procedures are, however, proposed for use in situations in which there is little information about the sources of specification error, and they should not be judged solely on the merits of the alternative hypothesis underlying the equivalent classical test.

ification can be calculated by adding a set of test variables to the null model and then assessing their joint significance. Special attention is paid to the problem of testing for omission of regressors when neither the null nor alternative model includes all relevant variables. This case has bearing on subsequent sections because it illustrates what happens when a misspecified model is tested against the wrong alternative. In view of the usual uncertainty about the nature of specification errors, this case has obvious practical relevance.

The origins and derivation of tests for misspecification are discussed in the context of a linear regression model of the form

$$y_t = \sum_{i=1}^{k} x_{ti}\beta_i + u_t, \; t = 1, 2, \ldots, n, \tag{1.1}$$

where y_t denotes the tth observation on the regressand, x_{ti} is the value of the tth observation on the ith regressor, β_i is the corresponding regression parameter, and u_t is the unobservable disturbance term. The full set of n observations on the null model of (1.1) will be written in matrix–vector notation as

$$y = X\beta + u, \tag{1.2}$$

where y and u are n-dimensional vectors with typical elements y_t and u_t, respectively, X is the n by k regressor matrix with typical element x_{ti}, and β is the k-dimensional vector of unknown parameters. It is assumed that X has full column rank, that is, $\text{rank}(X) = k$.

Since most of the previous work in this area has been based upon the linear regression model, the use of the model of (1.2) simplifies the task of relating new results to earlier contributions. This model also provides a useful first step towards the derivation of diagnostic checks for more flexible non-linear regression models of the form

$$y_t = f(x_t, \beta) + u_t, \tag{1.3}$$

where $x_t = (x_{t1}, \ldots, x_{tk})'$ and the function $f(\cdot)$ is known apart from the value of β. The equation corresponding to (1.2) for such non-linear models will be written as

$$y = f(X, \beta) + u. \tag{1.4}$$

The basic procedure adopted here for each type of problem is to provide a detailed discussion of only the case in which the null specification is a linear model, and then to outline the extensions (if any) required for non-linear equations at the end of the chapter.

In order to apply the results of the previous chapters, it is necessary to specify the distribution of the disturbances u_t in order to obtain the likelihood function which usually serves (in one way or another) as the basis for inference. It will be convenient to assume that the disturbances are normally and independently distributed with zero mean and variance σ^2 [NID(0, σ^2)]. Although this assumption is required to obtain exact finite sample results, it is not required for asymptotic validity.[2] If the assumption of normality is incorrect, then the LM, LR and W tests derived under this false assumption will still have the asymptotic null distributions derived from the conventional classical theory, provided quite weak regularity conditions are satisfied.[3] The misspecification of the likelihood does, however, imply that the (quasi) LM, LR, and W tests will no longer enjoy the local asymptotic optimality property.

Finally, different authors have made different assumptions about the nature of the regressors. It is sometimes assumed that the regressors are either non-stochastic or strictly exogenous, but asymptotic validity often requires only weak exogeneity. Engle, Hendry and Richard (1983) discuss in full the concepts of exogeneity and their implications for inference. Mention is made of such implications and, where appropriate, modifications are described that allow the procedures to be applied to more general models than those for which they were originally derived.

4.2   Tests for the omitted variables problem

First, consider a situation in which the model under investigation, namely,

$$y = X\beta + u, \tag{1.2}$$

is regarded as a potentially underspecified version of the extended relationship

$$y = X\beta + A\alpha + u, \tag{2.1}$$

where A is an n by p matrix containing observations on additional regressors. If the data are generated by (2.1) with $\alpha \neq 0$, then the omission of the variables of A will invalidate t and F tests relating to the parameters of β, and will, in general, render the estimators of these parameters biased and inconsistent.

In some cases, the variables of A will be directly observable – for example, when they are lagged values of regressors contained in X – but they can include artificial variables constructed from the estimation of the null model. The adequacy of (1.2) is then to be assessed by testing $H_0 \colon \alpha = 0$.

---

[2] The null model sometimes allows for heteroscedasticity or autocorrelation in the disturbances. Tests designed for such models will also be discussed.

[3] See, e.g., the results provided by Burguete et al. (1982).

Before proceeding to the details of the test procedures, it may be useful to comment on the interpretation of A and equation (2.1). When testing for misspecification, the variables of A are frequently selected bearing in mind general characteristics of possible departures from the null which are thought to be important. Thus the test of $\alpha = 0$ is not being undertaken in order to simplify a model presumed to be adequate. Next, the alternative of (2.1) is, in an important respect, much more general than it appears at first sight. The results of Chapter 3 on locally equivalent alternatives (LEAs) imply that many non-linear models which include (1.2) as a special case can be approximated by augmented regression equations like (2.1) without affecting the asymptotic properties of tests under the null and a sequence of local alternatives.

As a starting point for the derivation of tests, it will be assumed that the disturbances of (2.1) are independent $N(0, \sigma^2)$ variates. In this case, the standard approach to testing H_0 is to construct the F statistic

$$F = [(S_0 - S_1)/S_1] \cdot (n - k - p)/p, \tag{2.2}$$

where S_0 is the residual sum of squares from the regression of y on X alone and S_1 is the corresponding quantity from the regression of y on X and A.[4] If X and A are both non-stochastic, then the test statistic of (2.2) is distributed as central $F(p, n - k - p)$ when $\alpha = 0$ and as non-central F when $\alpha \neq 0$ (see Seber, 1966, chaps. 4 and 5). Under much weaker conditions, the F test is asymptotically valid with pF being asymptotically distributed as $\chi^2(p)$ on H_0 and as non-central χ^2 under a sequence of local alternatives. Also the F test is consistent against fixed alternatives $\alpha \neq 0$.

These standard results, however, relate to the situation in which (2.1) is taken to include an adequate model. There is often some uncertainty about the precise nature of specification errors, and alternative hypotheses are sometimes selected in the hope of generating convenient and reasonably effective checks of model adequacy. It therefore seems important to consider the behaviour of the test of (1.2) against (2.1) when the data are generated by some other alternative. The unconsidered alternative will be written as

$$y = X\beta + T\tau + u, \tag{2.3}$$

where T is n by q. It will be assumed that conventional asymptotic theory applies to the OLS estimators of the parameters of (2.3) under a sequence of local alternatives H_n: $\tau = \delta/\sqrt{n}$, $0 \leqslant \delta'\delta < \infty$. (The null model is obtained by setting δ equal to the q-dimensional null vector.)

---

[4] The relationships between the F statistic and the LR, LM and W tests are discussed in Chapter 2.

4.2.1   *Testing against an incorrect alternative*

In general, the F statistic of (2.2) will be $O_p(n)$ when the data process is (2.3) with the elements of τ being $O(1)$, implying that the restrictions of $\alpha = 0$ will be rejected with probability tending to one as $n \to \infty$. Consequently, in order to analyse the effects on asymptotic power of using the wrong alternative, it is necessary to consider behaviour under local alternatives.

It is convenient to proceed by examining the Wald tests of $\alpha = 0$ in (2.1) and of $\tau = 0$ in (2.3). The following notation is employed:

(i) the OLS estimators of the parameter vectors of (2.1) and (2.3) are denoted by $(\tilde{\beta}', \tilde{\alpha}')'$ and $(\dot{\beta}', \dot{\tau}')'$, respectively, with the associated estimators of σ^2 being $\tilde{\sigma}^2$ and $\dot{\sigma}^2$;

(ii) $M_x = I - X(X'X)^{-1}X'$; and

(iii) $A_x = M_x A$ and $T_x = M_x T$, so that, for example, A_x is the matrix of residuals from the multivariate least-squares regression of A on X.

The relevant Wald statistics are then

$$W_\alpha = \tilde{\alpha}'[A'M_xA]\tilde{\alpha}/\tilde{\sigma}^2$$
$$= \tilde{\alpha}'[A'_xA_x]\tilde{\alpha}/\tilde{\sigma}^2 \tag{2.4}$$

and

$$W_\tau = \dot{\tau}'[T'M_xT]\dot{\tau}/\dot{\sigma}^2$$
$$= \dot{\tau}'[T'_xT_x]\dot{\tau}/\dot{\sigma}^2. \tag{2.5}$$

Consider first the case in which the alternative is correctly specified. The OLS estimator $\dot{\tau}$ is given by

$$\dot{\tau} = [T'_xT_x]^{-1}T'_xy$$
$$= \tau + [T'_xT_x]^{-1}T'_xu,$$

or equivalently

$$\sqrt{n}\dot{\tau} = \sqrt{n}\tau + [T'_xT_x/n]^{-1}T'_xu/\sqrt{n}. \tag{2.6}$$

Equation (2.6) implies that, under H_n: $\tau = \delta/\sqrt{n}$,

$$\sqrt{n}\dot{\tau} \stackrel{a}{\sim} N(\delta, V_\tau),$$

where

$$V_\tau = \sigma^2 \, \text{plim}[T'_xT_x/n]^{-1}.$$

It follows that W_τ of (2.5) is asymptotically distributed as non-central χ^2 with q degrees of freedom and non-centrality parameter

$$NC_\tau = \text{plim} \, \delta'[T'_xT_x/n]\delta/\sigma^2.$$

Turning now to the case of the misspecified alternative, we have

$$\tilde{\alpha} = [A_x'A_x]^{-1}A_x'y$$
$$= [A_x'A_x]^{-1}A_x'T\tau + [A_x'A_x]^{-1}A_x'u,$$

or, using $A_x'T = A_x'T_x$,

$$\sqrt{n}\tilde{\alpha} = [A_x'A_x/n]^{-1}[A_x'T_x/n]\sqrt{n}\tau + [A_x'A_x/n]^{-1}A_x'u/\sqrt{n}. \qquad (2.7)$$

We deduce from equation (2.7) that, under H_n,

$$\sqrt{n}\dot{\alpha} \overset{a}{\sim} N(\alpha_\delta, V_\alpha),$$

where

$$\alpha_\delta = \text{plim}[A_x'A_x/n]^{-1}[A_x'T_x/n]\delta \qquad (2.8)$$

and

$$V_\alpha = \sigma^2 \, \text{plim}[A_x'A_x/n]^{-1}.$$

The statistic W_α defined by (2.4) is, therefore, asymptotically distributed as non-central χ^2 under H_n; the degrees-of-freedom parameter is p and the non-centrality parameter is

$$NC_\alpha = \text{plim} \, \delta'[T_x'A_x/n][A_x'A_x/n]^{-1}[A_x'T_x/n]\delta/\sigma^2.$$

The effects of choosing the wrong alternative depend upon the values of p and q, and the magnitudes of NC_τ and NC_α. The difference in non-centrality parameters is

$$NC_\tau - NC_\alpha = \text{plim}\{\delta'T_x'[I - A_x(A_x'A_x)^{-1}A_x']T_x\delta/n\sigma^2\}, \qquad (2.9)$$

which is the (non-negative) probability limit of the residual variance of the regression of $T\delta$ on (X, A) divided by σ^2. Thus $NC_\tau \geqslant NC_\alpha$, so that, if $q \leqslant p$, the W_α test based upon the false alternative will have lower asymptotic local power than W_τ. If, however, the false model of (2.1) is obtained by adding relatively few variables to the null model and $q > p$, then it is possible for W_α to have larger asymptotic local power than W_τ. Accordingly, picking the incorrect alternative can lead to a more effective check of model adequacy. A good choice of the alternative will lead to an A matrix with relatively few extra regressors which, with X, can provide a good approximation to the $T\delta$ term of the correct (LEA) model.

Note that under fixed alternatives with τ being $O(1)$ (or, equivalently, δ being $O(\sqrt{n})$) the W_α test will be consistent provided

$$\text{plim}[A_x'T_x/n]\tau \neq 0,$$

which is, in effect, the requirement that the probability limit of the OLS estimator of the coefficient vector of A in the regression of $T\tau$ on (X, A) should not be a null vector.

Although these results have been developed in the context of linear models with NID disturbances, they can be extended to more general specifications. For example, Engle (1982a) provides a theorem covering many non-linear regression models with non-spherical non-normal disturbances. Further, the analysis of Chapter 3 gives a general framework with estimation and testing allowing for specified types of heteroscedasticity and autocorrelation in the disturbances of the null model, and with the added regressors being partial derivatives evaluated at constrained estimates.

Whatever the nature of the generalization of the basic results, the success of misspecification tests will depend to some extent upon the ingenuity of the researcher who is faced with the problem of deciding which test variables to add to his null model. We now consider a solution to this problem which was proposed by Ramsey (1969) and has become quite popular in applied work.

4.2.2   Ramsey's RESET test

The distinctive feature of Ramsey's (1969) approach is his emphasis on the fact that the researcher will often have the same information available when deciding how to test the model as he or she had when choosing its specification. In the absence of guidance from extra information (which might consist of new theories or additional data), the test variables of A should reflect the paucity of information about alternatives. Ramsey (1969) assumes that the effect of the omitted variables can be proxied by some (unknown) analytic function of $X\beta$. If a polynomial approximation to this function is used and the unknown vector β replaced by the OLS estimate from the null model, that is, by

$$\hat{\beta} = (X'X)^{-1}X'y, \tag{2.10}$$

(1.1) is then tested against

$$y_t = \Sigma_1^k x_{ti}\beta_i + \Sigma_1^P[\Sigma_1^k x_{ti}\hat{\beta}_i]^{j+1}\alpha_j + u_t$$
$$= \Sigma_1^k x_{ti}\beta_i + \Sigma_1^P \hat{y}_t^{j+1}\alpha_j + u_t, \tag{2.11}$$

where $\hat{y}_t$ denotes the predicted value of v_t associated with the OLS estimation of (1.1).[5] (The term $\hat{y}_t$ does not appear as a test variable in (2.11) because it would be perfectly correlated with the k regressors of the original model.) Despite the fact that the test variables $\hat{y}_t^{j+1}$ of (2.11) are

---

[5] Ramsey's (1969) original exposition uses BLUS residuals, but the simpler approach discussed here is proposed in his later work; see Ramsey and Schmidt (1976).

stochastic, the F test of $H_0: \alpha_1 = \cdots = \alpha_p = 0$ is exact when the disturbances are $NID(0, \sigma^2)$ variates and the $\{x_{ti}\}$ are either non-stochastic or independent of the $\{u_t\}$. The exactness of Ramsey's regression equation specification error test (RESET) is implied by the general results of Milliken and Graybill (1970) on testing (1.2) against models of the form

$$y = X\beta + A(\hat{\beta})\alpha + u, \tag{2.12}$$

where $A(\hat{\beta})$ depends upon $y_1, \ldots, y_n$ only through $\hat{\beta}$.

The empirical implementation of the RESET test involves choosing a value of p. Since the value of p is irrelevant to the exactness of the RESET procedure, its importance lies in its impact on power. The results of Subsection 4.2.1 indicate that increasing p need not increase asymptotic local power. Ramsey and Gilbert (1972) report favourable evidence on the performance of RESET with $p = 3$ in Monte Carlo experiments.

The fundamental assumption of RESET, namely, that powers of $X\beta$ provide a good approximation to the omitted factor, is also open to question. Thursby and Schmidt (1977) suggest an alternative approach in which powers of the individual regressors (but not their cross-products) are added to the null specification. In a Monte Carlo study, Thursby and Schmidt (1977) find that this alternative procedure is superior to RESET and recommend augmenting the original set of regressors with their powers up to the fourth power.

In a subsequent paper, Thursby (1979) suggests that the Thursby–Schmidt test is robust to autocorrelation.[6] Strictly speaking, this is incorrect since autocorrelation invalidates the F test. The severity of the effects of autocorrelated disturbances will vary from one case to another and will depend, among other things, on the time series properties of the regressors. Porter and Kashyap (1984) consider different regressor sequences and obtain evidence which conflicts with Thursby's (1979) findings.

The RESET and Thursby–Schmidt procedures could be generalized to allow for some specified type of non-spherical errors, although such generalizations would only be valid in large samples. Alternatively, it might be useful to develop least-squares tests which have the correct asymptotic null distributions regardless of the form of any heteroscedasticity or autocorrelation in the disturbances. Such tests could be obtained by replacing the usual estimate of the variance–covariance matrix of $\tilde{\alpha}$, that is, $\tilde{\sigma}^2 [A'M_xA]^{-1}$, by an estimate of the type discussed by White and Domowitz (1984).

---

[6] Thursby (1979) refers to the Thursby–Schmidt procedure as the RESET test. We shall reserve 'RESET' for Ramsey's choice of test variables.

4.3   Testing for incorrect functional form

There are often close relationships between tests for incorrect functional form and tests for omitted variables. These relationships are sometimes direct; for example, a linear relationship might be tested against a more general relationship involving quadratic and higher-order terms in the regressors. Alternatively, if the null model

$$y = X\beta + u, \, u \sim N(0, \sigma^2 I), \tag{1.2}$$

is obtained by imposing the restrictions $\theta_2 = \theta_2^0$ on the parameters of the non-linear model

$$y = f(X; \theta_1, \theta_2) + u, \, u \sim N(0, \sigma^2 I), \tag{3.1}$$

then, provided $f(\cdot)$ is sufficiently smooth to permit a Taylor series expansion, the results on LEAs derived in Chapter 3 imply that the LR, LM and W tests of (1.2) against (3.1) are asymptotically equivalent to those of the null specification against

$$
\begin{aligned}
y &= f(X; \theta_1, \theta_2^0) + [\partial f(X; \hat{\theta}_1, \theta_2^0)/\partial \theta_2](\theta_2 - \theta_2^0) + u \\
&= X\beta + [\partial f(X; \hat{\theta}_1, \theta_2^0)/\partial \theta_2](\theta_2 - \theta_2^0) + u.
\end{aligned} \tag{3.2}
$$

Equation (3.2) is of the general form (2.1) with

$$A = [\partial f(X; \hat{\theta}_1, \theta_2^0)/\partial \theta_2] \text{ and } \alpha = \theta_2 - \theta_2^0,$$

$\hat{\theta}_1$ being the constrained least-squares estimate of θ_1.

If the non-linear alternative under consideration does not include (1.2) as a special case, then we have a case of non-nested models. A simple example would be competing linear and semi-log specifications

$$y_t = \beta x_t + u_t, \, t = 1, \ldots, n$$

and

$$y_t = \gamma \ln x_t + u_t, \, t = 1, \ldots, n.$$

A discussion of tests of non-nested hypotheses is outside the scope of this book, but, as pointed out by Plosser, Schwert and White (1982), the linear model can be viewed as a misspecified regression with an omitted variable $\ln x_t$ in the context of the comprehensive model

$$y_t = \beta x_t + \gamma \ln x_t + u_t, \, t = 1, \ldots, n.$$

Undoubtedly there will be situations in which there is little information about the precise form of the alternative. The usual strategy in such circumstances is to employ some variant of the RESET test or the

Thursby–Schmidt procedure.[7] An interpretation of the RESET test as a check for incorrect functional form can be obtained by regarding (2.11) as a computationally attractive LEA when the alternative is

$$y_t = \sum_{j=0}^{p} [z_t(\beta)]^{j+1} \alpha_j + u_t, \tag{3.3}$$

where $z_t(\beta) = \sum_{i=1}^{k} x_{ti} \beta_i$ and $\alpha_0 \equiv 1$. Equation (3.3) is non-linear in the parameters α_i and β_i, but reduces to (1.2) when $\alpha_1 = \alpha_2 = \cdots = \alpha_p = 0$.

Another test for incorrect functional form which can be used without the specification of an alternative has been proposed by White (1980a). White's test involves estimating (1.2) by OLS and by weighted least squares (WLS), and then comparing the two sets of estimates. The OLS estimator is, as before, denoted by $\hat{\beta}$ and the WLS estimator by

$$\tilde{\beta} = (X'\Omega^{-1}X)^{-1}X'\Omega^{-1}y, \tag{3.4}$$

where Ω^{-1} is a selected n by n diagonal matrix in which the elements are the positive weights w_i, $i = 1, \ldots, n$. The indicator of misspecification is then

$$q_\beta = \tilde{\beta} - \hat{\beta}, \tag{3.5}$$

which will tend to a null vector as $n \to \infty$ when there is no functional misspecification. White (1980a) provides a direct asymptotic χ^2 test of the joint significance of the elements of q_β using the result that, under the assumption of correct specification, $\sqrt{n}q_\beta$ is asymptotically normally distributed with zero mean vector and covariance matrix

$$\sigma^2 \operatorname{plim} n[(X'\Omega^{-1}X)^{-1}X'\Omega^{-2}X(X'\Omega^{-1}X)^{-1} - (X'X)^{-1}]. \tag{3.6}$$

It is shown in Section 4.10 that White's procedure is asymptotically equivalent to a test of $\alpha = 0$ in

$$y = X\beta + (\Omega^{-1}X)\alpha + u, \tag{3.7}$$

and so can be implemented as a check for omitted variables.[8] The power of this test will depend upon the choice of Ω^{-1}. White (1980a, p. 158) suggests trying two or three schemes and provides a numerical example.

It may be the case that functional misspecification is present because it is some transformation of y, rather than y itself, which is normally distributed. When such non-linearity is suspected, it will be useful to

---

[7] White's (1982) information matrix test is sometimes suggested as a general check for functional misspecification. This procedure is discussed later in this chapter; see Section 4.9.

[8] There are other examples of testing functional form by adding regressors to the null model; see, for example, Kmenta's (1967) work on production functions.

consider models of the form

$$f(y, X; \theta) = u, \tag{3.8}$$

which include the linear regression model as a special case. Models like (3.8) involve the new complication of a jacobian term $\|\partial f(y, X; \theta)/\partial y\|$ which will depend upon unknown parameters and be relevant to the construction of LR, LM and W test statistics.

The Box–Cox regression model

One non-linear relationship which has received considerable attention in econometrics is the Box–Cox (1964) regression model

$$y_t(\lambda) = \sum_{i=1}^{k} x_{ti}\beta_i + u_t, \, t = 1, \ldots, n, \tag{3.9}$$

where

$$y_t(\lambda) = (y_t^\lambda - 1)/\lambda, \, \lambda \neq 0, \, y \geqslant 0$$

$$= \ln y_t, \, \lambda = 0, \, y \geqslant 0,$$

and the parameters β_i include an intercept term.[9] The Box–Cox model can be extended by allowing some of the regressors to be defined by the same transformation as the dependent variable. This extended Box–Cox regression model has been studied by Savin and White (1978) and can be written as

$$y_t(\lambda) = \sum_{1}^{m} x_{ti}\beta_i + \sum_{m+1}^{k} x_{ti}(\lambda)\beta_i + u_t, \tag{3.10}$$

where

$$x_{ti}(\lambda) = (x_{ti}^\lambda - 1)/\lambda, \, \lambda \neq 0, \, x_{ti} \geqslant 0$$

$$= \ln x_{ti}, \, \lambda = 0, \, x_{ti} \geqslant 0.$$

The popularity of the Box–Cox model in econometrics is probably due to the fact that it includes the linear and log-linear specifications as special cases (obtained by setting λ equal to 1 and 0, respectively) which suggests that the choice between these widely used functional forms can be based upon one or other of the classical tests. The use of this transformation is, however, subject to an important limitation. The nature of the transformation implies that $y_t(\lambda)$ cannot be assumed to be normally distributed

---

[9] See Schlesselman (1971) for a discussion of the importance of the intercept term in the Box–Cox model.

unless $\lambda = 0$. Poirier (1978) proposed that a truncated normal distribution be adopted. Poirier's approach is more complicated than that of Amemiya and Powell (1981) in which the gamma distribution is used, and also implies some difficulty in the interpretation of regression coefficients (see Poirier and Melino, 1978). Notwithstanding the fact that $y_t(\lambda)$ can only be normally distributed when $\lambda = 0$, many empirical and theoretical contributions are based upon the assumption that the disturbances u_t of models like (3.9) and (3.10) are $\text{NID}(0, \sigma^2)$ variates. The practical consequences of the invalid assumption of normality will vary from case to case, but it is clearly unwise to employ this assumption in theoretical analyses of the Box–Cox model.

As mentioned above, one of the main incentives for considering the Box–Cox form is that it permits testing of the familiar linear and log-linear models which are often viewed as potentially useful specifications by applied workers. The relevant null hypotheses are $\lambda = 1$ and $\lambda = 0$ for the linear and log-linear variants, respectively.[10] Since estimation with λ unrestricted is relatively difficult, the LM principle is attractive. Godfrey and Wickens (1981) derive OPG forms of the LM statistics for testing the restrictions $\lambda = 0$ and $\lambda = 1$ for the case in which the disturbances have the symmetrically truncated normal distribution with probability density function (p.d.f.)

$$\gamma(u_t) = a(c)\rho(u_t;\ \sigma^2),\ u_t^2 \leqslant c^2\sigma^2,$$
$$= 0,\ u_t^2 > c^2\sigma^2, \tag{3.11}$$

where $\rho(u_t;\ \sigma^2)$ is the p.d.f. of a $N(0, \sigma^2)$ variate,

$$a(c) = \left\{ \int_{-c}^{c} (2\pi)^{-\frac{1}{2}} \exp(-z^2/2)dz \right\}^{-1},$$

$E(y_t)$ is never less than $c\sigma$ when $\lambda = 1$, and c is known. This form of truncated p.d.f. was used by Aneuryn-Evans and Deaton (1980) and, while leading to a much simpler analysis than Poirier's (1978) specification, it comprises a set of strong assumptions.[11]

Davidson and MacKinnon (1983, 1985) have examined the small sample performance of alternative forms of the LM tests of $\lambda = 0$ and $\lambda = 1$ using Monte Carlo techniques. They find that their DLR approach

[10] Imposing the restriction $\lambda = 1$ implies an unimportant redefinition of the intercept term.

[11] Unlike the disturbances of Poirier's (1978) model, the u_t with p.d.f. $\gamma(\cdot)$ can be regarded as a set of independently and identically distributed variates with zero means and common variance; see Godfrey and Wickens (1981, p. 491).

leads to procedures which have estimated trade-offs between power and size which are similar to those of the corresponding Godfrey–Wickens tests, but have the advantage of a much closer agreement between estimated and nominal significance levels. The OPG variants of the LM test tend to reject true models too frequently. The DLR approach, however, involves an estimate of the information matrix derived using properties of the multivariate normal distribution. Consequently, it is, strictly speaking, not applicable when the alternative is a Box–Cox regression model because

$$y_t(\lambda) \sim N\left(\sum_{i=1}^{m} x_{ti}\beta_i + \sum_{m+1}^{k} x_{ti}(\lambda)\beta_i, \ \sigma^2\right)$$

is not a proper statistical model (see Amemiya and Powell, 1981).

The work of Andrews (1971) on data transformations can also be used to obtain tests of linear and log-linear variants in the context of the Box–Cox model. The approach proposed by Andrews is claimed to provide exact tests, but this claim is only justified when the disturbances u_t of (3.9) or (3.10) are $NID(0,\sigma^2)$. It follows that an exact test can only be derived for the null hypothesis that the relationship is log-linear, that is, $\lambda = 0$. Furthermore, the evidence reported by Davidson and MacKinnon (1983, 1985) suggests that the Andrews-type tests of $\lambda = 0$ and $\lambda = 1$ are not as powerful as the LM procedures. These findings are in agreement with those of Atkinson (1973) on the small sample behaviour of some tests of $\lambda = -1$. In view of the relatively poor performance of Andrews's tests, these procedures are not described in detail here. The interested reader should consult Section 4 of the article by Godfrey and Wickens (1981).

To sum up, if the linear and log-linear regression models are both to be tested against the Box–Cox alternative using least-squares results, then the DLR method appears to be better than either the Godfrey–Wickens OPG approximation or the Andrews technique. It would, however, be very interesting to examine the robustness of the Davidson–MacKinnon tests to non-normality. The calculation of these tests is described in detail by Davidson and MacKinnon (1985), and involves substitution of

$$f_t(\theta) = \left[y_t(\lambda) - \sum_{1}^{m} x_{ti}\beta_i - \sum_{m+1}^{k} x_{ti}(\lambda)\beta_i\right]\bigg/ \sigma, \ \theta' = (\beta', \sigma, \lambda),$$

in the general formulae of Section 3.4.

4.4   Testing for autocorrelation

The implications of disturbance autocorrelation for OLS analysis will depend, in part, upon the nature of the regressors. If the regressors are strictly exogenous, then the OLS estimators, while remaining unbiased and consistent, are inefficient. Moreover the sampling theory based upon the assumption of independent disturbances will be inappropriate and so, for example, the usual t and F tests will be invalid. The OLS estimators are even less robust to autocorrelation when the regressors include lagged values of the dependent variable and are, in general, biased and inconsistent. These results indicate the importance of testing the hypothesis of independent errors, especially when estimating dynamic regression models.

If some particular form of autocorrelation is selected as the alternative hypothesis, then W and LR tests can be calculated. The estimation of the original regression equation subject to a specified autocorrelation scheme will, however, involve the solution of a set of non-linear first-order conditions. Consequently W and LR procedures are unattractive relative to tests such as LM that are based upon the OLS results obtained by estimating under the null hypothesis that the equation's error terms are independent.[12]

The choice of the alternative hypothesis will have an effect on the form of tests. It is not sufficient to test only against the widely used alternative of a first-order autoregressive process. Many dynamic models are estimated using quarterly data and/or derived as transformed versions of distributed lag models. There is, therefore, a need to consider general-order schemes and moving average processes as alternatives.

The plan of this section is as follows. First, various alternative hypotheses are considered and results on locally equivalent alternatives are used to obtain relationships between them. Next, convenient methods for calculating LM checks are described. These LM procedures are then compared to tests based upon other general approaches. Finally, since null specifications sometimes allow for autocorrelated disturbances, the problem of testing the adequacy of a specified autocorrelation model is discussed.

4.4.1   Autocorrelation models as alternatives

Consider a (possibly non-linear) regression model

$$y_t = f_t(\beta) + u_t \qquad\qquad (4.1)$$

and suppose that the assumption that the disturbances u_t are serially

[12] It might be argued that this preference is mistaken because the model must be re-estimated when the null hypothesis is rejected. It is, however, not always the case that unrestricted maximum likelihood estimation under the specified alternative is the correct response to significant evidence of residual serial correlation because the alternative model may itself be inadequate.

independent is to be tested against the alternative of a gth-order moving average [MA(g)] process

$$u_t = [1 + \alpha(L)]\varepsilon_t, \quad \varepsilon_t\text{NID}(0, \sigma_\varepsilon^2), \tag{4.2}$$

where L denotes the lag operator and $\alpha(L) = \alpha_1 L + \alpha_2 L^2 + \cdots + \alpha_g L^g$. The function $f_t(\beta)$ can be non-linear and involve lagged values of the dependent variable as well as exogenous variables. The moving average scheme is taken to be invertible.

The general alternative consisting of (4.1) and (4.2) can be written in the form

$$\varepsilon_t = [1 + \alpha(L)]^{-1}[y_t - f_t(\beta)], \quad \varepsilon_t\text{NID}(0, \sigma_\varepsilon^2), \tag{4.3}$$

and if θ_2 is defined to be the g-dimensional vector $(\alpha_1, \ldots, \alpha_g)$, then it is required to test $H_0: \theta_2 = 0$. The results of Chapter 3 can now be used to derive locally equivalent alternative (LEA) models. A typical element of $\partial\varepsilon_t/\partial\theta_2$ is

$$\partial\varepsilon_t/\partial\alpha_i = -[1 + \alpha(L)]^{-2}L^i[y_t - f_t(\beta)],$$

which reduces to $-L^i[y_t - f_t(\beta)]$, that is, $-u_{t-i}$, when θ_2 is set equal to a null vector.

A LEA to (4.3) is therefore

$$\varepsilon_t^* = [1 - \alpha_1 L - \cdots - \alpha_g L^g][y_t - f_t(\beta)]$$
$$= [1 - \alpha(L)][y_t - f_t(\beta)], \tag{4.4}$$

which is simply the autoregressive transform of the model (4.1) associated with the filter for the gth-order autoregressive [AR(g)] process

$$[1 - \alpha(L)]u_t = \varepsilon_t^*, \quad \varepsilon_t^*\text{NID}(0, \sigma_*^2). \tag{4.5}$$

Thus the AR(g) and MA(g) schemes are LEAs when the null is that the regression disturbances are serially uncorrelated.[13] This is a remarkable result with several interesting implications, for example, an LR test for AR(g) errors is asymptotically equivalent to the LR test for the MA(g) alternative despite the marked differences in unrestricted estimation under these alternatives. Perhaps more important to the applied worker, these results imply that, when testing the independence assumption, it is only necessary to specify the order of an alternative and not whether it is AR or MA.

[13] It should be noted that the AR(g) process of the alternative is assumed to be stationary and so, e.g., the random walk hypothesis is not covered. Berenblut and Webb (1973) consider non-stationary AR(1) schemes in the context of a regression model with fixed regressors and Gaussian disturbances.

Similar results can be developed for alternative models in which the parameters are subject to constraints. For example, consider the non-linear (in parameters) AR(5) model mentioned by Wallis (1972) as worthy of consideration when fitting quarterly models

$$(1 - \alpha_1 L)(1 - \alpha_4 L^4)u_t = \varepsilon_t, \quad \varepsilon_t \text{NID}(0, \sigma_\varepsilon^2). \tag{4.6}$$

The maximum likelihood estimation of the model consisting of (4.1) and (4.6) would be quite complicated, even if (4.1) were linear. It is, however, simple to show that (4.6) is locally equivalent to an AR(4) process with gaps, namely,

$$[1 - \alpha_1 L - \alpha_4 L^4]u_t = \varepsilon_t, \quad \varepsilon_t \text{NID}(0, \sigma_\varepsilon^2). \tag{4.7}$$

Models with autocorrelated errors

The model (4.1) itself can be regarded as the result of a transformation to eliminate serial correlation in some more basic economic formulation. Thus, if the null specification allows for a mixed autoregressive-moving average (p, q) [ARMA(p, q)] error process, then it is only necessary to decide on g, the number of additional coefficients, and not on whether to extend the AR or MA components, when testing for higher-order serial correlation. However, it is not possible to extend both parts of the ARMA (p, q) model. This result can be illustrated by considering the case of a null specification of ARMA $(0, 0)$ and an alternative of ARMA $(1, 1)$ errors.

If the ARMA $(1, 1)$ alternative is written as

$$(1 - \alpha_1 L)u_t = (1 + \mu_1 L)\varepsilon_t, \tag{4.8}$$

then partial linearizations yield as LEAs the AR(1) and MA(1) schemes

$$[1 - (\alpha_1 + \mu_1)L]u_t = \varepsilon_t \tag{4.9}$$

and

$$u_t = [1 + (\alpha_1 + \mu_1)L]\varepsilon_t. \tag{4.10}$$

(More generally, an ARMA (g, h) alternative is locally equivalent to the AR(j) and MA(j) alternatives when the null is ARMA $(0, 0)$, j being the larger of g and h.) The coefficients α_1 and μ_1 are obviously not locally identified and the information matrix will be singular under $H_0: \alpha_1 = \mu_1 = 0$. The problems associated with simultaneous tests of the significance of AR and MA coefficients have been noted in the literature (see, e.g., Fitts, 1973, p. 370; Hannan, 1970, pp. 388–9, 409–14).

Having decided upon the class of alternative hypotheses to be employed when testing the assumption that the errors u_t are independent, the next step is to choose a convenient method for calculating the associated test statistic.

4.4.2   *The implementation of autocorrelation tests*

Given the asymptotic local equivalence of the AR(g) and MA(g) alternatives, either can be used to discuss the implementation of serial correlation tests. It is convenient to employ the more widely used AR(g) model of (4.4) so that when the regression model of (4.1) is linear, the disturbance of the alternative, denoted by $\varepsilon_t(\theta)$, is defined by

$$\varepsilon_t(\theta) = u_t(\beta) - \alpha_1 u_{t-1}(\beta) - \cdots - \alpha_g u_{t-g}(\beta),$$

where

$$u_t(\beta) = y_t - x_t'\beta$$
$$\theta_1 = \beta$$
$$\theta_2' = (\alpha_1, \ldots, \alpha_g)$$

and $\theta' = (\theta_1', \theta_2')$.[14] The constrained maximum likelihood estimator is then $\hat{\theta}' = (\hat{\beta}', 0')$, where $\hat{\beta}$ is the OLS estimator.

There are several asymptotically equivalent algorithms for computing LM-type tests of the null hypothesis $H_0: \theta_2 = 0$. One of these methods involves regressing the OLS residual $\hat{u}_t$ on x_t and $(\hat{u}_{t-1}, \ldots, \hat{u}_{t-g})$, with the test statistic being calculated as n times the (uncentred) R^2 for this regression. The sample values of this statistic should be compared to the pre-specified critical value of a $\chi^2(g)$ distribution. This '$n \times R^2$' variant was independently suggested by several researchers working on the role of the LM principle in detecting misspecifications (see, e.g., Breusch, 1978a; Engle, 1984; Godfrey, 1978d).[15] Mizon and Hendry (1980) provide some quite favourable Monte Carlo evidence on the finite sample properties of '$n \times R^2$' tests for autocorrelation, but Kiviet (1986) finds that such tests can be poorly behaved when the regression model is overspecified. Kiviet suggests that it is safer to employ a modified LM procedure consisting of a

---

[14] The variance parameter σ_ε^2 can be ignored because its maximum likelihood estimator is asymptotically uncorrelated with those of the other parameters; i.e., the information matrix can be written in block-diagonal form.

[15] Breusch (1978a) and Godfrey (1978c) also propose alternative quadratic form tests for AR(g) and MA(g) errors using different estimates of the information matrix. The small sample performance of these tests does not appear to have been studied. Also the information matrix estimate appearing in (23) of Breusch (1978a) need not be positive definite.

simple (asymptotically valid) F test of the significance of the lagged residuals in the regression of $\hat{u}_t$ on x_t and $(\hat{u}_{t-1}, \ldots, \hat{u}_{t-g})$. Spencer (1975) also recommends this procedure which was suggested by Durbin (1970) for testing against AR(g) errors. The orthogonality of OLS-predicted values and residuals implies that an equivalent algorithm is to carry out the F test of $H_0 : \alpha_1 = \alpha_2 = \cdots = \alpha_g = 0$ for the alternative

$$y_t = x'_t \beta + \alpha_1 \hat{u}_{t-1} + \cdots + \alpha_g \hat{u}_{t-g} + \varepsilon_t. \tag{4.11}$$

The inclusion of lagged residuals in the regressors of (4.11) implies that either the estimation period should be reduced to $t = g + 1, \ldots, n$, or values of $\hat{u}_0, \ldots, \hat{u}_{1-g}$ must be supplied. If the latter strategy is adopted, then the pre-sample values $\hat{u}_0, \ldots, \hat{u}_{1-g}$ can all be set equal to zero without affecting the asymptotic properties of the tests. However, the asymptotic irrelevance of such starting values does not guarantee that their impact in small samples can always be neglected.

Non-linear regression models

The artificial regression model (4.11) is an augmented version of the null specification with considerable intuitive appeal. It is also easily recognized as a LEA of the $\varepsilon^+(\theta)$ type that was discussed in Section 3.2. The corresponding LEA for the case in which $f_t(\beta)$ of (4.1) is non-linear is given by

$$y_t = f_t(\beta) + \alpha_1 \hat{u}_{t-1} + \cdots + \alpha_g \hat{u}_{t-g} + \varepsilon_t, \tag{4.12}$$

where $\hat{u}_t$ denotes the residual $y_t - f_t(\hat{\beta})$, $\hat{\beta}$ being the minimizer of $\Sigma_1^n [y_t - f_t(\beta)]^2$. As (4.12) is non-linear, a direct test of the null hypothesis is unattractive, but the computational burden can be considerably reduced by linearizing $f_t(\beta)$ about $\beta = \hat{\beta}$. This linearization leads to the test model

$$\hat{u}_t = F_t(\hat{\beta})'b + \alpha_1 \hat{u}_{t-1} + \cdots + \alpha_g \hat{u}_{t-g} + \varepsilon_t, \tag{4.13}$$

where $F_t(\hat{\beta})$ is $\partial f_t(\beta)/\partial \beta$ evaluated at $\beta = \hat{\beta}$ (see Breusch and Pagan, 1980; Durbin, 1970; Godfrey and Wickens, 1982). The assumption of independent errors can then be checked by applying, for example, a pseudo-LR test of $\alpha_1 = \cdots = \alpha_g = 0$ in the context of (4.13).

To sum up, OV-type tests based upon augmented models like (4.11) and (4.13) offer simple procedures which are asymptotically optimal against both AR(g) and MA(g) alternatives. Further, Monte Carlo evidence for linear regression models suggests that this form of the LM test behaves quite well in finite samples (see Mizon and Hendry, 1980). The relationship of this and other variants of the general LM test to other procedures is now examined.

4.4.3   *Relationship of Lagrange multiplier-type tests to other procedures*

Let $\hat{U}_g$ denote the n by g matrix whose (t, i) element is $\hat{u}_{t-1}$ for $t > i$ and equal to zero for $t \leqslant i$. The LEA used to generate the OV variant of the LM test is then

$$y = X\beta + \hat{U}_g\theta_2 + \varepsilon, \tag{4.14}$$

with the OLS estimate of θ_2 being

$$\bar{\theta}_2 = [\hat{U}_g'M(X)\hat{U}_g]^{-1}\hat{U}_g'M(X)y$$

$$= [\hat{U}_g'M(X)\hat{U}_g]^{-1}\hat{U}_g'\hat{u}, \tag{4.15}$$

where $M(X)$ is the n by n projection matrix $I_n - X(X'X)^{-1}X'$.

Models with strictly exogenous regressors

Suppose first that the regressors of the linear null model are strictly exogenous. In this situation, $n^{-1}[\hat{U}_g'M(X)\hat{U}_g]$ and $n^{-1}[\hat{U}_g'\hat{U}_g]$ have the same probability limit which is $\sigma_u^2 I_g$ on H_0. It follows that $\bar{\theta}_2$ and $\hat{\sigma}_u^{-2}(\hat{U}_g'\hat{u}/n)$ differ by asymptotically negligible terms when X is fixed in repeated sampling and the disturbances u_t are independent, $\hat{\sigma}_u^2 = n^{-1}\hat{u}'\hat{u}$ being the constrained maximum likelihood estimator. A typical element of $\hat{\sigma}_u^{-2}(\hat{U}_g'\hat{u}/n)$ is

$$\Sigma\hat{u}_t\hat{u}_{t-j}/\Sigma\hat{u}_t^2 = r(j), \tag{4.16}$$

where $r(j)$ is the estimate of the jth-order autocorrelation coefficient based upon the OLS residuals. The OV variant of the LM test is, therefore, asymptotically equivalent to a check of the joint significance of a set of estimated autocorrelations. Since the regressors are exogenous, Bartlett's (1946) results can be applied and an asymptotically valid form of the test is

$$n[r(1)^2 + \cdots + r(g)^2] \overset{a}{\sim} \chi^2(g) \text{ on } H_0. \tag{4.17}$$

The expression of (4.17) is rather simpler to evaluate than the corresponding statistic derived by direct application of the LM principle, namely,

$$\hat{u}'\hat{U}_g[\hat{U}_g'M(X)\hat{U}_g]^{-1}\hat{U}_g'\hat{u}/\hat{\sigma}_u^2.$$

Some special cases of interest can be obtained by considering restricted AR(g) alternatives in which only the last coefficient is non-zero, for example, the simple AR(4) scheme $u_t = \alpha_4 u_{t-4} + \varepsilon_t$. The conventional tests for such restricted alternatives are the generalized Durbin–Watson statistics

$$DW_g = \Sigma_{g+1}^n(\hat{u}_t - \hat{u}_{t-g})^2/\Sigma_1^n\hat{u}_t^2 \tag{4.18}$$

(see Vinod, 1973). It is easily shown that DW_g of (4.18) is approximately equal to $2(1 - r(g))$ and so such generalizations of the Durbin–Watson test are asymptotically equivalent to the corresponding LM procedures.

If the alternative hypothesis specifies the sign of the coefficient of the simple $AR(g)$ error model, then the LM test has a finite sample optimality property as well as being asymptotically optimal. Consider the following model which covers the problem of testing for simple $AR(g)$ errors as a special case:

$$y = X\beta + u, \ u \sim N(0, \sigma^2 \Omega(\theta_2)),$$

where X is fixed and has full column rank, θ_2 is a non-negative scalar and $\Omega(0) = I_n$.[16] The null hypothesis is $H_0: \theta_2 = 0$ and the one-sided alternative is $H_1: \theta_2 > 0$. This problem is invariant under the group of transformations $y \to a_0 y + X a_1$, where a_0 is a positive scalar and a_1 is a k-dimensional vector (see Cox and Hinkley, 1974, Section 5.3, for a general discussion of invariant tests). King and Hillier (1985) show that a one-sided LM test is locally best invariant in finite samples; that is the power function of this test has maximum slope at the origin among all invariant tests of H_0 against H_1.

Dynamic regression models

The interpretation of the LM-type test as a check of the significance of a set of estimated autocorrelations $r(j)$ carries over to the case of a dynamic regression model. Breusch (1978a) and Godfrey (1978c) both apply a direct LM technique and show that the estimated multipliers are simply the $r(j)$, $j = 1, \ldots, g$. Note, however, that, when the regressors include lagged values of the dependent variable, the terms $\sqrt{n} r(j)$ are no longer asymptotically independent $N(0, 1)$ on the null hypothesis and so the form of the test statistic given in (4.17) is not appropriate.

Durbin's tests

The problem of deriving an asymptotically valid test for $AR(g)$ errors in dynamic regression models was discussed in Durbin's (1970) seminal paper. Durbin proposes a general procedure leading to a test of the significance of θ_2^*, the value of θ_2 maximizing the likelihood subject to $\beta = \hat{\beta}$. The conditional maximizer θ_2^* is given by

$$\theta_2^* = (\hat{U}_g' \hat{U}_g)^{-1} \hat{U}_g' \hat{u} = A\bar{\theta}_2, \tag{4.19}$$

---

[16] This model is used by King and Hillier (1985) who list several of the testing problems that it can represent.

where $A = (\hat{U}'_g \hat{U}_g)^{-1}(\hat{U}'_g M(X) \hat{U}_g)$. Equation (4.19) reveals that θ_2^* is a non-singular transformation of $\bar{\theta}_2$, so that differences in the sample values of the associated test statistics reflect asymptotically negligible differences in the implicit estimates of the asymptotic variance–covariance matrix of $\hat{U}'_g \hat{u}$ on H_0. Durbin (1970) deletes terms with a probability limit of zero when forming the estimate of the variance matrix of θ_2^*, but this can lead to estimates which are not positive definite (see Breusch, 1978a, for further discussion). In the case of testing against the AR(1) alternative, Durbin's technique leads to the familiar h statistic

$$h = n^{\frac{1}{2}}(1 - \tfrac{1}{2}DW_1)/(1 - n\hat{v})^{\frac{1}{2}},$$

where $(1 - \tfrac{1}{2}DW_1)$ is used as an approximation to $r(1)$ and $\hat{v}$ is the estimated variance of the OLS estimator of the coefficient of y_{t-1}. The statistic h will not be available if $n\hat{v} \geqslant 1$; Monte Carlo evidence on the frequency of this problem is provided by Maddala and Rao (1973) and Spencer (1975). Aldrich (1978) derives the h statistic using the LM approach. Durbin (1970) also outlines a test for AR(g) disturbances involving the regression of $\hat{u}$ on X and $\hat{U}_g$. This approach leads to the estimate $\bar{\theta}_2$ of (4.15) and so is equivalent to the LM-OV procedure.

The similarity between tests based upon the augmented model of (4.14) and Durbin's approach is much less marked when testing against a moving average alternative. The calculation of θ_2^* involves complex non-linear estimation when the MA(g) alternative is employed and so direct application of Durbin's (1970) theorem is unattractive. Fitts (1973) has, however, provided a test for MA(1) errors using Durbin's general approach. There is, of course, little incentive to consider a separate type of test for MA(g) errors since the results on asymptotic local equivalence imply that those for the AR(g) alternative are equally appropriate. Thus, for example, the h test is asymptotically equivalent to the procedure for detecting MA(1) errors derived by Fitts (1973).

Box–Pierce tests

If the regressors consist entirely of lagged values of the dependent variable, then the Q statistic of Box and Pierce (1970) is valid in large samples. The Box–Pierce statistic is defined by

$$Q = n\Sigma_1^m r(j)^2,$$

and if m is $O(n^{\frac{1}{2}})$, the limit null distribution of Q is $\chi^2(m - k)$, k now denoting the order of the autoregression of the null model. The similarity between Q and the LM procedures which also test the significance of a set of estimated $r(j)$ is, to some extent, superficial. The Q statistic was proposed as a pure significance test. No alternative hypothesis is supplied, and the number of estimated autocorrelations is instead allowed to tend to infinity with n, although at a rate which guarantees $m/n \rightarrow 0$ as $n \rightarrow \infty$.[17] Also, in the case of the Q test, the asymptotic variance–covariance matrix of the $r(j)$ is approximated in such a way that only the degrees-of-freedom parameter need be adjusted in (4.17) to allow for the presence of lagged dependent variables. However, in the LM approach, the number of autocorrelation estimates tested is fixed and finite, and need not exceed k; and the asymptotic variance–covariance matrix of the $r(j)$ is adjusted in dynamic models with the degrees-of-freedom parameter of (4.17) being unaffected.[18] It is also important to note that, unlike the LM test, the Q test is not valid when the regressors include both exogenous and lagged dependent variables.

4.4.4 *Testing for higher-order autocorrelation*

It is important to test the adequacy of the assumed error model when an econometric relationship has been estimated allowing for some specified form of autocorrelation in the disturbances (see, e.g., Granger and Newbold, 1977). Tests for the general case of an ARMA(p, q) error model and various special cases have been provided by Godfrey (1978d).[19] In practice, however, moving average processes are rarely estimated, and so details will only be given for models assumed to have purely autoregressive errors. The null model can, therefore, be written as

$$y_t = f_t(\beta) + u_t \tag{4.1}$$

$$[1 - \rho(L)]u_t = \varepsilon_t, \quad \varepsilon_t \text{NID}(0, \sigma_\varepsilon^2), \tag{4.20}$$

where $\rho(L) = \rho_1 L + \cdots + \rho_p L^p$. Let $\rho = (\rho_1, \ldots, \rho_p)'$.

The adequacy of (4.20) is to be judged by considering some more general process. It is, however, only necessary to decide upon g, the number of additional terms, since the AR($p + g$) and ARMA(p, g) models

---

[17] Note that m must be greater than k in order to ensure that the degrees-of-freedom parameter of the Q statistic is positive.

[18] Monte Carlo evidence suggests that neither the Box–Pierce procedure nor the Ljung–Box (1978) modified Q test is to be recommended for samples of the size normally encountered in econometric work; see Godfrey (1979a).

[19] Godfrey (1978d) presents the tests in the '$n \times R^2$' form, rather than as F tests for the appropriate artificial regression models. It seems reasonable to conjecture that the latter approach will lead to better small sample performance.

will be LEAs with respect to the null model. For simplicity of exposition, the former will be adopted and the alternative autocorrelation model is expressed as

$$[1 - \alpha(L)][1 - \rho(L)]u_t = \varepsilon_t, \quad \varepsilon_t \text{NID}(0, \sigma_\varepsilon^2), \tag{4.21}$$

where $\alpha(L) = \alpha_1 L + \cdots + \alpha_g L^g$. It will be convenient to introduce the g-dimensional vector $\alpha = (\alpha_1, \ldots, \alpha_g)'$. The consistency of the null specification with the sample data is then to be investigated by testing the g restrictions of $H_0: \alpha = 0$.

Artificial models of the general form (4.13) provide a convenient approach to calculating asymptotically optimal tests of $H_0: \alpha = 0$. First, equations (4.1) and (4.21) can be combined to form the restricted transformed equation which is a non-linear relationship with independent errors and so can be written as

$$y_t = s_t(\alpha, \beta, \rho) + \varepsilon_t, \quad \varepsilon_t \text{NID}(0, \sigma_\varepsilon^2)$$
$$= s_t(\theta) + \varepsilon_t, \quad \theta' = (\alpha', \beta', \rho'). \tag{4.22}$$

Next, if the constrained MLE is denoted by $\hat{\theta} = (0', \hat{\beta}', \hat{\rho}')'$ and $\hat{\varepsilon}_t = y_t - s_t(\hat{\theta})$, then (4.22) can be linearized about $\theta = \hat{\theta}$ and H_0 tested by checking the joint significance of the regressors $\partial s_t(\hat{\theta})/\partial \alpha$ in the least-squares regression of $\hat{\varepsilon}_t$ on $\partial s_t(\hat{\theta})/\partial \theta$. In the case of a linear regression model with autoregressive errors, we have $f_t(\beta) = x_t'\beta$ and $\partial s_t(\hat{\theta})/\partial \theta$ simplifies in such a way that it is possible to calculate the test of $AR(p)$ against $AR(p + g)$ as the usual least-squares F statistic for testing $\alpha_1 = \cdots = \alpha_g = 0$ in the model

$$y_t^* = \Sigma_1^k x_{ti}^* b_i + \Sigma_1^P \hat{u}_{t-i} c_i + \Sigma_1^g \hat{\varepsilon}_{t-i} \alpha_i + e_t, \tag{4.23}$$

where $\hat{u}_t = y_t - x_t'\hat{\beta}$ and '*' denotes an autoregressive transform estimated under the null, for example, $y_t^* = y_t - \Sigma_1^P \hat{\rho}_i y_{t-i}$.

If the autocorrelations of the $\hat{\varepsilon}_t$ are estimated by

$$r(j) = \Sigma_{j+1}^n \hat{\varepsilon}_t \hat{\varepsilon}_{t-j}/\Sigma_1^n \hat{\varepsilon}_t^2, j = 1, \ldots, m, \ m = O(n^{\frac{1}{2}}),$$

then the Box–Pierce statistic

$$Q = n\Sigma_1^m r(j)^2$$

provides a valid large sample test if the regressors are all exogenous, or if they are all lagged values of the dependent variable. However, even if the null specification corresponds to one of these two special cases, the Q test may well be markedly inferior to LM/score tests (see, e.g., Poskitt and Tremayne, 1981).

4.5 Testing for heteroscedasticity

As cross-section data sets have become more widely available for micro-econometric analyses, so there has been an increasing emphasis on the problems of estimation and testing in the presence of heteroscedasticity. The consequences of heteroscedasticity are in some ways similar to those of autocorrelation. If OLS is applied when the disturbances have been incorrectly assumed to have equal variances, then the estimators of the regression parameters will be inefficient and their estimated standard errors will be biased (see, e.g., Goldfeld and Quandt, 1972, pp. 83–4; Kmenta, 1971, pp. 255–6). Heteroscedasticity will also affect the validity of misspecification tests based upon OLS theory; for example, the statistic of Ramsey's (1969) RESET procedure will not be distributed as central F even when the conditional mean of y has been correctly specified.

Other general remarks made in the context of autocorrelation remain relevant in a discussion of heteroscedasticity. For example, reaction to a significant value of a heteroscedasticity test requires some thought because such checks can be powerful against more than one type of hetero-scedasticity as well as unconsidered alternatives such as incorrect func-tional form and omitted variables (see Pagan and Hall, 1983, p. 168).

There is, however, an important difference between constructing auto-correlation tests and deriving checks for heteroscedasticity. In the former case, there is a well-established and widely accepted class of alternatives, that is, linear ARMA models.[20] In contrast, there is often little information about the appropriate form of the alternative when testing the assumption of homoscedastic disturbances, and many different schemes and associated tests have been considered in the literature (see Judge et al., 1980, chap. 4).

Fortunately, considerable unification is possible, and many of the tests proposed can be interpreted as being derived for the following general alternative

$$y_t = x_t'\beta + u_t, \quad u_t \, \text{NID}(0, \sigma_t^2) \tag{5.1}$$

with

$$\sigma_t^2 = \sigma^2 h(z_t'\alpha), \tag{5.2}$$

where x_t and z_t are k-component and g-component non-stochastic vectors, and β and α are the corresponding unknown parameter vectors.[21] The function $h(\cdot)$ is assumed to be continuous and to possess at least first and

[20] Some work has also been done on non-linear time-series models; see Pagan and Hall (1983, p. 172).

[21] Nicholls and Pagan (1983) have shown that it is possible to extend the analysis to the case in which lagged values of y_t appear in x_t and z_t.

second derivatives, with its argument being a linear combination of exogenous variables which can be related to the regressors of x_t. The function $h(\cdot)$ will be specified so that $h(0) = 1$. Consequently the u_t are homoscedastic on $H_0: \alpha_1 = \cdots = \alpha_g = 0$ and are heteroscedastic if α contains non-zero elements. Finally, in order to ensure that the information matrix is non-singular under H_0, it is necessary to assume that the first derivative of $h(\cdot)$ is non-zero at the origin, that is, $h'(0) \neq 0$.

The variance model of (5.2) is sufficiently general to include most of the schemes considered in the literature. For example, if m denotes a prespecified integer, then the function

$$h(z_t'\alpha) = (1 + z_t'\alpha)^m \tag{5.3}$$

includes the models of Rutemiller and Bowers (1968) with $m = 2$, Glejser (1969) with $m = 1$ or 2, Goldfeld and Quandt (1972) and Amemiya (1977) with $m = 1$. Alternatively, the multiplicative (log-linear) heteroscedasticity model examined by Harvey (1976) can be represented by

$$h(z_t'\alpha) = \exp(z_t'\alpha), \tag{5.4}$$

which encompasses the schemes of Geary (1966), Lancaster (1968) and Park (1966).

In order to illustrate how the variables of z_t might be related to the regressors of x_t, suppose that $g = 1$ and $z_t = \ln(x_{ti})$, some i, then (5.2) and (5.4) yield $\sigma_t^2 = \sigma^2 x_{it}^\delta$ ($\delta = \alpha_1$) which is the familiar model discussed, for example, by Kmenta (1971, pp. 263–4). Also note that the additive model obtained by setting $m = 1$ in (5.3) includes many random coefficient specifications if the elements of z_t are taken as suitable functions of those of x_t. Suppose, for example, that

$$y_t = x_t'\beta_t, \ \beta_t \text{NID}(\beta, \Delta), \ t = 1, \ldots, n, \tag{5.5}$$

with x_t having as its first element an intercept dummy and Δ being a general symmetric positive-definite variance–covariance matrix.[22] (If x_t does not contain an intercept dummy, then the argument can be easily modified by adding a homoscedastic disturbance to the regression equation.) Now

$$\beta_t = \{\beta + (\beta_t - \beta)\}$$

and the vectors $(\beta_t - \beta)$ are NID$(0, \Delta)$, $t = 1, \ldots, n$. It follows that the random coefficient model of (5.5) can be expressed as

$$y_t = x_t'\beta + u_t, \ t = 1, \ldots, n,$$

---

[22] Hildreth and Houck (1968), following Rubin (1953), restricted Δ to be diagonal, but this constraint has been relaxed in subsequent work, e.g., see Swamy (1970).

where the disturbances $u_t = x_t'(\beta_t - \beta)$ are independent zero mean normal variates whose variances are given by

$$\sigma_t^2 = x_t'\Delta x_t = \sigma^2(1 + z_t'\alpha), \qquad (5.6)$$

where σ^2 denotes Δ_{11} and the vector z_t consists of the distinct elements of the k by k matrix $x_t x_t'$, excluding the $(1,1)$ element which equals unity.

Despite the generality of the alternative of (5.2), some familiar variance models cannot be obtained as special cases. One such model is $\sigma_t^2 = \sigma^2 Z_t$, for some scalar Z_t. This model does not allow the homoscedasticity assumption to be tested by standard methods because there is no parametric restriction which yields the null hypothesis $\sigma_t^2 = \sigma^2 \; \forall t$. Conventional tests will be available if the alternative is respecified as $\sigma_t^2 = \sigma^2 Z_t^\delta$ since homoscedasticity is then implied by $\delta = 0$. Another variance specification not included in (5.2) is

$$\sigma_t^2 = \sigma^2[E(y_t)]^2 = \sigma^2(x_t'\beta)^2 \qquad (5.7)$$

(see Theil, 1951; Amemiya, 1973). Bickel (1978) suggests that in such cases it is reasonable to use either

$$\sigma_t^2 = \sigma^2[1 + \alpha_1(x_t'\beta)]^2 \qquad (5.8)$$

or

$$\sigma_t^2 = \sigma^2 \exp[\alpha_1(x_t'\beta)] \qquad (5.9)$$

as an approximation and to test $H_0: \alpha_1 = 0$.[23]

4.5.1 Likelihood ratio, Wald and Lagrange multiplier tests for the alternative $\sigma_t^2 = \sigma^2 h(z_t'\alpha)$

When equation (5.2) characterizes the alternative hypothesis, unrestricted maximum likelihood estimation of the model's parameters – that is, the elements of α and β – requires the solution of a non-linear optimization problem. Thus, as is often the case, the LR and W tests of $\alpha = 0$ are unattractive relative to LM procedures. There are also special difficulties for LR and W in the case of the additive heteroscedasticity alternative $\sigma_t^2 = \sigma^2(1 + z_t'\alpha)$. As stressed by Amemiya (1977) in his discussion of regularity conditions, it is necessary to restrict z_t and α to satisfy $(1 + z_t'\alpha) > 0$ for all t. Further, if this heteroscedasticity specification has been derived from an underlying random coefficient model, then the

---

[23] It will be seen that (5.8) and (5.9) represent LEAs for $H_0: \alpha_1 = 0$ so that the asymptotic distribution of the test statistic under the null and local alternatives is the same whichever of these specifications is employed.

interpretation of the coefficients α_i in terms of variances and covariances will lead to other inequalities. Imposing such inequality constraints makes estimation even more complicated and prevents the use of the standard forms of the LR and W tests.[24] If, on the other hand, an attempt is made to obtain the MLEs of α and β without imposing inequality constraints, then difficulties may be found with the likelihood being unbounded. To see how such difficulties can arise, consider the contribution of the tth observation to the log-likelihood which is, apart from an irrelevant constant,

$$-\tfrac{1}{2} \ln \sigma_t^2 - (y_t - x_t'\beta)^2/2\sigma_t^2, \quad \sigma_t^2 = \sigma^2(1 + z_t'\alpha). \tag{5.10}$$

Let b^* be a value of β such that $y_t - x_t'b^* = 0$ and a^* be a value of α such that $(1 + z_t'a^*) = 0$ and $(1 + z_s'a^*) > 0$, $s \neq t$. When $\beta = b^*$, the likelihood will increase without bound as $\alpha \to a^*$. Although for sufficiently large n, the normal equations will yield a consistent asymptotically normally distributed estimator, Monte Carlo evidence reported by Breusch (1978b) indicates that severe difficulties can occur in finite samples even when the true parameter values are used to provide the starting point for maximum likelihood estimation.

The unrestricted estimation of the multiplicative heteroscedasticity model is free of such problems, but the LR and W tests have higher computational costs than the LM procedure and do not appear to have superior small sample performance (see Bera and Mackenzie, 1986). We shall therefore concentrate on the application of the LM principle and the associated concept of LEAs.

In order to derive results for LEAs which are similar to those obtained in the discussion of autocorrelation tests, consider the deflated disturbance

$$\varepsilon_t(\alpha, \beta) = [h(z_t'\alpha)]^{-\frac{1}{2}} u_t(\beta) \sim N(0, \sigma^2), \tag{5.11}$$

where $u_t(\beta) = y_t - x_t'\beta$. Linearization of $\varepsilon_t(\alpha, \beta)$ about $\alpha = 0$ yields the result that a LEA to (5.2) is represented by

$$\varepsilon_t^*(\alpha, \beta) = \varepsilon_t(0, \beta) - \tfrac{1}{2}h'(0)u_t(\beta)z_t'\alpha$$
$$= [1 - \tfrac{1}{2}h'(0)z_t'\alpha]u_t(\beta). \tag{5.12}$$

But for any specified function $h(\cdot)$ the term $-\tfrac{1}{2}h'(0)$ is a known non-zero constant and, since we are only interested in testing $H_0: \alpha = 0$, nothing of importance is altered by redefining $\varepsilon_t^*(\alpha, \beta)$ as

$$\varepsilon_t^*(\alpha, \beta) = [1 + z_t'\alpha]u_t(\beta). \tag{5.13}$$

---

[24] The standard LM procedure is unaffected because it uses only the estimates of the null model; see Section 3.5 above for a general discussion and the specific comments provided by Pagan and Hall (1983, p. 180).

Thus, given the choice of the vector z_t, the form of $h(\cdot)$ is irrelevant, and, whatever its specification, the resulting LR, W and LM tests of $\alpha = 0$ will be asymptotically equivalent to those derived for the alternative underlying (5.13). Further, the LM statistics for the simple additive model and the general alternative of (5.11) will be equal if a common estimate of the information matrix is employed.

As before, such results can be linked to the notion of a sequence of local alternatives. Consider for example the case in which z_t is a scalar and

$$\sigma_t^2 = \sigma^2 \exp(z_t \alpha)$$
$$= \sigma^2[1 + z_t\alpha + R]. \tag{5.14}$$

Under a sequence of local alternatives, $H_n : \alpha = n^{-\frac{1}{2}}\delta, \delta^2 < \infty$, the terms in R of (5.14) have coefficients which are at most $O(n^{-1})$ and so can be ignored.

The form of $h(\cdot)$, however, may have an indirect effect on test statistics via the choice of the vector z_t. If the alternative hypothesis is specified using

$$h(z_t'\alpha) = (1 + z_t'\alpha)^m, \ m \text{ a specified integer,}$$

then the *levels* of some regressors might be included in z_t, but if multiplicative heteroscedasticity is entertained with

$$h(z_t'\alpha) = \exp(z_t'\alpha),$$

then z_t might contain observations on the *logarithms* of some regressors. Since the power of a test is not independent of the specification of z_t, the choice between the general models of (5.3) and (5.4) may have important consequences for the detection of heteroscedasticity. We shall therefore first consider the implementation of LM tests, given z_t, and then discuss the choice of z_t. The discussion of the selection of the variables of z_t will include an examination of the relationships between LM checks and other tests for heteroscedasticity.

4.5.2 *The implementation of Lagrange multiplier tests*

As the specification of $h(\cdot)$ in (5.2) is irrelevant provided $h(0) = 1$ and $h'(0) \neq 0$, any convenient form can be adopted in order to derive the LM test of $\alpha = 0$. Suppose that Harvey's (1976) multiplicative heteroscedasticity scheme is used so that the log-likelihood function is

$$\ln L(\alpha, \beta, \sigma^2) = \text{cnst} - \tfrac{1}{2}\Sigma_1^n \ln(\sigma_t^2) - \tfrac{1}{2}\Sigma_1^n(y_t - x_t'\beta)^2/\sigma_t^2,$$

where $\sigma_t^2 = \sigma^2 \exp(z_t'\alpha)$ so that $\ln(\sigma_t^2) = \ln(\sigma^2) + z_t'\alpha$. The vector of multipliers appropriate for testing $H_0: \alpha = 0$ is $\partial \ln L(\alpha, \beta, \sigma^2)/\partial \alpha$ evaluated at $\alpha = \hat{\alpha} = 0$, $\beta = \hat{\beta}$ (the OLS estimate) and $\sigma^2 = \hat{\sigma}^2 = n^{-1}\Sigma_1^n \hat{u}_t^2$. This subvector of the score is given by

$$\partial \ln L(\hat{\alpha}, \hat{\beta}, \hat{\sigma}^2)/\partial \alpha = \tfrac{1}{2}\Sigma_1^n z_t(\hat{u}_t^2/\hat{\sigma}^2 - 1). \tag{5.15}$$

If r denotes the n-dimensional vector with typical element $r_t = (\hat{u}_t^2/\hat{\sigma}^2 - 1)$, then an alternative expression for the vector of (5.15) is $\tfrac{1}{2}Z'r$, where Z is the n by g matrix whose tth row is z_t. It will be useful to note that if $\iota' = (1, \ldots, 1)$, then $\iota' r = 0$ or equivalently $M_\iota r = r$, where $M_\iota = I - \iota\iota'/(\iota'\iota)$ is a projection matrix which removes the sample average of the elements of an n-dimensional vector.

Under the null hypothesis of homoscedasticity, the information matrix is

$$\begin{bmatrix} \sigma^{-2}(X'X) & 0 & 0 \\ 0 & \tfrac{1}{2}(Z'Z) & \tfrac{1}{2}\sigma^{-2}Z'\iota \\ 0 & \tfrac{1}{2}\sigma^{-2}\iota'Z & \tfrac{1}{2}\dfrac{n}{\sigma^4} \end{bmatrix},$$

so that, using $n = \iota'\iota$, the matrix required to construct the quadratic form of the score/LM test is

$$2[(Z'Z) - Z'\iota\iota'Z/\iota'\iota]^{-1} = 2(Z'M_\iota Z)^{-1}. \tag{5.16}$$

The test statistic for $H_0: \alpha = 0$ is, therefore, given by

$$s = \tfrac{1}{2}r'Z(Z'M_\iota Z)^{-1}Z'r$$
$$= \tfrac{1}{2}r'M_\iota Z(Z'M_\iota Z)^{-1}Z'M_\iota r$$
$$= \tfrac{1}{2}r'W(W'W)^{-1}W'r, \tag{5.17}$$

where $W = (\iota, Z)$. Thus the LM test for $\alpha = 0$ in the general alternative (5.2) can be calculated as one-half of the explained sum of squares from the OLS regression of $r = \{\hat{u}_t^2/\hat{\sigma}^2 - 1\}$ on (ι, Z).[25] Sample values of this test statistic should be compared to the prespecified critical value in the right-hand tail of the $\chi^2(g)$ distribution. The statistic of (5.17) was derived by Breusch and Pagan (1979) for unspecified $h(\cdot)$ and by Godfrey (1978b) for the specific case $h(\cdot) = \exp(\cdot)$.

There is some Monte Carlo evidence available on the behaviour of LM tests for heteroscedasticity. Godfrey (1978b) and Bera and McKenzie (1986) find that the estimated finite sample significance levels of the test

---

[25] An equivalent test can be obtained by regressing the squared residuals $\hat{u}_t^2$ on $(1, z_t)$, $t = 1, \ldots, n$, and then dividing the variance of the predicted values by $2\hat{\sigma}^4/n$; see Breusch and Pagan (1979).

based upon s of (5.17) tend to be a little smaller than those predicted by asymptotic theory; for example, 8 per cent at $n = 40$ as opposed to a nominal value of 10 per cent. Bera and McKenzie (1986) also report that the score test seems to be as powerful as the LR tests for the additive and multiplicative heteroscedasticity alternatives with the same choice of z_t.[26] This finding corroborates the results obtained by Godfrey (1981) on tests for autocorrelation and functional form. Thus little seems to be gained, as far as power of tests is concerned, by knowing which of a set of LEAs actually generated the data.

Despite this somewhat encouraging Monte Carlo evidence, there are arguments against the use of the statistic of (5.17). Koenker (1981) points out that its validity is dependent upon the normality assumption, or more precisely the assumption that $\mathrm{Var}(u_t^2/\sigma^2) = 2$ on $H_0: \sigma_t^2 = \sigma^2 \ \forall t$. This problem has also been noted by Bickel (1978), who remarks that for long-tailed non-normal distributions the actual asymptotic significance level will exceed the value based upon the normality assumption. Koenker (1981) suggests that a more robust form of the heteroscedasticity test can be obtained by using a direct estimate of the null variance of the variates u_t^2/σ^2, namely, $n^{-1}\Sigma_1^n(\hat{u}_t^2 - \hat{\sigma}^2)^2/\hat{\sigma}^4$. This suggestion leads to the 'studentized' statistic

$$s_R = n\{r'W(W'W)^{-1}W'r/r'r\}, \tag{5.18}$$

which is n times the uncentred R^2 from the regression of r on W. This form of the LM test was also proposed by Godfrey (1978e), while Bickel (1978) suggests the asymptotically equivalent variant $n^{-1}(n - k)s_R$. An omitted variables version of the studentized test could be obtained by calculating the asymptotically valid F test of $H_0: \alpha = 0$ in the regression model

$$\hat{u}_t^2 = a_0 + z_t'\alpha + error, \tag{5.19}$$

where a_0 denotes an intercept.[27]

It is also possible to check for heteroscedasticity by computing the F test for the relevance of a set of variables added to the original regression model (5.1). Godfrey and Wickens (1982) use LEA methods to show that if the alternative model

$$y_t = x_t'\beta + \Sigma_1^q\alpha_i\{(z_{ti} - \bar{z}_i)\hat{u}_t\} + v_t \tag{5.20}$$

[26] The LR tests have excessively high empirical significance levels and so Bera and McKenzie (1986) compare powers after making size corrections.

[27] Glejser (1969) suggests a test based upon a similar regression in which the dependent variable is $|\hat{u}_t|$, rather than $\hat{u}_t^2$. This test can be interpreted as a LM test when the u_t have a double exponential distribution.

is estimated, then dividing the F statistic for testing $\alpha_1 = \alpha_2 = \cdots = \alpha_g = 0$ by 2 yields a test which is asymptotically equivalent to s of (5.17). (A more robust procedure could presumably be obtained by dividing the F value by $n^{-1}r'r$, rather than by 2.) The computational device represented by (5.20) is, however, somewhat cumbersome and lacking in intuitive appeal. Moreover, equation (3.12) of Chapter 3 can be used to show that, as a result of asymptotic independence under the hypothesis of correct specification, the heteroscedasticity test can usually be calculated separately using (5.18), for example, and then can simply be added to a statistic designed to test against a set of other misspecifications.[28]

Suppose, for example, that a researcher wishes to test the null specification that the regression disturbances u_t are $NID(0, \sigma^2)$ against the alternative

$$u_t = \rho u_{t-1} + \varepsilon_t, \quad \varepsilon_t NID(0, \sigma_t^2)$$

with $Var(\varepsilon_t) = \sigma_t^2 = \sigma^2 h(z_t'\alpha)$. The results on LEAs imply that a test can be based upon testing $H_0^*: \rho = \alpha_1 = \cdots = \alpha_g = 0$ in the augmented regression

$$y_t = x_t'\beta + \rho\hat{u}_{t-1} + \Sigma_1^g \alpha_i(z_{ti} - \bar{z}_i)\hat{u}_t + v_t. \tag{5.21}$$

Further, the results on the asymptotic independence of tests of $\alpha_1 = \cdots = \alpha_g = 0$ and $\rho = 0$ justify adding the s_R statistic of (5.18) to t_ρ^2, the square of the t ratio of $\hat{u}_{t-1}$ arising from the OLS estimation of

$$y_t = x_t'\beta + \rho\hat{u}_{t-1} + e_t,$$

and treating the variate $(s_R + t_\rho^2)$ as being asymptotically distributed as $\chi^2(g + 1)$ under the null hypothesis.[29]

4.5.3   The choice of z_t, and the relationships between Lagrange multiplier tests and other procedures

The choice of variables to appear in z_t will sometimes be dictated by the general model being entertained as the alternative. In the case of the random coefficient model of (5.5), the z_t will consist of the distinct elements

---

[28] Pagan and Hall (1983) examine this issue and argue that the heteroscedasticity test will be asymptotically independent of several standard diagnostic checks when the null model is correct, provided the disturbances are symmetrically distributed; see Table I of Pagan and Hall (1983, p. 202).

[29] A more detailed discussion of testing for autocorrelated heteroscedastic errors is provided by Godfrey and Wickens (1982, pp. 88–90). It may be useful to test against such a combination of departures from the null if it is suspected that the regression parameters are random with serially correlated components; see Pagan and Hall (1983, p. 180).

of $x_t x_t'$ which remain after deletion of the term corresponding to the square of the intercept dummy. It is interesting that the vector z_t appropriate for this fairly specific alternative is also proposed by White (1980b) as the basis of a pure significance test of the homoscedasticity assumption.[30]

It is, however, not necessary to restrict the variables of z_t to be functions of the regressors of x_t. Indeed, the links between several established tests for heteroscedasticity and the LM principle can be demonstrated by restricting the z_t vector to contain a time trend and/or certain dummy variables.

One very common approach to detecting heteroscedasticity is based upon the assumption that, under the alternative, there is a known ordering of the data such that $\sigma_1^2 \leqslant \sigma_2^2 \cdots \leqslant \sigma_n^2$ with at least one strong inequality. Given this assumption, a natural strategy in the context of LM tests is to order the data and then to use the scalar $z_t = t$.[31] Indeed, this choice of z_t would correspond to a general procedure advocated by Szroeter (1978).

However, the use of trending test variables is not widespread, and the data are more frequently split into groups after ordering by increasing variance. This grouping of observations is appropriate when disturbance variances are constant within a group, but change between groups. The obvious LM strategy is, therefore, to employ a suitable set of dummy variables to construct the vector z_t.

In order to illustrate the relationships between tests based upon grouping and LM procedures, consider the simple case in which the data are put into two groups of n_1 and n_2 observations, $n_1 + n_2 = n$. The corresponding alternative hypothesis is then

$$\sigma_t^2 = \sigma_1^2 + \alpha z_t, \tag{5.22}$$

where

$z_t = 0$ for observations in the first group

$\quad = 1$ for observations in the second group.

It will be useful to denote $(\sigma_1^2 + \alpha)$ by σ_2^2.

The LM test can then be calculated from the regression of the squared OLS residual $\hat{u}_t^2$ on z_t of (5.22) and an intercept dummy, that is, from OLS estimation of

$$\hat{u}_t^2 = \sigma_1^2 + \alpha z_t + e_t. \tag{5.23}$$

---

[30] White (1980b) notes the interpretation of his test as a LM procedure, but does not discuss the corresponding set of alternative hypotheses; also see Waldman (1983).

[31] Strictly speaking, our assumptions on asymptotic orders of magnitude require the use of $z_t = n^{-1}t$, but such scaling is irrelevant.

The OLS estimate of α from (5.23) is $(\hat{\sigma}_2^2 - \hat{\sigma}_1^2)$, where $\hat{\sigma}_i^2$ denotes the average of the squared residuals $\hat{u}_t^2$ in the ith group, $i = 1, 2$. It follows that the LM procedure can be viewed as a Wald-type test based upon the difference between estimators of σ_1^2 and σ_2^2. Moreover, $\hat{\sigma}_1^2$ and $\hat{\sigma}_2^2$ maximize the likelihood for the model of the alternative hypothesis, conditional upon $\beta = \hat{\beta}$, so that this LM test is what Durbin (1970) terms a naive test. The block diagonality of the information matrix ensures that in this case the naive test is asymptotically equivalent to the W test derived from the unconditional maximum likelihood estimates of σ_1^2 and σ_2^2. It also ensures that a LR-type statistic calculated using $\hat{\sigma}_1^2$, $\hat{\sigma}_2^2$ and $\hat{\sigma}^2$ is asymptotically equivalent to the true LR criterion. The pseudo-LR statistic formed from $\hat{\sigma}_1^2$, $\hat{\sigma}_2^2$ and $\hat{\sigma}^2$ is in fact the Ramsey and Gilbert (1972) variant of Ramsey's (1969) BAMSET procedure.[32] These results are easily generalized to the case in which the data are divided into several groups.

The LM test of the significance of $\hat{\alpha} = (\hat{\sigma}_2^2 - \hat{\sigma}_1^2)$ from (5.23) is clearly asymptotically equivalent to one derived by considering $\hat{\sigma}_2^2/\hat{\sigma}_1^2$, and the use of a ratio of variance estimates is, at first sight, reminiscent of the familiar Goldfeld–Quandt (1965) test. There are, however, important distinguishing features of the Goldfeld–Quandt procedure:

(i)   The central set of c observations is omitted after ordering by increasing variance under the alternative.

(ii) Variance estimates, say s_1^2 and s_2^2, are calculated by running two separate regressions on the first $(n - c)/2$ and last $(n - c)/2$ of the remaining observations, and not from the residuals $\hat{u}_t$ which are associated with OLS estimation using the full data set.[33]

The Goldfeld–Quandt statistic s_2^2/s_1^2 is distributed as central $F(r, r)$, $r = (n - c)/2 - k$, if the errors are homoscedastic, with significantly large values indicating that the null hypothesis is inconsistent with the sample data.[34]

The implication of (i) is that, strictly speaking, an insignificant value of s_2^2/s_1^2 cannot be taken as evidence that the hypothesis $\{\sigma_t^2 = \sigma^2, \forall t\}$ is consistent with the data because the variances of the c central disturbances

---

[32] This equivalence holds provided that the same denominators are used when estimating variances. Ramsey (1969) follows Bartlett (1937) and uses degrees-of-freedom adjustments, rather than simply dividing by the relevant sample size.

[33] Clearly c must satisfy $(n - c)/2 > k$; see Goldfeld and Quandt (1965, 1972) for comments on the choice of c.

[34] Note that by running separate regressions, Goldfeld and Quandt are able to obtain an exact test. For alternative approaches to deriving exact tests, see Harvey and Phillips (1974) and Theil (1971).

have not been considered. (The practical relevance of this point should be limited, provided the ordering of the observations is more or less correct.) The use of the separate regressions described in (ii) implies that the Goldfeld–Quandt procedure does not require the constancy of the regression parameters under the null hypothesis of homoscedasticity and so it is completely robust to the misspecification which occurs when the regression parameters for the last $(n - c)/2$ observations do not equal those for other observations.

It is possible to obtain an LM statistic which corresponds to the Goldfeld–Quandt test, but this requires respecifying the regression model as

$$
y = \begin{bmatrix} X_1 & 0 & 0 \\ 0 & I_c & 0 \\ 0 & 0 & X_2 \end{bmatrix} \begin{bmatrix} \gamma_1 \\ \gamma_2 \\ \gamma_3 \end{bmatrix} + u, \tag{5.24}
$$

where X_1 and X_2 contain the first and last $(n - c)/2$ observations, respectively, and I_c is the c by c identity matrix. (The justification for using the regressor matrix of (5.24) to take into account features (i) and (ii) of the Goldfeld–Quandt procedure is provided in the next section, which is devoted to a discussion of testing parameter constancy.)

Finally, some researchers have suggested that z_t contain variables available as by-products from the estimation of the regression model (5.1). As mentioned earlier, Anscombe (1961) and Bickel (1978) consider the use of the OLS predicted values $\hat{y}_t = x_t'\hat{\beta}$, while Engle (1982b) proposes a test for autoregressive conditional heteroscedasticity (ARCH) which uses lagged values of $\hat{u}_t^2$ as the elements of z_t. Engle's ARCH model has proved useful in the analysis of economic time series (Engle and Kraft, 1983) and allows for conditional heteroscedasticity of the form

$$
\sigma_t^2 = \sigma^2 + \Sigma_1^q \alpha_i u_{t-i}^2.
$$

Estimation and testing for the ARCH specification are discussed by Engle (1982b). An LM test of $H_0: \alpha_1 = \cdots = \alpha_g = 0$ can be obtained by regressing $\hat{u}_t^2$ on $\hat{u}_{t-1}^2, \ldots, \hat{u}_{t-g}^2$ and an intercept term, and treating n times the R^2 for this regression as a $\chi^2(g)$ variate under H_0. Engle, Hendry and Trumble (1985) investigate the small sample behaviour of such a test using Monte Carlo methods and obtain mixed results.

4.5.4 *Heteroscedasticity consistent variance–covariance matrices*

As has been stressed above, there is often some uncertainty about the likely form of heteroscedasticity. Moreover, tests designed to have good power against a particular alternative may be quite sensitive to other types of departure from the null hypothesis of homoscedasticity. Accordingly, reacting to a significant value of a test statistic by re-estimation allowing for one of the LEAs for which the test is asymptotically optimal is not a strategy which can be strongly recommended. Choice of the wrong variance model will in general lead to inconsistent estimates of standard errors and invalidate inference.[35] The results of Eicker (1967), Fuller (1975) and White (1980b) may therefore be attractive since they offer the opportunity to carry out asymptotically valid inference using OLS estimates in the presence of unknown forms of heteroscedasticity.

Using standard notation, the OLS parameter estimator is

$$\hat{\beta} = (X'X)^{-1}X'y,$$

which has variance–covariance matrix

$$V = (X'X)^{-1}X'\Omega X(X'X)^{-1}, \tag{5.25}$$

Ω being the n by n diagonal matrix with non-zero elements $\omega_{tt} = \sigma_t^2$, $t = 1$, ..., n. The heteroscedasticity consistent estimate of V is

$$\hat{V} = (X'X)^{-1}X'WX(X'X)^{-1}, \tag{5.26}$$

where W is the n by n diagonal matrix with the squared OLS residuals $\hat{u}_t^2$ on the leading diagonal. Under quite general conditions, plim $\hat{V}V^{-1} = I$ whatever the form of the heteroscedasticity.

Heteroscedasticity robust tests of hypotheses concerning the elements of β can be based upon $\hat{V}$ of (5.26) and will be asymptotically valid. Further, nothing of importance is altered if X is reinterpreted to consist of the regressors of the original model and a specified set of test variables, provided that all variables in X satisfy appropriate conditions (for sets of regularity conditions covering time-series and cross-section applications see Hsieh, 1983; Nicholls and Pagan, 1983; White, 1980b). Consequently there is some scope for carrying out heteroscedasticity robust diagnostic checks of the omitted variables variety (see Pagan and Hall's, 1983, discussion and the comments by Domowitz, 1983).

In view of the potential usefulness of the heteroscedasticity-consistent variance–covariance matrix estimate of (5.26), it is worth describing how it can be computed using standard estimation programmes. Messer and White (1984) provide an IV interpretation of the OLS estimate $\hat{\beta}$ which leads to the calculation of the matrix $\hat{V}$. For any non-singular symmetric n by n matrix D, the following holds:

$$\hat{\beta} = [(DX)'D^{-1}X]^{-1}(DX)'D^{-1}y$$

$$= (Z^{*\prime}X^*)^{-1}Z^{*\prime}y^*, \tag{5.27}$$

---

[35] It is possible to carry out a test of the adequacy of an assumed model of heteroscedasticity; see Godfrey (1979b).

where $Z^* = DX$, $X^* = D^{-1}X$ and $y^* = D^{-1}y$. Equation (5.27) presents $\hat{\beta}$ in the form of an IV estimate for a transformed model, and the associated asymptotic variance–covariance matrix would be estimated by

$$V_{IV} = s_*^2(Z^{*'}X^*)^{-1}(Z^{*'}Z^*)(X^{*'}Z^*)^{-1}$$

$$= s_*^2(X'X)^{-1}(X'D^2X)(X'X)^{-1}, \tag{5.28}$$

where

$$s_*^2 = n^{-1}[y^* - X^*\hat{\beta}]'[y^* - X^*\hat{\beta}]$$

$$= n^{-1}\hat{u}'D^{-2}\hat{u}. \tag{5.29}$$

Putting D equal to the diagonal matrix with the OLS residuals $\hat{u}_t$ on its leading diagonal yields $s_*^2 = 1$, $D^2 = W$ of (5.26) and so $V_{IV} = \hat{V}$.[36] Thus, if the model

$$y_t = x_t'\beta + u_t, t = 1, 2, \ldots, n$$

is estimated by OLS to obtain $\hat{\beta}$ and $\hat{u}_t$, $t = 1, \ldots, n$, and we define

$$y_t^* = y_t/\hat{u}_t$$

$$x_t^{*'} = (x_{t1}/\hat{u}_t, \ldots, x_{tk}/\hat{u}_t)$$

$$z_t^{*'} = (x_{t1}\hat{u}_t, \ldots, x_{tk}\hat{u}_t),$$

then estimating the transformed relationship

$$y_t^* = x_t^{*'}\beta + u_t^*, t = 1, \ldots, n$$

by IV with the variables of z_t^* used as instruments yields heteroscedasticity consistent standard errors as a by-product of routine calculations.

Some small-scale Monte Carlo studies of the behaviour of heteroscedasticity-consistent variance–covariance matrix estimates have been reported, but their results are rather mixed. Hsieh (1983) and Nicholls and Pagan (1983) consider the simple dynamic regression equation

$$y_t = \beta y_{t-1} + u_t$$

and obtain encouraging results. Cragg (1983) uses the model

$$y_t = \beta_1 + \beta_2 x_t + u_t,$$

where the n values of x_t are independent drawings from a log normal distribution which are held fixed for all replications and reports that $\hat{V}$

---

[36] Some programmes calculate s_*^2 by dividing the sum of squared residuals by $(n - k)$, rather than by n, but this is asymptotically unimportant. Also if $\hat{u}_t = 0$, then the corresponding observation can be dropped, or the residual replaced by some small quantity; see Messer and White (1984, p. 183).

exhibits a serious downward bias.[37] The small sample performance of t ratios derived from alternative consistent estimators of V has been studied by MacKinnon and White (1985). On the basis of their sampling experiments, MacKinnon and White conclude that an estimator of V based upon the jackknife method performs best. This conclusion has been examined in a paper by Chesher and Austin (1987), who stress the importance of the regression design. Chesher and Austin find that all variants of the heteroscedasticity robust test perform well if a single leverage point is omitted from the data set used by MacKinnon and White (see Belsley, Kuh and Welsh, 1980, for a discussion of leverage and least-squares regression).

4.6   Testing the constancy of the regression parameters

It has already been noted that there is a close connection between models in which the regression parameters vary stochastically and those in which these parameters are constant but the disturbances are heteroscedastic. In particular, when the random coefficient model is that the parameter vectors β_t are independently distributed with common mean vector β and covariance matrix Δ, the appropriate test of the null hypothesis of parameter constancy is simply the heteroscedasticity test of White (1980b).[38] The analysis of random coefficient models can be extended by allowing the stochastic components to be serially correlated.[39] Problems do arise, however, if a random walk-type model

$$\beta_t = \beta_{t-1} + v_t, \ v_t \text{NID}(0, \Lambda)$$

is employed, and Tanaka (1983) shows that the LM test of $\Lambda = 0$ is not asymptotically distributed as χ^2 in the usual way (also see Garbade, 1977, who examines the properties of the LR test in this model).

Random coefficient models will not always be the most appropriate alternative, and a priori information may suggest that the null hypothesis be tested against the alternative that the regression parameters are influenced by economic forces. For example, Trivedi (1970) entertains the hypothesis that lag coefficients depend upon variables reflecting the state

[37] Cragg (1983) also proposes a technique for obtaining estimators which are asymptotically more efficient than OLS in the presence of hetero-scedasticity of unknown form.

[38] If some parameters are assumed to be fixed, then the corresponding test variables can be omitted.

[39] See Pagan and Hall (1983, pp. 180–4), who suggest that certain heteroscedasticity and autocorrelation tests might be usefully combined for such alternatives. See also Watson and Engle (1985).

of the queue when examining the relationship between the order–delivery lag and the rate of capacity utilisation. One general form for this sort of varying parameter model is

$$\beta_t = \beta + A z_t, \tag{6.1}$$

where z_t denotes a vector of variables and some of the elements of A can be specified as zero. The general alternative to be employed in a significance test is then

$$
\begin{aligned}
y_t &= x_t' \beta_t + u_t \\
&= x_t' \beta + x_t' A z_t + u_t \\
&= x_t' \beta + w_t' \alpha + u_t, \tag{6.2}
\end{aligned}
$$

where α contains the unrestricted elements of A and w_t contains the corresponding elements of $z_t x_t'$. Equation (6.2) indicates that the consistency of the hypothesis $\beta_t = \beta$ with the sample data can be investigated by testing the joint significance of the additional regressors appearing in w_t, so that a simple OV procedure is again available for testing the null model.

Perhaps the most commonly employed variant of (6.1) is the model in which z_t consists of a single dummy variable defined by

$$
\begin{aligned}
z_t &= 0, \, t = 1, \ldots, n_1 \\
&= 1, \, t = n_1 + 1, \ldots, n, \tag{6.3}
\end{aligned}
$$

where n_1 is a prespecified integer. Thus a single change in the regression parameter vector divides the sample into two disjoint sub-periods of sizes n_1 and $n_2 = n - n_1$.[40] This is the specification adopted by Chow (1960) in his seminal article on testing for structural change.

When applying Chow's results, it is essential that at least one of the sub-periods should contain sufficient observations to permit the estimation of the parameters of the null model. Without loss of generality, it will be assumed that the first sub-period satisfies this condition with $n_1 > k$. Chow (1960) describes two procedures which have become widely used. One of these tests is appropriate when $n_2 \geqslant k$ and involves calculating separate estimates of the regression coefficients from the two sub-periods. For situations in which $n_2 < k$ and separate estimation of all the coefficients in the second sub-period is not possible, Chow (1960) develops a test by considering the prediction errors when the estimates from the first sub-sample are used to predict the last n_2 values of the dependent variable.

It is convenient to introduce some additional notation. The null model

----

[40] The analysis can be generalized to allow for several changes in coefficients; see, for example, Dufour (1982).

will be written in partitioned form as

$$\begin{bmatrix} y_1 \\ y_2 \end{bmatrix} = \begin{bmatrix} X_1 \\ X_2 \end{bmatrix} \beta + \begin{bmatrix} u_1 \\ u_2 \end{bmatrix}, \tag{6.4}$$

with, for example, y_i being n_i by 1, $i = 1, 2$. Combining (6.1) and (6.3) yields the result that the alternative corresponding to (6.2) is

$$\begin{bmatrix} y_1 \\ y_2 \end{bmatrix} = \begin{bmatrix} X_1 \\ X_2 \end{bmatrix} \beta + \begin{bmatrix} 0 \\ X_2 \end{bmatrix} \alpha + \begin{bmatrix} u_1 \\ u_2 \end{bmatrix}, \tag{6.5}$$

or equivalently

$$\begin{bmatrix} y_1 \\ y_2 \end{bmatrix} = \begin{bmatrix} X_1 & 0 \\ 0 & X_2 \end{bmatrix} \begin{bmatrix} \beta_1 \\ \beta_2 \end{bmatrix} + \begin{bmatrix} u_1 \\ u_2 \end{bmatrix}, \tag{6.6}$$

where $\beta_1 = \beta$ and $\beta_2 = \beta + \alpha$. The null hypothesis of parameter constancy can, therefore, be stated as either $\alpha = 0$ in (6.5) or $\beta_1 = \beta_2$ in (6.6).

Whichever parameterization is adopted, it is clear that the problem is to construct a test of linear restrictions in the context of least-squares estimation of a linear model. Accordingly, the analysis of Chapter 2 indicates that a comparison of the unrestricted and restricted minima of the error sum of squares function is central to the derivation of an appropriate test statistic.

Consider first the case in which $n_1 > k$, $n_2 \geqslant k$; the alternative model is written as (6.6), and the null hypothesis is $\beta_1 = \beta_2$. Since

$$u'u = u'_1 u_1 + u'_2 u_2,$$

the error sum of squares function is

$$S(\beta_1, \beta_2) = (y_1 - X_1 \beta_1)'(y_1 - X_1 \beta_1) + (y_2 - X_2 \beta_2)'(y_2 - X_2 \beta_2). \tag{6.7}$$

The unrestricted minimum of $S(\beta_1, \beta_2)$ is clearly obtained by setting $\beta_i = \tilde{\beta}_i$, where

$$\tilde{\beta}_i = (X'_i X_i)^{-1} X'_i y_i \tag{6.8}$$

is the OLS parameter estimator from the regression using only the observations of the ith sub-period ($i = 1, 2$). The residual vectors and variance estimates associated with the unrestricted minimizers of $S(\beta_1, \beta_2)$ will be denoted by $\tilde{u}_i = y_i - X_i \tilde{\beta}_i$ and $\tilde{\sigma}_i^2 = n_i^{-1}(\tilde{u}'_i \tilde{u}_i)$, $i = 1, 2$.[41]

Minimizing $S(\beta_1, \beta_2)$ subject to the restriction $\beta_1 = \beta_2$ yields the constrained minimizers

$$\hat{\beta}_1 = \hat{\beta}_2 = \hat{\beta} = (X'X)^{-1} X'y, \tag{6.9}$$

[41] If $n_2 = k$, then $\tilde{u}_2 = 0$ and $\tilde{\sigma}_2^2 = 0$.

which is the OLS estimate based upon the entire sample, with associated residual vector and variance estimate $\hat{u} = y - X\hat{\beta}$ and $\hat{\sigma}^2 = n^{-1}\hat{u}'\hat{u}$, respectively.

The standard results described in Chapter 2 imply that a suitable test of $\beta_1 = \beta_2$ can be obtained by comparing the sample values of

$$\frac{[\hat{u}'\hat{u} - (\tilde{u}_1'\tilde{u}_1 + \tilde{u}_2'\tilde{u}_2)]}{(\tilde{u}_1'\tilde{u}_1 + \tilde{u}_2'\tilde{u}_2)} \cdot \frac{(n - 2k)}{k} \tag{6.10}$$

to a prespecified critical value in the right-hand tail of the central $F(k, n - 2k)$ distribution. The criterion of (6.10) is exactly equal to the statistic Chow proposed for this case. The corresponding LM, LR and W tests of $\beta_1 = \beta_2$ can be obtained by substituting in the formulae of Chapter 2, Section 3. For example, the LM statistic is

$$\text{LM} = n[\hat{u}'\hat{u} - (\tilde{u}_1'\tilde{u}_1 + \tilde{u}_2'\tilde{u}_2)]/\hat{u}'\hat{u}.$$

Turning to the case in which the second sub-period does not contain sufficient observations to permit the estimation of all regression parameters, that is, $n_2 < k$, it is convenient to adopt the (β, α) parameterization and to employ (6.5) as the alternative model. The restricted minimum of the error sum of squares function $S(\beta, \alpha)$ is, as before, $\hat{u}'\hat{u}$. In order to obtain the value of the unrestricted minimum, it is useful to note that

$$\min(u'u) \geqslant \min(u_1'u_1) + \min(u_2'u_2) \geqslant \min(u_1'u_1).$$

The form of the alternative model (6.5) implies that $u_1 = y_1 - X_1\beta$, so that u_1 is independent of α and $u_1'u_1$ is minimized by setting $\beta = \tilde{\beta}_1$, the OLS estimate calculated from the first n_1 observations. Next, since $k > n_2$, it will be possible to choose α so that $u_2'u_2 = 0$ when $\beta = \tilde{\beta}_1$. It follows that the unrestricted minimum of $S(\beta, \alpha)$ is $\tilde{u}_1'\tilde{u}_1$.

Some interesting insights and generalizations can be obtained by examining the conditions for an unrestricted minimum of $S(\beta, \alpha)$ in the $(n_1 > k, \ n_2 < k)$ case. Let $\tilde{\alpha}$ be a k-dimensional vector such that $y_2 - X_2\tilde{\beta}_1 - X_2\tilde{\alpha} = 0$, so that $u_2'u_2 = 0$ when $\beta = \tilde{\beta}_1$ and $\alpha = \tilde{\alpha}$. Also, let $\tilde{\delta} = X_2\tilde{\alpha}$. The first-order conditions for $\tilde{\beta}_1$ and the definition of $\tilde{\delta}$ imply that

$$X_1'y_1 - (X_1'X_1)\tilde{\beta}_1 = 0$$

$$y_2 - X_2\tilde{\beta}_1 - \tilde{\delta} = 0,$$

or equivalently

$$X'y - (X'X)\tilde{\beta}_1 - (X'W)\tilde{\delta} = 0$$

$$W'y - (W'X)\tilde{\beta}_1 - (W'W)\tilde{\delta} = 0, \tag{6.11}$$

where the n by n_2 matrix W is defined by

$$W = \begin{bmatrix} 0 \\ I_2 \end{bmatrix},$$

I_2 being the n_2 by n_2 identity matrix and 0 being the n_1 by n_2 null matrix. But the conditions of (6.11) are the normal equations for the OLS parameter estimates of the model

$$\begin{bmatrix} y_1 \\ y_2 \end{bmatrix} = \begin{bmatrix} X_1 \\ X_2 \end{bmatrix} \beta + \begin{bmatrix} 0 \\ I_2 \end{bmatrix} \delta + \begin{bmatrix} u_1 \\ u_2 \end{bmatrix},$$

or more compactly

$$y = X\beta + W\delta + u. \tag{6.12}$$

Thus the OLS estimate of δ in (6.12) equals $(y_2 - X_2\tilde{\beta}_1)$, but this is, of course, the vector of prediction errors upon which Chow's second test for structural stability is based. The joint significance of these prediction errors can, therefore, be assessed by means of a conventional F test of $\delta = 0$ in the augmented model of (6.12). This simple approach to the implementation of Chow's procedure was proposed by Salkever (1976).

The construction of the augmented model (6.12) implies that the unrestricted and restricted minima of the error sum of squares function are $\tilde{u}_1'\tilde{u}_1$ and $\hat{u}'\hat{u}$, respectively, with the corresponding degrees of freedom being $(n - k - n_2) = (n_1 - k)$ and $(n - k)$. Standard regression theory implies that, if the n_2 restrictions of $\delta = 0$ are valid, the statistic

$$F_p = \frac{(\hat{u}'\hat{u} - \tilde{u}_1'\tilde{u}_1)}{\tilde{u}_1'\tilde{u}_1} \cdot \frac{(n_1 - k)}{n_2} \tag{6.13}$$

is distributed as $F(n_2, n_1 - k)$ when the regressors are either non-stochastic or distributed independently of the disturbances. The F_p criterion of (6.13) is exactly equal to the statistic proposed by Chow.

It should be stressed that α of (6.5) is not estimable (the inequality $n_2 < k$ implies that the regressors of (6.5) are linearly dependent) and that F_p may have low power against some directions of parameter variation. The expected value of $\tilde{\delta}$ under the alternative is

$$E(y_2) - X_2 E(\tilde{\beta}_1) = X_2\alpha.$$

Consequently, as pointed out by Rea (1978), the prediction error test will not be sensitive to parameter changes such that $\alpha \neq 0$ but $X_2\alpha = 0$. The practical relevance of this point is open to question.

Salkever's interpretation of Chow's F_p test as a check of the validity of excluding the n_2 dummy variables of W from (6.12) facilitates several

interesting extensions. Nicholls and Pagan (1984) present generalizations
to cover dynamic and simultaneous equations with autocorrelated errors.
Also, since the value of F_p will not be altered by reordering and regrouping
the observations, (y_1, X_1) could be viewed as a central set of data with the
remaining n_2 values being shared between first and third sub-periods. This
rearrangement will generate Utt's (1982) 'rainbow' test.

A simpler form of the prediction error test can be obtained by noting
that if n_2 is fixed, then, as n_1 tends to infinity, the sampling variability
arising from the estimation of β is negligible. Consequently, on the null
hypothesis, the statistic

$$C_p = \tilde{\delta}'\tilde{\delta}/\tilde{\sigma}_1^2$$

is asymptotically distributed as $\chi^2(n_2)$. This variant of the test unfortunately tends to reject the true model far too frequently in finite sample
applications and so cannot be recommended (see Kiviet, 1986).

Since Chow's procedures can both be interpreted as OV tests, they are
vulnerable to the problems associated with this general class of checks. For
example, the values of n_1 may be unknown and if the switch-point is
chosen incorrectly, then the wrong set of test variables will be added to the
null model to form the alternative. This error will not affect the validity of
tests under the null hypothesis, but may have serious consequences for
power. Choosing the switch-point in order to maximize the value of the
test statistic will invalidate the usual theory, and the true significance level
will be greater than the nominal value (see Hawkins, 1977).

Further, Chow's tests will not be robust to violations of the assumption
that the disturbances are NID$(0, \sigma^2)$ variates. Autocorrelation, heteroscedasticity and non-normality will all affect the validity of the tests to
some degree. Some of their effects have been examined (see, e.g.,
Consigliere, 1981; Corsi, Pollock and Prakken, 1982; Schmidt and Sickles,
1977; Toyoda, 1974). The problems associated with heteroscedasticity
have received particular attention, perhaps because it is felt that the
variance of disturbances is unlikely to remain constant when the regression parameters change, so that it is reasonable to entertain the
heteroscedasticity model

$$\text{var}(u_t) = \sigma_1^2, t = 1, \ldots, n_1$$
$$= \sigma_2^2, t = n_1 + 1, \ldots, n. \tag{6.14}$$

Jayatissa (1977) provides a test of the hypothesis that the regression
parameters are constant, which is exact even when the errors have
variances given by (6.14). However, Jayatissa's procedure has been
criticized by Honda (1982) on the grounds that it does not make efficient

use of the data, is not unique and is complicated to compute. If n_1 and n_2 are both greater than k and are fairly large, then a simpler asymptotically valid heteroscedasticity robust Wald test can be calculated as

$$W = (\tilde{\beta}_1 - \tilde{\beta}_2)'[\tilde{s}_1^2(X_1'X_1)^{-1} + \tilde{s}_2^2(X_2'X_2)^{-1}]^{-1}(\tilde{\beta}_1 - \tilde{\beta}_2), \quad (6.15)$$

where

$$\tilde{\beta}_i = (X_i'X_i)^{-1}X_i'y_i, \quad i = 1, 2$$

and

$$\tilde{s}_i^2 = (y_i - X_i\tilde{\beta}_i)'(y_i - X_i\tilde{\beta}_i)/(n_i - k), \quad i = 1, 2$$

denote estimates based upon the two disjoint sub-periods. On the null hypothesis $\beta_1 = \beta_2$, W is asymptotically distributed as $\chi^2(k)$. Watt (1979) and Honda (1982) both provide Monte Carlo evidence on the small sample behaviour of W. Watt's results indicate that the asymptotically valid critical values can be rather smaller than the true ones and sometimes lead to estimated finite sample significance levels that are twice the nominal value. Honda (1982) reports that his results are more favourable and suggests that W performs well under null and alternative hypotheses, provided that neither sub-period contains fewer than 30 observations. Honda (1982) also argues that W outperforms Jayatissa's procedure.

Goldfeld and Quandt (1978), in an unpublished paper, propose a simple modification of Chow's test for the $n_1 > k$ and $n_2 > k$ case to overcome the problem of heteroscedasticity. If σ_1^2 and σ_2^2 were known, then the observations of the first sub-period could be divided by σ_1 and those of the second sub-period by σ_2. Chow's test could then be applied to the transformed data since the deflated disturbances would be homoscedastic with a common variance of unity. In order to obtain a feasible procedure, Goldfeld and Quandt suggest that $\tilde{s}_1$ and $\tilde{s}_2$ be employed to deflate the data in place of the unknown parameters σ_1 and σ_2. Monte Carlo experiments indicate that in reasonably small samples, asymptotic theory provides a good approximation to the null distribution and that the power is reasonable.[42]

Note that an insignificant value of a heteroscedasticity robust test of parameter constancy cannot be used by itself to justify the estimation of the null model by OLS, and that a check for heteroscedasticity is also required. The hypothesis that $\{\beta_1 = \beta_2, \sigma_1^2 = \sigma_2^2\}$ can be easily tested using

---

[42] Goldfeld and Quandt (1978) use the $F(k, n - 2k)$ distribution as the asymptotic approximation. Honda (1982) and Watt (1979) base their work on comparisons with the critical values of the $\chi^2(k)$ distribution.

the results of estimations for the sub-periods separately and the total sample. For example, the LR statistic is given by

$$LR = n \ln \hat{\sigma}^2 - n_1 \ln \tilde{\sigma}_1^2 - n_2 \ln \tilde{\sigma}_2^2,$$

and sample values should be compared with prespecified critical values of the $\chi^2(k + 1)$ distribution.[43]

Also note that the use of the test variable z_t of (6.3) is not the only candidate that has received attention in the literature. Farley and Hinich (1970) consider the case of the scalar $z_t = t$ and the use of a simple trend to capture parameter variation leads to testing $\alpha = 0$ in the alternative

$$y_t = x_t'\beta + (tx_t)'\alpha + u_t.[44] \tag{6.16}$$

Farley, Hinich and McGuire (1975) give some Monte Carlo results on the relative performance of this test and a Chow test with $n_1 = n_2$. As expected from the earlier analysis of the effects of using different sets of test variables, this version of the Chow test outperforms the Farley–Hinich procedure when there is a single change with the switch-point being near the middle of the sample period.

4.7   Testing for non-normality

Tests for the non-normality of the disturbances are not often carried out in applied econometric research. This apparent neglect may reflect a belief that the sample size is large enough to justify appeal to some asymptotic theory for quasi-maximum likelihood estimation and inference, for example, as exposited by Burguete et al. (1982). Alternatively, it may be thought that the effects of non-normality are unlikely to be serious.[45] Normality is, however, required to validate t and F tests in finite samples and certain asymptotic tests, such as the DLR tests of Davidson and MacKinnon (1984b) and the Breusch–Pagan (1979) check for heteroscedasticity. White and MacDonald (1980) cite several studies of the consequences of non-normality for OLS estimators and the usual t and F

[43] See Phillips and McCabe (1983) for a discussion of combining separate independent tests for heteroscedasticity and structural change in the context of classical normal regression models.

[44] The regressors of (6.16) may not be linearly independent; e.g., x_t might contain an intercept term and a linear trend variable. Redundant regressors should be omitted and the degrees-of-freedom parameters of the (possibly approximately valid) F distribution adjusted accordingly.

[45] It is important to distinguish between non-normal alternatives with finite variances and those with infinite variances; see the discussion of Judge et al. (1980, chap. 7).

tests. Not surprisingly, the magnitudes of these effects vary from one case to another.

An LM test for non-normality has been proposed by Jarque and Bera (1980). They embed the normal distribution in the Pearson family with density $f(u_t)$ determined by the equation

$$df(u_t)/du_t = (c_1 - u_t)f(u_t)/(c_0 - c_1u_t + c_2u_t^2), \tag{7.1}$$

with $-\infty < u_t < \infty$. The parametric restrictions which yield the normal p.d.f. as a special case are $c_1 = 0$ and $c_2 = 0$. The null hypothesis to be tested is, therefore, $H_0: c_1 = c_2 = 0$, and Jarque and Bera derive the direct LM test. Rather than provide details of this derivation, it is interesting to consider an indirect approach.

The null hypothesis $H_0: c_1 = c_2 = 0$ is equivalent to the hypothesis H_0^*: $\sqrt{\beta_1} = (\beta_2 - 3) = 0$, where $\beta_1 = \mu_3^2/\mu_2^3$, $\beta_2 = \mu_4/\mu_2^2$, and μ_r denotes $E(u_t^r)$.[46] This equivalence can be deduced from a result given by Kendall and Stuart (1969, p. 149, equation 6.4), and suggests that a test of the normality assumption be based upon the method of moments estimators

$$\sqrt{b_1} = n^{-1}\Sigma_1^n \hat{u}_t^3/\hat{\sigma}^3 = h_1(\hat{\beta})$$

and

$$b_2 = n^{-1}\Sigma_1^n \hat{u}_t^4/\hat{\sigma}^4 = h_2(\hat{\beta}),$$

where $\hat{\sigma}^2 = n^{-1}\Sigma_1^n \hat{u}_t^2$ and $\hat{u}_t$ denotes a typical OLS residual $y_t - x_t'\hat{\beta}$.

Under fairly general conditions, these estimators have the same asymptotic distributions as the unobservable variates $h_1(\beta)$ and $h_2(\beta)$ (see White and MacDonald, 1980). It is, therefore, possible to appeal to the work of Bowman and Shenton (1975) whose results imply that, under H_0, $n(\sqrt{b_1})^2/6$ and $n(b_2 - 3)^2/24$ are asymptotically distributed as independent $\chi^2(1)$ variates. An appropriate large sample test of the normality assumption can therefore be obtained by comparing the value of

$$LM = n\{(\sqrt{b_1})^2/6 + (b_2 - 3)^2/24\} \tag{7.2}$$

to the prespecified critical value of the $\chi^2(2)$ distribution. The statistic of (7.2) is exactly equal to the LM statistic obtained by Jarque and Bera (1980) and is asymptotically equivalent to the criterion derived by Kiefer and Salmon (1983) using an Edgeworth expansion of the p.d.f. of u_t.

The statistic of (7.2) has the useful property that it is asymptotically independent of more common diagnostic checks when the regression function is correctly specified and the disturbances are NID$(0, \sigma^2)$ variates (see Pagan and Hall, 1983, p. 202, Table I). Consequently, the overall

[46] It is assumed that $E(u_t) = \mu_1 = 0$ for all t.

nominal significance level for a collection of tests that includes the Jarque–Bera procedure is often easily determined. Asymptotic independence also permits the addition of individual test statistics to form the basis for a joint test. For example, Jarque and Bera note that, under the null hypothesis, the LM statistic for a joint test against autocorrelation, heteroscedasticity and non-normality can be evaluated as the sum of the three corresponding individual statistics. The importance of these asymptotic results should, however, not be overemphasized.

Jarque and Bera carry out simulation experiments and find that asymptotic theory provides a poor approximation to the actual finite sample behaviour of their test statistic. Jarque and Bera suggest that, in practice, finite sample critical values will have to be estimated by Monte Carlo experiments. Unfortunately, this modification has been neglected in empirical work.

A more general set of Monte Carlo results has been provided by White and MacDonald (1980) who consider several tests for non-normality of regression disturbances. No generally valid ranking emerges from this work, and no one test dominates the others. It is, however, interesting to note that, in deriving an omnibus test involving the $\sqrt{b_1}$ and b_2 statistics, White and MacDonald make use of adjustments suggested by Pearson, D'Agostino and Bowman (1977). These adjustments are designed to compensate for the lack of independence of $\sqrt{b_1}$ and b_2 in finite samples. The estimated small sample significance levels of the adjusted joint test are, unlike those of the Jarque–Bera procedure, in close agreement with the nominal values. This adjusted test, therefore, merits the consideration of workers interested in testing for non-normality.

4.8   Testing the independence of stochastic regressors and disturbances

Sargan (1975) has put forward the view that least-squares analysis based upon an untested assumption that stochastic regressors are independent of the disturbances is a 'pious fraud.' More recently, Hendry and Richard (1982) have also stressed the need to examine the validity of the assumption that the current conditioning variables are (weakly) exogenous. Since it is not often the case that all regressors are non-stochastic, tests of the independence assumption merit serious consideration. Many procedures test for correlations between disturbances and regressors. Note that since variables can be dependent and uncorrelated, such tests may lack power in some situations.

There are several possible causes of a lack of independence between stochastic regressors and the disturbances. One source of dependence which has received particular attention in the literature is the presence of measurement errors. Suppose that the true model for the dependent variable y is

$$y = X^*\beta + \varepsilon, \tag{8.1}$$

where X^* denotes an n by k non-stochastic matrix and ε is an n-dimensional vector whose elements are independently and identically distributed with zero mean and variance σ_ε^2. The data on the regressors are, however, contaminated by measurement errors according to

$$X = X^* + X^{**}, \tag{8.2}$$

where the n rows of the error matrix X^{**} are independently and identically distributed with zero mean vector and covariance matrix Ω and X denotes the stochastic regressor matrix.[47]

The equation that is available for estimation is then

$$y = X\beta + u,$$

where $u = (\varepsilon - X^{**}\beta)$. It follows that

$$\text{plim } n^{-1}X'u = \text{plim } n^{-1}(X^* + X^{**})'(\varepsilon - X^{**}\beta) = -\Omega\beta \neq 0,$$

indicating the existence of some dependence between the stochastic observable regressors of X and the disturbances of u. One implication of this dependence is that the OLS estimator

$$\hat{\beta} = (X'X)^{-1}X'y = \beta + (X'X)^{-1}X'u$$

will be inconsistent. Consistent estimators of the elements of β (and asymptotically valid tests) can, however, be obtained using the instrumental variable (IV) method.

Instrumental variable estimation and Durbin's test

If Z denotes an n by k matrix of valid instruments, then the IV estimator is

$$\tilde{\beta} = (Z'X)^{-1}Z'y. \tag{8.3}$$

In his seminal paper on IV estimation and the errors in variables problem, Durbin (1954) notes that the difference between $\tilde{\beta}$ and $\hat{\beta}$ can be used to obtain a test for measurement errors of the type represented by (8.2). Under the null hypothesis $\Omega = 0$ (i.e., $X = X^*$), $(\tilde{\beta} - \hat{\beta})$ has probability limit equal to a null vector since $\tilde{\beta}$ and $\hat{\beta}$ will both tend to β in probability;

---

[47] For simplicity of exposition, zero elements of Ω corresponding to correctly measured variables will not be shown explicitly.

but under the alternative hypothesis, $(\tilde{\beta} - \hat{\beta})$ has probability limit equal to minus the (non-zero) inconsistency of $\hat{\beta}$. Consequently, an asymptotic test can be derived by checking the joint significance of the elements of $(\tilde{\beta} - \hat{\beta})$.

When the regressors and disturbances are statistically independent, it can be shown that, under general conditions,

$$\sqrt{n}(\hat{\beta} - \beta) \overset{a}{\sim} N(0, V_{OLS})$$

and

$$\sqrt{n}(\tilde{\beta} - \beta) \overset{a}{\sim} N(0, V_{IV}),$$

where the asymptotic covariance matrices are given by

$$V_{OLS} = \sigma_u^2 \operatorname{plim} n(X'X)^{-1}$$

and

$$V_{IV} = \sigma_u^2 \operatorname{plim} n(Z'X)^{-1}Z'Z(X'Z)^{-1},$$

and moreover that the asymptotic null distribution of $\sqrt{n}(\tilde{\beta} - \hat{\beta})$ is multivariate normal with zero mean vector and covariance matrix $V_{IV} - V_{OLS}$. It follows that a valid large sample test for errors in variables can be obtained by constructing a quadratic form in $(\tilde{\beta} - \hat{\beta})$ using a consistent estimate of $V_{IV} - V_{OLS}$. An obvious choice for this statistic is

$$(\tilde{\beta} - \hat{\beta})'[\tilde{\sigma}_u^2(Z'X)^{-1}Z'Z(X'Z)^{-1} - \hat{\sigma}_u^2(X'X)^{-1}]^{-1}(\tilde{\beta} - \hat{\beta}), \qquad (8.4)$$

where $\tilde{\sigma}_u^2$ and $\hat{\sigma}_u^2$ are the IV and OLS residual variance estimates, both of which are consistent under the null. The test statistic of (8.4) should be compared to critical values of the $\chi^2(k)$ distribution. (If only a sub-set of, say, m regressors is stochastic, then (8.4) should be evaluated on the basis of a comparison of the corresponding sub-vectors of $\tilde{\beta}$ and $\hat{\beta}$, and critical points of the $\chi^2(m)$ distribution should be used.) Significantly large values indicate that the hypothesis that the stochastic regressors and the disturbances are independent is inconsistent with the data.

Related procedures

The misspecification indicator $(\tilde{\beta} - \hat{\beta})$ used by Durbin has been employed in several other tests of the independence assumption, for example, in the procedures described by Hausman (1978) and by Wu (1973). If the errors are normally distributed, then $\hat{\beta}$ is BAN under the null hypothesis and Hausman's (1978) general theorem can be used to derive the test of (8.4). In his own work on the errors in variables problem, Hausman replaces $\hat{\sigma}_u^2$ in (8.4) by $\tilde{\sigma}_u^2$ and suggests the criterion

$$(\tilde{\beta} - \hat{\beta})'[(Z'X)^{-1}(Z'Z)(X'Z)^{-1} - (X'X)^{-1}]^{-1}(\tilde{\beta} - \hat{\beta})/\tilde{\sigma}_u^2. \qquad (8.5)$$

Expressions (8.4) and (8.5) differ only in the choice of weighting matrix used to construct a quadratic form as a measure of the size of $(\tilde{\beta} - \hat{\beta})$. Several statistics derived from alternative specifications of this matrix are described by Wu (1973). However, as a result of a Monte Carlo study of relative power, Wu (1974) recommends the use of his T_2 statistic in preference to other forms. The motivation for the T_2 statistic in its original form is not transparent and, at first sight, its calculation appears difficult. Fortunately, Nakamura and Nakamura (1981) have shown that T_2 is exactly equal to the following OV test proposed by Hausman (1978).

An 'omitted variables' form of the test

The OV interpretation of a test which is asymptotically equivalent to those of (8.4) and (8.5) can be derived by replacing y in the expression for the IV estimator $\tilde{\beta}$ by $(X\hat{\beta} + \hat{u})$, where $\hat{u}$ denotes the OLS residual vector, so that (8.3) can be written as

$$\tilde{\beta} = \hat{\beta} + (Z'X)^{-1}Z'\hat{u}.$$

The misspecification indicator is therefore

$$q = (\tilde{\beta} - \hat{\beta}) = (Z'X)^{-1}Z'\hat{u}, \tag{8.6}$$

and since the non-singular matrix $(Z'X)^{-1}$ can be ignored, the test of the joint significance of the elements of q is equivalent to a test based upon $Z'\hat{u}$. The latter vector is, however, proportional to the score for the quasi-LM test of $\alpha = 0$ in the extended model

$$y = X\beta + Z\alpha + u. \tag{8.7}$$

Under the null hypothesis, the usual F test will be asymptotically valid and it will be exact if the u_t are $NID(0, \sigma_u^2)$.

Two comments should be made concerning the implementation of the simple OV test of the null model against (8.7). First, in some cases, a subset of regressors will be non-stochastic and can serve as their own instruments. Any redundant variables should be deleted from Z in (8.7) and the degrees-of-freedom parameters of the test adjusted accordingly. Second, modification is required if the matrix Z contains more variables than there are regressors in the original model. If the usual GIVE technique is used, then (8.3) is to be replaced by

$$\tilde{\beta} = (\hat{X}'X)^{-1}\hat{X}'y, \tag{8.8}$$

where $\hat{X}$ is the matrix of OLS predicted values from the regression of X on Z; that is, $\hat{X} = Z(Z'Z)^{-1}Z'X$. Substitution then leads to the null specification being tested against

$$y = X\beta + \hat{X}\alpha + u, \tag{8.9}$$

or equivalently against the model

$$y = X\beta + \hat{V}\gamma + u, \tag{8.10}$$

where $\hat{V} = X - \hat{X}$ is the matrix of OLS residuals from the regression of X on Z and $\gamma = -\alpha$.[48]

The choice of the IV matrix Z will, of course, affect the performance of the test since as Z is varied so is the set of test variables. No single choice of Z will be optimal for all possible alternatives, and, for any given IV matrix, the rejection probability of the test will vary according to the nature of the true data process. It is therefore of interest to determine the alternatives against which a test based upon (8.9) or (8.10) has good asymptotic power. Smith (1983) shows that if the general model is

$$y_t = x_t'\beta + u_t$$

$$x_t = \Pi z_t + v_t \, (\Pi \text{ unrestricted}),$$

with

$$\begin{bmatrix} u_t \\ v_t \end{bmatrix} \text{ being NID}\left(\begin{bmatrix} 0 \\ 0 \end{bmatrix}, \begin{bmatrix} \sigma_u^2 & \delta' \\ \delta & \Omega \end{bmatrix}\right), \, t = 1, \dots, n,$$

then the OV test calculated using either (8.9) or (8.10) is an LM type test of $\delta = 0$ (see Smith, 1983, for details).[49] Equation (8.10) has a special appeal in this context since it implies a score vector for $\gamma = 0$ equal to $\hat{V}'\hat{u}$ which is (apart from a factor of n^{-1}) an estimate of the covariance vector δ calculated from the constrained MLEs of the regression parameters of β and Π, thus immediately suggesting the possibility of an LM interpretation.

Sargan's test

As is often the case in applications of the LM principle, the estimated covariances of $n^{-1}\hat{V}'\hat{u}$ are inconsistent under the alternative hypothesis. Sargan (1975) suggests that a test be based upon covariance estimates that are consistent under the alternative, although he does not provide details of a procedure. At first sight, the use of the IV residuals $\tilde{u}$ to obtain the covariance vector estimate $n^{-1}\hat{V}'\tilde{u}$ appears attractive. However, despite the consistency of $n^{-1}\hat{V}'\tilde{u}$ under the alternative hypothesis $\delta \neq 0$, this

---

[48] As before, some columns of X may be contained in Z. In such cases, only non-redundant variables of $\hat{X}$ should be used as test variables in (8.9) and only non-zero columns of $\hat{V}$ should be employed in (8.10).

[49] In view of the assumption of multivariate normality, the restriction of $\delta = 0$ is equivalent to the hypothesis that u_t is distributed independently of the k elements of v_t.

choice does not lead to a new test. This result can be demonstrated by noting that

$$\hat{V}'\tilde{u} = (X - \hat{X})'\tilde{u} = X'\tilde{u} \text{ (since } \hat{X}'\tilde{u} = 0)$$

and also that

$$X'\tilde{u} = -(X'X)(\hat{X}'\hat{X})^{-1}\hat{X}'\hat{u}$$
$$= (X'X)(\hat{X}'\hat{X})^{-1}\hat{V}'\hat{u}.$$

Thus $\hat{V}'\tilde{u}$ is a non-singular linear transformation of the score vectors from (8.9) and (8.10), and so leads to an equivalent test.

4.9   The information matrix test

The main purpose of this section is not to provide the computational details of White's (1982) information matrix (IM) test in the context of linear regression models, but to draw upon Hall's (1987) work to show that the IM statistic can be written as the sum of a set of LM-type tests. This result helps to provide a unification of different approaches to testing for misspecification, indicates the sorts of alternatives against which the IM test will be powerful and simplifies the test's implementation.

It will be recalled from Section 1.6 that no alternative is to be specified, but the null model must be written in enough detail to permit the construction of the log-likelihood function. In this case, the model to be tested is

$$y_t = x_t'\beta + u_t, \ u_t \text{NID}(0, \sigma^2),$$

for $t = 1, \ldots, n$. It is convenient to define the $(k + 1)$-dimensional parameter vector θ_1 by $\theta_1' = (\beta', \sigma^2)$ with the associated MLE being $\hat{\theta}_1' = (\hat{\beta}', \hat{\sigma}^2)$, where $\hat{\beta}$ is the OLS estimator and $\hat{\sigma}^2 = n^{-1}\Sigma_1^n(y_t - x_t'\hat{\beta})^2$. The IM procedure is then a test of the joint significance of the non-redundant elements of the matrix

$$\Delta(\hat{\theta}_1) = \Sigma_1^n[\partial^2 l_t(\hat{\theta}_1)/\partial\theta_1\partial\theta_1' + \partial l_t(\hat{\theta}_1)/\partial\theta_1\partial l_t(\hat{\theta}_1)/\partial\theta_1'], \qquad (9.1)$$

where $l_t(\theta_1)$ is the log-likelihood for a typical observation. The quantities required for the evaluation of $\Delta(\hat{\theta}_1)$ are as follows:

$$\partial l_t(\hat{\theta}_1)/\partial\beta_i = x_{ti}\hat{u}_t/\hat{\sigma}^2(i = 1, k) \qquad (9.2a)$$

$$\partial l_t(\hat{\theta}_1)/\partial\sigma^2 = -1/(2\hat{\sigma}^2) + \hat{u}_t^2/(2\hat{\sigma}^4) \qquad (9.2b)$$

$$\partial^2 l_t(\hat{\theta}_1)/\partial\beta_i\partial\beta_j = -x_{ti}x_{tj}/\hat{\sigma}^2(i, j = 1, k) \qquad (9.2c)$$

$$\partial^2 l_t(\hat{\theta}_1)/\partial\beta_i\partial\sigma^2 = -x_{ti}\hat{u}_t/\hat{\sigma}^4 \ (i = 1, k) \qquad (9.2d)$$

$$\partial^2 l_t(\hat{\theta}_1)/\partial(\sigma^2)^2 = 1/(2\hat{\sigma}^4) - \hat{u}_t^2/\hat{\sigma}^6, \qquad (9.2e)$$

where, as usual, $\hat{u}_t$ denotes an OLS residual.

Consider first a typical element of the k by k sub-matrix of $\Delta(\hat{\theta}_1)$ corresponding to differentiation with respect to regression parameters only. Using (9.2a) and (9.2c), we have

$$\Sigma_1^n[\partial^2 l_t(\hat{\theta}_1)/\partial\beta_i\partial\beta_j + \partial l_t(\hat{\theta}_1)/\partial\beta_i\partial l_t(\hat{\theta}_1)/\partial\beta_j]$$
$$= \hat{\sigma}^{-4}\Sigma_1^n[x_{ti}x_{tj}(\hat{u}_t^2 - \hat{\sigma}^2)]. \quad (9.3)$$

Equation (9.3) implies that, under the null hypothesis of correct specification, this component of the IM misspecification indicator is asymptotically proportional to $\frac{1}{2}\Sigma_1^n[x_{ti}x_{tj}(\hat{u}_t^2 - \hat{\sigma}^2)]$, which is a typical element of the score for testing $\Sigma = 0$ in the random coefficient model

$$\beta_t = \beta + a_t, \quad a_t\text{NID}(0, \Sigma)$$

(see Breusch and Pagan, 1979).[50] This sub-set of the elements of $\Delta(\hat{\theta}_1)$ therefore corresponds to a LM test for parameter variation. The results of Section 4.5 of this chapter imply that an IM test of the significance of

$$\Sigma_1^n[\partial^2 l_t(\hat{\theta}_1)/\partial\beta\partial\beta' + \partial l_t(\hat{\theta}_1)/\partial\beta\partial l_t(\hat{\theta}_1)\partial\beta']$$

can also be interpreted as a version of White's (1980b) test for heteroscedasticity.

Turning now to that part of $\Delta(\hat{\theta}_1)$ based upon differences between $-\Sigma_1^n\partial^2 l_t(\hat{\theta}_1)/\partial\beta_i\partial\sigma^2$ and $\Sigma_1^n\partial l_t(\hat{\theta}_1)/\partial\beta_i\partial l_t(\hat{\theta}_1)/\partial\sigma^2$, equations (9.2a, b, d) imply that

$$\Sigma_1^n[\partial^2 l_t(\hat{\theta}_1)/\partial\beta_i\partial\sigma^2 + \partial l_t(\hat{\theta}_1)/\partial\beta_i\partial l_t(\hat{\theta}_1)/\partial\sigma^2]$$
$$= \Sigma_1^n x_{ti}\hat{u}_t^3/(2\hat{\sigma}^6), \quad i = 1, k. \quad (9.4)$$

The denominator again plays no real role in the analysis and this second component of the IM indicator consists of checks on the covariances between the regressors and the cubes of the residuals. If the model contains an intercept, then one member of (9.4) will be

$$\Sigma_1^n\hat{u}_t^3/(2\hat{\sigma}^6), \quad (9.5)$$

which is simply a non-singular transformation of $\sqrt{b_1} = n^{-1}\Sigma_1^n\hat{u}_t^3/\hat{\sigma}^3$ and so generates the familiar test for skewness.

Finally, the $(k + 1, k + 1)$ element of $\Delta(\hat{\theta}_1)$ is

$$\Sigma_1^n[\partial^2 l_t(\hat{\theta}_1)/\partial(\sigma^2)^2 + (\partial l_t(\hat{\theta}_1)/\partial\sigma^2)^2] = \Sigma_1^n(\hat{u}_t^4/\hat{\sigma}^4 - 3)/4\hat{\sigma}^4, \quad (9.6)$$

which obviously leads to the standard test for excess kurtosis based upon $b_2 = n^{-1}\Sigma_1^n\hat{u}_t^4/\hat{\sigma}^4$.

[50] The asymptotic constant of proportionality is $\sigma^4/2$. The relationship between the IM test and a check for parameter variation is implied by the more general results of Chesher (1984); see also Cox (1983).

Hall (1987) shows that the three χ^2 statistics which test the significance of the components defined by (9.3), (9.4) and (9.6) are, under the null, asymptotically independent, so that the IM statistic can be calculated as the sum of three quadratic forms. Given the limited sample sizes available in many empirical studies, it may sometimes be useful to reduce the number of degrees of freedom of the test by considering only a sub-set of the distinct elements of $\Delta(\hat{\theta}_1)$. One obvious strategy is to ignore $(k - 1)$ of the terms of (9.4) and to base a modified IM test on (9.3), (9.5) and (9.6). This modified IM statistic could then be calculated as

$$IM^* = n[R^2 + (\sqrt{b_1})^2/6 + (b_2 - 3)^2/24], \tag{9.7}$$

where R^2 is the coefficient of determination for the regression of $\hat{u}_t^2$ on the distinct elements of $x_t x_t' = \{x_{ti} x_{tj}\}$.[51] If there are $(q + 1)$ distinct elements of $x_t x_t'$, one of which corresponds to the square of the intercept dummy, then the asymptotic null distribution of IM^* is $\chi^2(q + 2)$ with significantly large values of IM^* suggesting that the model is misspecified.

The above remarks make it clear that White's IM statistic will be sensitive to heteroscedasticity/random parameter variation and non-normality, although the inclusion of unnecessary indicators implies that it will not be asymptotically optimal in the presence of only one of these departures from the null. The IM test will, however, not be powerful against autocorrelation when the regressors are fixed in repeated sampling, and so it may be more useful in cross-section applications than in such time-series models (also see Chesher, 1984).

4.10   Data transformation tests

We now consider a class of tests which, like the information matrix test, is intended for use when there is considerable uncertainty about the nature of specification errors.[52] This set of general checks for misspecification is derived by comparing two estimates of the regression parameter vector β. One estimate is calculated using the original observations, and it will be assumed that the other is obtained after the application of a linear transformation to the data. The basic idea of examining the difference between two estimators is reminiscent of the Durbin–Hausman–Wu procedures discussed in Section 4.7 of this chapter, but rather than

---

[51] Expression (9.7) is simpler than the one provided by the approach of Chesher (1983) and Lancaster (1984) because it incorporates much more information about the asymptotic covariance matrix of the distinct elements of $\Delta(\hat{\theta}_1)$.

[52] This section draws upon the articles by Davidson, Godfrey and MacKinnon (1985) and Breusch and Godfrey (1986).

choosing a set of instruments to obtain an estimator contrast, it is now necessary to specify the data transformation. There may be information to guide this specification. If not, it may be necessary to construct a pure significance test in some more or less arbitrary fashion.

The first part of this section contains some general results for data transformation tests, and it is shown that such tests can be implemented as checks for omitted variables. In the second part, the general results are applied to some well-known data transformation tests. These applications illustrate the general findings and also lead to new results.

The transformed model and some general results

Suppose that T is a non-stochastic m by n ($k < m \leqslant n$) transformation matrix with rank equal to m, and let the associated transformed data be denoted by $y^* = Ty$ and $X^* = TX$. If the null specification is

$$y = X\beta + u, u \sim N(0, \sigma^2 I), \tag{10.1}$$

then the transformed model is

$$y^* = X^*\beta + u^*, u^* \sim N(0, \sigma^2 TT').[53] \tag{10.2}$$

The OLS estimate from the original data is $\hat{\beta} = (X'X)^{-1}X'y$, and the estimate derived from (10.2) is denoted by β^*. Data transformation tests are then designed to test the null hypothesis of correct specification by examining $(\beta^* - \hat{\beta})$. Two cases must be considered, these cases being differentiated by whether or not (10.2) has as many observations as (10.1).

Case (i): $m = n$. When the original and transformed data contain the same number of observations, the OLS estimator is used for β^*; that is,

$$\beta^* = (X^{*'}X^*)^{-1}X^{*'}y^*$$

$$= (X'T'TX)^{-1}X'T'Ty, \tag{10.3}$$

which, under the null, is unbiased and consistent, but inefficient. The estimator $\hat{\beta}$ is BAN and so Hausman's (1978) general theorem can be applied to derive a test of the significance of $(\beta^* - \hat{\beta})$, but it is more convenient and useful to develop an OV variant.[54]

---

[53] The assumption of normality is required to obtain tests which are exact in finite samples, but can be relaxed without affecting the asymptotic validity of the results below.

[54] Strictly speaking, the absence of any alternative hypothesis puts the analysis outside Hausman's framework, but this point is irrelevant as far as asymptotic validity is concerned.

Replacing y in (10.3) by $(X\hat{\beta} + \hat{u})$ yields the following expression for the misspecification indicator:

$$(\beta^* - \hat{\beta}) = (X'T'TX)^{-1}X'T'T\hat{u}. \tag{10.4}$$

It follows that the data transformation test is equivalent to a test of the significance of $(X'T'T)\hat{u}$, which is proportional to the score vector for the quasi-LM test of $\alpha = 0$ in

$$y = X\beta + (T'TX)\alpha + u. \tag{10.5}$$

Thus, if there are equal numbers of observations available on the original and transformed models, the data transformation test of the former specification can be implemented by testing it against the augmented relationship of (10.5).

It is possible that the regressor matrix of (10.5) – namely, $(X, T'TX)$ – will not have rank equal to $2k$. In such cases, variables of $T'TX$ should be removed until all linear dependencies have been eliminated and then the F test for the remaining test variables can be calculated. If the rank of $(X, T'TX)$ equals $(k + q)$, sample values of the test statistic should be compared to right-hand tail critical values of the $F(q, n - k - q)$ distribution in the usual way.

Case (ii): m < n. In this second case, the number of observations is reduced by the transformation and β^* can be either the OLS estimator defined by (10.3) or the Aitken's generalized least-squares (AGLS) estimator

$$\beta^* = [X^{*\prime}(TT')^{-1}X^*]^{-1}[X^{*\prime}(TT')^{-1}y^*]$$

$$= [X'T'(TT')^{-1}TX]^{-1}[X'T'(TT')^{-1}Ty].{}^{55} \tag{10.6}$$

If the OLS estimator for the transformed model is used to construct the misspecification indicator, then the F test of $\alpha = 0$ in (10.5) is again appropriate. If, on the other hand, the AGLS estimator defined by (10.6) is compared to the OLS estimator for the original model, then, using substitutions similar to those of Case (i), it can be shown that the extended model corresponding to (10.5) is

$$y = X\beta + [T'(TT')^{-1}TX]\alpha + u,$$

or, more simply,

$$y = X\beta + \tilde{X}\alpha + u, \tag{10.7}$$

where $\tilde{X}$ is the matrix of predicted values from the OLS regression of X on T'. If $(X, \tilde{X})$ does not have full column rank, then redundant columns of $\tilde{X}$

---

[55] The application of AGLS to (10.2) in case (i) would, of course, yield the OLS estimate $\hat{\beta}$ of (10.1).

should be deleted and the degrees-of-freedom parameters of the F test adjusted to allow for their removal. The power of the test based upon (10.7) relative to that of the test calculated from (10.5) will depend upon the true data process. There is no reason to believe that using the AGLS estimator of the transformed model, rather than the OLS estimator, will always lead to a more powerful test.

Equations (10.5) and (10.7) represent convenient algorithms for the calculation of data transformation tests and imply that such procedures can be readily combined with the many other misspecification tests that can be interpreted as tests for omitted variables. Questions of test consistency and asymptotic power under various local alternatives can, of course, be examined using the general analysis of OV procedures provided in Section 4.2.

The application of the general results to some important special cases will now be considered.

Grouping tests

Perhaps the most familiar example of a data transformation test is the one in which the estimates calculated from the individual observations are compared to those derived from grouped data. In this case, the m by n matrix T is a grouping matrix whose elements equal either zero or one and are arranged so that the n micro-observations on any variable are converted to the m group totals. Since $m < n$, an appropriate set of test variables is $\tilde{X}$ of (10.7) which, in view of the definition of T, has typical element $\tilde{x}_{ti}$ equal to the average of the values of the ith regressor in the group to which the tth observation belongs.[56] Under classical assumptions, the usual F test of the significance of these test variables based upon estimation of (10.1) and (10.7) will be distributed as central $F(k, n - 2k)$ on the null hypothesis and is equivalent to Farebrother's (1979) grouping test for misspecification.

White's test for functional form

The second example is drawn from White's (1980a) work on testing the adequacy of a linear model viewed as an approximation to an unknown regression function.[57] White suggests that the OLS estimate $\hat{\beta}$ should be

---

[56] The grouping matrix is sometimes defined so that TX contains the group averages, rather than the group totals. This alternative definition of T leads to exactly the same set of test variables being added to the null model.

[57] This work was extended by White (1981) to cover the case of non-linear regression models.

compared to a weighted least-square (WLS) estimate

$$\tilde{\beta}_W = (X'WX)^{-1}X'Wy, \tag{10.8}$$

where W is an n by n diagonal matrix with non-zero elements $w_t, t = 1, \ldots,$ n. The weights w_t are assumed to be bounded and positive with

$$E(w_t x_t u_t) = 0. \tag{10.9}$$

If T now denotes a diagonal matrix with its diagonal elements being $\sqrt{w_t}$, $t = 1, \ldots, n$, then $T'T = W$ and White's WLS estimator can be interpreted as an indicator of the form (10.3). In terms of the corresponding transformed model, condition (10.9) can be written as

$$E(x_t^* u_t^*) = 0.$$

By substitution in (10.5), we obtain the result that White's check for functional misspecification can be implemented as a test of $\alpha = 0$ in

$$y = X\beta + (WX)\alpha + u. \tag{10.10}$$

This OV variant is rather simpler than White's equivalent test based upon Hausman's (1978) theorem, which can be expressed as

$$(\tilde{\beta}_W - \hat{\beta})'[s_W^2(X'WX)^{-1}(X'W^2X)(X'WX)^{-1} \\ - s^2(X'X)^{-1}]^{-1}(\tilde{\beta}_W - \hat{\beta}), \tag{10.11}$$

where s_W^2 and s^2 are the degrees-of-freedom adjusted variance estimates based upon the WLS and OLS residuals, respectively. In addition to the criterion of (10.11), White (1980a, p. 157, equations 8 and 9) provides a more complicated test statistic which is robust to heteroscedasticity. An asymptotically equivalent procedure could be obtained by computing the heteroscedasticity consistent estimate of the asymptotic covariance matrix of the OLS estimators for β and α in (10.10) and then calculating a Wald-type test of $\alpha = 0$.

The obvious practical difficulty with these potentially useful diagnostics lies in the selection of the weights w_t. A poor choice will lead to low power, but, without knowledge of the true data process, it is not possible to determine the optimal set of weight functions. White suggests that researchers experiment with several different schemes, but notes that the associated statistics will not be independent and that this dependence causes some problems. In particular, the generalization of (10.11), which permits a joint test, is unattractive since, in White's words, it requires the construction of a 'giant covariance matrix which explicitly takes account of covariances between' the various misspecification indicators $(\tilde{\beta}_W - \hat{\beta})$ associated with the different sets of weights. As a simpler alternative, White suggests that a separate test be conducted for each W matrix being entertained and the null be accepted if all statistics are insignificant. The problem with this approach is that the overall significance level is unknown (even asymptotically). An upper bound can be obtained by means of the Bonferroni inequality, but the true size might be much smaller than this bound.

The appropriate generalization of the OV form of the test is, in contrast, easy to implement and has known significance level, at least asymptotically. If q different sets of weights with corresponding matrices $W_1, W_2, \ldots, W_q$ are being considered, then the appropriate joint test is simply the F test of $\{\alpha_1 = 0, \alpha_2 = 0, \ldots, \alpha_q = 0\}$ in the augmented model

$$y = X\beta + \Sigma_1^q(W_iX)\alpha_i + u. \tag{10.12}$$

White also provides examples to illustrate the use of two schemes. In the first of these, w_t equals $\hat{y}_t^2$ ($\hat{y}_t$ being the OLS predicted value $x_t'\hat{\beta}$); and for the second set, w_t equals 0.001 if a regressor's value falls below a specified quantity and is equal to 1 otherwise. The former scheme is based upon work by Prais and Houthakker (1971), and since w_t depends upon y_1, $\ldots, y_n$ only through $\hat{\beta}$, the Milliken–Graybill (1970) result implies that the F test of $\alpha = 0$ in (10.10) will still be exact, provided the regressors of X are fixed or distributed independently of the NID$(0, \sigma^2)$ disturbance terms. The effect of the second choice of weights is very similar to dropping a subset of observations, and so it yields a test which resembles a check for parameter constancy.[58] The numerical examples show that different sets of weights can produce conflicting outcomes of significance tests.

Farebrother's (1979) grouping test and White's (1980a) check for model inadequacy share the feature that the researcher must decide upon the form of the matrix T in the light of available information, by partitioning the sample into m groups in the first case and by specifying a sequence of weights in the second procedure. The last data transformation test to be considered does not make this demand on the user and can be properly regarded as a pure significance test because it requires no information at all about the alternative.

The differencing test

This general specification test is proposed by Plosser, Schwert and White (1982), hereafter PSW, for application to linear time-series regression models, and uses the OLS estimate from the first differences of the data as

[58] Note that, however small the weights are, they must be non-zero and so the test is not equivalent to a Chow test.

β^*. More precisely, using a dot notation to indicate first differencing, for example,

$$\dot{y}_1 = 0$$

$$\dot{y}_t = y_t - y_{t-1}, \; t = 2, 3, \ldots,$$

we have

$$\tilde{\beta}_\Delta = (\dot{X}'\dot{X})^{-1}\dot{X}'\dot{y}.^{59} \tag{10.13}$$

PSW show that, under the null hypothesis of correct specification and the regularity conditions of their analysis, the statistic

$$\Delta = (\tilde{\beta}_\Delta - \hat{\beta})'\hat{V}^{-1}(\tilde{\beta}_\Delta - \hat{\beta}), \tag{10.14}$$

where

$$\hat{V} = \hat{\sigma}^2[(\dot{X}'\dot{X})^{-1}\dot{X}'\dot{X}(\dot{X}'\dot{X})^{-1} - (X'X)^{-1}], \tag{10.15}$$

is asymptotically distributed as $\chi^2(k)$, provided $\mathrm{plim}(n\hat{V})$ is non-singular. (The double-dot notation denotes second differencing, e.g., $\ddot{y}_t = y_t - 2y_{t-1} + y_{t-2}$.) The procedure based upon Δ is referred to as the differencing test, and PSW present Monte Carlo evidence in support of its use in empirical work.

In order to apply the previous results, it is only necessary to determine the specification of T that yields $\tilde{\beta}_\Delta$ of (10.13) as a special case of β^* of (10.3). It is easy to verify that the $(n-1)$ by n transformation matrix

$$T = \begin{bmatrix} -1 & 1 & 0 & \cdot & \cdot & \cdot & 0 \\ 0 & -1 & 1 & \cdot & & & \vdots \\ 0 & 0 & \cdot & & & & \vdots \\ \vdots & \vdots & & \cdot & & 1 & 0 \\ 0 & 0 & \cdots & 0 & & -1 & 1 \end{bmatrix}$$

generates the required first differences. In order to derive the test variables for (10.5), note that

$$T'T = \begin{bmatrix} 1 & -1 & & & 0 \\ -1 & 2 & \cdot\cdot & & \\ & \cdot\cdot & \cdot\cdot & & \\ 0 & & \cdot\cdot & 2 & -1 \\ & & & -1 & 1 \end{bmatrix},$$

---

[59] The treatment of the pre-sample values required for, e.g., $\dot{y}_1$ follows PSW. Other conventions are possible, e.g., $\dot{y}_1 = y_1$, but only lead to asymptotically negligible differences.

and so, given an appropriate treatment of terms for periods -1 and $n + 1$, a typical element of, for example, $T'Ty$ is $-y_{t-1} + 2y_t - y_{t+1}$, that is, $-\ddot{y}_{t+1}$. Thus $T'TX$ is $-\ddot{X}_{+1}$, and the differencing test is equivalent to a test of $\gamma = 0$ in the augmented model

$$y = X\beta + \ddot{X}_{+1}\gamma + u. \tag{10.16}$$

In practice, certain modifications of the basic form of the differencing test will be required. The matrix $(X, \ddot{X}_{+1})$ will often not have full column rank, for example, due to the presence of an intercept dummy or a sequence of lagged values of some variable in the regressors of X. The solution is simply to delete the redundant variables, making the necessary adjustments to the degrees-of-freedom parameters of the test statistic's null distribution.

A more serious problem arises when the regressors of X include the one-period lagged value of the dependent variable. The test variable corresponding to y_{t-1} is $y_t - 2y_{t-1} + y_{t-2}$ which is correlated with u_t even on H_0, thus invalidating OLS inference. PSW suggest that this difficulty be overcome by estimating the first differences model by IV, with the OLS estimate $\hat{\beta}$ being compared to the IV estimate, namely,

$$\bar{\beta} = (Z'\dot{X})^{-1}Z'\dot{y}.^{60} \tag{10.17}$$

Breusch and Godfrey (1984) show that (10.17) can also be interpreted as an IV estimate of the levels model with instruments $\dot{Z}_{+1} = Z_{+1} - Z$. The results for Durbin–Hausman–Wu tests then imply that the differencing test based upon $(\bar{\beta} - \hat{\beta})$ can be implemented by testing $\delta = 0$ in the extended model

$$y = X\beta + \dot{Z}_{+1}\delta + u. \tag{10.18}$$

(It may be necessary to omit some columns of $\dot{Z}_{+1}$ to ensure that the regressor matrix of (10.18) has full rank.)

The use of IV techniques to overcome the difficulties caused by the inclusion of y_{-1} in X is, however, unnecessary and a much simpler solution can be obtained by considering a non-singular transformation of the estimator contrast

$$\tilde{\beta}_\Delta - \hat{\beta} = (\dot{X}'\dot{X})^{-1}\dot{X}'_{+1}\hat{u}.$$

The irrelevance of $(\dot{X}'\dot{X})^{-1}$ implies that the PSW test involves investigating whether or not the sample values of the elements of $\dot{X}'_{+1}\hat{u}$ differ significantly from what is expected under the null hypothesis of correct specification. The element of $\dot{X}'_{+1}\hat{u}$ corresponding to the regressor y_{-1} is,

---

[60] The lagged variable y_{t-1} is not a valid instrument for the first differences model owing to the MA(1) structure of the $\dot{u}_t$.

using $\Sigma_1^n y_{t-1} \hat{u}_t = 0$, equal to

$$\Sigma_1^n (y_t + y_{t-2}) \hat{u}_t = \Sigma_1^n y_t \hat{u}_t + \Sigma_1^n y_{t-2} \hat{u}_t.$$

In the absence of specification errors, we have

$$\text{plim } n^{-1} \Sigma_1^n y_t \hat{u}_t = \sigma^2 \neq 0$$

and

$$\text{plim } n^{-1} \Sigma_1^n y_{t-2} \hat{u}_t = 0,$$

implying that

$$\text{plim } n^{-1} \Sigma_1^n (y_t + y_{t-2}) \hat{u}_t = \sigma^2.$$

Since $\hat{\sigma}^2 = n^{-1} \Sigma_1^n \hat{u}_t^2$ is consistent for σ^2 on the null hypothesis, it is appropriate to test whether

$$[n^{-1} \Sigma_1^n (y_t + y_{t-2}) \hat{u}_t - \hat{\sigma}^2]$$

is significantly different from zero. But the usual properties of OLS estimates imply that $n^{-1} \Sigma_1^n y_t \hat{u}_t = n^{-1} \Sigma_1^n \hat{u}_t^2$, and so the problem reduces to testing the significance of $\Sigma_1^n y_{t-2} \hat{u}_t$. The scalar $\Sigma_1^n y_{t-2} \hat{u}_t$ is, however, proportional to the LM criterion for testing the validity of excluding y_{t-2} from the original regression model. Thus the OV approach when applied to models with y_{t-1} as a regressor leads to the simple modification of using y_{t-2} as its test variable, rather than $\ddot{y}_t$, with the test variables for the remaining regressors being as in (10.16).[61]

Similar modifications could, of course, be employed for other stochastic regressors if they were to be regarded as predetermined, but not strictly exogenous. Thus if the regressors of the original model were all only weakly exogenous variables, the modified differencing test would be calculated as a test of $\alpha = 0$ in the augmented model

$$y = X\beta + X_{-1}\alpha + u,$$

where X_{-1} denotes the one-period lagged value of X, and so would be equivalent to the Wu (1973) test examined by PSW.

The OV interpretation of the differencing test simplifies implementation and the analysis of power. Breusch and Godfrey (1986) provide examples to show how the power properties of the PSW procedure depend upon the true data process; and Davidson, Godfrey and MacKinnon (1985) discuss asymptotic local power for quite general alternatives.

---

[61] This strategy is exactly equivalent to Pagan's suggestion described in footnote 7 of PSW (1982) and is, therefore, asymptotically equivalent to the IV procedure mentioned in the same footnote.

4.11   Concluding remarks and extensions

In this chapter we have attempted to describe and discuss a large number of tests designed to detect departures from the assumptions that underpin the standard methods of estimation, prediction and inference in regression analysis. Many of these tests have been developed in the form of checks of the significance of a set of additional regressors, and this simplifies implementation (and combination) of such tests. The OV interpretation of tests for a wide range of misspecifications also facilitates the analysis of (asymptotic local) power whether or not the correct alternative has been selected; thus, for example, the implications of choosing the wrong switch-point in a Chow test can be easily investigated.

Non-linear models

The null specification has usually been assumed to be a linear regression model, but the analysis can be extended for non-linear relationships of the form

$$y = f(X, \beta) + u, \tag{11.1}$$

provided attention is confined to asymptotic results. As Amemiya (1983) points out in his excellent survey, provided regularity conditions are satisfied, all the results on OV tests for the linear regression model can be extended to cover the non-linear specification of (11.1) by treating the matrix of partial derivatives

$$F(X, \hat{\beta}) = \partial f(X, \hat{\beta})/\partial \beta$$

as a regressor matrix, $\hat{\beta}$ denoting the non-linear least-squares estimate. A general class of asymptotic tests of the adequacy of (11.1) can then be obtained by testing $\alpha = 0$ in the pseudo-model

$$\hat{u} = F(X, \hat{\beta})b + W\alpha + \varepsilon, \tag{11.2}$$

where $\hat{u} = y - f(X, \hat{\beta})$ is the residual vector from estimation of the null model. As with some other diagnostic checks, the available evidence suggests that the F ratio based upon restricted and unrestricted sums of squared residuals provides a better test of $\alpha = 0$ than the corresponding Wald-type procedure (see Amemiya, 1983).

The asymptotically valid tests for normality and heteroscedasticity, as derived by Jarque and Bera (1980) and Breusch and Pagan (1979), respectively, are not conveniently implemented as OV tests. Fortunately, these procedures require no modification when the regression function is non-linear and the test statistics can be calculated using the residuals obtained by fitting (11.1). Exact tests such as the Goldfeld–Quandt test for heteroscedasticity are, however, invalid.

Separate and joint tests

Despite the enormous progress that has been made in developing and understanding tests for specification errors, important questions remain to be considered. Kmenta and Ramsey (1980) suggest that the 'chief difficulty occurs with the presence of more than one error and with the resulting problem of how to isolate and identify the separate effects.' The results of this chapter have shown that, in many situations, constructing a test for several types of error is perfectly straightforward, involving only the addition of an appropriate set of test variables to the null model and the calculation of a standard F test of the validity of their exclusion. It would be possible to carry out a separate test for each type of error, but this strategy is unattractive because the individual statistics will often be asymptotically correlated on the null hypothesis of correct specification, so that the overall significance level is either unknown or extremely difficult to calculate.

There are two exceptions to the general recommendation that joint tests should be carried out when several different misspecifications are being entertained, namely, tests for heteroscedasticity and the check for non-normality based upon $\sqrt{b_1}$ and b_2. These checks cannot be implemented by extending the set of test variables and applying a conventional F test (see Godfrey and Wickens, 1982, for a discussion of the problems associated with heteroscedasticity tests). Fortunately, under the null, these tests are asymptotically independent of each other and standard diagnostic checks for specification error, such as tests for incorrect functional form, omitted regressors and autocorrelation. The sample values of the separate tests for heteroscedasticity and non-normality can, therefore, be added together and their sum added to the value of whatever joint test has been calculated for the other specification errors being considered. Consequently, it should be fairly straightforward for researchers to devise tests against the particular combination of errors thought to be important in their own empirical work.

Model reformulation

Unfortunately, it is not possible to be so optimistic about the value of misspecification tests in isolating and identifying the separate errors. Many tests are not very specific and so there are several possible causes of significant values. The analysis of Section 4.2 can be used to investigate whether a particular criterion which is asymptotically distributed as χ^2 under the null is (generally) of $O_p(n)$ or $O_p(1)$ on any specified alternative.[62] If the statistic is $O_p(n)$, then the inadequate null will be rejected with probability tending to one as $n \to \infty$, even though the test is designed for a misspecification which is not present. On the other hand, if the criterion remains $O_p(1)$, then the test will not be consistent and the rejection probability may be smaller or larger than the nominal size.[63]

Another reason for doubting the usefulness of misspecification tests in model reformulation is that alternative hypotheses are frequently chosen because it is hoped that they will generate useful tests against likely errors, and not because they reflect precise and confidently held ideas about how the null differs from an adequate approximation.[64]

Choice of tests

In view of the above arguments, misspecification checks cannot be expected to act as simple and accurate guides to the reformulation of models that have been found to be inconsistent with the sample data. They should, however, be useful tools for the detection of inadequate models. The rejection of misspecified models with high probability will require careful use of available information on, for example, relevant economic theories, related empirical work and the nature of the data.[65] Thus, for example, it would be unwise to test only for first-order autocorrelation when estimating quarterly models. Pure significance tests such as the differencing and information matrix tests can, of course, be used when the researcher believes that there is no useful information to guide testing. There is, however, no need to regard pure significance tests and procedures derived for specified alternatives as being incompatible. Indeed the results above show how both types of test can often be easily combined.

[62] Sometimes the test statistic will be $O_p(n)$, except for relatively uncommon combinations of parameter vectors and limits of data covariance matrices.

[63] See, for example, the results of Schmidt and Sickles (1977) on the behaviour of the Chow test in the presence of heteroscedasticity.

[64] As Pagan and Hall (1983) point out, if a researcher was really sure about the alternative, it would be unwise not to include it in the specification from the start.

[65] Although a discussion of tests of non-nested models is outside the scope of this book, such procedures may prove useful in applied work.

CHAPTER 5

Tests for misspecification of simultaneous equation models

5.1   Introduction

Hausman (1983) has suggested that the simultaneous equation model is perhaps the most remarkable development in econometrics. In this chapter we shall be concerned with the problem of testing the specification of such models. The discussion is based for the most part on the linear structural model

$$YB + Z\Gamma = U, \tag{1.1}$$

where Y is the n by m matrix of endogenous variables, Z is the n by k matrix of predetermined variables, U is the n by m matrix of stochastic disturbances, B is the m by m matrix of structural coefficients of endogenous variables and Γ is the k by m matrix of structural coefficients of predetermined variables.

The special case in which B is a diagonal matrix and (1.1) represents a system of seemingly unrelated regression equations (SURE) will not be given separate consideration. The corresponding simplifications of tests derived for the general case are straightforward. The tests discussed below do not, however, include a check of the assumption that the disturbances of the system are contemporaneously uncorrelated. This assumption may be of interest in the context of SURE models, and Breusch and Pagan (1980, p. 247) derive an appropriate LM statistic.

Assumptions for the null model

Equation (1.1) will provide the null model to be tested. Its statistical analysis requires the usual sorts of assumptions. In order to simplify the exposition and to concentrate on the problem of testing, we shall employ the following:

(i)   The cross-product moment matrix

$$n^{-1}\begin{bmatrix} Y'Y & Y'Z \\ Z'Y & Z'Z \end{bmatrix}$$

tends to a finite non-singular matrix as $n \to \infty$.

164

(ii)   The matrix B is non-singular and is subject to the normalization rule $\beta_{ii} = 1$, $i = 1, 2, \ldots, m$.[1]

(iii) The coefficient matrices are subject to a priori restrictions which permit the identification of the equation(s) under scrutiny (see Hausman, 1983, and Hsiao, 1983, for discussions of identification). For simplicity, suppose that these restrictions are exclusions, so that certain elements of B and Γ are set equal to zero.

(iv)   The n rows of U are independently and identically distributed with zero mean vector and non-singular covariance matrix Σ.[2] The variance terms of the leading diagonal of Σ will be denoted by σ_i^2, $i = 1, 2, \ldots, m$.

If variables with zero coefficients are excluded, then the individual equations of the system (1.1) can be written as

$$y_i = Y_i\beta_i + Z_i\gamma_i + u_i = X_i\delta_i + u_i, \tag{1.2}$$

where Y_i is n by m_i, Z_i is n by k_i, $X_i = (Y_i, Z_i)$ is n by g_i $(g_i = m_i + k_i)$, and $\delta_i = (\beta_i', \gamma_i')'$ is a g_i-dimensional unrestricted coefficient vector, $i = 1, 2, \ldots, m$. The necessary condition for the elements of δ_i to be identified is that g_i should not exceed k, the number of predetermined variables in the complete model. The problem of testing equations like (1.2) for misspecification after estimation by instrumental variables (IV) will be considered below. The matrix of instruments used in such estimation will be denoted by W and so, in order to avoid confusion, 'Wald' will be written in full throughout this chapter.

The choice between limited information and system estimation

Several preliminary issues must be considered before undertaking a detailed discussion of tests for misspecification derived from particular alternative hypotheses. One important decision to be made is whether the system (1.1) is to be tested as a whole, using results obtained by some full information estimator, or whether it is to be checked one equation at a time after the application of a limited information technique. As will be seen below, the former approach can make quite heavy computational demands and may require relatively large sample sizes if asymptotic

---

[1] If B were singular, then it would be possible to form a non-stochastic combination of the predetermined variables which equalled a combination of the disturbances; see Fisk (1967, p. 7).

[2] It will be assumed that identities (equations with zero disturbances) have been eliminated by suitable substitutions. Also, the symmetric non-singular matrix Σ is unrestricted.

theory is to provide an adequate approximation. Moreover, contamination effects may lead to system rejection when only one or two structural equations are inadequately specified. The individual equation approach is more robust to such spill-over effects and involves less stringent regularity conditions (see Gallant and Jorgenson, 1979, p. 293).

The choice of estimation criterion

The details of the implementation of tests will also depend upon whether estimation is based upon the maximization of a quasi-log-likelihood function or the minimization of an IV criterion. The asymptotic theory of LM, LR and Wald-type tests for both approaches to estimation has been examined by Burguete et al. (1982). Owing to relative computational costs, IV methods (e.g., two-stage least squares) have in the past been much more popular than their quasi-maximum likelihood counterparts, and this situation seems likely to persist in the foreseeable future. Accordingly, the emphasis here is on checks of model adequacy designed to accompany IV estimation.

Contents

The assumptions that need to be tested when formulating and estimating the relationships of a simultaneous equation model are in many ways similar to those of relevance in the case of the (non-simultaneous) regression model which was the subject of the previous chapter. These similarities are reflected in the organization of this chapter. The remaining sections contain discussions of tests against the following types of misspecification:

  (i)   omitted variables (Section 5.2)
  (ii)   autocorrelated disturbances (Section 5.3)
  (iii) heteroscedastic disturbances (Section 5.4)
  (iv)   invalid exogeneity assumptions (Section 5.5)
  (v)   lack of parameter constancy (Section 5.6).

Tests for normality will not be considered. Existing tests (which are mentioned by Pagan and Hall, 1983, pp. 198–9) are only asymptotically valid and, if appeal is to be made to asymptotic theory, there is no need to assume normality in order to derive standard results relating to the analysis of system (1.1). More precisely, most results concerning the distributions of estimators and test statistics that are derived assuming normality remain asymptotically valid for many types of non-normality. One exception considered below is the case of testing for heteroscedasticity and robust test procedures are described (see Section 5.4).

Some concluding remarks are made in Section 5.7.

5.2 Asymptotic tests of significance for instrumental variable estimates

As in Chapter 4, it is possible to derive tests against a large number of alternatives simply by examining the significance of a set of suitable test variables added to the null model. Consequently, it will be useful to give a fairly detailed account of the asymptotic theory of IV tests for omitted variables (OV). This discussion can then be employed to derive tests against various different sorts of misspecification.

We first consider tests of hypotheses relating to the coefficients of a single structural equation and then extend the results so obtained to cover the case of a complete system. These tests are based upon the IV estimation criterion and so are similar in spirit to the LM, LR and Wald procedures. An approach proposed by Sargan (1976) is also examined. Sargan's procedure is a direct test for a relationship between estimated residuals and a specified set of instruments, and does not require the specification of an alternative hypothesis (see the related work of Newey, 1985b).

5.2.1 Tests for a single structural equation

In view of the results obtained for non-simultaneous regression equations, let us consider the null model (1.2) as being derived by setting $\alpha_i = 0$ in the more general model

$$y_i = X_i\delta_i + T_i\alpha_i + u_i, \tag{2.1}$$

where T_i is an n by p_i matrix of test variables and α_i is the associated p_i-dimensional parameter vector. The adequacy of (1.2) can then be assessed by testing the set of parametric restrictions $H_0: \alpha_i = 0$.

There are several asymptotically valid procedures for testing H_0 using IV estimates. Among these procedures are the IV analogues of the classical tests derived from a consideration of the log-likelihood function. In the context of the IV estimation of (2.1), the optimization criterion corresponding to minus the log-likelihood is

$$S_i(\alpha_i, \delta_i) = (y_i - X_i\delta_i - T_i\alpha_i)'P(W)(y_i - X_i\delta_i - T_i\alpha_i), \tag{2.2}$$

where W is an n by s ($s \geq p_i + g_i$) matrix of valid instruments and $P(W)$ is the projection matrix $W(W'W)^{-1}W'$.[3] The generalized instrumental variable estimators (GIVE) of α_i and δ_i are obtained by minimizing $S_i(\alpha_i, \delta_i)$ and will be denoted by $\tilde{\alpha}_i$ and $\tilde{\delta}_i$. Thus $\tilde{\alpha}_i$ and $\tilde{\delta}_i$ can be regarded as

---

[3] Strictly speaking, the instrument matrix of (2.2) should be denoted by W_i since it will usually vary from one equation to another, but little would be gained by this additional complication of the notation.

the unrestricted minimizers of the optimization criterion of (2.2). The associated function value $S_i(\tilde{\alpha}_i, \tilde{\delta}_i)$ will be denoted by $\tilde{S}_i$.

If, on the other hand, $S_i(\alpha_i, \delta_i)$ is minimized subject to the p_i constraints of $H_0: \alpha_i = 0$, then we obtain the restricted minimizers $\hat{\alpha}_i = 0$ and $\hat{\delta}_i$. Clearly, $\hat{\delta}_i$ minimizes

$$S_i(\delta_i) = (y_i - X_i\delta_i)'P(W)(y_i - X_i\delta_i) \tag{2.3}$$

and so is the GIVE for the null model (1.2) when it is estimated using the variables of W as instruments. Inspection of the first-order conditions for a minimum of the function of (2.3) yields

$$\hat{\delta}_i = (X_i'P(W)X_i)^{-1}X_i'P(W)y_i$$
$$= (\hat{X}_i'\hat{X}_i)^{-1}\hat{X}_i'y_i, \tag{2.4}$$

where $\hat{X}_i = P(W)X_i$ is the matrix of OLS predicted values for the regression of X_i on W. The restricted minimum, $S_i(\hat{\delta}_i)$, will be denoted by $\hat{S}_i$.

IV analogues of the LR test

Gallant and Jorgenson (1979) show that a simple test of $H_0: \alpha_i = 0$ can be derived by regarding the S_i functions as being similar to minus log-likelihood functions with the difference between restricted and unrestricted minima providing an asymptotic χ^2 test. More precisely, these authors demonstrate that, when $H_0: \alpha_i = 0$ is true,

$$\hat{S}_i - \tilde{S}_i \overset{a}{\sim} \sigma_i^2\chi^2(p_i), \tag{2.5}$$

with large values indicating that the sample evidence is not in accord with the null hypothesis. In fact, under the hypothesis that (1.2) is correctly specified, $\hat{S}_i$ and $\tilde{S}_i$ are asymptotically distributed as $\sigma_i^2\chi^2$ with degrees-of-freedom parameters $(s - g_i)$ and $(s - g_i - p_i)$, respectively. In order to derive a feasible test procedure, it is necessary to eliminate the unknown parameter σ_i^2 in (2.5). Gallant and Jorgenson prove that if $\dot{\sigma}_i^2$ is consistent for σ_i^2 when $\alpha_i = 0$, then

$$(\hat{S}_i - \tilde{S}_i)/\dot{\sigma}_i^2 \overset{a}{\sim} \chi^2(p_i) \tag{2.6}$$

on H_0.

The test statistic of (2.6) is viewed by Gallant and Jorgenson as an analogue of the LR test. It can be easily calculated by means of two artificial regressions. Let

$$\tilde{u}_i = y_i - X_i\tilde{\delta}_i - T_i\tilde{\alpha}_i \tag{2.7}$$

and

$$\hat{u}_i = y_i - X_i \hat{\delta}_i \tag{2.8}$$

denote the IV residual vectors obtained by unrestricted and restricted estimation of the alternative; then $\tilde{S}_i = \tilde{u}_i' P(W) \tilde{u}_i$ and $\hat{S}_i = \hat{u}_i' P(W) \hat{u}_i$. Thus $\tilde{S}_i$ (resp. $\hat{S}_i$) is simply the explained sum of squares from the OLS regression of $\tilde{u}_i$ (resp. $\hat{u}_i$) on the instruments W. The residual vectors of (2.7) and (2.8) can also be used to provide a suitable estimator $\dot{\sigma}_i^2$ since

$$\tilde{s}_i^2 = (n - g_i - p_i)^{-1} \tilde{u}_i' \tilde{u}_i,$$

$$\tilde{\sigma}_i^2 = n^{-1} \tilde{u}_i' \tilde{u}_i,$$

$$\hat{s}_i^2 = (n - g_i)^{-1} \hat{u}_i' \hat{u}_i$$

and

$$\hat{\sigma}_i^2 = n^{-1} \hat{u}_i' \hat{u}_i$$

are all consistent under H_0. Whichever of the available consistent estimators of σ_i^2 is employed, the test statistic of (2.6) will be non-negative. This property is not shared by a statistic described by Breusch and Godfrey (1981), which is based upon a comparison of the R^2 statistics from the two artificial regressions yielding $\tilde{S}_i$ and $\hat{S}_i$.

The Breusch–Godfrey variant can be derived by noting that the asymptotically valid criterion $(\hat{S}_i - \tilde{S}_i)/\hat{\sigma}_i^2$ can be written as

$$\hat{S}_i/\hat{\sigma}_i^2 - \tilde{S}_i/\tilde{\sigma}_i^2 + (\tilde{S}_i/\hat{\sigma}_i^2)[(\hat{\sigma}_i^2/\tilde{\sigma}_i^2) - 1]. \tag{2.9}$$

Under the null hypothesis, the third term of expression (2.9) can be neglected for large n since $\hat{S}_i/\hat{\sigma}_i^2 \underset{a}{\sim} \chi^2(s - g_i)$, $\tilde{S}_i/\tilde{\sigma}_i^2 \underset{a}{\sim} \chi^2(s - g_i - p_i)$ and $\mathrm{plim}[(\hat{\sigma}_i^2/\tilde{\sigma}_i^2) - 1] = 0$. Hence an asymptotically valid test of H_0 is provided by

$$(\hat{S}_i/\hat{\sigma}_i^2) - (\tilde{S}_i/\tilde{\sigma}_i^2) = n[R_r^2 - R_u^2], \tag{2.10}$$

where R_r^2 (resp. R_u^2) is the coefficient of determination for the OLS regression of $\hat{u}_i$ (resp. $\tilde{u}_i$) on the instruments W. This form of the IV analogue of the LR test can be easily calculated using standard estimation programmes, but sampling fluctuations can lead to negative values of the test statistic which are inconsistent with its asymptotic χ^2 distribution.

The statistics $\hat{S}_i/\hat{\sigma}_i^2$ and $\tilde{S}_i/\tilde{\sigma}_i^2$ are asymptotically equivalent to the IV analogue of the Anderson–Rubin (1949) statistic for testing overidentifying restrictions on the null model (1.2) and the alternative model (2.1), respectively. Consequently, a significance test is easily calculated when the estimation programme provides a test for overidentifying restrictions. If the

IV Anderson–Rubin statistics for (1.2) and (2.1) are denoted by ar_r and ar_u, respectively, then $(ar_r - ar_u)$ is asymptotically equivalent to the statistics of (2.6) and (2.10).

IV analogue of the Wald test

The Wald test of H_0: $\alpha_i = 0$ requires the evaluation of the quadratic form

$$\tilde{\alpha}_i'[\hat{T}_i'M(\hat{X}_i)\hat{T}_i]\tilde{\alpha}_i/\tilde{\sigma}_i^2, \tag{2.11}$$

where $\hat{T}_i = P(W)T_i$ and $M(\hat{X}_i) = [I - \hat{X}_i(\hat{X}_i'\hat{X}_i)^{-1}\hat{X}_i']$. As with the LR-type test of (2.6), sample values of the Wald criterion of (2.11) should be compared to prespecified critical values of the $\chi^2(p_i)$ distribution, or to p_i times those of the $F(p_i, n - g_i - p_i)$ distribution.[4]

If the number of instruments in W is strictly greater than $(p_i + g_i)$, a procedure proposed by Dhrymes (1969) can be used instead of the Wald test. This alternative test involves replacing the variance estimate $\tilde{\sigma}_i^2$ in (2.11) by $\tilde{S}_i/(s - g_i - p_i)$ and dividing the resulting quantity by p_i to obtain a large sample test based upon the $F(p_i, s - g_i - p_i)$ distribution. However, Hatanaka (1977) and Maddala (1974) both argue that the Dhrymes test is inferior to the more conventional Wald procedure based upon the statistic of (2.11).

IV analogue of the LM test

The derivation of LM/Score-type tests has been considered by several authors (e.g., Burguete et al., 1982; Engle, 1982a; Godfrey and Wickens, 1982). Application of their general results to the problem of testing $\alpha_i = 0$ in the alternative model (2.1) yields the statistic

$$\hat{u}_i'\hat{T}_i[\hat{T}_i'M(\hat{X}_i)\hat{T}_i]^{-1}\hat{T}_i'\hat{u}_i/\hat{\sigma}_i^2, \tag{2.12}$$

which can be shown to equal

$$\tilde{\alpha}_i'[\hat{T}_i'M(\hat{X}_i)\hat{T}_i]\tilde{\alpha}_i/\hat{\sigma}_i^2,$$

thus revealing that the only difference between the Wald and LM statistics is the choice of variance estimate in the denominator.[5] There is, however,

---

[4] These procedures are both asymptotically valid. As n tends to infinity so does $(n - g_i - p_i)$ for fixed g_i and p_i, and it is well known that $F(v_1, v_2) \to \chi^2(v_1)/v_1$ as $v_2 \to \infty$.

[5] It can be shown that the numerators of expressions (2.11) and (2.12) both equal the explained sum of squares for the OLS regression of $\hat{u}_i$ on $\hat{X}_i$ and $\hat{T}_i$.

no systematic inequality between the Wald and LM statistics of the type discussed in Chapter 2 because $\hat{\sigma}_i^2$ can be smaller than, equal to, or greater than $\tilde{\sigma}_i^2$. The LR statistic of (2.6) equals the LM statistic if $\dot{\sigma}_i^2 = \hat{\sigma}_i^2$ and equals the Wald statistic if $\dot{\sigma}_i^2 = \tilde{\sigma}_i^2$.

Choosing between tests and the use of LEAs

In the absence of comparative evidence on their small-sample behaviour, there is little to choose between the IV analogues of the LR, Wald and LM tests of $\alpha_i = 0$. It might be argued that, in the context of testing for misspecification, the LM procedure has smaller computational costs when the alternative is a non-linear generalization of the null specification. The strength of this argument is, however, considerably weakened by the fact that the previous results on LEAs for quasi MLE of non-simultaneous regression models carry over to IV estimation of structural equations. Consequently many misspecification tests can be implemented by means of extended models of the form (2.1) and there is no compelling case against the use of tests based upon overfitting the null model – namely, the Wald and LR type procedures – as long as they are applied to such augmented relationships and not to the actual non-linear alternative.

Consider, for example, a non-linear model of the type discussed by Amemiya (1983, Section 5) which can be written as

$$y_i = f_i(\theta_i) + u_i, \tag{2.13}$$

where $f_i(\cdot)$ depends upon the regressor data matrix X_i and possibly on observations on other variables, θ_i is a $(g_i + p_i)$-dimensional vector which will be written in partitioned form as $\theta_i' = (\delta_i', \alpha_i')$, and imposing $\alpha_i = 0$ yields $f_i(\delta_i, 0) = X_i\delta_i$. Thus the null hypothesis to be tested is $\alpha_i = 0$.

The restricted IV estimator $\hat{\theta}_i$ solves the constrained optimization problem

$$\min_{\theta_i} \ (y_i - f_i(\theta_i))'P(W)(y_i - f_i(\theta_i)) \text{ subject to } \alpha_i = 0,$$

but, if $\alpha_i = 0$, then

$$(y_i - f_i(\theta_i))'P(W)(y_i - f_i(\theta_i)) = (y_i - X_i\delta_i)'P(W)(y_i - X_i\delta_i).$$

It follows that the restricted estimator is given by the vector $\hat{\theta}_i = (\hat{\delta}_i', 0')'$. The analogue of the classical score vector is then

$$-F_i(\hat{\theta}_i)'P(W)\hat{u}_i, \tag{2.14}$$

where

$$F_i(\hat{\theta}_i) = \partial f_i(\hat{\theta}_i)/\partial\theta_i = [X_i, \partial f_i(\hat{\theta}_i)/\partial\alpha_i].$$

It is easy to verify that the vector of (2.14) is also appropriate for testing $\alpha_i = 0$ in the context of the artificial linear model

$$y_i = X_i\delta_i + [\partial f_i(\hat{\theta}_i)/\partial\alpha_i]\alpha_i + u_i. \tag{2.15}$$

It follows that equations (2.13) and (2.15) represent LEAs with respect to the null model (1.2). Since the alternative (2.15) is of the form (2.1) with $T_i = \partial f_i(\hat{\theta}_i)/\partial\alpha_i$, the variable addition tests discussed above can indeed be used to implement checks of the adequacy of the null specification relative to many non-linear generalizations.

A pure significance test

It is interesting to note that one of the quantities required when evaluating the LR-type tests of (1.2) against (2.1), namely $\hat{S}_i/\hat{\sigma}_i^2$, provides a pure significance test of the former specification. The variable

$$\hat{S}_i^2/\hat{\sigma}_i^2 = \hat{u}_i'P(W)\hat{u}_i/\hat{\sigma}_i^2 = nR_r^2 \tag{2.16}$$

is asymptotically distributed as $\chi^2(s - g_i)$ when the model is correctly specified and is $O_p(n)$ under many misspecifications. Alternatively, (2.16) can be regarded as a special case of either (2.6) or (2.10) since $\tilde{S}_i = 0$ for all alternatives (2.1) with $p_i = s - g_i$. In particular, when Z is used as the instrument matrix W, the resulting statistic $\hat{S}_i/\hat{\sigma}_i^2$ is asymptotically distributed as $\chi^2(k - g_i)$ under correct specification and can be interpreted as a test of (1.2) against any just identified alternative of the form (2.1) (see Hausman, 1983, p. 433, for a discussion of the relationship between this procedure and the Anderson–Rubin, 1949, test of overidentifying restrictions).[6]

5.2.2   Tests for systems of equations

The above tests of an individual structural equation against some more general model can be extended for application to complete systems. Let

y be the mn by 1 vector $(y_1', y_2', \ldots, y_m')'$
u be the mn by 1 vector $(u_1', u_2', \ldots, u_m')'$
δ be the g by 1 $(g = \Sigma_1^m g_i)$ vector $(\delta_1', \delta_2', \ldots, \delta_m')'$
X be the mn by g matrix diag$(X_1, X_2, \ldots, X_m)$.

The m equations of the form (1.2) can then be written as

$$y = X\delta + u. \tag{2.17}$$

---

[6] Overidentifying hypotheses are also discussed by Breusch (1986).

Suppose that the null specification of (2.17) is to be tested against the augmented structural form

$$y = X\delta + T\alpha + u, \tag{2.18}$$

where T is the mn by p $(p = \Sigma_1^m p_i)$ matrix of test variables, that is, $T = \text{diag}(T_1, T_2, \ldots, T_m)$, and α is the p by 1 vector $(\alpha_1', \alpha_2', \ldots, \alpha_m')'$.

For any suitable set of instruments W, the estimation function to be minimized is

$$(y - X\delta - T\alpha)'(\dot{\Sigma}^{-1} \otimes P(W))(y - X\delta - T\alpha), \tag{2.19}$$

where $\dot{\Sigma}$ is a consistent estimator of Σ. If the p restrictions of $H_0: \alpha = 0$ are imposed, then minimization of (2.19) will yield the usual full information GIVE of the parameters of the null model (2.17) (or equivalently (1.1)). For example, when $W = Z$ and $\dot{\Sigma}$ is constructed from two-stage least-squares (2SLS) residuals, the constrained minimizer of (2.19) is the three-stage least-squares (3SLS) estimator for (2.17).

As before, we shall denote the unrestricted GIVE by $\tilde{\alpha}$ and $\tilde{\delta}$, and the restricted GIVE of δ will be denoted by $\hat{\delta}$. It will again be useful to introduce the associated residual vectors $\tilde{u} = (y - X\tilde{\delta} - T\tilde{\alpha})$ and $\hat{u} = (y - X\hat{\delta})$. Gallant and Jorgenson (1979) show that, provided regularity conditions are satisfied,

$$\hat{u}'(\dot{\Sigma}^{-1} \otimes P(W))\hat{u} - \tilde{u}'(\dot{\Sigma}^{-1} \otimes P(W))\tilde{u} \tag{2.20}$$

is asymptotically distributed as $\chi^2(p)$ under $H_0: \alpha = 0$, thus generalizing their test of (2.6).

A pure significance test

As with the corresponding statistic for an individual structural equation, the component of the system test (2.20) associated with the estimation of the null model can serve as a pure significance test. The variable $\hat{u}'(\dot{\Sigma}^{-1} \otimes P(W))\hat{u}$ is asymptotically distributed as χ^2 $(ms - g)$ for a correctly specified system and, in general, will be $O_p(n)$ under many specification errors. Also, if $W = Z$, the criterion $\hat{u}'(\dot{\Sigma}^{-1} \otimes P(Z))\hat{u}$ provides a test of (2.17) against any generalization (2.18) in which each equation is just identified since $\tilde{u}'(\dot{\Sigma}^{-1} \otimes P(Z))\tilde{u}$ equals zero when $g_i + p_i = k$ for all i. The statistic $\hat{u}'(\dot{\Sigma}^{-1} \otimes P(Z))\hat{u}$ is, therefore, asymptotically equivalent to the usual quasi-likelihood ratio test of the restricted (null) structural form (1.1) against the unrestricted reduced form

$$Y = Z\Pi + V, \tag{2.21}$$

where Π is an unrestricted k by m coefficient matrix and $V = UB^{-1}$.

Hausman (1983, Section 5) provides a discussion of other complete systems tests of all overidentifying restrictions.

5.2.3 Sargan's tests for misspecification

The procedures described above, when combined with appropriately defined LEAs, provide a very flexible and easily implemented approach to checking for specification errors in simultaneous equation models. However, the IV analogues of classical tests discussed by Burgete et al. (1982) and Gallant and Jorgenson (1979) are not without their drawbacks. Even if only the null model is estimated, the instruments used must be sufficient in number to permit the estimation of the alternative and be valid for the latter model. We shall provide examples later in this chapter which illustrate that these restrictions can render the tests unattractive. It is, therefore, sometimes worth considering alternative approaches to testing for misspecification after estimation by IV.

In an important unpublished paper, Sargan (1976) proposes a general procedure which involves the examination of the covariances between the estimated IV residuals ($\hat{u}_i$ or $\hat{u}$ according to context) and a set of instruments that need not have been used in the estimation of the null model. This procedure can be illustrated by considering the problem of testing the specification of a single structural equation (1.2) estimated by the IV method with parameter vector estimate $\hat{\delta}_i$ and residual vector $\hat{u}_i$ given by (2.4) and (2.8), respectively.[7] Let Q_i denote an n by q_i matrix of instruments of rank q_i which may or may not overlap with W or Z. Sargan derives a χ^2 test criterion by obtaining the asymptotic null distribution of the scaled covariance vector $n^{-\frac{1}{2}}Q_i'\hat{u}_i = n^{\frac{1}{2}}(Q_i'\hat{u}_i/n)$. The elements of $n^{-\frac{1}{2}}Q_i'\hat{u}_i$ are shown to be asymptotically jointly normally distributed when the null model (1.2) is correct, having zero mean vector and a covariance matrix consistently estimated by

$$\hat{\Delta} = \hat{\sigma}_i^2 n^{-1}[Q_i'Q_i - Q_i'X_i(\hat{X}_i'\hat{X}_i)^{-1}\hat{X}_i'Q_i$$
$$- Q_i'\hat{X}_i(\hat{X}_i'\hat{X}_i)^{-1}X_i'Q_i + Q_i'X_i(\hat{X}_i'\hat{X}_i)^{-1}X_i'Q_i]. \qquad (2.22)$$

If, however, specification errors are present, then, in many cases, the residuals and instruments of Q_i will have non-zero asymptotic covariances, and so $n^{-\frac{1}{2}}Q_i'\hat{u}_i$ will be $O_p(n^{\frac{1}{2}})$. Large values of $n^{-\frac{1}{2}}Q_i'\hat{u}_i$ can, therefore, be taken as indicators of misspecification.

The covariance matrix estimate $\hat{\Delta}$ provides a natural metric for measuring whether $n^{-\frac{1}{2}}Q_i'\hat{u}_i$ is sufficiently close to the null vector to justify

---

[7] See Sargan (1976) for a more general discussion covering sets of equations that are non-linear in parameters.

acceptance of the hypothesis of correct specification. This matrix is, however, not a by-product of routine calculations for IV estimation, and so special subroutines will be required for its evaluation. Pagan and Hall (1983) feel that this problem constitutes a serious obstacle to would-be users and propose a restriction on the choice of Q_i in order to overcome it. The Pagan–Hall suggestion is that the variables of Q_i be selected only from W, the set of instruments employed for estimation. This restriction implies that $Q_i = \hat{Q}_i \equiv P(W)Q_i$ and that $X_i'Q_i = \hat{X}_i'Q_i = \hat{X}_i'\hat{Q}_i$. Substitution of these relationships in (2.22) yields

$$\hat{\Delta} = \hat{\sigma}_i^2 n^{-1}[\hat{Q}_i'\hat{Q}_i - \hat{Q}_i'\hat{X}_i(\hat{X}_i'\hat{X}_i)^{-1}\hat{X}_i'\hat{Q}_i]$$

$$= \hat{\sigma}_i^2 n^{-1}[\hat{Q}_i'M(\hat{X}_i)\hat{Q}_i].$$

If it is assumed that $[\hat{Q}_i'M(\hat{X}_i)\hat{Q}_i]$ is non-singular, then the Pagan–Hall modification of Sargan's check for model adequacy leads to the test statistic

$$\hat{u}_i'\hat{Q}_i[\hat{Q}_i'M(\hat{X}_i)\hat{Q}_i]^{-1}\hat{Q}_i'\hat{u}_i/\hat{\sigma}_i^2 \qquad (2.23)$$

since $Q_i'\hat{u}_i = \hat{Q}_i'\hat{u}_i$. The statistic of (2.23) is asymptotically distributed as χ^2 (q_i) under correct specification and is very similar to the LM-type criterion of (2.12). Indeed it is clear from (2.12) that the Pagan–Hall variant can be implemented by testing $\psi_i = 0$ in the alternative

$$y_i = X_i\delta_i + Q_i\psi_i + u_i. \qquad (2.24)$$

Thus, if the suggestion made by Pagan and Hall (1983) concerning the choice of test instruments Q_i is adopted, then Sargan's (1976) procedure loses its distinctive character and is reduced to a special case of the OV test in which only variables from W can be used as additional regressors to form an alternative to the null. This approach seems quite restrictive.

Note that in practice the matrix $[\hat{Q}_i'M(\hat{X}_i)\hat{Q}_i]$ will sometimes be singular, so that the criterion of (2.23) will not always be available. The problem and its solution can be discussed in the context of the extended model (2.24).[8] One potential cause of singularity is that (X_i, Q_i) does not have full column rank; for example, Q_i may contain some of the predetermined regressors of (1.2). The solution is simply to delete redundant variables of Q_i and to replace (2.24) by

$$y_i = X_i\delta_i + Q_i^*\psi_i^* + u_i, \qquad (2.25)$$

where (X_i, Q_i^*) is an n by $(g_i+q_i^*)$ matrix with full column rank. The next

---

[8] The solution to be described involves the deletion of a number of misspecification indicators and is equivalent to the use of a g-inverse in the quadratic form of (2.23).

aspect of the problem is whether or not there are sufficient instruments in W to permit testing of the q_i^* restrictions of $\psi_i^* = 0$. If $s \geqslant (g_i + q_i^*)$, no action is required, and standard omitted variables tests can be applied to test (1.2) against (2.25). On the other hand, if $s < (g_i + q_i^*)$, then $(g_i + q_i^* - s)$ of the variables of Q_i^* must be deleted from (2.25), leaving only $(s - g_i)$ zero restrictions to be tested. In this case, it does not matter which variables of Q_i^* are excluded, and the statistic $\hat{S}_i / \hat{\sigma}_i^2$ of (2.16) provides an appropriate test.

5.3   Testing for serial correlation

Although asymptotic results on the estimation of linear simultaneous equation models with vector autoregressive-moving average errors (VARMA) are available, most empirical work is conducted on the basis of the assumption that the disturbances are serially independent.[9] The presence of lagged endogenous variables in the system is almost as common as the assumption of serial independence and highlights the need to test this assumption since the usual estimators of the parameters of a dynamic model will be inconsistent if it is false. We shall, therefore, concentrate on the problem of checking the consistency of the hypothesis of serial independence with the sample evidence.

Many of the tests to be considered require the specification of an alternative hypothesis. For simplicity of exposition, results will be derived for the case of a first-order autocorrelation model, and the extensions required to cover other more complicated alternatives will just be outlined. In practice, however, it is important to use information about such features as the periodicity of the data and the form of any lag transformations employed to derive estimating equations from distributed lag relationships. The mechanical use of a single simple alternative model cannot be relied upon to yield a powerful test in all situations.

The simplest and most familiar autocorrelation scheme for the disturbances of a complete system is probably the first-order vector autoregressive (VAR(1)) process

$$U = U_{-1}R + E, \tag{3.1}$$

where U_{-1} denotes the one-period lagged value of U, R is an m by m coefficient matrix satisfying the conditions for stationarity and the n rows of E are independently distributed with zero mean vector and covariance matrix Φ.

---

[9] Reinsel (1979a, b) provides useful discussions of estimation in the presence of VARMA errors.

The VAR(1) model (3.1) may provide an attractive alternative hypothesis when the structural form is to be estimated by a systems method, but poses problems in the more common situation in which a limited information estimator is applied to each equation in turn. When an equation-by-equation approach to estimation is adopted, it is more convenient to employ scalar processes in the alternative model by restricting R to be diagonal. If the off-diagonal elements of R are set equal to zero, then (3.1) can be rewritten as

$$u_i = r_{ii}u_{i,-1} + e_i, \quad i = 1, m, \tag{3.2}$$

where $u_{i,-1}$ denotes the one-period lagged value of u_i, the ith column of U, r_{ii} is the (i, i) element of R, and e_i is the ith column of E and has n elements which have zero mean and common variance ϕ_i^2.

The disadvantage of considering only scalar processes is that the tests of $r_{ii} = 0$ may lack power for some non-diagonal R matrices, but the importance of this problem should not be overstated. Fisk (1967) argues that it is unlikely that cross-serial correlations will exist without autocorrelation along each series, so that it should be sufficient in most circumstances to test whether the errors in each equation are separately autocorrelated. As will be seen below, even if scalar processes like (3.2) are adopted as alternative models, some consideration must be given to the other equations when constructing an autocorrelation test for the equation of current interest.

There is, however, no need to consider autoregressive and moving average alternatives separately. The asymptotic theory is based upon analysis under the null and a sequence of local alternatives, and generalizations of the results of Section 4.4 apply. This feature can be illustrated by rewriting (3.1) as

$$U = E + E_{-1}R + E_{-2}R^2 + \cdots$$

and noting that when the elements of R are $O(n^{-\frac{1}{2}})$ the terms in $R^i(i > 1)$ can be ignored for the purposes of the analysis; so that the VAR(1) scheme (3.1) is locally equivalent to the VMA(1) alternative

$$U = E + E_{-1}R. \tag{3.3}$$

More generally, the VAR(p) and VMA(p) processes are locally equivalent alternatives (LEAs) when the null specification is that the disturbances are serially independent, and so nothing is lost by restricting attention to the more convenient autoregressive error models.

Portmanteau tests for serial correlation which do not involve the formulation of a specific alternative will also be considered. However, bounds tests and exact tests based upon the assumptions that the variables of Z are non-stochastic and the disturbances are normally distributed will not be examined.[10]

5.3.1   *Testing against vector serial correlation alternatives in dynamic models*

As a starting point, consider the alternative model comprising

$$YB + Z\Gamma = U \tag{1.1}$$

and

$$U = U_{-1}R + E. \tag{3.1}$$

The null hypothesis to be tested is H_0: $R = 0$. The FIML technique, therefore, provides the restricted MLE for (1.1). It will be convenient to denote the n by m matrix of FIML residuals by $\hat{U}$.

Direct application of the LM principle to the problem of testing H_0 is unattractive because this approach would require special sub-routines to be added to existing estimation programmes. An asymptotically equivalent indirect test based upon the results of Chapter 3 on LEAs may be much more convenient to implement. Godfrey (1981) shows that the alternative hypothesis under consideration is locally equivalent to

$$YB + Z\Gamma + \hat{U}_{-1}R = E, \tag{3.4}$$

where $\hat{U}_{-1}$ denotes the matrix of lagged FIML residuals. Thus it is only necessary to test the validity of excluding the matrix of test variables $\hat{U}_{-1}$ from (3.4).

Since estimation programmes often allow residuals to be lagged and then used as regressors, the LR test of $R = 0$ in the LEA (3.4) is quite attractive and requires no additional programming. It may be possible to reduce the computational costs of such an LR test by exploiting the fact that the matrix R is unrestricted and so can be eliminated by concentration of the likelihood for (3.4). This concentration simply leads to the original structural form being re-estimated with Y and Z being replaced by their residuals from OLS regressions on $\hat{U}_{-1}$; so that the unrestricted maximized log-likelihood is obtained by estimating

$$Y^*B + Z^*\Gamma = E^*$$

by FIML, where $Y^* = [I - \hat{U}_{-1}(\hat{U}'_{-1}\hat{U}_{-1})^{-1}\hat{U}'_{-1}]Y$ and $Z^* = [I - \hat{U}_{-1}(\hat{U}'_{-1}\hat{U}_{-1})^{-1}\hat{U}'_{-1}]Z$.

As noted by Godfrey (1981, p. 1448), the test derived from the

---

[10] See Harvey and Phillips (1980) for a discussion of such procedures.

augmented system (3.4) is a generalization of Durbin's (1970, p. 420) second test for autocorrelation in dynamic multiple regression models. It is also possible to generalize Durbin's first test, the h test; this approach has been used by Guilkey (1975). Unfortunately, as Maritz (1978) has pointed out, Guilkey's analysis contains errors which invalidate his expression for a test statistic.

Other computational schemes can be employed to produce procedures that are asymptotically equivalent to the direct LM test of $R = 0$. For example, Breusch and Godfrey (1981) describe $C(\alpha)$ tests that can be calculated using two-stage least-squares estimates.

Extensions for more general alternatives

As was noted above, the VAR(p) and VMA(p) schemes are LEAs with respect to the null hypothesis of serially independent disturbances and so there is no need for a separate treatment of LM-type tests despite the very real differences in estimation under these alternatives. The extension of previous results to allow for values of p greater than 1 is straightforward and, in general, the LEA corresponding to (3.4) can be written as

$$YB + Z\Gamma + \hat{U}_{-1}R_1 + \hat{U}_{-2}R_2 + \cdots + \hat{U}_{-p}R_p = E, \tag{3.5}$$

with the pm^2 restrictions of H_0 being

$$\text{vec}(R_1) = \text{vec}(R_2) = \cdots = \text{vec}(R_p) = 0.$$

Restricted alternatives can also be accommodated. For example, if quarterly data are being employed, then a test against a simple fourth-order vector moving average or autoregressive alternative can be calculated as a check of $R_4 = 0$ in the augmented model

$$YB + Z\Gamma + \hat{U}_{-4}R_4 = E.$$

Tests based upon IV estimates

The tests discussed above are based upon maximum likelihood estimators or asymptotically equivalent estimators. In practice, however, systems IV methods are sometimes used to obtain parameter estimates. The procedures of Gallant and Jorgenson (1979) described in Section 5.2 above can be employed to assess the significance of the estimated coefficients of lagged residuals, but require that the same instrument set be used to estimate the null and alternative specifications (this requirement is not imposed in the indirect LM approach using MLE since imposition of $H_0 : R = 0$ removes the variables of $\hat{U}_{-1}$ even though they are valid instruments under this hypothesis). Consequently, if the Gallant–

Jorgenson analogue of the LR test is to be adopted, then the null specification, that is, the original structural form with serially independent errors, must be estimated using an instrument set valid and adequate for the LEA.

5.3.2   Testing against scalar serial correlation alternatives in dynamic models

For ease of exposition, we shall again use a simple AR(1) alternative. A typical individual structural equation is then

$$y_i = Y_i \beta_i + Z_i \gamma_i + u_i = X_i \delta_i + u_i, \tag{1.2}$$

with the alternative to the serial independence assumption being

$$u_i = r_{ii} u_{i, -1} + e_i, \tag{3.2}$$

with the n elements of e_i being NID$(0, \phi_i^2)$ variates. In order to develop limited-information single-equation analogues of the LM tests of the previous sub-section, it would be necessary to make some assumption about the autocorrelation structure of the disturbances of the other $(m - 1)$ equations of the system. The likelihood function could then be obtained and concentrated to yield a criterion appropriate for the LIML estimation of δ_i and r_{ii}. For example, if Amemiya's (1966) Λ_0 specification is adopted with the system errors being VAR(1), then the concentrated log-likelihood is

$$l^*(\delta_i, r_{ii}) = \text{cnst} - \frac{n}{2} \ln e_i' e_i + \frac{n}{2} \ln e_i' M_F e_i, \tag{3.6}$$

where $M_F = I - F(F'F)^{-1} F'$, F contains the non-redundant variables of (Z, Y_{-1}, Z_{-1}), and e_i is regarded as a function of δ_i and r_{ii} defined by

$$e_i = y_i - X_i \delta_i - r_{ii} y_{i, -1} + X_{i, -1}(r_{ii} \delta_i) \tag{3.7}$$

(see Hatanaka, 1976, equation 14, p. 198).

However, this approach is somewhat unattractive because it seems likely that, in practice, revisions of specification and changes in the set of available instruments will occur as the researcher checks each equation of the model. Therefore it seems preferable to develop test criteria for the case in which the instruments can be selected in a fairly flexible fashion and need not be the regressors of a set of reduced-form relationships derived from an untested generalization of the null specification.

The estimation of econometric models with autoregressive disturbances by means of general sets of instruments was considered by Sargan (1959). Sargan proposed the Autoregressive Instrumental Variable (AIV) technique in which estimates of δ_i and r_{ii} are obtained as the minimizers of the quadratic form

$$S_i(\delta_i, r_{ii}) = e_i'P(W)e_i,$$

where $P(W) = W(W'W)^{-1}W'$, W being an n by s matrix of valid instruments, and e_i is given by (3.7) as a function of the unknown parameters. If θ is used to denote the $(g_i + 1)$ by 1 parameter vector $(\delta_i', r_{ii})'$, then the AIV estimator $\tilde{\theta}$ is consistent, with $n^{\frac{1}{2}}(\tilde{\theta} - \theta)$ being asymptotically normally distributed with zero mean vector and covariance matrix

$$\phi_i^2 \text{ plim } n^{-1}(\partial e_i/\partial \theta)'P(W)(\partial e_i/\partial \theta),$$

provided that the following conditions are satisfied:

(i) $n^{-1}W'W$ tends a finite non-singular s by s matrix M_{WW} as $n \to \infty$;
(ii) $n^{-\frac{1}{2}}W'e_i \underset{a}{\sim} N(0, \phi_i^2 M_{WW})$;
(iii) the probability that $n^{-1}W'(\partial e_i/\partial \theta)$ is a finite matrix with full column rank in a neighbourhood of the true parameter vector tends to one as $n \to \infty$.

Condition (iii) obviously requires that there be at least as many instruments as there are unknown parameters – that is, $s \geq (g_i + 1)$ – but it also places other restrictions on the choice of instruments. In order to determine the nature of these restrictions, note that

$$n^{-1}W'(\partial e_i/\partial \theta) = -[n^{-1}W'(X_i - r_{ii}X_{i,-1}):n^{-1}W'u_{i,-1}],$$

so that some of the instruments must be asymptotically correlated with the lagged disturbance $u_{i,-1}$ if condition (iii) is to be satisfied. Consequently, it is not valid to use only exogenous variables as instruments.

Having selected an appropriate set of instrumental variables, it would be possible to check the consistency of the assumption of independent errors with the data by testing the significance of the AIV estimate $\tilde{r}_{ii}$. This Wald-type test is, however, unattractive because it involves estimation under the alternative hypothesis. It is possible to obtain an asymptotically equivalent procedure which requires only estimation under the null hypothesis by extending Durbin's (1970) theorem.

Godfrey's test

Godfrey (1976) has modified Durbin's (1970) general theorem by using the AIV estimation criterion $S_i(\delta_i, r_{ii})$, rather than a log-likelihood function. Godfrey (1976) follows Durbin's analysis closely and derives an analogue of the latter author's h test, which he terms the π test. The π test and its generalizations for pth order autocorrelation alternatives are, however, not easily implemented using standard estimation programmes, and a much more convenient approach is available.

It can be shown that Godfrey's π test is asymptotically equivalent to a test of $r_{ii} = 0$ in the context of the expanded model

$$y_i = X_i\delta_i + r_{ii}\hat{u}_{i,-1} + e_i, \tag{3.8}$$

where the elements of e_i are taken to be NID$(0, \phi_i^2)$. The assumption that the disturbances of the ith equation are independent can, therefore, be checked by means of an asymptotically valid 't test' of $r_{ii} = 0$ in (3.8).

Extensions for more general alternatives

The usual arguments about LEAs imply that the π test of Godfrey (1976) and the asymptotically equivalent procedure based upon testing the validity of excluding the lagged IV residual from (3.8) are both appropriate for the MA(1) alternative

$$u_i = e_i + r_{ii}e_{i,-1}.$$

More generally, the tests against the AR(p) and MA(p) alternatives are asymptotically equivalent or identical depending upon which testing principle is adopted, and so only the former general scheme need be considered.

It will be convenient to write the AR(p) alternative as

$$u_i = U_{i,-p}\alpha + e_i, \tag{3.9}$$

where $U_{i,-p} = (u_{i,-1} \vdots u_{i,-2} \vdots \cdots \vdots u_{i,-p})$ and α is the p-dimensional vector containing the parameters of the autoregression (3.9). Use of Godfrey's (1976) extension of Durbin's (1970) method or the corresponding LM-type procedure leads to the result that the criterion to be tested for significance is $n^{-\frac{1}{2}}\hat{U}'_{i,-p}P(W)\hat{u}_i$, where $\hat{U}_{i,-p} = (\hat{u}_{i,-1} \vdots \hat{u}_{i,-2} \vdots \cdots \vdots \hat{u}_{i,-p})$. As before, the results of Section 5.2 can be employed to deduce that an asymptotically valid test can be implemented by applying one of the standard checks of $\alpha = 0$ in the augmented model

$$y_i = X_i\delta_i + \hat{U}_{i,-p}\alpha + e_i.^{11} \tag{3.10}$$

Thus it is only necessary to estimate the ith equation using at least $(g_i + p)$ instruments which are also valid for the estimation of (3.10), then to use the derived residual vector $\hat{u}_i$ to construct the matrix of lagged terms

---

[11] The IV analogue of the LR statistic given in (2.6) and the asymptotically equivalent Breusch–Godfrey criterion of (2.10) can be used to provide convenient checks of the null hypothesis. The direct implementation of LM and Wald procedures may, however, require special subroutines to be written.

$\hat{U}_{i,-p}$, and finally to assess the joint significance of the variables of $\hat{U}_{i,-p}$ in (3.10). This generalization and modification of Godfrey's π test will be referred to as the $\pi(p)$ test. (Rejection of $\alpha = 0$ indicates that the assumption of correct specification is inconsistent with the sample data, but, of course, does not imply that the disturbances of u_i are generated by either an AR(p) or MA(p) scheme.)

In some cases, it may be found that $(g_i + p)$, the number of parameters to be estimated in (3.10), exceeds k, the number of variables in Z. The variables of Z must then be augmented. While the researcher can choose which and how many 'outside' instruments to use in W, it would be valid to select them from the non-redundant variables of

$$(y_{i,-1}, X_{i,-1}; \ldots; y_{i,-p}, X_{i,-p})$$

that do not appear in Z. (There is, however, no need to restrict W to have Z as a sub-matrix when $(g_i + p) > k$.) Changes in the choice of instruments will not affect the asymptotic null distribution of the test statistic for a given value of p, but they will lead to variations in asymptotic local power, and this may be reflected by differences in small sample performance.

Residual autocorrelation tests for individual equations

Since the procedures discussed above are based upon a fairly arbitrary choice of instruments, they need not be asymptotically equivalent to the appropriate LR test, and so there may be other procedures which are superior to them in large samples. One obvious alternative approach to checking the adequacy of the specification that the elements of u_i are independent is to examine the significance of estimates of their autocorrelations. This approach does not require the specification of an alternative (AR or MA) hypothesis and yields a pure significance test similar in spirit (but not in detail) to the Box–Pierce (1970) procedure. Perhaps more importantly, residual autocorrelation tests place less restrictive conditions on the instrumental variables used to estimate the ith structural equation; the variables of W can all be exogenous and the number of instruments can be as small as g_i.

The autocorrelation estimates can be derived from the IV residuals of $\hat{u}_i$ and their general form will be taken to be

$$\hat{r}_{ii}(j) = \hat{u}_i'\hat{u}_{i,-j}/\hat{u}_i'\hat{u}_i, j = 1, 2, \ldots, \tag{3.11}$$

where pre-sample values appearing in $\hat{u}_{i,-j}$ are set equal to zero.[12] Under

---

[12] The treatment of pre-sample values is asymptotically irrelevant. Also the implicit estimate of σ_i^2, namely, $n^{-1}\hat{u}_i'\hat{u}_i$, could be replaced by any estimator which is consistent under the null hypothesis without affecting the results provided by large sample theory.

the null hypothesis of serial independence, the IV estimator $\hat{\delta}_i$ will be consistent, and consequently each $\hat{r}_{ii}(j)$ will converge in probability to the corresponding population value of zero. Thus, if the first p estimated autocorrelations are examined, a test of the joint significance of the elements of

$$\hat{U}'_{i,-p}\hat{u}_i/\hat{u}'_i\hat{u}_i = \{\hat{r}_{ii}(j)\} \tag{3.12}$$

is required. The vector of (3.12) can be written as $Q'_i\hat{u}_i$, where $Q_i = (\hat{u}'_i\hat{u}_i)^{-1}\hat{U}_{i,-p}$, and is, therefore, a special case of Sargan's (1976) misspecification indicator since the variables of $\hat{U}_{i,-p}$ are valid instruments under the null hypothesis.

Substitution in (2.22), the general expression for Sargan's statistic, yields the result that

$$\theta(p) = \hat{u}'_i\hat{U}_{i,-p}[\hat{U}'_{i,-p}\hat{U}_{i,-p} - \hat{U}'_{i,-p}X_i(\hat{X}'_i\hat{X}_i)^{-1}\hat{X}'_i\hat{U}_{i,-p}$$
$$- \hat{U}'_{i,-p}\hat{X}_i(\hat{X}'_i\hat{X}_i)^{-1}X'_i\hat{U}_{i,-p}$$
$$+ \hat{U}'_{i,-p}X_i(\hat{X}'_i\hat{X}_i)^{-1}X'_i\hat{U}_{i,-p}]^{-1}\hat{U}'_{i,-p}\hat{u}_i/\hat{\sigma}^2_i, \tag{3.13}$$

where $\hat{\sigma}^2_i = n^{-1}\hat{u}'_i\hat{u}_i$ and $\hat{X}_i = P(W)X_i$, is the appropriate criterion for testing the significance of $(\hat{r}_{ii}(1), \ldots, \hat{r}_{ii}(p))'$.[13] The statistic $\theta(p)$ is asymptotically distributed as $\chi^2(p)$ when the disturbances of the ith structural equation are serially independent. It is, of course, simple to modify the $\theta(p)$ statistic in order to restrict attention to some sub-set of the first p residual autocorrelations; for example, if a quarterly dynamic relationship is being considered, then $\hat{r}_{ii}(4)$, $\hat{r}_{ii}(8)$, and so on, might be of particular interest. The actual calculation of $\theta(p)$, or of modified versions of this statistic, may, however, require additional programming.

The implementation of the $\theta(p)$ test is considerably simplified by choosing the instrument matrix W so that

$$P(W)\hat{U}_{i,-p} = \hat{U}_{i,-p}. \tag{3.14}$$

If the equality of (3.14) holds, then $\theta(p)$ of (3.13) takes the simpler form

$$\hat{u}'_i\hat{U}_{i,-p}[\hat{U}'_{i,-p}M(\hat{X}_i)\hat{U}_{i,-p}]^{-1}\hat{U}'_{i,-p}\hat{u}_i/\hat{\sigma}^2_i,$$

and the discussion of the Pagan–Hall (1983) suggestion provided in Section 5.2 implies that an asymptotically equivalent test can be obtained by testing $\alpha = 0$ in

$$y_i = X_i\delta_i + \hat{U}_{i,-p}\alpha + e_i.[14]$$

---

[13] The notation $\theta(p)$ for the statistic of (3.23) is suggested by the work of Godfrey (1978a) on the special case of $p = 1$, and is not to be confused with the use of θ to denote the parameter vector of some alternative model.

[14] This simplified form arises naturally if the variables of $\hat{X}_i$ are true

Consequently, the simplifying restriction on the choice of instruments removes the distinctive character of the $\theta(p)$ test and reduces it to a quasi–'LM with LEA' procedure. This restriction on W may also imply that a large number of instruments will have to be used to estimate the ith structural equation. For example, if $p = 4$, then for the lagged residuals to be linear combinations of the columns of W, W will have to include the non-redundant variables of

$$(y_{i,-1}, X_{i,-1}; y_{i,-2}, X_{i,-2}; y_{i,-3}, X_{i,-3}; y_{i,-4}, X_{i,-4}).^{15}$$

Given the limited numbers of observations available in empirical work, it seems ill-advised to achieve computational savings at the risk of harming small sample performance by having too many instruments. Equally relative computational costs do not provide sufficient justification for using the $\pi(p)$ test based upon variable addition rather than the $\theta(p)$ procedure – the properties of these tests must also be considered.

Comparison of the properties of $\pi(p)$ and $\theta(p)$ tests

Conventional asymptotic theory does not provide assistance in choosing between the $\pi(p)$ and $\theta(p)$ tests. Under the null hypothesis, the $\pi(p)$ and $\theta(p)$ statistics are both asymptotically distributed as $\chi^2(p)$. Further, both tests are consistent against fixed $AR(p)$ and $MA(p)$ alternatives. If behaviour under a sequence of local alternatives is considered, it can be shown that

$$\pi(p) \underset{a}{\sim} \chi^2(p, \mu_\pi^2)$$

and

$$\theta(p) \underset{a}{\sim} \chi^2(p, \mu_\theta^2),$$

but the sign of the difference between the non-centrality parameters, that is, $(\mu_\pi^2 - \mu_\theta^2)$, cannot, in general, be determined.[16] Hence comparison of asymptotic local powers does not yield a generally valid ranking of the two tests.

It seems unlikely that exact finite sample distributions of $\pi(p)$ and $\theta(p)$ will be available in the near future. There is clearly a need for Monte Carlo

reduced-form predictions (i.e., $W = Z$) and all the disturbances of the system are serially independent. Pagan and Hall (1983) express the view that these two conditions are very unlikely to be satisfied.

[15] Pagan and Hall (1983) suggested that lagged residuals $\hat{u}_{i,-j}$ are natural candidates for inclusion in W, but these variables are by-products of estimation and are not available before it takes place.

[16] Breusch (1978b) provides details for the $p = 1$ case.

studies to be carried out as a first step towards gaining useful information about the small sample properties of these important checks.

5.4   Testing for heteroscedasticity

As in the discussion of checks for serial correlation presented in Section 5.3, we shall distinguish between test procedures derived from the complete system and those appropriate for individual structural equations. A distinction will also be made between tests based upon the likelihood function and those calculated from estimates obtained using an arbitrary set of instruments.

Despite the widespread recognition of the need to check for heteroscedastic disturbances in the analysis of the non-simultaneous multiple regression model, the problems of inference and estimation for simultaneous equation systems with varying error covariance matrices have not received a great deal of attention.[17] In particular, there is very little information available about the finite sample behaviour of the asymptotically valid tests to be examined below. Harvey and Phillips (1981) present Monte Carlo results for the special case in which the model is static and the errors are normally distributed.

The large sample procedures to be discussed are the following: a system check calculated from FIML residuals; simple individual equation tests similar to the LM statistics described in Section 4.5; and a more robust form of the individual equation test.

5.4.1   *Systems tests for heteroscedasticity*

In their discussion of testing linear simultaneous equation models for heteroscedasticity, Godfrey and Wickens (1982) adopt the alternative hypothesis

$$u_{ti} = (1 + q_t(i)'\alpha_i)e_{ti}, \ i = 1, 2, \ldots, m, \tag{4.1}$$

where the $q_t(i)$ are r_i-dimensional non-stochastic vectors with uniformly bounded elements and the disturbances e_{ti} are such that the vectors $e_t = (e_{t1}, \ldots, e_{tm})'$ are independent $N(0, \Sigma)$ variates, $t = 1, 2, \ldots, n$. Equation (4.1) implies that

$$\sigma_{tij} = E(u_{ti}u_{tj})$$

$$= \sigma_{ij}(1 + q_t(i)'\alpha_i)(1 + q_t(j)'\alpha_j), \tag{4.2}$$

---

[17] Changes in the error covariance matrix, i.e., $E(u_tu_t')$, might reflect the fact that some coefficients of exogenous variables are random.

thus permitting time-varying variances $(i = j)$ and covariances $(i \neq j)$; i, $j = 1, 2, \ldots, m$ and $t = 1, 2, \ldots, n$.

Let $\theta'_2 = (\alpha'_1, \alpha'_2, \ldots, \alpha'_m)$. The disturbances of the system are homoscedastic under the null hypothesis $H_0: \theta_2 = 0$, and Godfrey and Wickens propose an LM test of H_0. However, the LM statistic given by Godfrey and Wickens (1982) is in outer-product gradient (OPG) form, and Monte Carlo evidence on the performance of OPG variants in other applications is far from encouraging (see Davidson and MacKinnon, 1985; Orme, 1987). Details of the calculation of the test statistic are provided by Godfrey and Wickens (1982, p. 94) and will not be reproduced here.

In view of the likely uncertainty about the form of the alternative hypothesis, it is worth pointing out that Kelejian (1982) has considered the following generalization of the single-equation framework used by Amemiya (1977):

$$\sigma_{tij} = \sigma_{ij} + q_t(i, j)' \alpha^*_{ij},$$

which can be rewritten as

$$\sigma_{tij} = \sigma_{ij}(1 + q_t(i, j)' \alpha_{ij}), \tag{4.3}$$

where $q_t(i, j)$ is the vector of non-stochastic variables thought to affect the covariance between u_{ti} and u_{tj}, α^*_{ij} is the corresponding parameter vector, and $\alpha_{ij} \equiv \alpha^*_{ij}/\sigma_{ij}$; $i, j = 1, 2, \ldots, m$ and $t = 1, 2, \ldots, n$. Comparison of (4.2) and (4.3) reveals that the Godfrey–Wickens model is a special case of Kelejian's alternative hypothesis.[18]

The test statistics proposed by Godfrey and Wickens (1982) and Kelejian (1982) are not simple to implement.[19] As yet, little is known about their finite sample behaviour, but it is possible that agreement with asymptotic theory will not be good. One potential problem lies in the number of degrees of freedom for the limit null distribution. In practice, it seems likely that the number of restrictions to be tested will be quite large relative to the sample size and that asymptotic results will not provide a good approximation.

For example, consider the application of Kelejian's procedure to a nine-equation model with each $q_t(i, j)$ vector having three elements; the system test for heteroscedasticity would then be based upon the $\chi^2(135)$ distribution. The approach outlined by Godfrey and Wickens (1982) leads

---

[18] In contrast to Kelejian's formulation, the model adopted by Godfrey and Wickens constrains correlations between disturbances to be constant.

[19] Kelejian (1982) describes a fairly cumbersome GLS procedure in which $\hat{u}_{ti}\hat{u}_{tj}$ variates are regressed on terms representing the constants σ_{ij} and appropriate $q_t(i, j)$.

to a procedure involving fewer degrees of freedom (27 in this example) by constraining the cross-equation error correlations to be constant. The cost of this constraint is that the test will be consistent against a smaller set of alternative hypotheses than the procedure given by Kelejian. It would, of course, be possible to modify Kelejian's test so that only the m variance terms were examined.[20] It seems, however, more natural to pursue the issue of tests for variances in the context of individual structural equations.

5.4.2   *Individual equation tests for heteroscedasticity*

Suppose that the relationship under investigation is the ith structural equation

$$y_i = X_i \delta_i + u_i,$$

and, as an alternative to the assumption of homoscedasticity, consider the additive heteroscedasticity model

$$\text{Var}(u_{ti}) = \sigma_{ti}^2 = \sigma_i^2 + q_t(i)' \alpha_i, \; t = 1, \ldots, n, \tag{4.4}$$

where the number of elements in α_i will again be denoted by r_i and, for the moment, the u_{ti} will be assumed to be independently and normally distributed.[21] The usual results on LEAs apply and the additive hetero-scedasticity form given in (4.4) is adopted to facilitate reference to previous work (e.g., Kelejian, 1982; Pagan and Hall, 1983).

As with the problem of testing the assumption of serial independence using limited information estimates, it is necessary to make some assumption about the disturbances of the other $(m - 1)$ structural equations of the model. The simplest strategy is to assume that it is certain that all other equations have homoscedastic errors, so that only the ith row and column of $Eu_t u_t'$ are suspected of varying with t. Kelejian (1982) proves that in this special case the procedure proposed by Breusch and Pagan (1979) and Godfrey (1978b) for (non-simultaneous) multiple regression models need only be modified by using, for example, 2SLS residuals in place of the OLS residuals.[22] Kelejian also provides two useful extensions.

---

[20] Kelejian (1982) discusses the case in which heteroscedasticity is only suspected in a sub-set of the equations of the system. If it is certain that some errors are homoscedastic, then this information will justify a test involving fewer degrees of freedom.

[21] The alternative of (4.4) is, after an irrelevant reparameterization, locally equivalent to the form specified by Godfrey and Wickens (1982).

[22] Such simple modifications do not always lead to valid large sample tests for simultaneous equation models; see, e.g., Godfrey's (1978a) comments on Durbin's (1970) h test.

First, Kelejian (1982) allows the disturbances u_{ti} to have a non-normal distribution, provided that the first eight moments are finite. The asymptotic test of $H_0^i : \alpha_i = 0$ against $H_1^i : \alpha_i \neq 0$ can then be carried out by inspecting the significance of the R^2 statistic for the OLS regression of $\hat{u}_{ti}^2$ on an intercept term and $q_t(i)$. More precisely, if this R^2 statistic is denoted by R_h^2, then, under H_0^i, nR_h^2 is asymptotically distributed as $\chi^2(r_i)$ (or equivalently, the usual F statistic for testing the significance of R_h^2 is distributed as $F(r_i, n - r_i - 1)$ in large samples). This result extends the work of Koenker (1981) on studentizing tests for heteroscedasticity.

Kelejian (1982) also shows that it is not necessary to estimate the equation of interest by LIML, 2SLS or some asymptotically equivalent estimator. The nR_h^2 statistic can be calculated using the squares of the residuals associated with virtually any consistent estimator of δ_i without affecting the asymptotic validity of the test.

So far, it has been assumed that the researcher is able to specify the variables appearing in the alternative model

$$\sigma_{ti}^2 = \sigma_i^2 + q_t(i)'\alpha_i$$

(or some LEA). The nR_h^2 test can, however, be employed when, instead of adopting a precise specification, it is assumed that there is a known ordering of the observations such that, under the alternative, the variances are non-decreasing. (This is, of course, the sort of alternative underlying the Goldfeld–Quandt, 1965, test for the multiple regression model with normal errors.) If the data are ordered so that the alternative takes the form $H_1 : \sigma_{ti}^2 \geqslant \sigma_{t-1,i}^2$, then it seems reasonable to conjecture that a useful one-degree-of-freedom test will be obtained by setting $r_i = 1$ and $q_t(i) = t$.[23] In fact, using nR_h^2 with $r_i = 1$ and $q_t(i) = t$ yields a studentized version of the procedure recommended by Szroeter (1978, p. 1320).

Since the procedures described by Harvey and Phillips (1981), Kelejian (1982) and Szroeter (1978) can be calculated as significance tests of $\alpha_i = 0$ in

$$\hat{u}_{ti}^2 = \sigma_i^2 + q_t(i)'\alpha_i + a_{ti}, \quad t = 1, \ldots, n, \tag{4.5}$$

they are clearly simple to implement and so, at first sight, represent attractive tests for heteroscedasticity. However, these simple procedures are based upon restrictive assumptions about the variances and covariances of the errors of the other $(m - 1)$ structural equations. In order to make use of standard asymptotic theory to justify these tests, it is necessary

---

[23] Strictly speaking, the use of a time trend violates the assumptions on asymptotic orders of magnitudes of cross-product moment matrices, but clearly nR_h^2 is the same whether t or t/n is used as the scalar $q_t(i)$.

to assume that the covariance matrix of the reduced form errors, $E(v_t v_t')$, is almost always constant or exhibits asymptotically negligible changes generated by some sequence of local alternatives (see, e.g., Szroeter, 1978, Section 6). In view of the fact that the reduced-form disturbances are linear transformations of those of the structural form, this assumption implies that the null hypothesis $H_0^i: \alpha_i = 0$ is being tested conditional upon the other structural equations having homoscedastic disturbances; this point is stressed by Kelejian (1982).[24] This approach to equation-by-equation testing would presumably have to be abandoned after a significant test result had been obtained.

Pagan and Hall (1983) provide a detailed analysis of the special circumstances required to justify the tests based upon the artificial regression model of (4.5) and argue that it is important to derive a heteroscedasticity test which is applicable to an individual equation estimated by IV and robust to heteroscedasticity elsewhere in the system. By studying the asymptotic properties of the OLS estimators of the parameters of (4.5) under the null hypothesis, Pagan and Hall (1983) are able to derive an individual equation test which is unaffected by heteroscedasticity in the remaining equations and also by non-normality of the disturbances.

As a first step to the construction of a suitable test statistic, Pagan and Hall (1983) prove the following theorem:

> **Theorem.** Let ζ_i denote the $(r_i + 1)$-dimensional parameter vector for (4.5) and $\tilde{\zeta}_i$ denote the corresponding OLS estimator with $\tilde{\zeta}_i' = (\tilde{\sigma}_i^2, \tilde{\alpha}_i')$. If $\alpha_i = 0$ then, under standard conditions, $n^{\frac{1}{2}}(\tilde{\zeta}_i - \zeta_i)$ is asymptotically normally distributed with zero mean vector and covariance matrix given by
>
> $$\text{plim } n\{(\mu_{4i} - \sigma_i^4)(M_i'M_i)^{-1} - 2\mu_{3i}(M_i'M_i)^{-1}M_i'\hat{X}_i(\hat{X}_i'\hat{X}_i)^{-1}J_i'$$
> $$+ 4\sigma_i^2 J_i(\hat{X}_i'\hat{X}_i)^{-1}J_i'\}, \qquad (4.6)$$
>
> where: $M_i = (\iota, Q_i)$, ι being an n-dimensional vector with every element equal to unity and Q_i being the n by r_i matrix with typical row $q_t(i)'$; J_i is the $(r_i + 1)$ by g_i matrix of coefficient estimates in the regression of $E(x_t(i)u_{ti})$ against an intercept term and $q_t(i)$, $x_t(i)$ being the tth row of X_i; and μ_{3i} and μ_{4i} are the third and fourth moments of the disturbance (which are constant under $H_0^i: \alpha_i = 0$).[25]

[24] As mentioned by Godfrey and Wickens (1982), the errors of the $(m - 1)$ equations not being examined may exhibit asymptotically negligible heteroscedasticity, but this point has little empirical relevance.

[25] Pagan and Hall (1983, p. 192) also provide a simpler expression for the special case of normally distributed errors.

It is simple to use the IV residuals to construct estimators of σ_i^2, μ_{3i} and μ_{4i} which are consistent under H_0^i; so that the only difficulty in obtaining a consistent estimator of the covariance matrix of (4.6) lies in estimating the matrix J_i. Pagan and Hall (1983, p. 196) suggest that J_i be estimated by regressing $x_t(i)\hat{u}_{ti}$ on an intercept term and $q_t(i)$. By replacing unknown quantities in (4.6) by consistent estimators and then deleting the first row and column of the matrix so obtained, it is possible to derive a consistent estimator of the covariance matrix of $\tilde{\alpha}_i$ which can be employed to construct a Wald-type test of $\alpha_i = 0$.

5.5   Tests of the independence of variables and disturbances

The problem of testing whether or not some set of variables can be taken to be independent of disturbances has received considerable attention (see, e.g., Engle, 1982a; Hausman and Taylor, 1981; Hwang, 1985; Smith, 1984, 1985; Spencer and Berk, 1981, 1982; Wu, 1983a). The procedures which have been developed are often referred to as asymptotic orthogonality tests because independence implies that the asymptotic covariances between the variables and the disturbances all equal zero. This asymptotic orthogonality is, of course, only a necessary condition for the variables under scrutiny to serve as valid instruments in estimation and inference.

This section provides details of the derivation, properties and implementation of tests designed to accompany limited information and full information estimation. As in other sections, emphasis is placed upon deriving an equivalent 'omitted variables' problem so that asymptotic orthogonality tests can be calculated using standard estimation programmes (see equations (5.14) and (5.16)). The relevance of time-series 'causality' tests is also discussed.

5.5.1   *Limited information tests*

Much of the research in this area has been addressed to the problem in which a single structural equation is estimated by an IV method and the independence of its disturbance and a sub-set of its regressors is to be tested.[26] It will, therefore, be convenient to write a typical equation of the system as

$$y_i = Y_{i1}\beta_{i1} + Y_{i2}\beta_{i2} + Z_i\gamma_i + u_i, \tag{5.1}$$

where y_i and Y_{i1} contain observations on endogenous variables, Z_i is a

---

[26] Engle (1982a) considers a more general framework in which a sub-system, rather than a single equation, is under consideration and derives LM tests.

matrix of predetermined or weakly exogenous variables, and the status of the variables of the n by m_{i2} matrix Y_{i2} is to be investigated.[27] The null hypothesis is then that the regressors of Y_{i2} are independent of the disturbance.

Let W be an n by $s(s \geqslant g_i)$ matrix of instruments valid for the estimation of (5.1) under the alternative hypothesis that the variables of Y_{i2} must be treated as endogenous when estimating the parameters of interest, namely the elements of β_{i1}, β_{i2} and γ_i. It will be assumed that the predetermined regressors of Z_i are used as instruments, so that Z_i is a sub-matrix of W. Under the null hypothesis of independence, Y_{i2} is a valid instrument matrix with

$$\text{plim } n^{-1} Y'_{i2} u_i = 0, \tag{5.2}$$

and so can be combined with W to form the matrix $\dot{W} = (W, Y_{i2})$.

The IV estimators of δ_i associated with W and $\dot{W}$ will be written as

$$\hat{\delta}_i = [X'_i P(W) X_i]^{-1} [X'_i P(W) y_i] \tag{5.3}$$

and

$$\dot{\delta}_i = [X'_i P(\dot{W}) X_i]^{-1} [X'_i P(\dot{W}) y_i], \tag{5.4}$$

respectively. If the regressors of Y_{i2} and the disturbance u_i are independent, then $\dot{\delta}_i$ is consistent and asymptotically efficient relative to $\hat{\delta}_i$, the latter estimator being consistent under the alternative hypothesis. This relationship between the two estimators of δ_i suggests the use of a generalization of Hausman's (1978) test, and so the vector of differences $(\hat{\delta}_i - \dot{\delta}_i)$ merits consideration.

Before studying the behaviour of $(\hat{\delta}_i - \dot{\delta}_i)$, it is useful to note that since W is known to be a valid IV matrix, the asymptotic orthogonality condition of (5.2) can be replaced by

$$\text{plim } n^{-1} \tilde{Y}_{i2} u_i = 0, \tag{5.5}$$

where $\tilde{Y}_{i2}$ is the matrix of OLS residuals from the multivariate regression of Y_{i2} on W; that is, $\tilde{Y}_{i2} = M(W) Y_{i2}$. Also the value of the IV estimate $\dot{\delta}_i$ of (5.4) is not changed if $\dot{W}$ is redefined to be the matrix $(W, \tilde{Y}_{i2})$. This redefinition of $\dot{W}$ will be adopted in what follows and implies that the projection matrix $P(\dot{W})$ can be decomposed with

$$P(\dot{W}) = P(W) + P(\tilde{Y}_{i2}). \tag{5.6}$$

It will also be useful to note that the normal equations for $\dot{\delta}_i$ can be

---

[27] Equation (5.1) contains a minor change of notation since β_{i1} and β_{i2} now denote sub-vectors of β_i, and not elements in the matrix B.

partitioned and written as

$$Y'_{i1}P(\dot{W})\dot{u}_i = 0 \tag{5.7}$$

$$Y'_{i2}P(\dot{W})\dot{u}_i = Y'_{i2}\dot{u}_i = 0 \tag{5.8}$$

and

$$Z'_iP(\dot{W})\dot{u}_i = Z'_i\dot{u}_i = 0, \tag{5.9}$$

where $\dot{u}_i$ is the residual vector $y_i - X_i\dot{\delta}_i$.

The Hausman-type estimator contrast is then

$$\begin{aligned}
(\hat{\delta}_i - \dot{\delta}_i) &= [X'_iP(W)X_i]^{-1}[X'_iP(W)y_i] - \dot{\delta}_i \\
&= [X'_iP(W)X_i]^{-1}[X'_iP(W)(X_i\dot{\delta}_i + \dot{u}_i)] - \dot{\delta}_i \\
&= [X'_iP(W)X_i]^{-1}X'_iP(W)\dot{u}_i. \tag{5.10}
\end{aligned}$$

The usual arguments on the irrelevance of non-singular linear transformations imply that a test of the significance of $(\hat{\delta}_i - \dot{\delta}_i)$ is equivalent to the corresponding test for the elements of $X'_iP(W)\dot{u}_i$ which has sub-vectors

$$Y'_{i1}P(W)\dot{u}_i \tag{5.11}$$

$$Y'_{i2}P(W)\dot{u}_i \tag{5.12}$$

and

$$Z'_iP(W)\dot{u}_i = Z'_i\dot{u}_i. \tag{5.13}$$

The normal equations of (5.9) indicate that the term of (5.13) is a null vector, so that the asymptotic null distribution of $(\hat{\delta}_i - \dot{\delta}_i)$ cannot be non-singular. There are, in fact, additional linear dependencies. Combining equations (5.6) and (5.7) yields

$$0 = Y'_{i1}P(\dot{W})\dot{u}_i = Y'_{i1}[P(W) + P(\tilde{Y}_{i2})]\dot{u}_i,$$

or

$$\begin{aligned}
Y'_{i1}P(W)\dot{u}_i &= -Y'_{i1}P(\tilde{Y}_{i2})\dot{u}_i \\
&= -[Y'_{i1}\tilde{Y}_{i2}][\tilde{Y}'_{i2}\tilde{Y}_{i2}]^{-1}[\tilde{Y}'_{i2}\dot{u}_i],
\end{aligned}$$

but

$$0 = Y'_{i2}\dot{u}_i = [P(W)Y_{i2} + \tilde{Y}_{i2}]'\dot{u}_i$$

(see (5.8)). It follows that

$$Y'_{i1}P(W)\dot{u}_i = [Y'_{i1}\tilde{Y}_{i2}][\tilde{Y}'_{i2}\tilde{Y}_{i2}]^{-1}Y'_{i2}P(W)\dot{u}_i,$$

and so the indicator sub-vector of (5.11) is simply a linear transformation of the term given in (5.12). The Hausman-type test based upon $(\hat{\delta}_i - \dot{\delta}_i)$, therefore, reduces to a test of the joint significance of the elements of $Y'_{i2}P(W)\dot{u}_i$, and so an asymptotic χ^2 test with at most m_{i2} degrees of freedom is to be anticipated.

Hausman and Taylor (1981) propose a statistic suitable for testing the significance of $(\hat{\delta}_i - \dot{\delta}_i)$, but their formulation requires the use of a generalized inverse to take account of the linear dependencies described above. Wu (1983a) derives an equivalent test based upon $\hat{\beta}_{i2} - \dot{\beta}_{i2}$, the difference between the two estimators of the coefficients of the variables whose orthogonality is under test.[28] Wu's strategy is, however, not entirely straightforward to implement because it requires separate calculation of the difference between the estimated covariance matrices of $\hat{\beta}_{i2}$ and $\dot{\beta}_{i2}$. We shall, therefore, show how the asymptotic orthogonality test can be implemented by adding variables to the original equation and then checking their joint significance.

An 'omitted variables' test

Since the misspecification indicator $Y'_{i2}P(W)\dot{u}_i$ equals $-\tilde{Y}'_{i2}\dot{u}_i$ and $P(\dot{W})\tilde{Y}_{i2}$ equals $\tilde{Y}_{i2}$, the orthogonality test can be calculated as a test of the significance of $-\tilde{Y}'_{i2}P(\dot{W})\dot{u}_i$. The vector $-\tilde{Y}'_{i2}P(\dot{W})\dot{u}_i$ is, however, proportional to the quasi score for testing $\psi = 0$ in the augmented model

$$y_i = Y_{i1}\beta_{i1} + Y_{i2}\beta_{i2} + Z_i\gamma_i + \tilde{Y}_{i2}\psi + u_i, \tag{5.14}$$

when the instrument matrix for estimating the restricted model (5.1) and the unrestricted model (5.14) is $(W, \tilde{Y}_{i2})$ or equivalently (W, Y_{i2}). Thus the independence assumption can be checked by using one of the significance tests described in Section 5.2 with the LR-type statistics of (2.6) and (2.10) being especially easy to calculate.

If W contains as many variables as X_i, – that is, $s = g_i$ – then it is only necessary to compare sample values of

$$n[\dot{u}'_iP(\dot{W})\dot{u}_i/\dot{u}'_i\dot{u}_i] \tag{5.15}$$

to pre-specified critical values of the $\chi^2(m_{i2})$ distribution. The criterion of (5.15) is, of course, the usual IV analogue of the Anderson–Rubin (1949) overidentification test statistic, and equals n times the (possibly uncentred) R^2 statistic for the regression of $\dot{u}_i$ on (W, Y_{i2}).

---

[28] Wu (1983a) also provides results on asymptotic distributions under a sequence of local alternatives.

Disturbance covariance tests

It should be noted that the validity of the orthogonality assumption implies that

$$\text{plim } n^{-1} \tilde{Y}'_{i2} \hat{u}_i = \text{plim } n^{-1} V'_{i2} u_i,$$

where V_{i2} is the matrix of disturbances of the reduced-form equations for the variables of Y_{i2}. Hence the test of $\psi = 0$ can be regarded as a test of the hypothesis that the covariances between these reduced-form disturbances and the structural disturbance of (5.1) all equal zero. Several authors have worked with direct tests of this hypothesis in the context of a system consisting of (5.1) and a set of unrestricted reduced-form equations (see, e.g., Hwang, 1985; Smith, 1984, 1985). Hwang (1985) demonstrates that the Hausman test is algebraically equivalent to the LM test of zero covariances in such models, provided the same estimate of σ_i^2 is used.[29]

5.5.2 *A more general class of limited information tests*

A more general class of orthogonality tests can be obtained by relaxing the assumption that the variables of uncertain status are regressors of the equation being estimated. Consider an n by q_i matrix W_i^* of variables whose independence of the disturbance of the individual structural equation (5.1) is to be tested without imposing the restriction that W_i^* is a sub-matrix of X_i. It will be useful to let $\tilde{W}_i^*$ denote the OLS residual matrix $M(W)W_i^*$.

Equation (5.14) suggests that an asymptotically valid orthogonality test can be obtained by testing the q_i restrictions of $\psi_i^* = 0$ in the context of the extended relationship

$$y_i = X_i \delta_i + \tilde{W}_i^* \psi_i^* + u_i, \tag{5.16}$$

where IV estimates under both the null hypothesis and alternative hypothesis are calculated employing the instrument matrix $(W, \tilde{W}_i^*)$, or equivalently (W, W_i^*).

Application of one of the IV analogues of the classical procedures to the problem of testing $\psi_i^* = 0$ in (5.16) would lead to an asymptotic test based upon the $\chi^2(q_i)$ distribution with significantly large values of the test statistic resulting in rejection of the independence assumption. It could, however, be argued that it is the elements of δ_i which are of interest and

---

[29] Many of the asymptotic orthogonality tests proposed in the literature have been derived using either the LM principle or Hausman's approach. Smith (1984, 1985), however, presents results for LR and Wald tests.

that ψ_i^* has no intrinsic importance because it is only introduced to provide a check of the orthogonality hypothesis. This argument could be employed as part of a justification for using LM techniques in preference to overfitting methods, but it is also used by Hausman and Taylor (1981) in support of Hausman's (1978) class of specification tests.

In examining the application of the various procedures to the problem of testing $\psi_i^* = 0$ in the augmented model given by (5.16), it will be useful to introduce some additional notation. Let $\bar{W}$ denote the n by $(s + q_i)$ matrix $(W, \tilde{W}_i^*)$ to be used for the estimation of the unrestricted model (5.16) and its restricted version (5.1), $\tilde{\delta}_i$ and $\tilde{\psi}_i^*$ be the unrestricted IV estimators of δ_i and ψ_i^*, respectively, and $\bar{\delta}_i$ be the constrained estimator of δ_i obtained when the q_i restrictions of $\psi_i^* = 0$ are imposed. These estimators are given by

$$\tilde{\delta}_i = [\bar{X}_i' M(\tilde{W}_i^*) \bar{X}_i]^{-1} [\bar{X}_i' M(\tilde{W}_i^*) y_i] \tag{5.17}$$

and

$$\bar{\delta}_i = (\bar{X}_i' \bar{X}_i)^{-1} \bar{X}_i' y_i, \tag{5.18}$$

where the projection matrix $M(\cdot)$ has its usual meaning and

$$\bar{X}_i = P(\bar{W}) X_i = P(W) X_i + P(\tilde{W}_i^*) X_i, \tag{5.19}$$

since

$$W' \tilde{W}_i^* = W' M(W) W_i^* = 0.$$

Equation (5.19) implies that

$$M(\tilde{W}_i^*) \bar{X}_i = M(\tilde{W}_i^*) P(W) X_i = P(W) X_i, \tag{5.20}$$

because $M(\tilde{W}_i^*) P(\tilde{W}_i^*) = 0$ and W is orthogonal to $\tilde{W}_i^*$. Substituting (5.20) in (5.17) yields the result that $\tilde{\delta}_i$ can be written as

$$\tilde{\delta}_i = [X_i' P(W) X_i]^{-1} [X_i' P(W) y_i]$$
$$= \hat{\delta}_i \text{ of equation (5.3)}.$$

This result leads to a very convenient form of the LR test of $H_0: \psi_i^* = 0$.

If $\tilde{u}_i$ denotes the residual vector derived from $\tilde{\delta}_i$ and $\tilde{\psi}_i^*$, then combining $\tilde{\delta}_i = \hat{\delta}_i$ with the normal equations for $\tilde{\psi}_i^*$ implies that

$$\tilde{u}_i' P(\bar{W}) \tilde{u}_i = \hat{u}_i' P(W) \hat{u}_i.$$

It follows that a LR-type test of $\psi_i^* = 0$ can be implemented without estimating the unrestricted model (5.16). Instead the restricted model (5.1) can be estimated twice: first using only the variables of W as instruments, and second using the augmented set $(W, \tilde{W}_i^*)$ or equivalently (W, W_i^*).

Under H_0, the test statistic

$$[\bar{u}_i' P(\bar{W}) \bar{u}_i / \bar{\sigma}_i^2] - [\hat{u}_i' P(W) \hat{u}_i / \hat{\sigma}_i^2] \tag{5.21}$$

is asymptotically distributed as $\chi^2(q_i)$, where $\bar{u}_i$ and $\bar{\sigma}_i^2$ (resp. $\hat{u}_i$ and $\hat{\sigma}_i^2$) denote the residual vector and variance estimate associated with $\tilde{\delta}_i$ (resp. $\hat{\delta}_i$). The variate of (5.21) is simply the change in the IV version of the Anderson–Rubin statistic for testing overidentifying restrictions when the instrument set is expanded from W to (W, W_i^*).

The algebraic equivalence of $\tilde{\delta}_i$ and $\hat{\delta}_i$ also implies that the Hausman test of the hypothesis $\psi_i^* = 0$ based upon $(\tilde{\delta}_i - \bar{\delta}_i)$ is the same as the procedure proposed by Hausman and Taylor (1981) for testing the predeterminedness of the variables of W_i^*. Hausman and Taylor derive the asymptotic distribution of $(\hat{\delta}_i - \bar{\delta}_i)$ under the null hypothesis and show that the statistic for testing the joint significance of the elements of this vector should be compared to pre-specified critical values of a χ^2 distribution with degrees of freedom not exceeding $\min(m_i, q_i)$, where m_i equals the dimension of β_i. The appearance of m_i, rather than g_i, in $\min(\cdot, q_i)$ reflects the fact that W contains Z_i, so that, after an irrelevant non-singular transformation, the specification error indicator has at most $m_i = g_i - k_i$ non-zero elements.[30] As the covariance matrix of the asymptotic null distribution of $(\hat{\delta}_i - \bar{\delta}_i)$ cannot have full rank except in special cases with $k_i = 0$ and $m_i \leqslant q_i$, the χ^2 criterion given by Hausman and Taylor involves a generalized inverse (see Hausman and Taylor, 1981, pp. 242–4).

Holly's (1982) likelihood-based results on the relative asymptotic local power of Hausman's procedure and the LM, LR and Wald tests generalize to the case of IV estimation. If $q_i \leqslant m_i$, then all four tests have the same asymptotic local power, provided assumptions corresponding to those stated by Holly are satisfied (see Holly, 1982, pp. 755–6). If $q_i > m_i$, then the asymptotic local power of Hausman's test can be smaller than, equal to or greater than that shared by the classical tests.[31]

5.5.3   *Full information tests*

Although the analysis so far has been devoted to the examination of tests based upon limited information estimation, the validity of asymptotic orthogonality conditions can be assessed using full information estimates.

Suppose that it is desired to test the restrictions

$$\text{plim } n^{-1} W^{*\prime} u_i = 0, \quad i = 1, 2, \dots, m,$$

---

[30] The proof of this proposition follows the discussion of the $W_i^* = Y_{i2}$ case; see, in particular, the comments in relation to equation (5.13).

[31] Holly (1982, pp. 756–7) discusses this sort of situation in some detail.

where W^* is an n by q matrix. Let W be an n by s, $s \geqslant \max(g_1, \ldots, g_m)$, matrix of instruments whose validity is not in question. A full information test can be implemented as follows.

(i)   Estimate the system $y = X\delta + u$ using W as the instrument matrix and obtain the value of

$$\hat{\Lambda} = \hat{u}'(\dot{\Sigma}^{-1} \otimes P(W))\hat{u}.$$

(ii)   Re-estimate the model using $\bar{W} = (W, W^*)$ as the instrument matrix and calculate

$$\tilde{\Lambda} = \tilde{u}'(\dot{\Sigma}^{-1} \otimes P(\bar{W}))\tilde{u},$$

where $\tilde{u}$ denotes the residual associated with full information IV estimation based upon $\bar{W}$.

(iii)   Compare the value of $(\tilde{\Lambda} - \hat{\Lambda})$ to a pre-specified right-hand tail critical value of the $\chi^2(mq)$ distribution.

The quantities $\tilde{\Lambda}$ and $\hat{\Lambda}$ are often available as a by-product of estimation being tests of overidentifying restrictions (see Hausman, 1983, p. 432, footnote 48). The evaluation of the test statistic using these (or asymptotically equivalent) criteria should, therefore, be simple. It is worth noting that if the use of a common estimate of Σ in obtaining $\hat{\Lambda}$ and $\tilde{\Lambda}$ is inconvenient, then different estimates can be used, provided both are consistent for Σ under the null hypothesis.

5.5.4   *'Causality' tests*

Finally, it may be useful to offer some explanation of the absence of a discussion of time-series–based checks for 'causality' of the types described by Granger (1969) and Sims (1972). The relationships between Granger non-causality, (strict) exogeneity, and predeterminedness have been examined by several authors, and it has been shown that Granger non-causality is neither necessary nor sufficient for predeterminedness (see, e.g., Engle et al., 1983, especially p. 290; Wu, 1983b). Consequently, tests for Granger causality are not helpful in checking the assumption that a variable is predetermined, rather than endogenous, and so do not provide tests of the validity of instruments.[32] Thus Granger causality tests are not relevant to the problem of validating estimation and hypothesis testing

---

[32] Hausman (1983, Section 5) provides a useful discussion of Granger–Sims tests in the context of testing the specification of a simultaneous equation model.

conditional upon a sub-set of variables. These time-series procedures are, of course, important in certain analyses of dynamic simulation exercises (see Engle et al., 1983; Hendry and Richard, 1982). A discussion of the role of dynamic simulation in checking the adequacy of econometric models is, however, outside the scope of this book.

5.6   Tests of parameter constancy

Evidence of a lack of parameter constancy during the sample period clearly casts doubt upon the usefulness of conventional estimators and tests which are appropriate for systems with fixed coefficients. It is, therefore, not surprising that the importance of structural stability tests has been recognized for some time (e.g., see Dhrymes et al., 1972; Menges and Diehl, 1964). Most of the available results concerning such tests have been obtained within the framework of Chow's (1960) influential article. More precisely, the alternative hypothesis is that there is a single change in the parameter vector which takes place at a known point in time. Thus a sample of n observations can be regarded as being split by the alternative hypothesis into two distinct sub-samples containing, say, n_1 and n_2 observations $(n = n_1 + n_2)$.[33]

The procedures to be discussed are based upon the assumption that at least one of these two sub-samples contains enough observations to permit the estimation of the complete parameter vector. Without loss of generality, it will be assumed that the first sub-sample meets this condition. As in Chow's (1960) analysis, it is useful to distinguish between cases in which the second sub-sample is also large enough to allow separate estimation of the model's parameters and those in which it is not. In the former case, it is natural to compare the two sub-sample estimates of the parameter vector: if these estimates are significantly different, then there is evidence against the assumption that the model is correctly specified and has constant parameters.[34] In the latter case, the work by Chow (1960) suggests that it will be useful to consider prediction errors. More precisely, coefficient

---

[33] In principle, it is simple to extend the analysis to allow for several changes at known points in time. There may, however, be practical problems when the number of observations is not large. Also Kelejian (1974) provides some discussion of random parameters.

[34] As Klein (1964) and Hendry (1979) have pointed out, significant values of test statistics should not be taken as indicating that the original specification should be re-estimated allowing for a change in its parameter vector. The test for parameter constancy may be powerful against some other misspecifications.

estimates derived using only the first n_1 observations are used to predict values of the endogenous variables in the last n_2 periods. A comparison of actual and predicted values then yields a set of prediction errors which can be tested for significance.

5.6.1　*Systems tests of parameter constancy*

Discussions of systems tests have usually been based upon the likelihood principle. We shall, therefore, concentrate on cases in which maximum likelihood estimates have been obtained, but the Gallant–Jorgenson (1979) analogue of the LR test is applicable if some 3SLS type estimator has been employed. Consider first the case in which both sub-samples contain enough observations to permit the estimation of the null model by FIML. The alternative hypothesis is that there is a single switch-point after n_1 periods when the structural coefficient vector changes from δ to $(\delta + d\delta)$ and the disturbance covariance matrix changes from Σ to $(\Sigma + d\Sigma)$. The null hypothesis then consists of the $g + m(m + 1)/2$ restrictions of $d\delta = 0$ and $d\Sigma = 0$.[35]

Under the null hypothesis, standard FIML using all n observations is the appropriate restricted MLE and the associated maximized log-likelihood function will be denoted by $\hat{l}$. Given the form of the alternative hypothesis and the serial independence of the disturbance vectors $u_t, t = 1, \ldots, n$, the unrestricted MLE can be derived by obtaining two separate sets of sub-sample FIML estimates, say, $(\tilde{\delta}_{(1)}, \tilde{\Sigma}_{(1)})$ and $(\tilde{\delta}_{(2)}, \tilde{\Sigma}_{(2)})$, and then using $\tilde{\delta}_{(2)} - \tilde{\delta}_{(2)}$ and $-\tilde{\Sigma}_{(2)}$ to estimate $d\delta$ and $d\Sigma$, respectively. Further, if the maximized log-likelihood derived from the first n_1 observations is $\tilde{l}_{(1)}$ and that calculated from the last n_2 observations is $\tilde{l}_{(2)}$, then (ignoring any asymptotically negligible initial value effects) the unrestricted maximum of the log-likelihood of the alternative model is $\tilde{l}_{(1)} + \tilde{l}_{(2)}$. It follows that a joint test of parameter constancy and homoscedasticity can be based upon the LR statistic

$$\mathrm{LR}_{pch} = 2(\tilde{l}_{(1)} + \tilde{l}_{(2)} - \hat{l}) \tag{6.1}$$

which is asymptotically distributed as $\chi^2(g + m(m + 1)/2)$ under the null hypothesis if n_1 and n_2 are both $O(n)$.

The two sub-sample FIML estimates $\tilde{\delta}_{(1)}$ and $\tilde{\delta}_{(2)}$ can be used to derive an asymptotic test of $d\delta = 0$, which is robust to heteroscedasticity with $d\Sigma \neq 0$.[36] If the estimated asymptotic covariance matrices of $\tilde{\delta}_{(1)}$ and $\tilde{\delta}_{(2)}$

---

[35] The number of restrictions is the sum of the number of elements in $d\delta$, i.e., g, and the number of distinct elements in the m by m symmetric matrix $d\Sigma$.

[36] Anderson and Mizon (1983) derive an LR test for testing $d\delta = 0$, conditional upon $d\Sigma = 0$.

are denoted by $\mathscr{V}_{(1)}$ and $\mathscr{V}_{(2)}$ respectively, then

$$(\tilde{\delta}_{(1)} - \tilde{\delta}_{(2)})'[\mathscr{V}_{(1)} + \mathscr{V}_{(2)}]^{-1}(\tilde{\delta}_{(1)} - \tilde{\delta}_{(2)}) \tag{6.2}$$

is asymptotically distributed as $\chi^2(g)$ whether or not $d\Sigma = 0$. The test statistic of (6.2) is a simple generalization of the criterion proposed by Watt (1979) in the context of OLS analysis.

Consider next the case in which n_2 is too small to allow sub-sample FIML estimation. The tests of (6.1) and (6.2) are not available, but Chow's (1960) prediction error test is easily generalized. In order to describe prediction error tests for systems, it will be convenient to introduce some additional notation. Let Y and Z be partitioned according to the sub-sample split as $Y' = (Y'_{(1)}, Y'_{(2)})$ and $Z' = (Z'_{(1)}, Z'_{(2)})$, where $Y_{(i)}$ is an n_i by m matrix and $Z_{(i)}$ is an n_i by k matrix, $i = 1, 2$. Also, let D be an n by n_2 matrix of Salkever-type dummy variables defined by $D' = (0, I_2)$, where 0 is an n_2 by n_1 matrix with every element equal to zero and I_2 is the n_2 by n_2 identity matrix (see Salkever, 1976).

The reduced-form (RF) equations are $Y = Z\Pi + V$ and, given an estimate $\dot{\Pi}_{(1)}$ derived using only $Y_{(1)}$ and $Z_{(1)}$, the prediction errors $\dot{V}_{(2)} = Y_{(2)} - Z_{(2)}\dot{\Pi}_{(1)}$ can be calculated and tested for significance. As in the case of the multiple regression model of Chapter 4, it is possible to implement a test by variable addition. More precisely, a test of $\Delta = 0$ in the augmented RF system

$$Y = Z\Pi + D\Delta + V \tag{6.3}$$

is appropriate.

For the purposes of obtaining a suitable test statistic, the original RF and the expanded system (6.3) can be estimated by either unrestricted multivariate least squares or maximum likelihood, taking into account any overidentifying restrictions. The general form of the LR statistic is the same whichever estimator is used and is given by

$$n[\ln|\hat{V}'\hat{V}| - \ln|\tilde{V}'_{(1)}\tilde{V}_{(1)}|], \tag{6.4}$$

where $\hat{V}$ is the n by m residual matrix obtained by fitting the original RF (i.e., (6.3) with $\Delta = 0$) using the complete sample, and $\tilde{V}_{(1)}$ is the corresponding n_1 by m matrix derived from estimation using only the first sub-sample.[37] If n_2 is fixed and $\Delta = 0$, then the statistic of (6.4) is asymptotically distributed as $\chi^2(mn_2)$, as are the corresponding LM and Wald statistics.[38]

---

[37] The derivation of (6.4) by means of the results of Lawton and Sylvestre (1971) is straightforward.

[38] Dhrymes et al. (1972) argue that, if multivariate least-squares estimation is employed, it is possible to derive an exact test of $\Delta = 0$. Jayatissa (1976) shows that their argument is invalid.

It can be shown that the discrepancy between Π and any consistent estimator can be neglected in large samples when constructing a test for predictive failure. Consequently, asymptotic theory provides no guidance for choosing between ordinary least-squares and FIML estimators of Π since both are consistent. Indeed it would be asymptotically valid to ignore the variability of a consistent estimator of Π about the true value in order to obtain a multi-equation analogue of Hendry's (1979, p. 222) z_4 test. In view of the poor small sample performance of the single-equation variant reported in Chapter 4, it is difficult to be optimistic about the usefulness of such a strategy (see the related work of Schmidt, 1977).

Finally, note that Nicholls and Pagan (1984) provide results which are applicable when predictions are only required for a sub-set of endogenous variables and extend their analysis to allow for autocorrelated disturbances.

5.6.2   *Limited information tests of parameter constancy*

As Pagan (1984) has remarked, there are few results available on testing for parameter variation after IV estimation of a single equation from a system. The results that have been published are derived using Chow's (1960) two-sub-sample framework in the context of a typical structural equation

$$y_i = X_i \delta_i + u_i.$$

It is assumed that the g_i-dimensional vector δ_i is to be estimated with the instruments being the variables of the n by s matrix W $(s \geqslant g_i)$. The alternative hypothesis divides the complete sample of n observations into one group of $n_1 > s$ observations and another group containing n_2 observations $(n = n_1 + n_2)$. Thus δ_i can be estimated using all observations or just the first n_1 of them.

Suppose that $n_2 > s$ and that an IV estimate of δ_i can be calculated for each sub-sample. Let the estimator of δ_i based upon the jth sub-sample be denoted by $\tilde{\delta}_{i(j)}$ and the estimator of its asymptotic covariance matrix be denoted by $\mathscr{V}_{i(j)}, j = 1, 2$. Lo and Newey (1985) propose that the stability of the coefficient vector be tested using the statistic

$$(\tilde{\delta}_{i(1)} - \tilde{\delta}_{i(2)})'[\mathscr{V}_{i(1)} + \mathscr{V}_{i(2)}]^{-1}(\tilde{\delta}_{i(1)} - \tilde{\delta}_{i(2)}). \tag{6.5}$$

The statistic of (6.5) is the limited information analogue of the criterion of (6.2) and is asymptotically distributed as $\chi^2(g_i)$ (as n_1 and n_2 both tend to infinity) under the hypothesis of parameter constancy. If $\tilde{\delta}_{i(1)}$ and $\tilde{\delta}_{i(2)}$ are significantly different, then it may be useful to consider estimation using the methods of Barten and Bronsard (1970).

The Lo–Newey procedure for the $(n_1 > s, n_2 > s)$ case is a straightforward extension of the Wald test proposed by Watt (1979) for application to multiple regression models estimated by OLS. This sort of simple generalization is, however, not available for the case in which $(n_1 > s, n_2 < s)$, and it is not possible to estimate δ_i using only the last n_2 observations. Consider the extension of Salkever's (1976) approach to the construction of a prediction error test. The obvious generalization of the OLS analysis is to examine the IV estimation of the expanded model

$$y_i = X_i\delta_i + D\alpha_i + u_i, \tag{6.6}$$

using the instruments of $W^+ = (W, D)$, where D is the n by n_2 matrix of dummy variables discussed in the preceding sub-section.

Let the partitioning of the data into sub-sets of n_1 and n_2 observations be represented by

$$y_i = \begin{bmatrix} y_{i(1)} \\ y_{i(2)} \end{bmatrix}, \quad X_i = \begin{bmatrix} X_{i(1)} \\ X_{i(2)} \end{bmatrix} \quad \text{and} \quad W = \begin{bmatrix} W_{(1)} \\ W_{(2)} \end{bmatrix}.$$

It can be shown that the estimation of (6.6) using W^+ leads to the IV estimates

$$\delta_i^+ = \tilde{\delta}_{i(1)} = [\hat{X}'_{i(1)}\hat{X}_{i(1)}]^{-1}\hat{X}'_{i(1)}y_{i(1)}, \tag{6.7}$$

and

$$\alpha_i^+ = y_{i(2)} - X_{i(2)}\tilde{\delta}_{i(1)}, \tag{6.8}$$

where $\hat{X}_{i(1)}$ is the n_1 by g_i matrix of predicted values from the OLS regression of $X_{i(1)}$ on $W_{(1)}$. Equation (6.7) indicates that δ_i^+ is the IV estimate of δ_i based upon the original set of instruments and calculated using only the first n_1 observations. It follows from (6.8), therefore, that α_i^+ is the vector of prediction errors when the endogenous regressors of $X_{i(2)}$ are treated as known. This treatment of endogenous variables is, however, inappropriate since, as argued by Nicholls and Pagan (1984), reduced-form predictions should be obtained. One possible solution might be to combine the structural equation of interest with unrestricted reduced-form relationships for its endogenous regressors and then to derive a system-type test, but this is clearly a long way from a simple 'IV for OLS' substitution in Chow's (1960) original prediction error test. Erlat (1983) proposes a finite sample test for the $(n_1 > s, n_2 < s)$ case which is valid when Z is strictly exogenous and the disturbances are normally distributed.

5.7   Concluding remarks

It is difficult to argue with Pagan's (1981) statement that 'the reality of model construction demands that diagnostic and specification tests be neither expensive nor cumbersome to construct. Once methods begin to cause trouble on either of these criteria, they are likely to be ignored.' It is, therefore, encouraging that several important checks for misspecification can be calculated simply as omitted variables/variable addition tests. The strategy of adding a set of test variables to the null specification is helpful in communicating results, analyzing asymptotic local power, and implementing checks in empirical work. There are, of course, several asymptotically equivalent procedures available for assessing the joint significance of the regressors added to detect misspecification, for example, the various IV analogues of classical tests. It would be very useful to have some evidence on the relative merits of these procedures in finite samples.

The testing of simultaneous equation models poses some problems not encountered in the analysis of the multiple regression model of Chapter 4. For example, it may be important to consider the consequences of misspecification in the rest of the system when deriving limited information single-equation tests: the comments on Szroeter's (1978) test for heteroscedasticity illustrate this problem. Also, in contrast to the OLS results of Chapter 4, tests of the assumption of serial independence based upon IV residual autocorrelations are not, in general, equivalent to LM-type tests. In view of the importance of testing for serial correlation in dynamic models, it would be valuable to have some results to help applied workers to choose between the π tests derived for specified alternatives and the θ tests which check the significance of a specified set of estimated autocorrelations.

Non-linear models

There are few detailed discussions of checks against specific alternatives in the context of non-linear simultaneous equation models (for general discussions see Burguete et al., 1982; Gallant and Jorgenson, 1979; Newey, 1985b). However, one important general point relating to the choice of estimator should be made. The non-linear FIML estimator based upon the assumption that the disturbances are normally distributed is, in general, inconsistent when this assumption is false.[39] Thus it is inappropriate to rely upon the results of quasi-maximum likelihood estimators derived in the context of linear simultaneous equation models. The non-

---

[39] See Amemiya (1983, Section 5.5).

linear systems IV estimator, referred to as the non-linear three-stage least-squares (N3SLS) estimator by Gallant and Jorgenson (1978), is, on the other hand, consistent and asymptotically normally distributed when the errors are non-normal, provided regularity conditions are satisfied.[40] Similarly, the non-linear two-stage least-squares (N2SLS) procedure provides a consistent and asymptotically normally distributed estimator of the parameter vector of a single implicit non-linear structural equation under quite general conditions (see Gallant and Jorgenson, 1979).

In addition to being robust to many types of non-normality, the N3SLS and N2SLS estimators provide a basis for asymptotically valid inference. Indeed, the results of Gallant and Jorgenson (1979) on analogues of classical tests were derived for the N3SLS and N2SLS estimators of parameters of an implicit non-linear equation system (see also Burguete et al., 1982, Sections 5, 6 and 7). Large sample tests for specification error can, therefore, be constructed by nesting the null model in some more general formulation and then testing the relevant parametric restrictions in the context of a LEA by means of one of the tests discussed by Burguete et al. (1982) and Gallant and Jorgenson (1979). As Hausman (1983) has suggested, the further development of misspecification tests is an important next step in the use and analysis of non-linear simultaneous equation models.

[40] See Amemiya (1983, Section 5.5) and Hausman (1983, Section 6).

CHAPTER 6

Tests for qualitative and limited dependent variable models

6.1   Introduction

Models in which the dependent variable is qualitative or has its range limited in some way are being increasingly used in applied work. Amemiya (1981, 1984) and Maddala (1983) have given detailed accounts of estimation techniques for such models, but unfortunately few results on misspecification tests were available when these authors published their works. This chapter presents checks of model adequacy for some well-known and widely used specifications: the logit and probit models of binary choice and the Tobit (censored regression) model.[1]

Classical likelihood-based procedures and Hausman-type tests are considered in the following sections. Section 6.2 deals with tests for binary choice models. Checks for limited dependent variable (LDV) models are discussed in Section 6.3. In both of these sections, the effects of certain misspecifications are summarized and the corresponding test statistics are described. The test procedures considered are all based upon asymptotic theory and, where possible, reference is made to Monte Carlo evidence on small sample behaviour. Section 6.4 contains some concluding remarks.

6.2   Qualitative dependent variable models

We shall assume that the dependent variable y is binary taking on the values 0 or 1 with the null specification being of the general form

$$y_i^* = x_i'\beta + u_i, \quad i = 1, \ldots, n, \tag{2.1}$$

with

$$y_i = 1 \text{ if } y_i^* > 0$$
$$= 0 \text{ otherwise,} \tag{2.2}$$

---

[1] Some tests for more complicated models are available; see, for example, the work by Hausman and McFadden (1984) on multinomial logit models, and Lee's (1984) tests for selectivity models.

206

where y_i^* is an unobservable latent variable, x_i is a k-dimensional vector of exogenous variables and β is the k-dimensional vector of unknown parameters.[2] The disturbances u_i are assumed to be independently and identically distributed with zero mean and variance σ^2, $i = 1, \ldots, n$. Equations (2.1) and (2.2) imply that

$$\text{prob}(y_i = 0) = \text{prob}(u_i \leqslant -x_i'\beta) = F(-x_i'\beta), \tag{2.3}$$

and so

$$\text{prob}(y_i = 1) = 1 - F(-x_i'\beta), \tag{2.4}$$

where $F(\cdot)$ denotes the cumulative distribution function for the disturbance u_i. In order to complete the stochastic specification of the model, it is necessary to make an assumption about the distribution of the disturbances since this will lead to a specific form of $F(\cdot)$. We shall provide detailed results only for the two most popular distributional assumptions, namely those employed in the logit and probit models; results for other choices can be obtained using the general formulae below.

In the logit model, the disturbances are assumed to have a logistic distribution, so that

$$\text{prob}(y_i = 0) = F(-x_i'\beta) = 1/[1 + \exp(x_i'\beta)] \tag{2.3a}$$

and

$$\text{prob}(y_i = 1) = 1 - F(-x_i'\beta)$$
$$= \exp(x_i'\beta)/[1 + \exp(x_i'\beta)]. \tag{2.4a}$$

The probit model is based upon the assumption that the disturbances are independent standard normal variates, that is $u_i \sim IN(0, 1)$, and in this case

$$\text{prob}(y_i = 0) = F(-x_i'\beta) = \Phi(-x_i'\beta) \tag{2.3b}$$

and

$$\text{prob}(y_i = 1) = 1 - F(-x_i'\beta) = 1 - \Phi(-x_i'\beta), \tag{2.4b}$$

where $\Phi(\cdot)$ denotes the cumulative distribution function for an $N(0, 1)$ variable. The properties of the $N(0, 1)$ distribution imply that $\Phi(-x_i'\beta)$ and $1 - \Phi(-x_i'\beta)$ equal $1 - \Phi(x_i'\beta)$ and $\Phi(x_i'\beta)$, respectively, and it will be convenient to use the latter expressions for the probabilities of the probit model. An LM test of the normality assumption underlying the probit model is given by Bera, Jarque and Lee (1984).

---

[2] Many of the results of this section are taken from an article by Davidson and MacKinnon (1984a).

At first sight, it might appear restrictive to assume that the u_i are $N(0, 1)$ variates, rather than $N(0, \sigma^2)$ variates with the parameter σ^2 unspecified. However, no generality is lost by this restriction. Consider, for example, the probability that y_i equals 1, which is

$$\text{prob}(y_i = 1) = \text{prob}(\beta' x_i > -u_i)$$
$$= \text{prob}(\lambda(\beta' x_i) > -\lambda u_i)$$

for all positive scalars λ, and so, while the vector of ratios β/σ can be estimated, it is not possible to obtain estimates of the elements of β and σ^2 separately. Thus, putting $\sigma^2 = 1$ in the probit model simply amounts to a convenient normalization. (The corresponding normalization implicit in the logit model is $\sigma^2 = \pi^2/3$.)

In order to obtain a classical likelihood-based test of the adequacy of the null model given by (2.1), (2.2) and a particular form of $F(\cdot)$, it is necessary to specify some more general alternative model. Consider the alternative in which (2.1) is replaced by

$$y_i^* = g(x_i'\beta, z_i'\alpha) + u_i, \tag{2.5}$$

where z_i is a q-dimensional vector of exogenous variables, α is a q-dimensional vector of unknown parameters, and the function $g(\cdot)$ satisfies regularity conditions and is such that

$$g(x_i'\beta, 0) = x_i'\beta.$$

As in previous applications of the LM principle, model adequacy is to be assessed by testing the set of parametric restrictions $H_q: \alpha = 0$.

The construction of an appropriate test statistic will require the evaluation of the first-order partial derivatives of the log-likelihood function for the alternative (and, of course, the MLE of the null model). In order to simplify the notation for these derivatives, it will be useful to introduce the following definitions: $\theta' \equiv (\alpha', \beta')$; $g_i(\theta) \equiv g(x_i'\beta, z_i'\alpha)$, $i = 1,$ $\ldots, n$; $g_{ir}(\theta) \equiv \partial g_i(\theta)/\partial \theta_r$, $i = 1, \ldots, n$ and $r = 1, \ldots, k + q$; and $F_i(\theta) \equiv F(-g_i(\theta))$, $i = 1, \ldots, n$. The restricted MLE will be denoted by $\hat{\theta} = (0', \hat{\beta}')'$. The log-likelihood for a single observation on the general qualitative dependent variable model can then be written as

$$l_i(\theta) = (1 - y_i)\ln F_i(\theta) + y_i \ln[1 - F_i(\theta)], \tag{2.6}$$

and the log-likelihood function for the whole sample is

$$l(\theta) = \sum_{i=1}^{n} l_i(\theta). \tag{2.7}$$

The vector of first-order partial derivatives $d(\theta)$, therefore, has typical element

$$d_r(\theta) = \partial l(\theta)/\partial \theta_r = \sum_{i=1}^{n} \partial l_i(\theta)/\partial \theta_r, \qquad (2.8)$$

where

$$\partial l_i(\theta)/\partial \theta_r = [(y_i - 1)g_{ir}(\theta)f_i(\theta)/F_i(\theta)]$$
$$+ [y_i g_{ir}(\theta)f_i(\theta)/(1 - F_i(\theta))], \qquad (2.9)$$

and $f_i(\theta)$ denotes the p.d.f. of the disturbance term, $f(u)$, evaluated at $u = -g_i(\theta)$. For the logit model, the p.d.f. $f(\cdot)$ is given by

$$f(u) = \exp(-u)/[1 + \exp(-u)]^2,$$

and, in the case of the probit model, $f(\cdot)$ is $\phi(\cdot)$, the standard normal density.

The construction of the LM test of $H_\alpha: \alpha = 0$ also requires an estimate of the information matrix based upon the restricted MLE $\hat{\theta}$. Davidson and MacKinnon (1984a) suggest that calculation of the matrix of second-order partial derivatives

$$\partial^2 l(\hat{\theta})/\partial \theta \partial \theta' = \sum_{i=1}^{n} \partial^2 l_i(\hat{\theta})/\partial \theta \partial \theta'$$

is sufficiently complicated to render it inconvenient as a basis for estimating the information matrix. A much more convenient approach is to use the OPG estimate $W'(\hat{\theta})W(\hat{\theta})$, where $W(\hat{\theta})$ is the n by $(k + q)$ matrix with typical element $w_{ir}(\hat{\theta}) = \partial l_i(\hat{\theta})/\partial \theta_r$, since the score test can then be calculated as $LM_1 = nR_w^2$, where R_w^2 is the uncentred R^2 for the OLS regression of a vector of ones on the matrix $W(\hat{\theta})$. An asymptotically equivalent F-test variant of LM_1 can be derived from this regression and can be written as

$$F_1 = [R_w^2/(1 - R_w^2)] \times [(n - k - q)/q]$$
$$= [LM_1/q] \times [(n - k - q)/n(1 - R_w^2)]. \qquad (2.10)$$

Since $(n - k - q)/n \to 1$ as $n \to \infty$ and $\text{plim}(1 - R_w^2) = 1$ under the null hypothesis, an asymptotically valid test of $H_\alpha: \alpha = 0$ can be obtained by assuming that the null distribution of F_1 is central $F(q, n - k - q)$. Unfortunately, the evidence for other types of econometric models suggests that the computational convenience of the LM_1 and F_1 statistics may be bought at the price of poor finite sample performance (see Chapter 3). There is, however, another convenient method for estimating the information matrix and calculating LM tests.

The basic information matrix equality implies that

$$-E[\partial^2 l_i(\theta)/\partial\theta_r\partial\theta_s] = E[\partial l_i(\theta)/\partial\theta_r\partial l_i(\theta)/\partial\theta_s],$$

and so the information matrix for the total sample has typical element

$$\sum_{i=1}^{n} E[\partial l_i(\theta)/\partial\theta_r\partial l_i(\theta)/\partial\theta_s],$$

which can be easily shown to be

$$\sum_{i=1}^{n} [g_{ir}(\theta)g_{is}(\theta)f_i(\theta)^2]/[F_i(\theta)(1 - F_i(\theta))]. \tag{2.11}$$

The required estimate of the information matrix can then be constructed by evaluating terms like (2.11) at $\theta = \hat{\theta}$.

As with the OPG variant, the estimate based upon (2.11) can be used to provide an artificial regression model that serves as a tool for computing LM statistics (see Davidson and MacKinnon, 1984a; Engle, 1984). If $s(\hat{\theta})$ denotes the n-dimensional vector with typical element

$$s_i(\hat{\theta}) = (y_i - 1)[(1 - F_i(\hat{\theta}))/F_i(\hat{\theta})]^{\frac{1}{2}} + y_i[(1 - F_i(\hat{\theta}))/F_i(\hat{\theta})]^{-\frac{1}{2}}$$

$$= [y_i - (1 - F_i(\hat{\theta}))]/[F_i(\hat{\theta})(1 - F_i(\hat{\theta}))]^{\frac{1}{2}}, \tag{2.12}$$

and $S(\hat{\theta})$ denotes the n by $(k + q)$ matrix with typical element

$$S_{ir}(\hat{\theta}) = [F_i(\hat{\theta})(1 - F_i(\hat{\theta}))]^{-\frac{1}{2}}f_i(\hat{\theta})g_{ir}(\hat{\theta}), \tag{2.13}$$

then it is easy to verify that $S_{ir}(\hat{\theta})s_i(\hat{\theta}) = \partial l_i(\hat{\theta})/\partial\theta_r$, so that $S'(\hat{\theta})s(\hat{\theta}) = d(\hat{\theta})$, the score vector for the LM test.[3] Moreover, equation (2.13) implies that

$$S_{ir}(\hat{\theta})S_{is}(\hat{\theta}) = [g_{ir}(\hat{\theta})g_{is}(\hat{\theta})f_i(\hat{\theta})^2]/[F_i(\hat{\theta})(1 - F_i(\hat{\theta}))],$$

and it follows that $S(\hat{\theta})'S(\hat{\theta})$ is the information matrix estimate associated with (2.11) since the former matrix has typical element $\sum_{i=1}^{n} S_{ir}(\hat{\theta})S_{is}(\hat{\theta})$. Consequently, an asymptotically valid form of the LM test statistic is

$$LM_2 = s'(\hat{\theta})S(\hat{\theta})[S(\hat{\theta})'S(\hat{\theta})]^{-1}S(\hat{\theta})'s(\hat{\theta}), \tag{2.14}$$

which is the explained sum of squares for the OLS regression of $s(\hat{\theta})$ on $S(\hat{\theta})$. The null hypothesis $H_a: \alpha = 0$ can, therefore, be tested by performing this artificial regression and comparing the sample value of LM_2 to the pre-specified critical value of the $\chi^2(q)$ distribution.

The artificial regression of $s(\hat{\theta})$ on $S(\hat{\theta})$ provides two other variants of the LM test. As noted by Engle (1984), under $H_a: \alpha = 0$,

$$\text{plim } s(\hat{\theta})'s(\hat{\theta})/n = 1,$$

---

[3] Note that $s_i(\hat{\theta})$ of (2.12) can be regarded as a standardized residual in so far as $E(y_i) = 1 - F_i(\theta)$ and $\text{Var}(y_i) = F_i(\theta)(1 - F_i(\theta))$.

and so LM_2 is asymptotically equivalent to n times R_s^2, the uncentred R^2 statistic for this regression. Also, as pointed out by Davidson and MacKinnon (1984a), there is the corresponding F test form, namely,

$$F_2 = [LM_2/q] \times [(n - k - q)/n(1 - R_s^2)], \tag{2.15}$$

which is analogous to F_1 of (2.10).

The results above are applicable to the problem of testing $H_\alpha: \alpha = 0$ whatever the choice of $F(\cdot)$, provided regularity conditions are not violated. Before examining misspecification tests for the logit and probit models, it will be useful to provide expressions relevant to these two special cases.

We have already noted that the p.d.f. $f(\cdot)$ has the form

$$f(u) = \exp(-u)/[1 + \exp(-u)]^2$$

for the logit model and $f(u) = \phi(u)$ for the probit model; the corresponding cumulative distribution functions are

$$F(u) = 1/(1 + \exp(-u))$$

and $F(u) = \Phi(u)$. Specializing equation (2.9) to obtain formulae for contributions to the vector of first-order derivatives $d(\theta)$ yields

$$\partial l_i(\theta)/\partial \theta_r = y_i g_{ir}(\theta) - g_{ir}(\theta) \exp(g_i(\theta))/[1 + \exp(g_i(\theta))], \tag{2.16}$$

and

$$\partial l_i(\theta)/\partial \theta_r = g_{ir}(\theta)\phi(g_i(\theta))[y_i - \Phi(g_i(\theta))]/\Phi(g_i(\theta))[1 - \Phi(g_i(\theta))] \tag{2.17}$$

for the logit and probit models, respectively. (In obtaining (2.17), we have made use of the results that $\phi(u) = \phi(-u)$ and $\Phi(-u) = 1 - \Phi(u)$.) Finally, turning to expression (2.11), which gives a typical element of the information matrix and provides the basis of the LM_2 and F_2 tests, the form for the logit model can be shown to be

$$\sum_{i=1}^{n} [\exp(g_i(\theta))/(1 + \exp(g_i(\theta)))^2] g_{ir}(\theta) g_{is}(\theta), \tag{2.18}$$

with the corresponding expression for the probit model being

$$\sum_{i=1}^{n} \{\phi^2(g_i(\theta))/[\Phi(g_i(\theta))(1 - \Phi(g_i(\theta)))]\} g_{ir}(\theta) g_{is}(\theta). \tag{2.19}$$

6.2.1 *Testing for omitted variables in logit and probit models*

A test for the omission of variables from (2.1) can be obtained by using

$$g_i(\theta) = x_i'\beta + z_i'\alpha \tag{2.20}$$

as the regression function of the alternative model. As in the case of the standard multiple regression model, the constrained MLE $\hat{\beta}$ will not be consistent for β if $\alpha \neq 0$. Unfortunately, while formulae for estimator inconsistencies are easily derived for linear regression equations, the results available for logit and probit models are only approximate. These results have been obtained by Kiefer and Skoog (1984) and Yatchew and Griliches (1985) on the basis of the assumption that the elements of α are all close to zero. The basic strategy of these authors is to take linear Taylor series expansions of the probability limits of the first-order conditions. Since the results of Kiefer and Skoog (1984) and Yatchew and Griliches (1985) are derived for small departures from the null hypotheses, it is perhaps not surprising that the same approximations can be obtained by considering the mean vector of the asymptotic distribution of $n^{\frac{1}{2}}(\hat{\theta} - \theta)$ under a sequence of local alternatives H_n: $\alpha = n^{-\frac{1}{2}}\delta$, $\delta'\delta < \infty$.

Let $d_2(\theta) = \partial l(\theta)/\partial\beta$, $D_{21}(\theta) = \partial^2 l(\theta)/\partial\beta\partial\alpha'$ and $D_{22}(\theta) = \partial^2 l(\theta)/\partial\beta\partial\beta'$. The constrained MLE $\hat{\theta}$ satisfies $d_2(\hat{\theta}) = 0$ and, under H_n, we have

$$d_2(\hat{\theta}) \underset{a}{=} d_2(\theta) - D_{21}(\theta)\alpha + D_{22}(\theta)(\hat{\beta} - \beta),$$

so that

$$n^{\frac{1}{2}}(\hat{\beta} - \beta) \underset{a}{=} -n^{\frac{1}{2}}[D_{22}(\theta)]^{-1}d_2(\theta) + [D_{22}(\theta)]^{-1}D_{21}(\theta)\delta.$$

$$(2.21)$$

The first term on the right-hand side of (2.21) is asymptotically normally distributed with zero mean vector and finite covariance matrix, while the second term converges in probability to a vector with finite elements, not all of which are zero. The mean vector of the asymptotic distribution of $n^{\frac{1}{2}}(\hat{\beta} - \beta)$ is, therefore, $\text{plim}\,[D_{22}(\theta)]^{-1}D_{21}(\theta)\delta$. The approximate effect ('local inconsistency' of $\hat{\beta}$) due to the omission of the variables of z can then be estimated by

$$n^{-\frac{1}{2}}[D_{22}(\hat{\theta})]^{-1}D_{21}(\hat{\theta})\delta = [D_{22}(\hat{\theta})]^{-1}D_{21}(\hat{\theta})\alpha, \qquad (2.22)$$

which is the general expression provided by Kiefer and Skoog (1984, p. 876) evaluated at $\theta = \hat{\theta}$.[4]

Expression (2.22) can be combined with equations (2.18), (2.19) and (2.20) to yield simple formulae for the logit and probit models. A little manipulation leads to the result that the local inconsistency of $\hat{\beta}$ due to omitted variables is

$$\eta(\hat{\beta}) = (X'\Omega X)^{-1}X'\Omega Z\alpha, \qquad (2.23)$$

---

[4] The term 'local inconsistency' is not entirely accurate. The estimator $\hat{\beta}$ is consistent for β under H_n with $(\hat{\beta} - \beta)$ being $O_p(n^{-\frac{1}{2}})$.

where X and Z are the data matrices with ith row x_i' and z_i', respectively, and Ω is the n by n diagonal matrix with ith diagonal element given by

$$\omega_{ii} = \exp(x_i'\beta)/[1 + \exp(x_i'\beta)]^2 \tag{2.24}$$

in the case of the logit specification, and

$$\omega_{ii} = \phi(x_i'\beta)^2/[\Phi(x_i'\beta)(1 - \Phi(x_i'\beta))] \tag{2.25}$$

for probit models. It is clear from (2.23) that $\eta(\hat{\beta})$ is the weighted least squares estimator for the regression of $Z\alpha$ on X when the weighting matrix is Ω, so that this equation is a generalization of Theil's (1957) globally valid expression for linear regression models which has $\Omega = I$. The approximate effects of leaving out the variables of z when they play only a minor role can then be estimated by evaluating the matrix Ω in (2.23) at $\beta = \hat{\beta}$.

It is obviously important to devise checks for the omitted variables problem. The LR test is not difficult to implement because the estimation programme required for the alternative is in any case required for the null specification, and so it is worth examining the relative computational costs and small-sample behaviour of LR- and LM-type tests. Davidson and MacKinnon (1984a) report Monte Carlo results that are relevant to this issue. They find that, even for their quite simple specifications, the computational cost of the LR test is much higher than that of LM procedures, and that the LR test has a tendency to reject a true null hypothesis too frequently. Accordingly, LM checks of the restrictions $\alpha = 0$ merit consideration.

As discussed above, several variants of the LM statistic can be calculated easily using artificial regressions. Davidson and MacKinnon (1984a) examine the finite sample properties of these alternative forms, including the nR_s^2 test suggested by Engle (1984), and find that the LM_2 statistic of (2.14) has by far the best performance under the null and also has good relative power properties. The use of LM_2 is, therefore, recommended and, since $\partial g_i(\theta)/\partial \alpha = z_i$ and $\partial g_i(\theta)/\partial \beta = x_i$ for the model of (2.20), it can be calculated as the explained sum of squares for the OLS regression of the standardized residual

$$[y_i - (1 - F_i(\hat{\theta}))]/[F_i(\hat{\theta})(1 - F_i(\hat{\theta}))]^{\frac{1}{2}}$$

on

$$(x_i', z_i')f_i(\hat{\theta})/[F_i(\hat{\theta})(1 - F_i(\hat{\theta}))]^{\frac{1}{2}},$$

with

(i) $f_i(\hat{\theta})/[F_i(\hat{\theta})(1 - F_i(\hat{\theta}))]^{\frac{1}{2}} = [F_i(\hat{\theta})(1 - F_i(\hat{\theta}))]^{\frac{1}{2}}$

and

$$F_i(\hat{\theta}) = 1/(1 + \exp(x_i'\hat{\beta}))$$

for the logit model; and

(ii) $F_i(\hat{\theta}) = 1 - \Phi(x_i'\hat{\beta})$ and $f_i(\hat{\theta}) = \phi(x_i'\hat{\beta})$

for the probit model.

Finally, note that the results on locally equivalent alternatives (LEAs) derived in previous chapters for regression models and simultaneous equation systems can also be obtained in the context of qualitative dependent variable models. In particular, if $h(\cdot)$ is some twice differentiable function with $h(0) = 0$ and $h'(0) \neq 0$, then the LM test of $\alpha = 0$ for the alternative

$$g_i(x_i'\beta, z_i'\alpha) = x_i'\beta + h(z_i'\alpha)$$

is exactly the same as that derived for the apparently more restrictive alternative of (2.20).[5]

6.2.2   *Heteroscedasticity*

It is often acknowledged that heteroscedasticity may be encountered when analyzing cross-section data and, since logit and probit models are usually estimated using such data, tests of the homoscedasticity assumption should form part of routine calculations. Indeed, it is very important to test for heteroscedasticity in qualitative dependent variable models because this misspecification leads to inconsistent estimators. This inconsistency reflects the fact that heteroscedasticity of the errors in this type of model is similar to misspecification of functional form and omitted variables in classical linear regression models. This similarity can be shown by considering the specification consisting of equations (2.1) and (2.2) which has

$$y_i^* = x_i'\beta + u_i, \quad u_i \text{ i.i.d.}(0, \sigma^2)$$

$$y_i = 1 \text{ if } y_i^* > 0$$

$$= 0 \text{ otherwise,}$$

for $i = 1, 2, \ldots, n$.

---

[5] Strictly speaking, it is the score vectors for the two alternatives that will be identical. The value of the test statistic depends upon the choice of information matrix estimate.

Recall that it was argued above that since only the sign of y_i^* is observable and

$$\text{prob}(y_i^* > 0) = \text{prob}(\lambda(\beta'x_i) > -\lambda u_i) \text{ for all } \lambda > 0,$$

it is impossible to estimate β and σ^2 separately. This difficulty can, of course, be resolved easily by imposing a normalization rule with the variance parameter σ^2 restricted to equal some specified positive constant. The general form of the normalization can be written as $\sigma^2 = \sigma_0^2$. The conventional logit and probit models have $\sigma_0^2 = \pi^2/3$ and $\sigma_0^2 = 1$, respectively. Suppose, however, that the disturbances u_i are heteroscedastic with

$$\text{Var}(u_i) = \sigma_i^2 = \sigma_0^2\tau_i^2, \quad i = 1, 2, \ldots, n,$$

with the τ_i not all being equal. In this case, the deflated disturbances $u_i^* = u_i/\tau_i$ are homoscedastic and since

$$\text{prob}(x_i'\beta > -u_i) = \text{prob}((x_i/\tau_i)'\beta > -u_i^*), \ i = 1, \ldots, n,$$

the normalization $\sigma^2 = \sigma_0^2$ is only appropriate if deflated regressor values are used.[6]

In practice, the quantities τ_i will usually be unknown. It will be assumed that they depend upon exogenous variables z_i and an unknown q-dimensional parameter vector α according to

$$\tau_i = h(z_i'\alpha), \quad i = 1, \ldots, n, \tag{2.26}$$

where $h(\cdot)$ is a twice differentiable function satisfying $h(0) = 1$ and $h'(0) \neq 0$, e.g., $h(\cdot) = \exp(\cdot)$.[7] In view of the specification (2.26), the function

$$g_i(\theta) = x_i'\beta/h(z_i'\alpha), \quad \theta' \equiv (\alpha', \beta') \tag{2.27}$$

should be used in place of $x_i'\beta$ for estimating standard logit and probit models.

As before, the null hypothesis to be tested is H_α: $\alpha = 0$ and the approximate effects of small departures from this assumption can be investigated using the general local inconsistency formula of (2.22). If the elements of α are taken to be close to zero, then a linear Taylor series approximation can be employed to yield

$$g_i(\theta) = x_i'\beta/h(z_i'\alpha) \simeq x_i'\beta - h'(0)(x_i'\beta)z_i'\alpha, \tag{2.28}$$

which reinforces the omitted variable/incorrect functional form interpre-

---

[6] Strictly speaking, it is not necessary to deflate the elements of x_i by τ_i and the deflators $\lambda\tau_i$ (λ some positive quantity) would serve.

[7] This choice of $h(\cdot)$ function was made by Davidson and MacKinnon (1984a) and is very convenient.

tation of heteroscedasticity outlined above. The term $-h'(0)$ can be deleted from (2.28) without loss because it is irrelevant when testing $H_a: \alpha = 0$, and then this approximation can be used with the local inconsistency formula (2.23) developed for the omitted variables problem.

Kiefer and Skoog (1984) and Yatchew and Griliches (1985) consider the special case in which a probit model is estimated and the heteroscedasticity function (2.26) takes the simple form

$$\tau_i = 1 + \alpha_1 z_i, \quad i = 1, \ldots, n \qquad (2.29)$$

with

$$z_i = 0 \quad \text{for } i = 1, \ldots, n_1$$

$$= 1 \quad \text{for } i = n_1 + 1, \ldots, n.$$

This specification corresponds to a situation in which $\text{Var}(u_i) = \sigma_1^2$ for $i = 1, \ldots, n_1$, $\text{Var}(u_i) = \sigma_2^2$ for $i = n_1 + 1, \ldots, n$, and the elements of β are associated with the normalization obtained by dividing by σ_1.[8] The parameter α_1 of (2.29) can then be interpreted as $(\sigma_2 - \sigma_1)/\sigma_1$ and so the variable omitted from (2.28) to obtain the null specification is $[(\sigma_2 - \sigma_1)/\sigma_1](x_i'\beta) z_i$, which is an n by 1 vector with the first n_1 elements equal to zero and the last $n_2 = n - n_1$ elements being $[(\sigma_2 - \sigma_1)/\sigma_1]x_i'\beta$, $i = n_1 + 1, \ldots, n$. Substituting this vector for $Z\alpha$ in (2.23) with Ω defined by (2.25) yields the local inconsistency of $\hat{\beta}$, the MLE obtained by restricting $\alpha_1 = 0$, or equivalently $\sigma_1 = \sigma_2$.

Viewing the problem of heteroscedastic disturbances as being equivalent to a misspecification of the $g_i(\theta)$ function in standard logit and probit models also simplifies the derivation of test statistics. The general results on testing $\alpha = 0$ apply to the heteroscedasticity-equivalent specification $g_i(\theta)$ of (2.27) just as much as they do to the omitted variables alternative of (2.20). Consequently, it is only necessary to choose a form of LM-test, for example, LM_1, F_1, LM_2, or F_2, and to obtain the information required for its evaluation.

Davidson and MacKinnon (1984a) provide valuable Monte Carlo evidence on comparative behaviour and, as with the omitted variables problem, the LM_2 variant of (2.14) is to be preferred. The marginal cost of the heteroscedasticity check is quite small and the only new terms required to calculate the LM_2 statistic are the partial derivatives $g_{ir}(\hat{\theta}) = \partial g_i(\hat{\theta})/\partial \theta_r$ which appear in (2.18) and (2.19). These derivatives are the elements of $\partial g_i(\hat{\theta})/\partial \theta$ which can be partitioned as

$$\partial g_i(\hat{\theta})/\partial \theta' = [\partial g_i(\hat{\theta})/\partial \alpha' : \partial g_i(\hat{\theta})/\partial \beta']$$

---

[8] This set-up corresponds to normalization 1 of Kiefer and Skoog (1984, p. 877).

and, since $g_i(\theta)$ is defined by (2.27), the sub-vectors are

$$\partial g_i(\hat{\theta})/\partial \alpha = -(x_i'\hat{\beta})z_i$$

and

$$\partial g_i(\hat{\theta})/\partial \beta = x_i.$$

To sum up, a check against heteroscedasticity of the form $\sigma_i^2 \propto h(z_i'\alpha)$ can be carried out by calculating LM_2, the explained sum of squares for the OLS regression of the variable

$$[y_i - (1 - F_i(\hat{\theta}))]/[F_i(\hat{\theta})(1 - F_i(\hat{\theta}))]^{\frac{1}{2}}$$

on the $(k + q)$ variables

$$[-(x_i'\hat{\beta})z_i', \ x_i']f_i(\hat{\theta})/[F_i(\hat{\theta})(1 - F_i(\hat{\theta}))]^{\frac{1}{2}},$$

where

(i) $f_i(\hat{\theta})/[F_i(\hat{\theta})(1 - F_i(\hat{\theta}))]^{\frac{1}{2}} = [F_i(\hat{\theta})(1 - F_i(\hat{\theta}))]^{\frac{1}{2}}$

and $F_i(\hat{\theta}) = 1/(1 + \exp(x_i'\hat{\beta}))$ for the logit model; and

(ii) $F_i(\hat{\theta}) = 1 - \Phi(x_i'\hat{\beta})$ and $f_i(\hat{\theta}) = \phi(x_i'\hat{\beta})$ for the probit specification.

Sample values of LM_2 should be compared to pre-specified upper-tail critical values of the $\chi^2(q)$ distribution. The fact that LM_2 does not depend upon the form of the function $h(\cdot)$ reflects the usual invariance property of LM tests (cf. Breusch and Pagan, 1979).

6.3   Tobit models

In his survey of the econometrics of Tobit models, Amemiya (1984) provides a likelihood-based classification of different types of Tobit model. The standard Tobit model (which Amemiya calls the type I Tobit model) is by far the most widely used, and we shall concentrate on this variant. It can be written as

$$y_i^* = x_i'\beta + u_i, \quad i = 1, 2, \ldots, n \tag{3.1}$$

$$y_i = \max(y_i^*, 0), \tag{3.2}$$

where the disturbances u_i are assumed to be $\text{NID}(0, \sigma^2)$. This specification is not as restrictive as it appears at first sight and is easily modified to allow for $y_i = \max(y_i^*, y_i^0)$, where the terms y_i^0 are known (possibly unequal) constants (see Amemiya, 1973, p. 997, fn. 2). The k-dimensional vectors x_i and β are constants, with only the former vector being known. The regularity conditions required to justify appeal to the conventional asymptotic theory of MLE are set out by Amemiya (1973).

The likelihood function for the standard Tobit model of (3.1) and (3.2) is given by

$$L(\theta_1) = \prod_0 [1 - \Phi(x_i'\beta/\sigma)] \prod_1 \sigma^{-1}\phi[(y_i - x_i'\beta)/\sigma], \qquad (3.3)$$

where Π_0 denotes the product over values of i such that $y_i^* \leqslant 0$, Π_1 denotes the product over values of i such that $y_i^* > 0$, $\theta_1' = (\beta', \sigma^2)$, and $\Phi(\cdot)$ and $\phi(\cdot)$ have their usual meanings. The form of the likelihood function (3.3) reflects the fact that, when $y_i^* \leqslant 0$, only x_i is observed; that is to say, the sample $y_1, y_2, \ldots, y_n$ is censored. If neither y_i nor x_i is observed when $y_i^* \leqslant 0$, then we have a truncated sample and the appropriate likelihood function can be written as

$$L^t(\theta_1) = \prod_1 \Phi(x_i'\beta/\sigma)^{-1}\sigma^{-1}\phi[(y_i - x_i'\beta)/\sigma]. \qquad (3.4)$$

Truncated regression models have been used in econometric applications (e.g., Hausman and Wise, 1977), and are discussed by Maddala (1983, Section 6.9).

It will be useful to note that there is a simple relationship between the likelihood functions (3.3) and (3.4). Clearly

$$L(\theta_1) = \left\{ \prod_0 [1 - \Phi(x_i'\beta/\sigma)] \prod_1 \Phi(x_i'\beta/\sigma) \right\}$$

$$\times \left\{ \prod_1 \Phi(x_i'\beta/\sigma)^{-1}\sigma^{-1}\phi[(y_i - x_i'\beta)/\sigma] \right\}. \qquad (3.5)$$

The first term in $\{\cdot\}$ on the right-hand side of (3.5) is just the likelihood for the probit model, say $L^P(\theta_1)$, and the second such term is the truncated Tobit model's likelihood $L^t(\theta_1)$ of (3.4). If $l^P(\theta_1)$ and $l^t(\theta_1)$ denote the log-likelihood functions for the probit and truncated Tobit models, respectively, then it will be useful to record for future reference that

$$l(\theta_1) = l^P(\theta_1) + l^t(\theta_1), \qquad (3.6)$$

where $l(\theta_1)$ is the corresponding function for the standard (censored) Tobit model. It should also be observed that the probit log-likelihood $l^P(\theta_1)$ is not capable of providing estimates of β and σ^2 separately, but does permit estimation of the vector of ratios $\gamma \equiv \beta/\sigma$. The MLE for the null specification of (3.1) and (3.2) will, as usual, be denoted by $\hat{\theta}_1' = (\hat{\beta}', \hat{\sigma}^2)$ and yields the MLE of γ, viz. $\hat{\gamma} = \hat{\beta}/\hat{\sigma}$.

As indicated by the results given by Amemiya (1984, Section 5), the estimator $\hat{\theta}_1$ is inconsistent in the presence of several different types of specification error, and so it is extremely important to carry out checks of model adequacy. Since Tobit models are usually estimated using cross-section data, we shall concentrate on the specification errors likely to occur when employing this type of data.[9] These errors include omitted variables, heteroscedasticity and non-normality, and, after summarizing results on inconsistencies, LM test procedures will be outlined. Results based upon Hausman's (1978) approach will also be discussed.

6.3.1 Omitted variables

Consider first the misspecification that arises when there are, say, q variables left out from the right-hand side of (3.1). This equation can then be regarded as an underspecified version of the more general relationship

$$y_i^* = x_i'\beta + z_i'\alpha^* + u_i, \quad i = 1, \ldots, n. \tag{3.7}$$

We shall consider the calculation of tests of the q exclusion restrictions of $\alpha_* = 0$ using the MLE for the null model. This MLE will, in general, be inconsistent if $\alpha_* \neq 0$. For small values of the elements of α_*, the effects of misspecification can be approximated by evaluating the local inconsistency function of (2.22) at $\hat{\theta}' = (\hat{\beta}', 0', \hat{\sigma}^2)$, where $\theta = (\beta', \alpha^{*\prime}, \sigma^2)'$ is the parameter vector associated with the alternative of (3.7) and (3.2), and $\hat{\beta}$ and $\hat{\sigma}^2$ are MLE for the null specification. The second-order partial derivatives required for calculating the value of the vector of local inconsistencies can be derived from the expressions provided by Amemiya (1973, p. 1000); it is only necessary to reinterpret Amemiya's notation with his vectors β' and x_t' being replaced by $(\beta', \alpha^{*\prime})$ and (x_i', z_i'), respectively. The formulae so obtained are, however, somewhat cumbersome and will not be reproduced here. Rather simpler expressions for second-order partial derivatives result from a transformation of parameters, and this reparameterization will be adopted for the purpose of constructing checks for omitted variables.

Following Tobin (1958), we divide both sides of (3.7) by σ to obtain

$$\rho y_i^* = (\rho\beta)'x_i + (\rho\alpha^*)'z_i + v_i, \tag{3.8}$$

$$\rho y_i = \max(\rho y_i^*, 0), \tag{3.9}$$

where $\rho = \sigma^{-1}$ and the disturbances v_i are NID(0, 1), $i = 1, 2, \ldots, n$. Let

[9] An examination of the asymptotic properties of the estimators of LDV models for time-series data has been provided by Robinson (1982). Robinson proves that the Tobit MLE is consistent and asymptotically normal even when the disturbances are serially correlated. He also suggests an autocorrelation consistent estimate of its asymptotic covariance matrix.

$\alpha = \rho\alpha^*$ and $w_i' = (x_i', z_i')$.[10] Since ρ is finite and positive, $\alpha^* = 0$ if and only if $\alpha = 0$, and it will be convenient to derive checks of the validity of excluding the variables of z_i by testing the null hypothesis $H_\alpha: \alpha = 0$. We have already defined $\gamma = \beta/\sigma = \rho\beta$, and so if $\delta' = (\gamma', \alpha')$, equation (3.8) can be written in a more compact form as

$$\rho y_i^* = \delta' w_i + v_i. \tag{3.10}$$

The log-likelihood for the Tobit model in terms of the transformed parameters is

$$l(\psi) = \sum_0 \log[1 - \Phi(w_i'\delta)] + n_1 \log(\rho) - \tfrac{1}{2} \sum_1 (\rho y_i - w_i'\delta)^2, \quad (3.11)$$

where Σ_0 (resp. Σ_1) denotes summation over observations for which $y_i = 0$ (resp. $y_i > 0$), n_1 is the number of observations for which $y_i > 0$, and ψ is the $(k + q + 1)$ vector of transformed parameters defined by $\psi' = (\gamma', \alpha', \rho) = (\delta', \rho)$. The first-order partial derivatives of this function are the elements of

$$d(\psi)' = [\partial l(\psi)/\partial\delta', \ \partial l(\psi)/\partial\rho], \tag{3.12}$$

where

$$\partial l(\psi)/\partial\delta = -\sum_0 \phi(w_i'\delta)[1 - \Phi(w_i'\delta)]^{-1}w_i + \sum_1 [\rho y_i - w_i'\delta]w_i, \tag{3.13}$$

and

$$\partial l(\psi)/\partial\rho = n_1/\rho - \sum_1 (\rho y_i - w_i'\delta)y_i. \tag{3.14}$$

The second-order partial derivatives (which are less complicated than those for the original parameterization) are the elements of

$$D(\psi) = \begin{bmatrix} D_{\delta\delta}(\psi) & D_{\delta\rho}(\psi) \\ D_{\rho\delta}(\psi) & D_{\rho\rho}(\psi) \end{bmatrix}, \tag{3.15}$$

where

$$D_{\delta\delta}(\psi) = \partial^2 l(\psi)/\partial\delta\partial\delta' = \sum_0 \phi(w_i'\delta)[1 - \Phi(w_i'\delta)]^{-1}(w_i'\delta)w_i w_i'$$

---

[10] The vector w_i' should not be confused with a typical row of the matrix $W(\hat{\theta})$ which appeared in the discussion of LM tests for logit and probit models.

$$- \sum_0 \{\phi(w_i'\delta)[1 - \Phi(w_i'\delta)]^{-1}\}^2 w_i w_i'$$

$$- \sum_1 w_i w_i'; \tag{3.16}$$

$$D_{\rho\delta}(\psi) = [D_{\delta\rho}(\psi)]' = \sum_1 y_i w_i'; \tag{3.17}$$

and

$$D_{\rho\rho}(\psi) = -n_1/\rho^2 - \sum_1 y_i^2. \tag{3.18}$$

The calculation of the LM statistic involves the evaluation of the derivatives given by (3.12) to (3.18) at $\psi = \hat{\psi}$, the estimator that maximizes $l(\psi)$ subject to $\alpha = 0$. This restricted MLE can be easily derived from β and $\hat{\sigma}^2$, the MLEs of the original parameters of the standard Tobit model. Partitioning $\hat{\psi}$ as

$$\hat{\psi}' = (\hat{\gamma}', \hat{\alpha}', \hat{\rho}),$$

the invariance property of MLE implies that $\hat{\gamma} = \hat{\beta}/\hat{\sigma}$, $\hat{\alpha} = 0$ and $\hat{\rho} = (\hat{\sigma}^2)^{-\frac{1}{2}}$. The LM statistic $-d(\hat{\psi})'[D(\hat{\psi})]^{-1}d(\hat{\psi})$ is asymptotically distributed as $\chi^2(q)$ under the null hypothesis $H_\alpha: \alpha = 0$, with significantly large values indicating the inadequacy of (3.1).

However, it must be acknowledged that, even with the simplifying reparameterization, the LM test for omitted variables will be difficult to implement unless the estimation program being used by the researcher includes a subroutine for its evaluation.[11] If such a subroutine is not available, the asymptotically equivalent LR test of $\alpha^* = 0$ is completely straightforward, requiring the ML estimation of the Tobit models based upon (3.1) and (3.7).

6.3.2   *Heteroscedasticity*

If the assumption of a common variance is relaxed, the model can be written as

$$y_i^* = x_i'\beta + u_i, \ u_i \sim N(0, \sigma_i^2) \tag{3.19}$$

$$y_i = \max(y_i^*, 0), \quad i = 1, \ldots, n, \tag{3.20}$$

where the disturbances u_i are independent and $\sigma_i^2 \neq \sigma_j^2$ for some i and j.

[11] The problem of calculating second-order partial derivatives could be avoided by using the OPG variant of the LM procedure, but the Monte Carlo evidence obtained for several different types of econometric model strongly suggests that such a test would be poorly behaved in finite samples.

The standard censored Tobit model is obtained by imposing $\sigma_i^2 = \sigma^2$ for all i. When this assumption is false, the likelihood fumction of (3.3) is inappropriate and, not surprisingly, its maximizers will not provide a consistent estimator of β.

Maddala (1983, p. 179) seeks to shed some light on the source of the inconsistency by considering the expected value of y_i under the homoscedasticity assumption and the more general form of (3.19). When the disturbances are heteroscedastic, the expected value of y_i is given by

$$E(y_i) = [\Phi(x_i'\beta/\sigma_i)]x_i'\beta + \sigma_i\phi(x_i'\beta/\sigma_i), \tag{3.21}$$

which depends upon the value of σ_i. The conventional Tobit MLE, however, is based upon the restriction that $\sigma_i^2 = \sigma^2$ for all i, which implies an expected value function of the form

$$[\Phi(x_i'\beta/\sigma)]x_i'\beta + \sigma\phi(x_i'\beta/\sigma). \tag{3.22}$$

Comparison of (3.21) and (3.22) reveals the misspecification resulting from incorrectly imposing the assumption that the variances σ_i^2 are all equal.

Maddala (1983) also points out that, even if attention is restricted to simple examples of heteroscedasticity, it is very difficult to say much about the direction of inconsistencies. Some expressions for asymptotic biases in quite special cases have been obtained and may be of interest (see Arabmazar and Schmidt, 1981, for an analysis of censored Tobit models, and Hurd, 1979 for an investigation in the context of the truncated Tobit model; also, some Monte Carlo evidence on the impact of heteroscedasticity on the Tobit MLE is provided by Warner, 1976).

As usual, the LM test against heteroscedasticity will be obtained by setting up an alternative hypothesis of the type employed by Breusch and Pagan (1979). In order to simplify reference to other work, it will be useful to write the heteroscedasticity function of the alternative model as

$$\sigma_i^2 = h(\sigma^2 + z_i'\alpha), \quad i = 1, \ldots, n, \tag{3.23}$$

where z_i and α are q-dimensional vectors with the variables of z_i being exogenous and satisfying the necessary regularity conditions.[12] The function $h(\cdot)$ is twice differentiable and $h'(\sigma^2) \neq 0$. The null hypothesis to be tested is then H_α: $\alpha = 0$. Let $\theta' = (\beta', \sigma^2, \alpha')$ denote the parameter vector for the alternative and $\hat{\theta}' = (\hat{\beta}', \hat{\sigma}^2, 0')$ denote the constrained MLE obtained by imposing H_α.

The log-likelihood for the heteroscedastic censored Tobit model de-

---

[12] Clearly, z_i cannot contain an intercept dummy. The model of (3.23) is used by Jarque and Bera (1982) and Lee and Maddala (1985).

fined by (3.19), (3.20) and (3.23) is

$$l(\theta) = \sum_0 \ln[1 - \Phi(x_i'\beta/\sigma_i)] - \tfrac{1}{2}\sum_1 \{\ln(\sigma_i^2) + (y_i - x_i'\beta)^2/\sigma_i^2\},$$

(3.24)

where σ_i^2 is regarded as a function of α and σ^2 determined by (3.23). The LM test of H_α is an asymptotic test of the joint significance of the elements of $\hat{d}_2 = \partial l(\hat{\theta})/\partial\alpha$. Partial differentiation of $l(\theta)$ of (3.24) with respect to α and evaluation at $\theta = \hat{\theta}$ yields

$$\partial l(\hat{\theta})/\partial\alpha = \left[\frac{h'(\hat{\sigma}^2)}{2}\right] \sum_0 \left[\frac{\hat{\phi}_i}{1 - \hat{\Phi}_i}\right]\left[\frac{(x_i'\beta)}{\hat{\sigma}^3}\right] z_i$$
$$+ \left[\frac{h'(\hat{\sigma}^2)}{2}\right] \sum_1 \left[\frac{(\hat{u}_i^2 - \hat{\sigma}^2)}{\hat{\sigma}^4}\right] z_i,$$

(3.25)

where $\hat{\phi}_i = \phi(x_i'\beta/\hat{\sigma})$, $\hat{\Phi}_i = \Phi(x_i'\beta/\hat{\sigma})$ and $\hat{u}_i = y_i - x_i'\hat{\beta}$ for $y_i > 0$. The value of the LM statistic is not altered by taking non-singular transformations of the score of (3.25) and so the term $h'(\hat{\sigma}^2)$ can be ignored. Thus the functional form of $h(\cdot)$ is irrelevant, as would be expected from the results on locally equivalent alternatives (LEAs). Note, however, that the form of $h(\cdot)$ may well have indirect influence through its relationship to the choice of the variables in z_i; for example, if $h(\cdot)$ represents additive heteroscedasticity, the z_i may contain one or more of the variables of x_i, whereas if $h(\cdot)$ implies multiplicative heteroscedasticity, it may be the logs of x-variables that appear in z_i (see Chapter 4, Section 4.5).

Whatever the choice of the variables z_i, it remains to construct the asymptotic χ^2 criterion that serves to check the significance of $\partial l(\hat{\theta})/\partial\alpha$. The 'efficient score statistic' form of this criterion is $d(\hat{\theta})'[\mathscr{I}(\hat{\theta})]^{-1}d(\hat{\theta})$, where $d(\hat{\theta})' = (0', 0, \partial l(\hat{\theta})/\partial\alpha')$ and $\mathscr{I}(\hat{\theta})$ is an estimate of the information matrix based upon $\hat{\theta}$. Expressions for the elements of suitable $\mathscr{I}(\hat{\theta})$ estimates are quite complicated and if, without any loss of generality, we set $h'(\hat{\sigma}^2) = 1$ in (3.25), we can use the formulae provided by Jarque and Bera (1982) (see also Jarque, 1981).

An alternative approach to testing for heteroscedasticity is to estimate the alternative model and then to apply the Wald or LR test of $\alpha = 0$. The LR test is straightforward in principle, but, unlike the LM procedure, requires that $h(\cdot)$ be specified.[13] Maddala (1983) discusses the specification

$$\sigma_i^2 = (\sigma + \alpha'z_i)^2, \quad i = 1, \ldots, n,$$

(3.26)

[13] The LR statistics for LEAs will be asymptotically equivalent, but not numerically equal in finite samples.

which is used by Fishe, Maddala and Trost (1979). The derivation of the unrestricted MLE obviously requires the application of some non-linear optimization technique. The problem of calculating the second derivatives sometimes required in iterative schemes is avoided by Fishe et al. (1970) who employ the method of Berndt et al. (1974) involving only first-order partial differentiation. It should be emphasized that while a specification like (3.26) may prove to be a useful tool for the rejection of a false assumption of homoscedasticity, there is no guarantee that it is itself adequate. Consequently, deriving the unrestricted MLE for a specified alternative is not the same as 'solving' the problem of residual hetero-scedasticity. Indeed, evidence of apparent heteroscedasticity may reflect inconsistencies caused by omission of relevant x-variables.

6.3.3   *Non-normality*

In contrast to the OLS estimator for a linear multiple regression model, the MLE of the Tobit model is inconsistent when the errors are incorrectly assumed to be normally distributed. Robinson (1982) discusses the causes of inconsistency by considering the probability limits of first-order derivatives of the 'Gaussian' log-likelihood and also illustrates the general problem by looking at the special case in which the term $x_i'\beta$ is simply a constant, so that $y_i^* = \mu + u_i$. This special case is also examined by Arabmazar and Schmidt (1982), who calculate inconsistencies for various non-normal distributions. Some Monte Carlo evidence on the effects of non-normality on the 'Gaussian' Tobit MLE is reported by Paarsch (1984).

In view of the sensitivity of the Tobit MLE to non-normality and the fact that there is rarely a compelling reason for believing that the disturbances are jointly normally distributed, a test for misspecification of the p.d.f. $f(u)$ would appear to be desirable in any thorough empirical study. The tests proposed by Jarque and Bera (1980) and by Kiefer and Salmon (1983) for linear regression models are invalid, but have been generalized to cover Tobit models by Jarque and Bera (1982). Under the alternative hypothesis, the distribution of u is a member of the Pearson family and so the p.d.f. $f(u)$ is determined by

$$df(u_i)/du_i = f(u_i)(c_1 - u_i)/(c_0 - c_1 u_i + c_2 u_i^2), \tag{3.27}$$

with $-\infty < u_i < \infty$. The normal distribution of the null hypothesis is the special case obtained by imposing $c_1 = c_2 = 0$ in (3.27). The form of the LM statistic described by Jarque and Bera is complicated and will not be reproduced here.[14] Empirical applications of this test are provided by Bera, Jarque and Lee (1984).[15]

6.3.4   *The common structure of tests against omitted variables,*
          heteroscedasticity and non-normality

Full expressions for the LM statistics for the alternatives of omitted
variables, heteroscedasticity and non-normality are themselves cumbersome and of limited intuitive appeal. Some unifying results can, however,
be obtained by restricting attention to the score vectors. Lee and Maddala
(1985) have shown that the scores relevant to several types of misspecification can be interpreted as certain sample conditional moments, and, as will
be seen below, their results are analogous to those derived for the linear
regression model.

For simplicity of exposition, we shall start by considering the problem
of checking for omitted variables. It will be recalled that the LM test was
derived in the context of a reparameterized model obtained by dividing by
σ, and the standardized disturbances u_i/σ were denoted by v_i, $i = 1, 2, \ldots,$
n. The score for the reparametrized Tobit model is given by (3.13) and
(3.14), and the former equation can be rewritten as

$$\partial l(\psi)/\partial \delta = \sum_{i=1}^{n} \{ y_i^+ (\rho y_i - w_i'\delta) - (1 - y_i^+)\phi(w_i'\delta)[1 - \Phi(w_i'\delta)]^{-1} \} w_i,$$

$$(3.28)$$

where y_i^+ is an indicator variable defined by

$$y_i^+ = 1 \text{ if } y_i > 0$$

$$= 0 \text{ otherwise.}$$

Now $v_i = (\rho y_i - w_i'\delta)$ when $y_i^+ = 1$ and

$$E(v_i|y_i^+ = 0) = E(v_i|v_i \leqslant -w_i'\delta) = -\phi(w_i'\delta)[1 - \Phi(w_i'\delta)]^{-1}.$$

It follows that

$$E(v_i|y_i^+, v_i y_i^+) = y_i^+ v_i - (1 - y_i^+)\phi(w_i'\delta)[1 - \Phi(w_i'\delta)]^{-1},$$

so that the derivative vector of (3.28) can be expressed as

$$\partial l(\psi)/\partial \delta = \sum_{i=1}^{n} w_i E(v_i|y_i^+, v_i y_i^+).$$

[14] Jarque and Bera (1982) give a formula for a joint test against heteroscedasticity and non-normality, but explain how it should be modified if
only one of these misspecifications is being considered.

[15] If the assumption of normality is not made, the researcher may wish to
consider estimators based upon non-normal distributions or transformations to normality; see Maddala (1983, pp. 187–92) and Poirier and
Ruud (1983).

Evaluation at the constrained MLE implies that the only non-zero component of the score is

$$\partial l(\hat{\psi})/\partial\alpha = \sum_{i=1}^{n} z_i \hat{E}(v_i|y_i^+, v_i y_i^+), \tag{3.29}$$

where z_i contains the exogenous variables whose relevance is under scrutiny and $\hat{E}(\cdot|\cdot)$ denotes the function $E(\cdot|\cdot)$ evaluated at $\psi = \hat{\psi}$. In terms of the original parameters,

$$\hat{E}(v_i|v_i, 1) = \hat{v}_i = (y_i - x_i'\hat{\beta})/\hat{\sigma}$$

and

$$\hat{E}(v_i|0, 0) = -\phi(x_i'\hat{\beta}/\hat{\sigma})[1 - \Phi(x_i'\hat{\beta}/\hat{\sigma})]^{-1}.$$

The right-hand side of (3.29) is, apart from a factor of n^{-1}, a vector of sample conditional moments (covariances) evaluated at the Tobit MLE.

Equations like (3.29) can be derived for other misspecifications. Lee and Maddala (1985) show that the LM test for heteroscedasticity based upon (3.25) is asymptotically equivalent to an asymptotic test of the joint significance of the elements of the vector

$$\sum_{i=1}^{n} z_i [\hat{E}(v_i^2|y_i^+, v_i y_i^+) - 1], \tag{3.30}$$

and state that the two non-zero elements of the score employed in the Jarque–Bera (1982) test for non-normality are equivalent to

$$\sum_{i=1}^{n} \hat{E}(v_i^3|y_i^+, v_i y_i^+) \tag{3.31}$$

and

$$\sum_{i=1}^{n} [\hat{E}(v_i^4|y_i^+, v_i y_i^+) - 3]. \tag{3.32}$$

In the linear regression equation, the moments (sample sums) corresponding to (3.29), (3.30), (3.31) and (3.32) are

$$\sum_{i=1}^{n} z_i(\hat{u}_i/\hat{\sigma})$$

$$\sum_{i=1}^{n} z_i[(\hat{u}_i^2/\hat{\sigma}^2) - 1]$$

$$\sum_{i=1}^{n} (\hat{u}_i^3/\hat{\sigma}^3)$$

and

$$\sum_{i=1}^{n} [(\hat{u}_i^4/\hat{\sigma}^4) - 3],$$

respectively, where $\hat{u}_i$ denotes a typical OLS residual and $\hat{\sigma}^2 = n^{-1}\Sigma_1^n \hat{u}_i^2$.

It is of course interesting that moments and covariances involving conditional expectations evaluated at the Tobit MLE can be used to provide a unifying scheme for diagnostic checks, and that links can be forged between these procedures and those developed for the conventional multiple regression model. It remains the case, however, that LM tests for the Tobit model will be difficult to implement unless specially written computer subroutines are available.

6.3.5 Hausman specification tests

Since omitted variables, heteroscedasticity, and non-normality all cause the Tobit MLE to be inconsistent with $(\hat{\beta} - \beta)$ being $O_p(1)$, all three of the corresponding LM statistics are likely to be $O_p(n)$ when one of these misspecifications is present. Therefore, it seems reasonable to conjecture that the LM tests discussed above will usually have power against general misspecification and will not just be sensitive to the specific alternatives for which they were derived.[16] In view of this feature and the fact that the calculation of these statistics may be fairly inconvenient, it is worth considering alternative specification tests that are simpler to implement. The estimator contrast tests proposed by Hausman (1978) are designed to detect errors that lead to estimator inconsistency and often require little more than the standard output of estimation programmes. They are, therefore, potentially attractive in this context.[17]

Nelson (1981) suggests that one way in which Hausman's general approach can be used in Tobit models is to compare alternative estimates of the vector $E_{xy} \equiv n^{-1}E(X'y)$, where X is the n by k matrix with typical row x_i' and y is the n-dimensional vector with elements y_i, $i = 1, 2, \ldots, n$. If the standard Tobit specification of (3.1) and (3.2) is correct, then equation (3.22) is valid and implies that

$$E_{xy} = n^{-1}E(X'y) = n^{-1} \sum_{i=1}^{n} x_i[\Phi(x_i'\beta/\sigma)x_i'\beta + \sigma\phi(x_i'\beta/\sigma)].$$

$$(3.33)$$

---

[16] This property of LM tests for the Tobit model is mentioned by Lee and Maddala (1985) in their concluding remarks.

[17] Hausman and McFadden (1984) examine the relative merits of Hausman tests and classical procedures for checking the adequacy of multinomial logit models.

A consistent and asymptotically efficient estimator of E_{xy}, denoted by $\hat{E}_{xy}$, is obtained by replacing β and σ in (3.33) by $\hat{\beta}$ and $\hat{\sigma}$, respectively.

Hausman's method requires that $\hat{E}_{xy}$ be compared to an estimator which is consistent and inefficient relative to $\hat{E}_{xy}$ under the null hypothesis and is consistent under the alternative hypothesis. The method of moments estimator, $n^{-1}X'y$, is used by Nelson to play this role in his analysis. In order to assess whether or not the differences between $\hat{E}_{xy}$ and $n^{-1}X'y$ are small enough to be consistent with the hypothesis of correct specification, it is necessary to estimate the asymptotic covariance matrix of $(n^{-1}X'y - \hat{E}_{xy})$. Hausman's (1978) results imply that this matrix equals the difference of the covariance matrices of the estimates being compared.

Let the asymptotic covariance matrices of $n^{\frac{1}{2}}(\hat{E}_{xy} - E_{xy})$ and $n^{\frac{1}{2}}(n^{-1}X'y - E_{xy})$ be denoted by V_0 and V_1, respectively.[18] Nelson's test statistic for general misspecification can then be written as

$$n(n^{-1}X'y - \hat{E}_{xy})'[\hat{V}_1 - \hat{V}_0]^{-1}(n^{-1}X'y - \hat{E}_{xy}), \tag{3.34}$$

where $\hat{V}_0$ (resp. $\hat{V}_1$) is an estimate of V_0 (resp. V_1) based upon $\hat{\beta}$ and $\hat{\sigma}^2$. The asymptotic null distribution of the criterion of (3.34) is $\chi^2(k)$, with significantly large values indicating some sort of model inadequacy.

Unfortunately, although the expression for $V_1 - V_0$, the covariance matrix of $n^{\frac{1}{2}}(n^{-1}X'y - \hat{E}_{xy})$, is much less cumbersome than those defining the information matrix estimates for LM tests against, for example, heteroscedasticity and/or non-normality, its estimation still requires separate and non-trivial calculations after the researcher has carried out the basic task of obtaining the values of $\hat{\beta}$ and $\hat{\sigma}^2$. Also, Amemiya (1984, p. 26) suggests that it would be better to compare estimates of the original parameters, rather than functions of these parameters such as E_{xy}.

Ruud (1984) shows that both of these problems can be overcome if Hausman's original framework is extended to cover situations in which neither estimator is asymptotically efficient under the null hypothesis and/or neither estimator is consistent under the alternative hypothesis. The extended Hausman test will, in general, be consistent when the two estimators being compared have different probability limits under the alternative hypothesis.

The estimators considered by Ruud (1984) in devising a test of the Tobit model are the Tobit MLE, the truncated regression estimator derived by using only observations for which y_i^* is positive, and the probit MLE obtained using only information about the sign of y_i^*. These estimators maximize the likelihood functions $L(\theta_1)$, $L^t(\theta_1)$ and $L^p(\theta_1)$, respectively; see

---

[18] Details of the formulae for V_0 and V_1 are given by Nelson (1981) and Maddala (1983, Section 6.15).

equations (3.3), (3.4) and (3.5) for the definitions of these likelihoods. It will be recalled that $L(\theta_1)$ can be factorized as the product of $L^t(\theta_1)$ and $L^P(\theta_1)$; see equation (3.6). Consequently the log-likelihood functions satisfy

$$l(\beta, \sigma^2) = l^t(\beta, \sigma^2) + l^P(\beta/\sigma). \tag{3.35}$$

Our purpose in introducing (3.35), rather than retaining (3.6), is to emphasize that the probit specification does not provide a basis for the separate estimation of all the elements of $\theta_1' = (\beta', \sigma^2)$.

The key result of Ruud's (1984) analysis is a likelihood factorization theorem, which implies the asymptotic equivalence of the three tests based upon pair-wise comparisons between the estimators obtained by maximizing $l(\beta, \sigma^2)$, $l^t(\beta, \sigma^2)$ and $l^P(\beta/\sigma)$. This result may appear surprising at first sight since the vector of differences between the maximizers of $l(\beta, \sigma^2)$ and $l^t(\beta, \sigma^2)$ has $(k + 1)$ elements, whereas the two contrasts involving the probit MLE have only k elements. There is, however, no real difference in the degrees-of-freedom parameters of the three pair-wise comparison tests. There is a singularity in the asymptotic null distribution of the contrast calculated from the censored Tobit MLE and the MLE of the truncated regression model, and one redundant element must be dropped. All three criteria will be asymptotically distributed as $\chi^2(k)$ under the null hypothesis of correct specification.

It only remains to choose which of the three available contrasts to use for the specification test. It seems reasonable to include the Tobit MLE in the analysis. This estimator has intrinsic interest as the (asymptotically) efficient estimator for the model specified by the researcher and also satisfies Hausman's (1978) criterion for inclusion. The Tobit MLE of γ, namely, $\hat{\gamma} = \hat{\beta}/\hat{\sigma}$, could be compared to the probit MLE. The associated test statistic would be of the general form

$$(\bar{\gamma} - \hat{\gamma})'[\bar{V}_\gamma - \hat{V}_\gamma]^{-1}(\bar{\gamma} - \hat{\gamma}), \tag{3.36}$$

where $\bar{\gamma}$ denotes the probit MLE, and $\bar{V}_\gamma$ and $\hat{V}_\gamma$ are the estimated asymptotic covariance matrices of $\bar{\gamma}$ and $\hat{\gamma}$, respectively. The matrix $\bar{V}_\gamma$ will be available as a by-product of estimation, as will $\hat{V}_\gamma$ if the Tobit model is fitted in reparameterized form, that is, with parameter vector $\psi_1' = (\beta/\sigma, \sigma^{-1})$ (see Maddala, 1983, Section 6.4). The calculation of $\hat{V}_\gamma$ will, however, be something of a chore if the programme for the Tobit MLE is designed to estimate the parameters of the original form of the model, namely, β and σ^2. In such cases, it may be simpler to consider the difference between the Tobit MLE and the MLE for the truncated regression model.

If the truncated regression MLE is denoted by $\dot{\theta}_1' = (\dot{\beta}', \dot{\sigma}^2)$, then the first step in constructing a Hausman-type test is to drop an element of

$(\dot{\theta}_1 - \hat{\theta}_1)$ in order to remove the singularity mentioned above. It seems natural to omit the difference between the estimates of σ^2 and to use only the alternative estimates of β. The specification test so obtained is

$$(\dot{\beta} - \hat{\beta})'[\dot{V}_\beta - \hat{V}_\beta]^{-1}(\dot{\beta} - \hat{\beta}), \tag{3.37}$$

where $\dot{V}_\beta$ and $\hat{V}_\beta$ are the estimated asymptotic covariance matrices of $\dot{\beta}$ and $\hat{\beta}$, respectively. The matrices $\dot{V}_\beta$ and $\hat{V}_\beta$ are routinely calculated by estimation programmes, and so the test based upon (3.37) is easy to implement.

Finally, if the researcher is willing to incur the costs of obtaining all three estimators, an LR form of the extended Hausman test which is asymptotically equivalent to (3.36) and (3.37) can be derived (see Ruud, 1984, p. 232). This LR variant is based upon the criterion

$$-2[l(\hat{\beta}, \hat{\sigma}^2) - l^t(\dot{\beta}, \dot{\sigma}^2) - l^P(\bar{\gamma})], \tag{3.38}$$

which is asymptotically distributed as $\chi^2(k)$ if the model of (3.1) and (3.2) represents a correct specification. Ruud (1984) remarks that since maximized log-likelihoods are usually included in the results provided by standard software, the statistic of (3.38) is much simpler to calculate than quadratic forms like (3.36) and (3.37), and is moreover guaranteed to be non-negative, as is required if it is to be interpreted as a χ^2 variate.

6.4   Conclusions

It has been argued that the maximum likelihood estimators of qualitative and limited dependent variable models are not robust to several misspecifications that may be reasonably regarded as potential problems in empirical work. Since the number of applied studies involving such models is growing, thorough testing should become part of standard econometric practice. If such testing is not undertaken, the results reported will be of uncertain status and may be very misleading.

In the case of logit and probit models, LM checks are fairly simple to implement and Monte Carlo evidence suggests that a variant, LM_2, derived from an artificial OLS regression will be useful when testing for omitted variables or heteroscedasticity. The OPG version of the LM test based upon the regression of a vector of ones on a matrix of first-order partial derivatives is, however, not to be recommended, despite the fact that it is probably the easiest form to calculate.

The LM tests for the Tobit specification are not so attractive.[19] They

---

[19] The LM procedures discussed in Section 6.3 cover many important misspecifications, but other tests are available. For example, Lee and Maddala (1985) derive an LM test of the Tobit model against a selectivity model.

often involve quite cumbersome expressions which require separate calculation after estimation of the basic model. Also it seems likely that these tests will act as general, rather than specific, checks so that there may be little incentive to prepare subroutines for the evaluation of a number of individual test statistics. Ruud's (1984) specification tests based upon Hausman-type estimator contrasts are more easily calculated and represent an interesting alternative means of evaluating Tobit models. It would be interesting to have some Monte Carlo evidence on their performance.

The adequacy of a Tobit specification can also be tested by applying White's (1982) information matrix (IM) test. Chesher, Lancaster and Irish (1985) provide numerical examples in which IM statistics are calculated by means of pseudo-regressions, for example, the OPG regression described in Section 1.6. Unfortunately, such pseudo-regressions can lead to substantial differences between the asymptotic properties of the IM statistic and its finite sample behaviour (see Orme, 1987).

Bibliography

Aitchison, J. and S. D. Silvey (1958). Maximum-likelihood estimation parameters subject to restraints. *Annals of Mathematical Statistics, 29*, 813–28.

Aitchison, J. and S. D. Silvey (1960). Maximum-likelihood estimation procedures and associated tests of significance. *Journal of Royal Statistical Society,* Series B, *22*, 154–71.

Aldrich, J. (1978). An alternative derivation of Durbin's h statistic. *Econometrica, 46*, 1493–4.

Amemiya, T. (1966). Specification analysis in the estimation of parameters of a simultaneous equation model with autoregressive residuals. *Econometrica, 34*, 283–306.

Amemiya, T. (1973). Regression analysis when the variance of the dependent variable is proportional to the square of its expectation. *Journal of the American Statistical Association, 68*, 928–34.

Amemiya, T. (1977). A note on a heteroscedastic model. *Journal of Econometrics, 6*, 365–70.

Amemiya, T. (1981). Qualitative response models: a survey. *Journal of Economic Literature, 19*, 1483–1536.

Amemiya, T. (1983). Non-linear regression models. In *Handbook of econometrics,* Vol. I, ed. Z. Griliches and M. D. Intriligator, 333–89. Amsterdam: North Holland.

Amemiya, T. (1984). Tobit model: a survey. *Journal of Econometrics, 24*, 3–61.

Amemiya, T. and J. L. Powell (1981). A comparison of the Box–Cox maximum likelihood estimator and the non-linear two stage least squares estimator. *Journal of Econometrics, 17*, 351–81.

Anderson, G. J. and G. E. Mizon (1983). Parameter constancy tests: old and new. Unpublished paper, University of Southampton (DP8325).

Anderson, T. W. and H. Rubin (1949). Estimation of the parameters of a single equation in a complete system of stochastic equations. *Annals of Mathematical Statistics, 20*, 46–63.

Andrews, D. F. (1971). A note on the selection of data transformations. *Biometrika, 58*, 249–54.

Aneuryn-Evans, G. and A. S. Deaton (1980). Testing linear versus logarithmic regression models. *Review of Economic Studies, 47*, 275–91.

Anscombe, F. J. (1961). Examination of residuals. In *Proceedings of the Fourth Berkeley Symposium on Mathematical Statistics and Probability, 4*, 1–36. Berkeley: University of California Press.

Arabmazar, A. and P. Schmidt (1981). Further evidence on the robustness of the Tobit estimator to heteroscedasticity. *Jounal of Econometrics, 17*, 253–8.

Arabmazar, A. and P. Schmidt (1982). An investigation of the robustness of the Tobit estimator to non-normality. *Econometrica, 50*, 1055–63.

232

Atkinson, A. C. (1973). Testing transformations to normality. *Journal of the Royal Statistical Society*, Series B, *35*, 473–8.

Bahadur, R. R. (1960). Stochastic comparison of tests. *Annals of Mathematical Statistics*, *31*, 276–95.

Barten, A. P. and L. Silvas Bronsard (1970). Two stage least squares estimation with shifts in the structural form. *Econometrica*, *38*, 938–41.

Bartlett, M. S. (1937). Properties of sufficiency and statistical tests. *Proceedings of the Royal Society*, Series A, *160*, 268.

Bartlett, M. S. (1946). On the theoretical specification of sampling properties of autocorrelated time series. *Journal of the Royal Statistical Society*, Series B, *8*, 27–41.

Belsley, D. A., E. Kuh and R. E. Welsch (1980). *Regression Diagnostics*. New York: Wiley.

Bera, A. K. (1982). *Aspects of Econometric Modelling*. Unpublished Ph.D. thesis, Australian National University.

Bera, A. K. and C. M. Jarque (1981). Efficient tests for normality, homoscedasticity and serial independence of regression residuals: Monte Carlo evidence. *Economic Letters*, *7*, 313–18.

Bera, A. K. and C. M. Jarque (1982). Model specification tests: a simultaneous approach. *Journal of Econometrics*, *20*, 59–82.

Bera, A. K., C. M. Jarque and L.-F. Lee (1984). Testing the normality assumption in limited dependent variable models. *International Economic Review*, *25*, 563–78.

Bera, A. K. and C. R. McKenzie (1986). Alternative forms and properties of the score test. *Journal of Applied Statistics*, *13*, 13–25.

Berenblut, I. I. and G. I. Webb (1973). A new test for autocorrelated errors in the linear regression model. *Journal of the Royal Statistical Society*, Series B, *35*, 33–50.

Berndt, E. R., B. H. Hall, R. E. Hall and J. A. Hausman (1974). Estimation and inference in nonlinear structural models. *Annals of Economic and Social Measurement*, *3*, 653–66.

Berndt, E. R. and N. E. Savin (1977). Conflict among criteria for testing hypotheses in the multivariate linear regression model. *Econometrica*, *45*, 1263–78.

Bickel, P. J. (1978). Using residuals robustly I: test for heteroscedasticity, nonlinearity. *The Annals of Statistics*, *6*, 266–91.

Bowman, K. O. and L. R. Shenton (1975). Omnibus contours for departures from normality based upon $\sqrt{b_1}$ and b_2. *Biometrika*, *62*, 243–50.

Box, G. E. P. and D. R. Cox (1964). An analysis of transformations. *Journal of the Royal Statistical Society*, Series B, *26*, 211–52.

Box, G. E. P. and D. A. Pierce (1970). Distribution of residual autocorrelations in autoregressive-integrated moving average time series models. *Journals of the American Statistical Association*, *65*, 1509–26.

Breusch, T. S. (1978a). Testing for autocorrelation in dynamic linear models. *Australian Economic Papers*, *17*, 334–55.

Breusch, T. S. (1978b). *Some Aspects of Statistical Inference for Econometrics*. Unpublished Ph.D. thesis, Australian National University.

Breusch, T. S. (1979). Conflict among criteria for testing hypotheses: extensions and comments. *Econometrica*, *47*, 203–7.

Breusch, T. S. (1986). Hypothesis testing in underidentified models. *Review of Economic Studies*, *53*, 635–51.

Breusch, T. S. and L. G. Godfrey (1981). A review of recent work on testing for autocorrelation in dynamic simultaneous models. In *Macroeconomic Analysis*, ed. D. Currie, A. R. Nobay and D. Peel, 63–105. London: Croom Helm.

Breusch, T. S. and L. G. Godfrey (1984). Implementation, power and interpretation of the differencing test. Unpublished paper, University of Southampton (DP8412).

Breusch, T. S. and L. G. Godfrey (1986). Data transformation tests. *Economic Journal* (Supplement), *96*, 47–58.

Breusch, T. S. and A. R. Pagan (1979). A simple test for heteroscedasticity and random coefficient variation. *Econometrica, 47*, 1287–94.

Breusch, T. S. and A. R. Pagan (1980). The Lagrange multiplier test and its applications to model specification in econometrics. *Review of Economic Studies, 47*, 239–53.

Brillingsley, P. (1961). *Statistical Inference for Markov Processes.* Chicago: University of Chicago Press.

Burguete, J. F., A. R. Gallant and G. Souza (1982). On unification of the asymptotic theory of nonlinear econometric models. *Econometric Reviews, 1*, 151–90.

Chant, D. (1974). On asymptotic tests of composite hypotheses in non-standard conditions. *Biometrika, 61*, 291–9.

Chen, C.-F. (1983). Score tests for regression models. *Journal of the American Statistical Association, 78*, 158–61.

Chen, C.-F. (1985). Robustness aspects of score tests for generalized linear and partially linear regression models. *Technometrics, 27*, 277–83.

Chernoff, H. (1954). On the distribution of the likelihood ratio. *Annals of Mathematical Statistics, 25*, 573–8.

Chesher, A. D. (1983). The information matrix test: simplified calculation via a score test interpretation. *Economics Letters, 13*, 45–8.

Chesher, A. D. (1984). Testing for neglected heterogeneity. *Econometrica, 52*, 865–71.

Chesher, A. D. and G. Austin (1987). Finite sample behaviour of heteroskedasticity robust Wald statistics. Unpublished paper, University of Bristol (DP87/187).

Chesher, A. D., T. Lancaster and M. Irish (1985). On detecting the failure of distributional assumptions. *Annales de l'INSEE, 59/60*, 7–45.

Chow, G. C. (1960). Tests of equality between sets of coefficients in two linear regressions. *Econometrica, 28*, 591–605.

Chow, G. C. (1981a). Evaluation of econometric models by decomposition and aggregation. In *Large-Scale Macro-Econometric Models*, ed. J. Kmenta and J. B. Ramsey, 423–44. Amsterdam: North-Holland.

Chow, G. C. (1981b). Selection of econometric models by the information criterion. In *Proceedings of the Econometric Society European Meeting, 1979*, ed. E. G. Charatsis, 199–214. Amsterdam: North-Holland.

Chow, G. C. (1982). Note on maximum-likelihood estimation of misspecified models. Unpublished paper, Princeton University.

Chow, G. C. and P. Corsi (1982). *Evaluating the Reliability of Macroeconomic Models.* London: Wiley.

Consigliere, I. (1981). The Chow test with serially correlated errors. *Rivista Internatazionale di Scienze Sociali, 89*, 125–37.

Corsi, P., R. Pollock and J. Prakken (1982). The Chow test in the presence of serially correlated errors. In Chow and Corsi (1982), 163–92.

Cox, D. R. (1961). Tests of separate families of hypotheses. *Proceedings of the Fourth Berkeley Symposium on Mathematical Statistics and Probability, 1,* 105–23. Berkeley: University of California Press.

Cox, D. R. (1962). Further results on tests of separate families of hypotheses. *Journal of the Royal Statistical Society,* Series B, *24,* 406–24.

Cox, D. R. (1983). Some remarks on overdispersion. *Biometrika, 70,* 269–74.

Cox, D. R. and D. V. Hinkley (1974). *Theoretical Statistics.* London: Chapman and Hall.

Cragg, J. G. (1983). More efficient estimation in the presence of heteroscedasticity of unknown form. *Econometrica, 51,* 751–63.

Cramér, H. (1946). *Mathematical Methods of Statistics.* Princeton University Press.

Cramer, J. S. (1986). *Econometric Applications of Maximum Likelihood Methods.* Cambridge: Cambridge University Press.

Crowder, M. J. (1976). Maximum likelihood estimation for dependent observations. *Journal of the Royal Statistical Society,* Series B, *38,* 45–53.

Das Gupta, S. and M. D. Perlman (1974). Power of the non-central F-test: effect of additional variates on Hotelling's T^2-test. *Journal of the American Statistical Association, 69,* 174–80.

Davidson, R., L. G. Godfrey and J. G. MacKinnon (1985). A simplified version of the differencing test. *International Economic Review, 26,* 639–47.

Davidson, R. and J. G. MacKinnon (1983). Small sample properties of alternative forms of the Lagrange multiplier test. *Economics Letters 12,* 269–75.

Davidson, R. and J. G. MacKinnon (1984a). Convenient specification tests for logit and probit models. *Journal of Econometrics, 25,* 241–62.

Davidson, R. and J. G. MacKinnon (1984b). Model specification tests based upon artificial linear regressions. *International Economic Review, 25,* 485–502.

Davidson, R. and J. G. MacKinnon (1985). Testing linear and log-linear regressions against Box–Cox alternatives. *Canadian Journal of Economics, 18,* 499–517.

Davies, R. B. (1977). Hypothesis testing when a nuisance parameter is present only under the alternative. *Biometrika, 64,* 247–54.

Davies, R. B. (1987). Hypothesis testing when a nuisance parameter is present only under the alternative. *Biometrika, 74,* 33–43.

Desai, M. (1974). Pooling as a specification error–a note. *Econometrica, 42,* 389–91.

Dhrymes, P. J. (1969). Alternative asymptotic tests of significance and related aspects of two stage least squares and three stage least squares estimators. *Review of Economic Studies, 36,* 213–26.

Dhrymes, P. J., E. P. Howrey, S. H. Hymans, J. Kmenta, E. E. Leamer, R. E. Quandt, J. G. Ramsey, H. T. Shapiro and V. Zarnowitz (1972). Criteria for evaluation of econometric models. *Annals of Economic and Social Measurement, 1,* 291–324.

Domowitz, I. (1983). Comment on diagnostic tests as residual analysis. *Econometric Reviews, 2,* 159–218.

Domowitz, I. and H. White (1982). Misspecified models with dependent observations. *Journal of Econometrics, 20,* 35–58.

Dufour, J. M. (1982). Generalised Chow tests for structural change: a coordinate free approach. *International Economic Review, 23,* 565–75.

Durbin, J. (1954). Errors in variables. *Review of the International Statistical Institute, 22,* 23–32.

Durbin, J. (1970). Testing for serial correlation in least squares regression when some of the regressors are lagged dependent variables. *Econometrica, 38,* 410–421.

Efron, B. and D. V. Hinkley (1978). Assessing the accuracy of the maximum likelihood estimator: observed versus expected Fisher information. *Biometrika, 65,* 457–82.

Eicker, F. (1967). Limit theorems for regressions with unequal and dependent errors. *Fifth Berkeley Symposium on Mathematical Statistics and Probability, 1,* 59–82. Berkeley: University of California.

Engle, R. F. (1982a). A general approach to Lagrange multiplier model diagnostics. *Journal of Econometrics, 20,* 83–104.

Engle, R. F. (1982b). Autoregressive conditional heteroscedasticity with estimates of the variance of United Kingdom inflation. *Econometrica, 50,* 987–1007.

Engle, R. F. (1984). Wald, likelihood ratio, and Lagrange multiplier tests in econometrics. In *Handbook of Econometrics*, Vol. 2, ed. Z. Griliches and M. Intriligator, 775–826. Amsterdam: North-Holland.

Engle, R. F., D. F. Hendry and J.-F. Richard (1983). Exogeneity. *Econometrica, 51,* 277–304.

Engle, R. F., D. F. Hendry and D. Trumble (1985). Small sample properties of ARCH estimators and tests. *Canadian Journal of Economics, 18,* 66–93.

Engle, R. F. and D. F. Kraft (1983). Multiperiod forecast error variances of inflation estimated from ARCH models. In *Applied Time Series Analysis of Economic Data*, ed. A. Zellner, 293–302. Bureau of Census.

Erlat, H. (1983). A note on testing structural change in a single equation belonging to a simultaneous system. *Economics Letters, 13,* 185–9.

Evans, G. B. A. and N. E. Savin (1982). Conflict among the criteria revisited; the W, LR and LM tests. *Econometrica, 50,* 737–48.

Evans, G. B. A. and N. E. Savin (1983). Conflict among test procedures in a linear regression model with lagged dependent variables. In *Advances in Econometrics*, ed. W. Hildenbrand, 263–83. Cambridge: Cambridge University Press.

Farebrother, R. W. (1979). A grouping test for misspecification. *Econometrica, 47,* 209–10.

Farley, J. U. and M. Hinich (1970). Testing for a shifting slope coefficient in a linear model. *Journal of the American Statistical Association, 65,* 1320–9.

Farley, J. U., M. Hinich and T. W. McGuire (1975). Some comparisons of tests for a shift in the slopes of multivariate linear time series model. *Journal of Econometrics, 3,* 297–318.

Fishe, R. P. H., G. S. Maddala and R. P. Trost (1979). Estimation of a heteroscedastic Tobit model. Unpublished paper, University of Florida.

Fisk, P. R. (1967). *Stochastically Dependent Equations.* London: Griffin.

Fitts, J. (1973). Testing for autocorrelation in the autoregressive moving average error model. *Journal of Econometrics, 1,* 363–76.

Fuller, W. A. (1975). Regression analysis for sample survey. *Sankhya*, Series C, *37,* 117–32.

Gallant, A. R. and D. W. Jorgenson (1979). Statistical inference for a system of simultaneous, non-linear, implicit equations in the context of instrumental variable estimation. *Journal of Econometrics, 11,* 275–302.

Garbade, K. (1977). Two methods for examining the stability of regression coefficients. *Journal of the American Statistical Association, 72,* 54–63.

Geary, R. C. (1966). A note on residual heterovariance and estimation efficiency in regression. *American Statistician, 20*, 30–1.

Glejser, H. (1969). A new test for heteroscedasticity. *Journal of the American Statistical Association, 64*, 316–23.

Godfrey, L. G. (1976). Testing for serial correlation in dynamic simultaneous equation models. *Econometrica, 44*, 1077–84.

Godfrey, L. G. (1978a). A note on the use of Durbin's h-test when the equation is estimated by instrumental variables. *Econometrica, 46*, 225–8.

Godfrey, L. G. (1978b). Testing for multiplicative heteroscedasticity. *Journal of Econometrics, 8*, 227–36.

Godfrey, L. G. (1978c). Testing against general autoregressive and moving average error models when the regressors include lagged dependent variables. *Econometrica, 46*, 1293–302.

Godfrey, L. G. (1978d). Testing for higher order serial correlation in regression equations when the regressors include lagged dependent variables. *Econometrica, 46*, 1303–10.

Godfrey, L. G. (1978e). Some tests for specification error. Unpublished paper, University of York.

Godfrey, L. G. (1979a). Testing the adequacy of a time series model. *Biometrika, 66*, 67–72.

Godfrey, L. G. (1979b). A diagnostic check of the variance model in regression equations with heteroscedastic disturbances. Unpublished paper, University of York.

Godfrey, L. G. (1981). On the invariance of the Lagrange multiplier test with respect to certain changes in the alternative hypothesis. *Econometrica, 49*, 1443–55.

Godfrey, L. G. and M. R. Wickens (1981). Testing linear and log-linear regressions for functional form. *Review of Economic Studies, 48*, 487–96.

Godfrey, L. G. and M. R. Wickens (1982). Tests of misspecification using locally equivalent alternative models. In Chow and Corsi (1982), 71–99.

Goldfeld, S. M. and R. E. Quandt (1965). Some tests for homoscedasticity. *Journal of the American Statistical Association, 60*, 539–47.

Goldfeld, S. M. and R. E. Quandt (1972). *Nonlinear Methods in Econometrics.* Amsterdam: North-Holland.

Goldfeld, S. M. and R. E. Quandt (1978). Asymptotic tests for the constancy of regressions in the heteroscedastic case. Princeton University, Econometric Research Program, Research Memorandum no. 229.

Gouriéroux, C., A. Holly and A. Monfort (1982). Likelihood ratio test, Wald test, and Kuhn-Tucker test in linear models with inequality constraints on the regression parameters. *Econometrica, 50*, 63–80.

Gouriéroux, C., A. Monfort and A. Trognon (1984). Psuedo maximum likelihood methods: theory, *Econometrica, 52*, 681–99.

Granger, C. W. J. (1969). Investigating causal relations by econometric models and cross spectral methods. *Econometrica, 37*, 428–38.

Granger, C. W. J. and P. Newbold (1977). The time series approach to econometric model building. In *New Methods in Business Cycle Research: Proceedings from a Conference*, ed. C. A. Sims, 7–21. Minneapolis: Federal Reserve Bank of Minneapolis.

Gregory, A. W. and M. R. Veall (1985). Formulating Wald tests of nonlinear restrictions. *Econometrica, 53*, 1465–8.

Guilkey, D. K. (1975). A test for the presence of first order vector autoregressive errors when lagged endogenous variables are present. *Econometrica, 43*, 711–18.

Hall, A. (1987). The information matrix test for the linear model. *Review of Economic Studies, 54*, 257–63.

Hannan, E. J. (1970). *Multiple Time Series*. New York: Wiley.

Harvey, A. C. (1976). Estimating regression models with multiplicative heteroscedasticity. *Econometrica, 44*, 461–5.

Harvey, A. C. and G. D. A. Phillips (1974). A comparison of the power of some tests for heteroscedasticity in the general linear model. *Journal of Econometrics, 2*, 307–16.

Harvey, A. C. and G. D. A. Phillips (1980). Testing for serial correlation in simultaneous equation models. *Econometrica, 48*, 747–59.

Harvey, A. C. and G. D. A. Phillips (1981). Testing for heteroscedasticity in simultaneous equation models. *Journal of Econometrics, 15*, 311–40.

Hatanaka, M. (1976). Several efficient two-step estimators for the dynamic simultaneous equations model with autoregressive disturbances. *Journal of Econometrics, 4*, 189–204.

Hatanaka, M. (1977). Hypothesis testing in the large macro-economic models. *International Economic Review, 18*, 607–27.

Hausman, J. (1975). An instrumental variable approach to full information estimators for linear and certain nonlinear econometric models. *Econometrica, 43*, 727–37.

Hausman, J. (1978). Specification tests in econometrics. *Econometrica, 46*, 1251–71.

Hausman, J. (1983). Specification and estimation of simultaneous equation models. In *Handbook of Econometrics*, Vol. I, ed. Z. Griliches and M. D. Intriligator, 391–448. Amsterdam: North-Holland.

Hausman, J. and D. McFadden (1984). Specification tests for the multinomial logit model. *Econometrica, 52*, 1219–39.

Hausman, J. and W. E. Taylor (1981). A generalised specification test. *Economics Letters, 8*, 239–45.

Hausman, J. and D. A. Wise (1977). Social experimentation, truncated distributions and efficient estimation. *Econometrica, 45*, 319–39.

Hawkins, D. M. (1977). Testing a sequence of observations for a shift in location. *Journal of the American Statistical Association, 72*, 180–6.

Hendry, D. F. (1976). The structure of simultaneous equations estimators. *Journal of Econometrics, 4*, 51–88.

Hendry, D. F. (1979). Predictive failure and econometric modelling in macroeconomics: the transactions demand for money. In *Economic Modelling*, ed. P. Omerod, 217–42. London: Heinemann Educational Books.

Hendry, D. F. (1980). Econometrics: alchemy or science? *Economica, 47*, 387–406.

Hendry, D. F. and J.-F. Richard (1982). On the formulation of empirical models in dynamic econometrics. *Journal of Econometrics, 20*, 3–33.

Hendry, D. F. and J.-F. Richard (1983). The econometric analysis of economic time series. *International Statistical Review, 51*, 111–63.

Hildreth, C. and J. P. Houck (1968). Some estimators for a linear model with random coefficients. *Journal of the American Statistical Association, 63*, 584–95.

Holly, A. (1982). A remark on Hausman's specification test. *Econometrica, 50*, 749–59.

Holly, A. and A. Monfort (1986). Some useful equivalence properties of Hausman's test. *Economics Letters, 20,* 39–43.

Honda, Y. (1982). On tests of equality between sets of coefficients in two linear regressions when disturbance variances are unequal. *Manchester School, 50,* 116–25.

Hsiao, C. (1983). Identification. In *Handbook of Econometrics,* Vol. I, ed. Z. Griliches and M. D. Intriligator, 223–83. Amsterdam: North-Holland.

Hsieh, D. A. (1983). A heteroscedasticity-consistent covariance matrix estimator for time series regressions. *Journal of Econometrics, 22,* 281–90.

Hurd, M. (1979). Estimation in truncated samples when there is heteroscedasticity. *Journal of Econometrics, 11,* 247–58.

Hwang, H. (1985). The equivalence of Hausman and Lagrange multiplier tests of independence between disturbance and a subset of stochastic regressors. *Economics Letters, 17,* 83–6.

Jarque, C. M. (1981). A test for heteroscedasticity in a limited dependent variable model. *Australian Journal of Statistics, 23,* 159–63

Jarque, C. M. and A. K. Bera (1980). Efficient tests for normality, homoscedasticity and serial independence of regression residuals. *Economics Letters, 6,* 255–9.

Jarque, C. M. and A. K. Bera (1982). Efficient specification tests for limited dependent variable models. *Economics Letters, 9,* 153–60.

Jayatissa, W. A. (1976). Criteria for evaluation of econometric models: a correction. *Annals of Social and Economic Measurement, 5,* 161.

Jayatissa, W. A. (1977). Tests of equality between sets of coefficients in two linear regressions when disturbance variances are unequal. *Econometrica, 45,* 1291–2.

Johnston, J. (1984). *Econometric Methods,* 3d ed. London: McGraw-Hill.

Judge, G. G., W. E. Griffiths, R. Carter Hall and T.-C. Lee (1980). *The Theory and Practice of Econometrics.* New York: Wiley.

Judge, G. G. and T. Takayama (1966). Inequality restrictions in regression analysis. *Journal of the American Statistical Association, 61,* 166–81.

Kelejian, H. H. (1974). Random parameters in a simultaneous equation framework: identification and estimation. *Econometrica, 42,* 517–27.

Kelejian, H. H. (1982). An extension of a standard test for heteroscedasticity to a systems framework. *Journal of Econometrics, 20,* 325–33.

Kendall, M. G. and A. Stuart (1969). *The Advanced Theory of Statistics,* Vol. I. London: Griffin.

Kent, J. T. (1982). Robust properties of likelihood ratio tests. *Biometrika, 88,* 19–27.

Kiefer, N. M. and M. Salmon (1983). Testing normality in econometric models. *Economics Letters, 11,* 123–7.

Kiefer, N. M. and G. R. Skoog (1984). Local asymptotic specification error analysis. *Econometrica, 52,* 873–85.

King, M. H. and G. H. Hillier (1985). Locally best invariant tests of the error covariance matrix of the linear regression model. *Journal of the Royal Statistical Society,* Series B, *47,* 98–102.

Kiviet, J. (1986). On the rigour of some specification tests for modelling dynamic relationships. *Review of Economic Studies, 53,* 241–62.

Klein, L. R. (1964). Discussion of 'Time stability of structural parameters,' by Menges and Diehl (1964).

Kmenta, J. (1967). On the estimation of the CES production function. *International Economic Review, 8,* 180–9.

Kmenta, J. (1971). *Elements of Econometrics.* New York: Macmillan.

Koenker, R. (1981). A note on studentizing a test for heteroscedasticity. *Journal of Econometrics, 17,* 107–12.

Lafontaine, F. and K. J. White (1986). Obtaining any Wald statistic you want. *Economics Letters, 21.* 35–40.

Lancaster, T. (1968). Grouping estimators on heteroscedastic data. *Journal of the American Statistical Association, 63,* 182–91.

Lancaster, A. (1984). The covariance matrix of the information matrix test. *Econometrica, 52,* 1051–3.

Lawton, W. H. and E. A. Sylvestre (1971). Elimination of linear parameters in nonlinear regression. *Technometrics, 13,* 461–7.

Lee, L.-F. (1984). Tests for the bivariate normal distribution in econometric models with selectivity. *Econometrica, 52,* 843–63.

Lee, L.-F. and A. Chesher (1986). Specification testing when score test statistics are identically zero. *Journal of Econometrics, 31,* 121–49.

Lee, L.-F. and G. S. Maddala (1985). The common structure of tests for selectivity bias, serial correlation, heteroscedasticity and nonnormality in the Tobit model. *International Economic Review, 26,* 1–20.

Liew, C. K. (1976). Inequality constrained least squares estimation. *Journal of the American Statistical Association, 71,* 746–51.

Ljung, G. M. and G. E. P. Box (1978). On a measure of lack of fit in time series models. *Biometrika, 65,* 297–303.

Lo, A. W. and W. K. Newey (1985). A large sample Chow test for the linear simultaneous equation. *Economics Letters, 18,* 351–3.

McAleer, M. (1983). Specification tests for separate models: a survey. In *Specification Analysis in the Linear Model,* ed. M. L. King and D. E. A. Giles, pp. 146–96. London: Routledge and Kegan Paul.

MacKinnon, J. G. (1983). Model specification tests against nonnested alternatives. *Econometric Reviews, 2,* 85–110.

MacKinnon, J. G. and H. White (1985). Some heteroskedasticity-consistent covariance matrix estimators with improved finite sample properties. *Journal of Econometrics, 29,* 305–25.

McLeish, D. L. (1974). Dependent central limit theorems and invariance principles. *Annals of Probability, 2,* 620–8.

Maddala, G. S. (1974). Some small sample evidence on tests of significance in simultaneous equations models. *Econometrica, 42,* 841–52.

Maddala, G. S. (1983). *Limited-Dependent and Qualitative Variables in Econometrics.* Cambridge: Cambridge University Press.

Maddala, G. S. and F. D. Nelson (1975). Specification errors in limited dependent variable models. NBER working paper 96.

Maddala, G. S. and A. S. Rao (1973). Tests for serial correlation in regression models with lagged dependent variables and serially correlated errors. *Econometrica, 41,* 761–74.

Malinvaud, E. (1981). Econometrics faced with the needs of macroeconomic policy. *Econometrica, 49,* 1363–75.

Mann, H. B. and A. Wald (1943). On stochastic limit and order relationships. *Annals of Mathematical Statistics, 14,* 217–26.

Maritz, A. (1978). A note of correction to Guilkey's test for serial independence in simultaneous equations models. *Econometrica, 46,* 471.

Menges, G. and H. Diehl (1964). Time stability of structural parameters. In

Econometric Analysis for National Economic Planning, ed. P. E. Hart, G. Mills and J. K. Whitaker, 299–317. London: Butterworths.

Messer, K. and H. White (1984). A note on computing the heteroscedasticity consistent covariance matrix using IV techniques. *Oxford Bulletin of Economics and Statistics, 46*, 181–4.

Milliken, G. A. and F. A. Graybill (1970). Extensions of the general linear hypothesis model, *Journal of the American Statistical Association, 65*, 797–807.

Mizon, G. E. (1977a). Model selection procedures. In *Studies in Modern Economic Analysis*, ed. M. J. Artis and A. R. Nobay. Oxford: Basil Blackwell.

Mizon, G. E. (1977b). Inferential procedures in nonlinear models: an application in a U.K. industrial cross-section study of factor substitution and returns to scale. *Econometrica, 45*, 1221–42.

Mizon, G. E. and D. F. Hendry (1980). An empirical application and Monte Carlo analysis of tests of dynamic specification. *Review of Economic Studies, 47*, 21–45.

Mizon, G. E. and J.-F. Richard (1986). The encompassing principle and its application to testing nonnested hypotheses. *Econometrica, 54*, 657–77.

Moran, P. A. P. (1971a). The uniform consistency of maximum likelihood estimators. *Proceedings of the Cambridge Philosophical Society, 70*, 435–9.

Moran, P. A. P. (1971b). Maximum likelihood estimation in non-standard conditions. *Proceedings of the Cambridge Philosophical Society, 70*, 441–50.

Nakamura, A. and M. Nakamura (1981). On the relationships between several specification tests presented by Durbin, Wu and Hausman. *Econometrica, 49*, 1583–8.

Nelson, F. D. (1981). A test for misspecification in the censored normal model. *Econometrica, 49*, 1317–29.

Newey, W. K. (1985a). Maximum likelihood specification testing and conditional moment tests. *Econometrica, 53*, 1047–70.

Newey, W. K. (1985b). Generalized method of moments specification testing. *Journal of Econometrics, 29*, 229–56.

Neyman, J. (1959). Optimal asymptotic tests of composite statistical hypotheses. In *Probability and Statistics, the Harald Cramer Volume*, ed. U. Grenander. New York: Wiley.

Nicholls, D. F. and A. R. Pagan (1983). Heteroscedasticity in models with lagged dependent variables. *Econometrica, 51*, 1233–42.

Nicholls, D. F. and A. R. Pagan (1984). Estimating predictions, prediction errors and their standard deviations using constructed variables. *Journal of Econometrics, 24*, 293–310.

Orme, C. D. (1987). The small sample performance of the information matrix test. Unpublished paper, University of York.

Paarsch, H. J. (1984). A Monte Carlo comparison of estimators for censored regression models. *Journal of Econometrics, 24*, 197–213.

Pagan, A. R. (1981). Reflections on Australian macro-modelling. Unpublished paper, Australian National University.

Pagan, A. R. (1984). Model evaluation by variable addition. In *Econometrics and Quantitative Economics*, ed. D. F. Hendry and K. F. Wallis, 103–33. Oxford: Blackwell.

Pagan, A. R. and A. D. Hall (1983). Diagnostic tests as residual analysis. *Econometric Reviews, 2*, 159–218.

Park, R. E. (1966). Estimation with heteroscedastic error terms. *Econometrica, 34,* 888.

Pearson, E. S., R. B. D'Agostino and K. O. Bowman (1977). Tests for departure from normality: comparison of powers. *Biometrika, 64,* 231–46.

Pesaran, M. H., R. P. Smith and J. S. Yeo (1985). Testing for structural stability and predictive failure: a review. *Manchester School, 53,* 280–95.

Phillips, G. D. A. and B. McCabe (1983). The independence of tests for structural change in regression models. *Economics Letters, 12,* 283–7.

Plosser, C. I., G. W. Schwert and H. White (1982). Differencing as a test of specification. *International Economic Review, 23,* 535–52.

Poirier, D. (1978). The use of the Box–Cox transformation in limited dependent variable models. *Journal of the American Statistical Association, 73,* 284–7.

Poirier, D. and A. Melino (1978). A note on the interpretation of regression coefficients within a class of truncated distributions. *Econometrica, 46,* 1207–9.

Poirier, D. J. and P. A. Ruud (1983). Diagnostic testing in missing data models. *International Economic Review, 24,* 537–46.

Porter, R. D. and A. K. Kashyap (1984). Autocorrelation and the sensitivity of RESET. *Economics Letters, 14,* 229–33.

Poskitt, D. S. and A. R. Tremayne (1981). An approach to testing linear time series models. *The Annals of Statistics, 9,* 974–86.

Prais, S. J. and H. S. Houthakker (1971). *The Analysis of Family Budgets.* Cambridge: Cambridge University Press.

Ramsey, J. B. (1969). Tests for specification errors in classical linear least-squares regression analysis. *Journal of the Royal Statistical Society,* Series B, *31,* 350–71.

Ramsey, J. B. (1974). Classical model selection through specification error tests. In *Frontiers of Econometrics,* ed. P. Zarembka, 13–47. New York: Academic Press.

Ramsey, J. B. and R. Gilbert (1972). A Monte Carlo study of some small sample properties of tests for specification error. *Journal of the American Statistical Association, 67,* 180–6.

Ramsey, J. B. and J. Kmenta (1980). Problems and issues in evaluating econometric models. In *Evaluation of Econometric Models,* ed. J. Kmenta and J. B. Ramsey, 1–11. New York: Academic Press.

Ramsey, J. B. and P. Schmidt (1976). Some further results in the use of OLS and BLUS residuals in specification error tests. *Journal of the American Statistical Association, 71,* 389–90.

Rao, C. R. (1948). Large sample tests of statistical hypotheses concerning several parameters with applications to problems of estimation. *Proceedings of Cambridge Philosophical Society, 44,* 50–57.

Rao, C. R. (1973). *Linear Statistical Inference and Its Applications.* New York: Wiley.

Rao, C. R. and S. K. Mitra (1971). *Generalised Inverse of Matrices and Its Applications.* New York: Wiley.

Rea, J. D. (1978). Indeterminancy of the Chow test when the number of observations is insufficient. *Econometrica, 46,* 229.

Reinsel, G. (1979a). Maximum likelihood estimation of stochastic linear difference equations with autoregressive moving average errors. *Econometrica, 47,* 129–52.

Reinsel, G. (1979b). FIML estimation of the dynamic simultaneous equations model with ARMA disturbances. *Journal of Econometrics, 9*, 263–81.

Robinson, P. M. (1982). On the asymptotic properties of estimators of models containing limited dependent variables. *Econometrica, 50*, 27–41.

Rothenberg, T. J. (1971). Identification in parametric models. *Econometrica, 39*, 577–91.

Rothenberg, T. J. (1973). *Efficient Estimation with a priori Information.* New Haven: Yale University Press.

Rothenberg, T. J. (1983). Comparing alternative asymptotically equivalent tests. In *Advances in Econometrics*, ed. W. Hildenbrand, 255–62. Cambridge: Cambridge University Press.

Rothenberg, T. J. (1984). Hypothesis testing in linear models when the error covariance matrix is nonscalar. *Econometrica, 52*, 827–41.

Rothenberg, T. J. and C. T. Leenders (1964). Efficient estimation of simultaneous equation systems. *Econometrica, 32*, 57–76.

Roy, S. N. (1953). On a heuristic method of test construction and its use in multivariate analysis. *Annals of Mathematical Statistics, 24*, 220–38.

Rubin, H. (1953). A note on random coefficients. In *Studies in Econometric Method*, ed. W. C. Hood and T. C. Koopmans. New York: Wiley.

Rutemiller, H. C. and D. A. Bowers (1968). Estimation in a heteroscedastic regression model. *Journal of the American Statistical Association, 63*, 552–7.

Ruud, P. A. (1984). Tests of specification in econometrics. *Econometric Reviews, 3*, 211–42.

Salkever, D. S. (1976). The use of dummy variables to compute predictions, prediction errors and confidence intervals. *Journal of Econometrics, 4*, 393–7

Sargan, J. D. (1959). The estimation of relationships with autocorrelated residuals by the use of instrumental variables. *Journal of the Royal Statistical Society, Series B, 21*, 91–105.

Sargan, J. D. (1975). Discussion on misspecification. In *Modelling the Economy*, ed. G. A. Renton, 321–2. London: Heinemann.

Sargan, J. D. (1976). Testing for misspecification after estimating using instrumental variables. Unpublished paper, London School of Economics.

Sargan, J. D. (1980). Some tests of dynamic specification for a single equation. *Econometrica, 48*, 879–97.

Sargan, J. D. and F. Mehta (1983). A generalisation of the Durbin significance test and its application to dynamic specification. *Econometrica, 51*, 1551–67.

Savin, N. E. (1976). Conflict among testing procedures in a linear regression model with autoregressive disturbances. *Econometrica, 44*, 1303–15.

Savin, N. E. and K. J. White (1978). Estimation and testing for functional form and autocorrelation: a simultaneous approach. *Journal of Econometrics, 8*, 1–12.

Schlesselman, H. (1971). Power families: a note on the Box and Cox transformation. *Journal of the Royal Statistical Society, Series B, 33*, 307–11.

Schmidt, P. (1976). *Econometrics.* New York: Marcel Dekker.

Schmidt, P. (1977). Some small sample evidence on the distribution of dynamic simulation forecasts. *Econometrica, 45*, 997–1005.

Schmidt, P. and R. Sickles (1977). Some further evidence on the use of the Chow test under heteroscedasticity. *Econometrica, 45*, 1293–8.

Seber, G. E. F. (1966). *The Linear Hypothesis: a General Theory.* London: C. Griffin.

Silvey, S. D. (1959). The Lagrange multiplier test. *Annals of Mathematical Statistics, 30*, 387–407.

Sims, C. A. (1972). Money, income and causality. *American Economic Review, 62*, 540–52.

Smith, R. (1983). On the classical nature of the Wu–Hausman statistics for the independence of stochastic regressors and disturbances. *Economics Letters, 11*, 357–64.

Smith, R. J. (1984). A note on likelihood ratio tests for the independence between a subset of stochastic regressors and disturbances. *International Economic Review, 25*, 263–9.

Smith, R. J. (1985). Wald tests for the independence of stochastic variables and disturbance of a single linear stochastic simultaneous equation. *Economics Letters, 17*, 87–90.

Spencer, B. G. (1975). The small sample bias of Durbin's tests for serial correlation when one of the regressors is the lagged dependent variable and the null hypothesis is true. *Journal of Econometrics, 3*, 249–54.

Spencer, D. E. and K. N. Berk (1981). A limited information specification test. *Econometrica, 49*, 1079–85.

Spencer, D. E. and K. N. Berk (1982). Erratum. *Econometrica, 50*, 1087.

Stroud, T. W. F. (1971). On obtaining large sample tests from asymptotically normal estimators. *Annals of Mathematical Statistics, 42*, 1412–24.

Swamy, P. A. V. B. (1970). Efficient estimation in a random coefficient regression model. *Econometrica, 38*, 311–23.

Szroeter, J. (1978). A class of parametric tests for heteroscedasticity in linear econometric models. *Econometrica, 46*, 1311–28.

Tanaka, K. (1983). Non-normality of the Lagrange multiplier statistic for testing the constancy of regression coefficients. *Econometrica, 51*, 1577–82.

Tauchen, G. (1985). Diagnostic testing and evaluation of maximum likelihood models. *Journal of Econometrics, 30*, 415–43.

Theil, H. (1951). Estimates and their sampling variance of parameters of certain heteroscedastic distributions. *Review of the International Statistical Institute, 19*, 141–7.

Theil, H. (1957). Specification errors and the estimation of economic relations. *Review of the International Statistical Institute, 25*, 41–51.

Theil, H. (1971). *Principles of Econometrics.* New York: Wiley.

Thursby, J. (1979). Alternative specification error tests: a comparative study. *Journal of the American Statistical Association, 74*, 222–3.

Thursby, J. and P. Schmidt (1977). Some properties of tests for specification error in a linear regression model. *Journal of the American Statistical Association, 72*, 635–41.

Tobin, J. (1958). Estimation of relationships for limited dependent variables. *Econometrica, 26*, 24–36.

Toyoda, T. (1974). Use of the Chow test under heteroscedasticity. *Econometrica, 42*, 601–8.

Trivedi, P. K. (1970). The relation between the order–delivery lag and the rate of capacity utilisation in the engineering industry in the United Kingdom, 1958–1967. *Economica, 37*, 54–67.

Ullah, A. and V. Zinde-Walsh (1984). On the robustness of LM, LR and W tests in regression models. *Econometrica, 52*, 1055–65.

Ullah, A. and V. Zinde-Walsh (1985). Estimation and testing in a regression model with spherically symmetric errors. *Economics Letters, 17*, 127–32.

Utt, J. M. (1982). The rainbow test for lack of fit in regression. *Communications in Statistics, 11*, 2801–15.

Vinod, H. D. (1973). Generalisations of the Durbin–Watson statistic for higher order autoregressive processes. *Communications in Statistics, 2*, 115–44.

Waldman, D. M. (1983). A note on the algebraic equivalence of White's test and a variation of the Godfrey/Breusch–Pagan test for heteroscedasticity. *Economics Letters, 13*, 197–200.

Wallis, K. F. (1972). Testing for fourth order autocorrelation in quarterly regression equations. *Econometrica, 40*, 617–36.

Warner, D. (1976). A Monte Carlo study of limited dependent variable estimators. In *Studies in Non-linear Estimation*, ed. S. M. Goldfeld and R. E. Quandt. Cambridge, Mass.: Ballinger.

Watson, M. (1982). A test for regression coefficient stability when a parameter is identified only under the alternative. Discussion paper 906, Harvard University.

Watson, M. W. and R. F. Engle (1985). Testing for regression coefficient stability with a stationary AR(1) alternative. *Review of Economics and Statistics, 67*, 341–6.

Watt, P. A. (1979). Tests of equality between sets of coefficients in two linear regressions when disturbance variances are unequal: some small sample properties. *Manchester School, 47*, 391–6.

White, H. (1980a). Using least squares to approximate unknown regression functions. *International Economic Review, 21*, 149–70.

White, H. (1980b). A heteroscedastic-consistent covariance matrix and a direct test for heteroscedasticity. *Econometrica, 48*, 421–48.

White, H. (1981). Consequences and detection of misspecified nonlinear regression models. *Journal of the American Statistical Association, 76*, 419–33.

White, H. (1982). Maximum likelihood estimation of misspecified models. *Econometrica, 50*, 1–25.

White, H. (1983a). Corrigendum. *Econometrica, 51*, 513.

White, H. (1983b). Editor of *Non-nested models. Annals of Applied Econometrics*, Supplement to *Journal of Econometrics*, vol. 21.

White, H. and I. Domowitz (1984). Nonlinear regression with dependent observations. *Econometrica, 52*, 141–61.

White, H. and G. M. MacDonald (1980). Some large sample tests for non-normality in the linear regression model. *Journal of the American Statistical Association, 75*, 16–28.

Wu, D.-M. (1973). Alternative tests of independence between stochastic regressors and disturbances. *Econometrica, 41*, 733–50.

Wu, D.-M. (1974). Alternative tests of independence between stochastic regressors and disturbances: finite sample results. *Econometrica, 42*, 529–46.

Wu, D.-M. (1983a). A remark on a generalised specification test. *Economics Letters, 11*, 365–70.

Wu, D.-M. (1983b). Tests of causality, predeterminedness and exogeneity. *International Economic Review, 24*, 547–58.

Yatchew, A. and Z. Griliches (1985). Specification error in probit models. *Review of Economics and Statistics, 18*, 134–9.

Zellner, A. (1976). Bayesian and non-Bayesian analysis of the regression model with multivariate Student t error terms. *Journal of the American Statistical Association, 71*, 400–5.

Zinde-Walsh, V. and A. Ullah (1987). On robustness of tests of linear restrictions in regression models with elliptical error distributions, in *Time Series and Econometric Modelling*, eds. B. MacNeill and G. J. Umphrey. The Netherlands: D. Reidel.

Index